REVISITING THE 'IDEAL VICTIM'
Developments in critical victimology

Edited by Marian Duggan

First published in Great Britain in 2018 by

Policy Press
University of Bristol
1-9 Old Park Hill
Bristol
BS2 8BB
UK
t: +44 (0)117 954 5940
pp-info@bristol.ac.uk
www.policypress.co.uk

North America office:
Policy Press
c/o The University of Chicago Press
1427 East 60th Street
Chicago, IL 60637, USA
t: +1 773 702 7700
f: +1 773-702-9756
sales@press.uchicago.edu
www.press.uchicago.edu

© Policy Press 2018

British Library Cataloguing in Publication Data
A catalogue record for this book is available from the British Library

Library of Congress Cataloging-in-Publication Data
A catalog record for this book has been requested

ISBN 978-1-4473-3876-5 hardcover
ISBN 978-1-4473-3916-8 ePub
ISBN 978-1-4473-3917-5 Mobi
ISBN 978-1-4473-3915-1 ePdf

The right of Marian Duggan to be identified as editor of this work has been asserted by her in accordance with the Copyright, Designs and Patents Act 1988.

The statements and opinions contained within this publication are solely those of the editor and contributors and not of the University of Bristol or Policy Press. The University of Bristol and Policy Press disclaim responsibility for any injury to persons or property resulting from any material published in this publication.

Policy Press works to counter discrimination on grounds of gender, race, disability, age and sexuality.

Cover design by Jess Augarde
Front cover image: AdobeStock
Printed and bound in Great Britain by CPI Group (UK) Ltd,
Croydon, CR0 4YY
Policy Press uses environmentally responsible print partners

Contents

Contents

List of abbreviations

ACCC	Australian Competition and Consumer Commission
ASB	Anti-social behaviour
CAFC	Canadian Anti-Fraud Centre
CPS	Crown Prosecution Service
CSEW	Crime Survey for England and Wales
DNA	Deoxyribonucleic acid
DVA	Domestic violence and abuse
DVDS	Domestic Violence Disclosure Scheme
ECHR	European Court of Human Rights (in references)
ECtHR	European Court of Human Rights (in text)
HMICP	Her Majesty's Chief Inspectorate of Prisons
HMIP	Her Majesty's Inspectorate of Prisons
IACtHR	Inter-American Court of Human Rights
IDVA	Independent Domestic Violence Adviser
IPCC	Independent Police Complaints Commission
ISIS	Islamic State of Iraq and Syria
LGB and/or T	Lesbian, gay, bisexual and transgender
MTT	Moral Typecasting Theory
NCVS	National Crime and Victimisation Survey
NSIR	National Standard for Incident Recording
ODIHR	Office for Democratic Institutions and Human Rights
ONS	Office for National Statistics
OSCE	Organisation for Security and Co-operation in Europe
PSPO	Public Spaces Protection Order
RTA Ltd	Rio Tinto Alcan Limited
SCM	Stereotype Content Model
UKIP	United Kingdom Independence Party

Notes on contributors

Editor

Marian Duggan is a Senior Lecturer in Criminology at the University of Kent. Her research interests cover gender, sexuality and victimisation, particularly in relation to hate crimes and violence prevention. She is currently researching domestic violence prevention policies and gendered experiences of hate crime. Marian is the author of *Queering Conflict: Examining Lesbian and Gay Experiences of Homophobia in Northern Ireland* (Ashgate, 2012; Routledge, 2016), and (with Vicky Heap) *Administrating Victimization: The Politics of Anti-Social Behaviour and Hate Crime Policy* (Palgrave, 2014). She is also the co-editor (with Malcolm Cowburn, Anne Robinson and Paul Senior) of *Values in Criminology and Community Justice* (Policy Press, 2013).

Contributors

Rebecca Barnes is Lecturer in Criminology at the University of Leicester. She has been researching domestic violence in lesbian, gay, bisexual and/or transgender (LGB and/or T) people's relationships for 15 years. Rebecca was Co-Investigator (with Catherine Donovan) on the Economic and Social Research Council (ESRC)–funded Coral Project (2012–14), which explored partners' use of abusive behaviours in LGB and/or T people's relationships and the availability of inclusive relationships and domestic abuse interventions. More recently, she has been researching churchgoers' perceptions and experiences of domestic abuse in Cumbria, and is currently leading a participatory research study to improve understandings of, and provision for, the mental health needs of LGB and/or T people in Nottingham.

Alice Bosma LLM MSc is finalising her PhD project at the International Victimology Institute Tilburg (INTERVICT), Tilburg University. For this project, she examined observer reactions towards emotional victims of crime: positive reactions such as support and compensation versus negative reactions such as victim blaming. Alice compared the reactions of laypersons to those of legal professionals and worked with judges, public prosecutors and victim support workers in the Netherlands. Next to her PhD project, she worked on other interdisciplinary victimological topics, such as human trafficking (together with C. Rijken) and sexual abuse (together with the Dutch National Rapporteur on Human Trafficking and Child Sexual Abuse).

Hannah Bows is an Assistant Professor in Criminal Law at Durham University. Her research interests cover gender, ageing, violence and victimisation, with a focus on sexual violence, crimes against older people and criminal justice responses to ageing. Her current projects include the homicide of older people and the stalking of male victims. Her monograph, *Sexual Violence Against Older People*, is due to be published by Routledge in 2018. She is the co-author (with Professor Nicole Westmarland) of *Researching Gender, Violence and Abuse: Methods, Theory, Policy*, also due to be published in 2018 by Routledge. She is the editor of a two-volume collection on *Violence Against Older Women* (Palgrave Macmillan, 2019).

Claire Cohen is a Senior Lecturer in Criminology at Nottingham Trent University, and is presently a Doctoral Candidate at the University of Nottingham. Claire is a Critical Criminologist and Foucauldian. Her research interests are varied, but are unified by a passion for epistemology and subscription to the critical stances, including critical victimology. She has a particular interest in gendered knowledges and gendered injustices. Her recent monograph *Male Rape is a Feminist Issue: Feminism, Governmentality and Male Rape*, was published with Palgrave Macmillan in 2014. She is currently working on her second monograph, due for publication with Policy Press in 2019.

Karen Corteen is a Senior Lecturer in Criminal Justice at Liverpool John Moores University. Her research interests cover critical criminology, victimology, crime, harm and victimisation. This includes an interest in crimes of the powerful, particularly in relation to professional wrestling and sports entertainment. Her current joint research project is titled 'Miniature Prisons in the Community: The Secretive World of Police Custody Suites'. Karen is co-editor of a serious of four Companions concerned with criminology, victimology and criminal justice (Policy Press, 2014–17).

Cassandra Cross is a Senior Lecturer in the School of Justice, Queensland University of Technology. Previously, she worked as a research/policy officer with the Queensland Police Service, where she commenced research on the topic of online fraud. In 2011, she was awarded a Churchill Fellowship to examine the prevention and support of online fraud victims worldwide. Since taking up her position at Queensland University of Technology in 2012, she has continued her research into online fraud, across the policing, prevention and victim support aspects. With colleagues, she has received highly competitive Criminology Research Grants, the first in 2013 to conduct the first Australian study into the reporting experiences and support needs of online fraud victims, and another in 2016 to examine the policing of cybercrime in Australia. She is co-author (with Professor Mark Button) of the book *Cyber Frauds, Scams and their Victims* (Routledge, 2017).

Pamela Davies is Professor of Criminology at Northumbria University. Her research interests centre on gender, crime and victimisation, particularly the gendered nature of harm and violence and how this can be prevented and reduced while victims are protected and supported. Pam has a strong interest in theoretical developments in criminology and victimology and her work in this respect is shaped by her concerns about criminal and non-criminal victimisation and experiences of harm, especially women and children as victims and survivors. Pam has written about victimisation in different contexts, including domestic violence and green crime and victimisation. She has authored and edited numerous books, including *Gender, Crime and Victimisation* (Sage, 2011), *Victims, Crime and Society* (2nd edn) (with Peter Francis and Chris Greer) (Sage, 2017), *Invisible Crimes and Social Harms* (with Peter Francis and Tanya Wyatt) (Palgrave Macmillan, 2014) and *Doing Criminological Research* (3rd edn) (with Peter Francis) (Sage, 2018).

Catherine Donovan is Professor in Social Relations and leads research in the Centre for Applied Social Studies in the School of Social Sciences at the University of Sunderland. She has spent nearly 30 years researching the intimate and family lives of lesbians, gay men and, more recently, bisexual and trans people. Currently, she is co-authoring (with Rebecca Barnes) a book on the use of violent and/or abusive behaviour in the relationships of those who are LGB and/or T. Other work includes work on hate crime, particularly on hate relationships, and campus safety. As part of her latter work, Catherine is an institutional lead for a pilot Bystander Intervention Programme.

Stephanie Fohring is a Lecturer in Criminology at Edinburgh Napier University. Her research interests cover victims and victim identity and labelling, crime surveys, and the psychological impact of crime, particularly in relation to crime reporting and the criminal justice system. She is currently researching stereotypes and the social stigma attached to being a victim of crime. Stephanie has previously held a British Academy Post-Doctoral Fellowship and an Economic and Social Research Council (ESRC)/Scottish Government Studentship. She is the author of a growing number of articles and chapters based on her research, and has also recently edited a special issue of the *International Review of Victimology*, titled 'Victim Identities and Hierarchies'.

Carolina Yoko Furusho is an Erasmus Mundus Fellow under the auspices of the European Commission. Carolina is currently a PhD candidate at the Joint Doctorate in Cultural and Global Criminology (DCGC) at the University of Kent and the University of Hamburg. Her research focus lies on international and comparative human rights, feminist and postcolonial approaches to inequality and vulnerability, global victimology, and social justice. She was awarded an LLM with Distinction by University College London and a BCL by the University of São Paulo. She previously worked as a lawyer licensed by the Brazilian Bar Association.

Jorge Gracia teaches Victimology at Escola de Criminologia (School of Criminology), FDUP (Faculty of Law University of Oporto) – Porto (Portugal). His main field of expertise is elder abuse and domestic violence in general. However, his interests include vulnerable groups, discrimination and human rights, social policy, and the connection between cinema and the law. He is also a researcher in the Laboratorio de Sociología Jurídica (Laboratory of Sociology of Law) at the University of Zaragoza (Spain) and collaborates with the Open University of Catalonia (UOC, Barcelona, Spain) as a course instructor of criminology online in the field of the sociology of law. Jorge is author of *Elder Abuse in the Family. a Socio Legal Approach* (*El maltrato familiar hacia las personas mayores. Un análisis sociojurídico*) (PUZ, 2012).

Vicky Heap is a Senior Lecturer in Criminology and Fellow of the Sheffield Institute for Policy Studies at Sheffield Hallam University. She conducts research and lectures in the areas of anti-social behaviour, crime prevention and research methods. Her current research examines victims' experiences of anti-social behaviour and the implementation of the Community Trigger and Community Remedy policies from the Anti-Social Behaviour, Crime and Policing Act 2014. Vicky is editor of the *Safer Communities* journal and co-authored (with Marian Duggan) *Administrating Victimization: The Politics of Anti-Social Behaviour and Hate Crime Policy* (Palgrave, 2014).

Hannah Mason-Bish is a Lecturer in Criminology and Sociology at the University of Sussex and the Director of the Centre for Gender Studies. Hannah's research interests address the development of hate crime policy, with a particular focus on gender-related violence and street harassment. Additionally, she looks at how social problems are constructed and how groups of victims are defined and given policy attention. Hannah is the co-editor (with Alan Roulstone) of *Disability, Hate Crime and Violence* (Routledge, 2013).

Eva Mulder MSc is a PhD researcher at the International Victimology Institute Tilburg (INTERVICT), with a background in social psychology and victimology. Her PhD thesis focuses on negative observer reactions towards stereotypical and non-stereotypical victims of sexual violence, with a specific interest in gender and the 'normalisation' of sexual violence. She has additionally worked on projects involving deradicalisation, victim rights and narratives of victimisation.

Antony Pemberton is Professor of victimology and director of the International Victimology Institute Tilburg (INTERVICT) at Tilburg University in the Netherlands. He is a political scientist and a criminologist. His research interests concern the broad topic of victims and society, including victims' perspectives on justice, societal reactions to victims and processes of victimisation, cultural victimology, narrative victimology, and the ethics of victimology. He has published over 80 articles, book chapters and books on the subject of victimology. Most of his current ideas are reflected in his inaugural address in Tilburg, *Victimology with a Hammer: The Challenge of Victimology* (Prismaprint, 2015).

Jennifer Anne Sloan Rainbow is a Senior Lecturer in Criminology at Sheffield Hallam University. Her research interests include prisons, gender, sexual violence and masculinities. She is author of *Masculinities and the Adult Male Prison Experience* (Palgrave Macmillan, 2016) and co-editor (with Dr Deborah H. Drake and Dr Rod Earle) of the *Palgrave Handbook of Prison Ethnography* (Palgrave Macmillan, 2015).

Sinéad Ring is a Senior Lecturer in Law at the University of Kent. Her research interests lie in law's regulation of sexual violence and law's relationship to history. Her current research explores legal responses to reports of historical child sexual abuse, in particular, what these responses reveal about how a particular society understands itself, and the position of survivors within it. Sinéad's work has been published in *Social and Legal Studies*, *The International Journal of Evidence and Proof* and *The International Journal for Crime, Justice and Social Democracy*.

Irene Zempi is a Lecturer in Criminology, Department of Sociology, Nottingham Trent University. Irene is the co-author of the books *Islamophobia: Lived Experiences of Online and Offline Victimisation* (with Imran Awan) (Policy Press, 2016) and *Islamophobia, Victimisation and the Veil* (with Neil Chakraborti) (Palgrave Macmillan, 2014). Irene is also a board member of Tell MAMA (Measuring Anti-Muslim Attacks), Nottinghamshire Hate Crime Steering Group, Sociological Research Online – Associate Editorial Board, and Sociology Consultative Forum OCR (Oxford, Cambridge and RSA).

Acknowledgements

I would like to sincerely thank all of the contributors to this collection for their time, input and chapters. There are some excellent perspectives and critiques provided in the book, and all delivered bang on schedule – much appreciated! Thanks also to Rebecca Tomlinson and Victoria Pittman at Bristol University Press for their invaluable assistance in the development and production of this edited collection.

I am delighted that David Scott agreed to provide the Foreword to this collection. David was a very supportive influence during my undergraduate studies, embodying and demonstrating the hallmarks of a truly critical scholar that set me on an academic path that helped produce this collection. Thanks Dave!

To the many students that I have taught over the years: our lively debates and discussions have helped shape my thinking and writing around victimology for the better. I want to thank you for your contributions and I hope you took as much from our classes as I did. Victimology is still woefully represented in many UK university Criminology/Criminal Justice degrees, but those of us working in the area shall not be deterred!

Finally, I would like to dedicate this book to my family. Your unwavering support means the world to me; even though some of you are still not entirely sure what I do for a living, knowing that you care is enough. Thank you!

Foreword: thinking beyond the ideal

David Scott, The Open University

This is a timely book and a fitting tribute to the writings and intellectual legacy of the great Norwegian anti-criminologist Nils Christie (1928–2015). The 16 original chapters comprising this excellent collection not only provide an innovative interpretation, but also substantially develop upon one the most important ideas that Christie explored in his long career: the 'ideal victim'. Collectively, the chapter authors evidence the continued relevance of this concept for our understanding of the denial and acknowledgement of harmful outcomes that fall both inside and outside the remit of the criminal law. Indeed, the durability and flexibility of the concept of the 'ideal victim' is perfectly illustrated in the breadth of themes covered in this book, which include chapters on environmental harms, structural violence, sexual violence, hate crime, sex work, Islamophobia and online fraud. I think Nils Christie would have been delighted to see his work applied in such sophisticated and original ways.

Nils Christie was a leading member of the European Group for the Study of Deviance and Social Control and his work is closely associated with the tradition of 'penal abolitionism'. Like his great friend Stanley Cohen (2001), Christie was concerned with the recognition, or not, of human suffering. A 'moral imperialist' and humanist, many of his writings are a direct call to limit unnecessary and useless human suffering. For Christie, it was crucial that, as a society, we attempt to limit and heal pain rather than increase it. This was one of the main reasons why he so strongly opposed harms deliberately initiated through the penal law (Christie, 1981) and why his work has been so influential in victim studies.

Although the intellectual connections between 'penal abolitionism' and 'victimology' are largely underexplored, the links between them are clearly strong as both traditions are grounded in a commitment to acknowledge and subsequently reduce human suffering. Both penal abolitionism and victimology place the person harmed at the centre of their analysis and their top priority is to meet the needs of the victim. Through their reflections on the 'ideal victim', the chapters in this book shine a spotlight on just how important such a victim-centred approach is. The range of topics explored, the nature of the harms interrogated and the invisibility and denial of the victimhood of people on the margins of society demonstrate how dynamic, vibrant and fruitful such an approach can be. A further strength of this collection is the manner in which a number of authors highlight victims of injustice and structural violence. In so doing, they not only further open up important avenues for a victim-centred approach, but also remind us of how victims and offenders can sometimes be the same people, albeit perhaps at different points in their life-course. Abolitionism and victimology stand side by side in the recognition of such victims of injustice, and it should perhaps come as no surprise that the ideas of Christie are associated with ideas of 'transformative justice'.

Nils Christie published his analysis of the social construction of the 'ideal victim' in 1986, and this single contribution provides the starting point for this book (Christie, 1986). His chapter on the 'ideal victim' (included in this volume) is remarkable and groundbreaking, both for its insights and for the ease with which he makes his argument. His analysis is understandable and convincing, although, as a number of chapters in this book highlight, not without its limitations. Providing inspiration for this book is testament that his concept of the 'ideal victim' deserves continued attention, albeit in a critical way.

Nils Christie had a long-standing interest in the denial of victimhood. Indeed, this theme permeates much of his writings. For his masters' thesis, he investigated the attitudes of Norwegian guards who had worked at Nazi camps holding Yugoslavian partisans in Norway during the Second World War. The Nazi camps had been terrible places: in one year, 70% of prisoners died. Christie found that those guards who had treated prisoners worst had been able to deny their captives' common humanity (for discussion, see Christie, 2004). Anticipating the insights of Zygmunt Bauman (1989) some three decades later, Christie noted that the prisoners had been successfully distanced, dehumanised and constructed as 'non-victims' by the guards. Christie (1993) recognised that the more we know someone and accept their basic similarities to us as fellow humans, the more sympathetic we are likely to be towards them. Conversely, the less we know someone, the less likely we are to acknowledge what we share in common or empathise with them. Social and psychic distancing underscored the failure to recognise the pain and suffering of the 'non-ideal' victim.

Empathy and sympathy for a victim may also depend upon who the perpetrator is and if they could be considered an 'ideal enemy' (Christie, 1986). The 'ideal enemy' is the exact opposite of the 'ideal victim' – the ideal enemy is a person easy to dislike and resent. The ideal enemy conforms to the fears and stereotypes touted in populist media. For Christie (1993), the appetite for 'ideal enemies' grows as societies become more and more unequal as inequalities undermine social solidarity and create the conditions for social distance to widen. Marginalised outsiders become raw materials for social control – a population to be blamed and subjected to pain – highlighting that the denial of victimhood should be understood within wider social, economic and political contexts. The respectability, power and status of victim and perpetrator count. Through engaging with a diverse range of harms and actors, the chapters in this book brilliantly tease out such important factors shaping the social construction of the 'ideal victim'.

Nils Christie's work is, then, helpful for understanding how social categories around victimhood are constructed, while, at the same time, also providing a subtle critique of such stereotyping. In his writings, Christie emphasises time and time again how human relationships transcended the artificial barriers and simplifications of human life. In one of his lesser-known works, *Beyond Loneliness and Institutions* (Christie, 1997), he describes life in a rural Norwegian community called Vidaråsen; a place, he tells us in the English translation, that he frequently visited for more than 20 years. Vidaråsen is a commune for extraordinary people who, in wider society, would probably be stereotyped as disabled or as having an illness. For Christie (1997), being separated from such extraordinary people was a great loss to wider society because these extraordinary people, with all of their diversity and difference, would add so much to everyday social life. Christie (1997) highlights here: what we lose collectively when we Other people; what we lose collectively when we fail to acknowledge and assist; and what we lose collectively when we operate on simplified stereotypes and fail to think beyond social constructions of the 'ideal'.

This book provides us with an opportunity to scrutinise and critically reflect upon how we categorise and classify other people, and the implications that this has on the level of care, support and solidarity that they receive. Marian Duggan has done an excellent job in bringing this edited collection together; the original chapters are analytically rigorous and take the concept of the 'ideal victim' in new and interesting directions. This important collection will generate interest and further critical engagement with the ideas of Nils Christie in the coming years, which is all that could ever be asked of it.

References

Bauman, Z. (1989) *Modernity and the Holocaust*, Cambridge: Polity Press.

Christie, N. (1981) *Limits to Pain*, Oxford: Wiley-Blackwell.

Christie, N. (1986) 'The ideal victim', in E.A. Fattah (ed) *From Crime Policy to Victim Policy*, London: Macmillan.

Christie, N. (1993) *Crime Control as Industry?*, London: Routledge.

Christie, N. (1997) *Beyond Loneliness and Institutions: Communes for Extraordinary People*, Oslo: Scandinavian University Press.

Christie, N. (2004) *A Suitable Amount of Crime*, London: Routledge.

Cohen, S. (2001) *States of Denial*, Cambridge: Polity Press.

Preface

This collection has been compiled in memory of Professor Nils Christie, Professor of Criminology at the University of Oslo, who sadly passed away on 27 May 2015. There are many excellent tributes to him and his work in the wake of his death published by those who knew him best and that expertly capture the enormous impact that he had on the criminological domain. This collection seeks to offer an alternative form of tribute through scholarly engagement with his ideas, specifically, his seminal work on the 'ideal victim', by those who have been inspired by his work over the years.

I first read Nils Christie's papers during my undergraduate studies, which was an excellent introduction to the world of critical criminology at the University of Central Lancashire, UK. The passion imparted by many of the lecturers there (including David Scott, who has graciously written the Foreword) emulated the sentiments espoused by Christie and his cohort. They embodied a desire to challenge, question and change (for the better) the status quo; this was a position I readily adopted and have continued to impart (often via Christie's teachings) to my own students over the years. Christie's work resonates with me personally as my research interests focus on gendered and sexual/sexual identity victimisation. My explorations into people's experiences of and responses to domestic violence, sexual violence, violence against women and homophobic violence are founded by a desire to know more about the interconnection between misogyny and homophobia, particularly in light of the emergence of 'hate crime' studies. As such, I find myself straddling various research camps: part 'violence against women' and part 'hate crime'; increasingly more 'gender and sexuality' than 'gender' and 'sexuality'; and ever-more 'victimologist' than 'criminologist'.

Victimology has grown significantly as a topic of both academic study and scholarly research. As most victimological texts assert, the study of victims was initiated by several researchers working to understand the role of victim precipitation in crime prevention. However, like criminology, the positivistic approach adopted by many early victim researchers led to a significant backlash from an emerging cohort of critical and radical scholars, particularly those concerned with the impact of 'victim precipitation' discourses on female victims of sexual and domestic violence. This is evidenced clearly in Christie's writings, with many references made to the societal inequalities informing additional hardships faced by women victims of crime. This critique broadened to address other identity factors, resulting in a more inclusive victimological scholarship that now encompasses a range of competing and complementary perspectives.

It has been a pleasure to see the adaptation of Christie's work emerge across various themes. The chapters in this book can be read independently or as a whole, but I would recommend reading Christie's chapter first if you are unfamiliar with it. For readers who like the format adopted in this volume, you will be pleased to know that a similar version exists! *Values in Criminology and Community Justice* is a collection of responses to Howard Becker's 1967 seminal article 'Whose side are we on?', also published by Policy Press. My co-editors (Malcolm Cowburn, Anne Robinson and Paul Senior) and I brought together 16 scholars who, over 22 chapters, demonstrated clear links between the application of Becker's theoretical debates to a range of criminal justice areas. It was a great experience and very favourably received among colleagues. I am therefore delighted to have been given the opportunity to undertake a similar endeavour with the present volume, and I very much hope you enjoy reading it.

Marian Duggan
4 January 2018

Introduction

Marian Duggan

Revisiting the 'Ideal Victim': Developments in Critical Victimology presents a collection of academic responses to the late Nils Christie's (1986) seminal chapter, in which he addressed the socially constructed concept of an idealised form of victim status or identity. In unpacking what it was to be a 'victim' in a given society, Christie highlighted the complex factors informing the application or rejection of such a status while illustrating the role of subjective/objective perspectives on personal/societal responses to victimisation. In sum, he outlined the existence of an 'ideal victim': '*a person or category of individuals, who – when hit by crime – most readily are given the complete and legitimate status of being a victim*' (Christie 1986: 18, emphasis in original). It is his example of the little old lady who is hit on the head by a big, bad man who grabs her bag (and uses the money for liquor or drugs while she is on her way home in the middle of the day after having cared for her sick sister) that forms the basis for the first five of the six key attributes highlighted in the construction of the 'ideal victim' (Christie, 1986: 19):

> (1) The victim is weak. Sick, old or very young people are particularly well suited as ideal victims. (2) The victim was carrying out a respectable project – caring for her sister [as per Christie's example]. (3) She was where she could not possibly be blamed for being – in the street during the daytime. (4) The offender was big and bad. (5) The offender was unknown and in no personal relationship to her.

This piece of writing and the concept Christie outlined within it has become a most frequently cited theme of victimological (and, where relevant, criminological) academic scholarship over the past 30 years. Recognising this, the proposed volume seeks to celebrate and commemorate Nils Christie's contribution to victimology by analysing, evaluating and critiquing the current nature and impact of victim identity, experience, policy and practice in light of this 'ideal victim' concept. Within this, it has been imperative to recognise that the decision regarding what is and is not a 'crime' often reflects political power and interests. All this requires scholars working in and around the field of victim studies to critically engage with how 'victims' and 'victimhood' are conceptualised in the current climate.

This edited collection is original in that it is the first volume of its kind to take Christie's work and apply a thematically focused response from a range of different issues. It is also the first to do this from a victimology perspective in a manner that showcases the breadth and depth of current victimological work. The chapters in this volume offer comprehensive, timely and topical analyses of Christie's key text in a manner that evidences how it has been instrumental in informing victimology and victim studies. The thematic evaluation and application of the concept to a range of victim issues and identities encompasses a multiplicity of people, experiences, spaces and activities, which, in turn, demonstrates the varied and vast nature of this topic. The contributions are provided by a selection of leading scholars who are actively engaged in their relative fields of research. They have produced cutting-edge commentary on their respective topics while demonstrating the application of research and/or theory to specialist areas of criminological and victimological knowledge and practice. Their brief was to evaluate the impact and applicability of Christie's 'ideal victim' concept in a variety of victim-specific domains in order to address and analyse elements of change or continuity. This has allowed for the progression and expansion of the focus and remit of 'victim studies' to encompass new and diverse identities, experiences and discourses in a rapidly changing environment. The contributions in this volume offer and seek to inspire critical commentary on a range of new, emerging and developed areas of victim studies.

Background to the book

Criminology is increasing in popularity in most UK universities, becoming one of the fastest-growing and stable degree pathways and, more recently, being offered as a module in Sociology A Level courses. Coverage of the victim and related victimisation studies can be considered a core component within criminology. Victimology, victim studies and victim policy are also becoming more visible on undergraduate criminology degrees in the UK and elsewhere. Within this developing academic domain, a victimological divide has become evident in research produced by scholars in the US compared to those based in the UK/Western Europe. Publications emerging from the US tend to focus heavily on a quantitative and/or positivist approach to identifying, addressing and understanding victimisation, whereas in the UK and Western Europe, a broader, more qualitative and often critical approach has been evident. Nonetheless, scholarship that can be defined as 'victimological' in nature has tended to focus on the same interpersonal issues addressed within criminological research.

For years, criminological inquiry focused predominantly on the offender, the criminal justice system (CJS) and society at large. However, as Christie (1986: 28) notes, this was not *all* offenders, but 'ideal' offenders: those who are 'distant', 'foreign', 'less humane', a 'non-person' – the more so the better. Certainly, this has been a central critique of the discipline; there is still much to research around corporate, white-collar and upper-class crimes. Compared to the overall expansion of criminology as an academic discipline during the 20th century, which resulted in a wealth of research, theory and knowledge regarding the CJS, victims of harm have been described as the 'forgotten players' in the CJS. Victims have occupied a lesser focus in statutory and academic rhetoric, but this state of affairs has begun to change significantly over the past three decades.

The notion of the 'victim' has undergone considerable theorisation, analysis and re-conceptualisation since Christie published his chapter (Mawby and Walklate, 1994; Spencer and Walklate, 2016). These developments have been informed by factors ranging from the changing nature of societies to the growth in mobile technologies and social networking, as well as a broader consideration of victimisation to include issues such as zemiology (Hillyard et al, 2004). Victimology, therefore, has grown significantly as a topic of both academic study and scholarly research. As most victimological texts assert, the study of victims was initiated by several researchers working to understand the role of victim precipitation in crime prevention. Scholars such as Mendelsohn (1947), Von Hentig (1948) and Wolfgang (1957) pioneered the foregrounding of the victim in understanding and responding to crime. Indeed, the links between Christie's and Mendelsohn's work on atrocities committed during the Holocaust evidence the continuation of this broader approach to addressing victimhood.

The positivistic approach that many early victim studies academics adopted, however, led to a significant backlash from an emerging cohort of critical and radical scholars, particularly those concerned with the impact of 'victim precipitation' discourses on female victims of sexual violence. This is evidenced clearly in Christie's writing, with many references made to the societal inequalities informing additional hardships faced by women victims of crime. Evident (although not always explicitly addressed) is the role that gender plays in determining victim status. The examples he uses to convey the attributes that support or refute this 'ideal victim' status being conferred upon a person are grounded in gender relations. These include where a rape victim is a 'young virgin', an 'experienced lady' or a prostitute, as well as how 'family violence' – including sexual abuse, domestic violence and child abuse – is not prioritised in societal concerns (Christie, 1986: 19).

This critique broadened to address other identity factors, resulting in a more inclusive victimological scholarship that now encompasses a range of competing and complementary perspectives. Many victimology texts have since moved on from addressing the origins and developments of this discipline (often categorised as a sub-discipline of criminology) to applying a victimological analysis of specific issues. For example, violence against women has progressed significantly from the narrow understandings and restricted definitions of sexual victimisation which meant that many women could not seek justice for harms that did not fit the specifics of demarcated acts or assailants. Similar developments have been witnessed in the recognition of, and response to, child abuse (sexual or otherwise). In the UK, the ongoing investigations as part of Operation Yewtree have prompted discussions about historical child sexual abuse and the treatment of victims, both at the time of the offences taking place (in many cases, decades before the perpetrators were apprehended, if, indeed, they ever were) and later at the point of disclosure.

In another sign of changing times, legal protections now exist for those who once faced persecution on the basis of their minority racial, religious, sexual orientation, disability or gender identities. The emergence of 'hate crime' discourses, policies and legislation in the US and UK over the past 30 years has demonstrated significant changes in the recognition and socio-political response to people persecuted on the basis of their minority status. However, with these macro-changes have come other, more subtle, shifts. Victim hierarchies are becoming more evident within and across groups; take, for example, the perceived trajectory of harm and culpability affiliated to victims in cases of sexual violence, where differentiations are made between 'real' (stranger) and 'date' (acquaintance) rapes. Similarly, the differing media responses and rewards for information about missing children Madeline McCann and Shannon Matthews indicated a significant class bias. Discrepancies are also evident in responses to hate crime victimisation, with this largely being dependent on the identity of the victim (see Duggan and Heap, 2014). Developments have also been evident in a move away from person-centred crimes and towards scholarly analyses of crime and victimisation linked to environmental studies, animal abuse and artificial intelligence. While not all of these themes are evident in the present collection, they are indicative of the leaps made in victimology and the potential areas of future development for established and emergent researchers.

Outline of the collection

The degree to which Christie's 'ideal victim' concept is informing and sustaining diversification in victimological inquiry will be illustrated throughout the chapters in this book. By adopting a thematic approach, each author invokes Christie's concept and evaluates this in relation to their own area or subject of expertise. Explorations of research, theory, policy and practice are supplemented with case studies, media analyses, political rhetoric, international comparisons (where relevant) and gendered/raced/classed critiques to emulate the holistic – yet critically evaluative – tone of the existing sociological and criminological works. Several key themes evidently inherent to the chapters are critiques of power, knowledge, identity, status, the ability to recognise harm experienced or imparted, comparisons over time/space/place, and so forth. The chapters have been selected on the basis of topicality, relevance and contemporary applicability to global issues. The chapters address: conceptual and practical issues; identity characteristics within and beyond those highlighted in Christie's work; international perspectives; policy and procedure; idealised versus contested victim experience and identity; interdisciplinary foci; and a range of harms, from interpersonal to historical to financial. Christie's concept of the 'non-ideal' victim is also addressed by several contributors to the volume.

The book begins with Christie's chapter before dividing into two sections: Part One: Exploring the Ideal Victim; and Part Two: Exploring the Non-Ideal Victim. As the first chapter in Part One, Alice Bosma, Eva Mulder and Antony Pemberton expand on and react to Christie's key arguments, particularly his assumption that the most important reasons for perceiving a victim as legitimate and blameless lie in the specific attributes of the victim, and those of the relationship between victim and offender. Using more contemporary theories in victimology, such as the Stereotype Content Model and the Moral Typecasting Theory, they emphasise the importance of two observer-related aspects that Christie leaves underdeveloped: the individual's sense of threat and subsequent coping when confronted with a victim; and society's particular interests and values at the time of victimisation. They show how the concept of framing can be used to explain how victims may (ex post) be accepted as ideal or non-ideal, irrelevant of their 'objective' attributes, but dependent on the *framer*, either on a collective or individual level. In Chapter Two, Hannah Mason-Bish, suggests that problems around the perception of the nature of hate crime mean that disabled victims of hate crime are often overlooked. Born out of an identity politics that sought recognition for the specific harms of hate crime, the development of policy has been shaped by sometimes simplistic perceptions of what it is to be victimised. This reliance on identity politics has often meant that victims of disablist hate crime are portrayed as weak and vulnerable, a situation that Christie suggests can contribute to anxiety and a questionable focus on the need for severe punishments. Mason-Bish argues that Christie's notion of the ideal victim is relevant today, with an increasing emphasis on identity politics used to demonstrate that some victims are both 'deserving' and 'legitimate'.

In Chapter Three, Irene Zempi discusses how Muslim women who wear the veil in public are stigmatised as 'other' and demonised as 'dangerous'. Specifically, the wearing of the veil is understood as a practice synonymous with religious fundamentalism and Islamist extremism. Correspondingly, media discourses and political rhetoric about Islamist extremism are often illustrated by the image of a Muslim woman in a veil. Veiled Muslim women who experience hate crime are likely to fall into this ideal victim category. However, they are often denied this identity due to the demonisation and criminalisation of the veil, especially in light of it being banned in European countries such as France and Belgium. Rather, they are seen as hate crime victims on the margins. The issue of identity is furthered in Chapter Four by Catherine Donovan and Rebecca Barnes, who identify the need to make victimised lesbian, gay, bisexual and/or transgender (LGB and/or T) people visible within discussions of eligibility for ideal victim status. Using two examples of victimisation, the authors consider why LGB and/or T people can more easily access an ideal victim status when victimised by hate than is possible for those victimised by (or enacting) domestic violence and abuse. The contrasting examples demonstrate that LGB and/or T individuals' status as ideal victims (or offenders) is tenuous and dependent on the type of victimisation experienced. In both cases, they illustrate how the importance of raising awareness, countering victim-blaming and building trust and the accessibility of support services is critical to improving responses to LGB and/or T people. Taking a more gendered approach, in Chapter Five, Karen Corteen evaluates the degree to which sex workers have been included in criminal justice hate crime policies and practices. Hate crime laws are important symbolically in the messages that they convey to offenders, victims, institutions and society, strongly censuring crimes and victimisation motivated by bias and/or hatred. They acknowledge and signal the harms experienced by the victim and the group to which they belong. Given that female sex workers challenge the concept of the 'ideal victim', the introduction and acceptance of sex worker hate crime victimisation invites a re-evaluation of this central historical and contemporaneous victimological concept.

In Chapter Six, Carolina Yoko Furusho focuses on the polarised debate surrounding the limits of ethical state responses to migration. She shows how, on the one hand, there is the deviant and dangerous migrant 'Other' in the societal imagination, which bears an intimate link to the moral panics underlying national security discourses and increasingly stricter 'crimmigration' laws. The ascension of this derogatory stereotype resonates with Christie's assessment that the more foreign and the less human someone is, the closer to the notion of the 'ideal offender' they become. However, on the other hand, the expansion of globalised networks of solidarity has propelled a powerful, albeit double-edged, discourse on migrant vulnerability in human rights advocacy, framing migrants as 'ideal vulnerable victims' of human rights violations as a means to tackle the anti-migrant discourse that purports to construct the image of migrants as *a priori* offenders until proven otherwise. In Chapter Seven, a similarly topical issue is addressed by Sinéad Ring, who examines the salience of Christie's conceptualisation of the ideal victim/offender in the context of legal and political responses to reports of historic childhood sexual abuse in Ireland. She demonstrates how abusers were typically perceived as monstrous while the survivors were not 'ideal' because they threatened the established order of Church and state. This shows how non-ideal victims may still be effective in informing and sustaining values and meanings in society. Ring argues that, contrary to Christie, non-ideal victims may still gain political purchase if their offenders fit preconceived, idealised notions.

In Chapter Eight, Marian Duggan addresses the age-old issue of domestic violence victimisation, an area that has long been contested with regards to 'idealised' victims. Socio-political rhetoric often poses the question 'Why didn't she leave?', yet feminist research indicates that leaving a violent partner increases a victim's vulnerability to escalated violence and fatality. Drawing on the ideal victim concept and the 'cultural heritage of male dominance' (Christie, 1986: 20), Duggan's research into the Domestic Violence Disclosure Scheme, also known as 'Clare's Law', demonstrates how this policy may be putting applicants at greater risk through expectations of safeguarding measures, as well as the potential impact the increased independence underpinning this scheme may have on wider victim-blaming discourses linked to domestic violence. Finally, in Chapter Nine, Pamela Davies addresses an area that has emerged since Christie's publication: green criminology. This is broadly concerned with an analysis of environmental harms from a criminological and victimological perspective, exploring how victims suffer as a result of environmental damage, how environmental harms might be prevented and how criminal and non-criminal forms of such harms might be responded to. Invoking a case study of the closure of an aluminium smelter at Lynemouth, Northumberland, North-East England, Davies reflects on how green criminology in general clearly illustrates the diffuse nature of crime and victimisation and how this conceptualisation of criminality – but, more significantly for this chapter, how this conceptualisation of *victimisation* – is at complete odds with the individualised concept of the 'ideal victim'.

Part Two begins with Chapter Ten, in which Stephanie Fohring focuses on those who do not want to be associated with a victim label. She demonstrates how some people go to great lengths to avoid the negative societal reactions affiliated with this identity, rendering evident the potential for psychological distress. Fohring's analysis is explained via social psychological theory and cognitive processing – the idea that in order to go about our daily lives, we need to hold a number of fundamental (though not necessarily accurate) beliefs about ourselves and the world. She argues that avoiding victimisation, or at least avoiding the victim identity and label, is thereby potentially an effective means of protecting one's foundational belief system and maintaining personal well-being. Following this, in Chapter Eleven, Vicky Heap centres on the creation of anti-social behaviour (ASB) legislation to govern nuisance and sub-criminal behaviour. She notes that from 1998, a vast number of ASB tools and powers have been introduced to tackle behaviour that causes (or is likely to cause) harassment, alarm or distress to one or more persons not of the same household. Heap critically deconstructs notions of ASB victimisation by focusing on conceptualising individual and community experiences of ASB, assessing how far Christie's ideal victim framework can be applied to this area. In doing so, she takes into account victims' perceptions of their own victim status, attributes such as vulnerability and the extent to which individuals' victim status is legitimised by society.

Legitimation is also the theme of Chapter Twelve, in which Hannah Bows draws on data from the first national study to examine the extent of recorded rape offences involving a victim aged 60 or over to challenge the depiction of the 'ideal' older rape victim that dominates the media coverage of such cases. Noting how feminists have largely distanced themselves from issues relating to older women, her analysis demonstrates how older rape victims do not fit the 'real-rape' stereotype of a young attractive woman who is attacked, late at night, because of her sexual desirability. However, when cases of rape involving older people hit the headlines, the 'ideal' victim that Christie describes is crucial in framing and conceptualising their victimisation. In particular, older people are portrayed in the media as inherently vulnerable, old and frail, seemingly making them ideal victims. Validity is also addressed by Cassandra Cross in Chapter Thirteen, where she assesses online fraud victimisation – a crime that affects millions of individuals globally and often with devastating effects. These extend far beyond pure financial losses to a deterioration of physical health and emotional well-being, depression, relationship breakdown, unemployment, homelessness, and, in extreme cases, suicide. Despite the prevalence of victimisation and the severity of its impact, it remains a contested and fraught area, whereby there is a strong victim-blaming attitude towards those who respond to fraudulent approaches. Using the narratives of 80 online fraud victims in Australia, Cross examines how online fraud victims are often denied victim status despite the offences perpetrated against them.

In Chapter Fourteen, Jennifer Anne Sloan Rainbow also draws on her empirical research with men in prison to show how they are often seen as the creators of victims, and are positioned as completely opposed to the 'ideal victim'. Yet, many prisoners are actually victims themselves, in their past, present and future lives, physically, mentally and emotionally. Drawn from interviews conducted as part of an ethnographic study, Rainbow examines the vulnerabilities of men in prison and the unseen victimisation processes that they undergo. Male prisoners may, in many cases, be victims of the socio-structural inequalities and class-based 'structural violence' that Christie (1986: 24) highlighted; however, in addressing the subjective identities occupied by these 'non-ideal' victims, a greater understanding of the truths and experiences of the 'non-ideal' offender is provided. Taking a similar position in Chapter Fifteen, Claire Cohen employs the highly publicised case of Lynndie England, for crimes that included photographically documented acts of sexual violence against male detainees in her care, to question the absence of a sea-change of criminological inquiry into female sexual offending against male victims. Employing a Foucauldian analysis of knowledge production in the academy, Cohen examines the gender stasis that surrounds sexual violence research, and articulates the discursive mechanisms underlying it – arguing that the ideal victim binary, in the area of sexual violence, constitutes a gender-normative taxonomy that functions as a governmentalised 'regime of truth'.

In Chapter Sixteen, Jorge Gracia suggests that challenging some of the inadequate understandings of 'compassion' and its limits may help provide scholars with a useful policy of compassion as a public virtue. In turn, this may generate stronger and more accurate institutions for victim support. Such an approach requires being especially aware of the processes of differentiation and hierarchies that ultimately distinguish between 'good' and 'bad' victims: those deemed worthy of support and compassion; and those that inspire only oblivion or contempt. Further reflections on and developments of the impacts and negative effects of the stereotype of the 'ideal victim' present in Nils Christie's work are a good starting point to achieving an inclusive and critical victimology. Considering the criticisms levied at victimology over the years, this approach may be a way to recover some of the lost prestige of the discipline. Finally, the collection ends with a concluding chapter that summarises the key messages imparted across the various contributions and where discussions may lead on to from here.

References

Christie, N. (1986) 'The ideal victim', in E.A. Fattah (ed) *From Crime Policy to Victim Policy: Reorienting the Justice System*, London: Macmillan.

Duggan, M. and Heap, V. (2014) *Administrating Victimization: The Social Politics of Anti-Social Behaviour and Hate Crime Policy*, Basingstoke: Palgrave Macmillan.

Hillyard, P., Pantazis, C., Tombs, S. and Gordon, D. (eds) (2004) *Beyond Criminology: Taking Harm Seriously*, London: Pluto Press.

Mawby, R. and Walklate, S. (1994) *Critical Victimology*, London: Sage.

Mendelsohn, B. (1947) 'New biopsychosocial horizons: victimology', paper presented to the Psychiatric Society of Bucharest, Coltzea State Hospital, Hungary.

Spencer, D. and Walklate, S. (eds) (2016) *Critical Victimology: Reconceptualizations, Interventions and Possibilities*, Maryland, MD: Lexington Books.

Von Hentig, H. (1948) *The Criminal and His Victim: Studies in the Socio-Biology of Crime*, Cambridge, MA: Yale University Press.

Wolfgang, M. (1957) 'Victim precipitated criminal homicide', *Journal of Criminal Law, Criminology and Police Science*, 48(1): 1–11.

The Ideal Victim

Nils Christie[1]

On being a victim

It is often useful within the social sciences to rely on personal experiences, or at least take this as our point of departure. So, given the challenge to lecture on the topic "Society and the victim", I started out with some reflections on my own past history. Had I ever been a victim, and if so, when and how? And I will ask you in this audience to engage in the same exercise. Have you ever been victims? When was that? Where was it? What characterized the situation? How did you react? How did your surroundings react? Maybe I could ask you to scribble down just a few words from your own personal histories as a victim, not for my use, but for your own. Such personal memories might prove valuable during my presentation, and particularly during our later discussions.

My personal conclusion as a result of my reflections came actually as a certain surprise, at least to myself. It turned out that I had great trouble in finding any example at all of having been a victim. The closest to being one was a summer night far back in time. It was in Finland. The night was light as nights are in the North during summer, and in addition it had the soft blue qualities so particular to Finland. A colleague, we were some 20 to 30 criminologists out in the forest, proposed a running competition down to a nearby lake and back again.

I was the only one who accepted. Before I had reached the shore, he was up again to the point of departure. When I came up there, the group had gone home. At that time, I felt like a *loser*. When I later got to know that the man who proposed the competition was a Swedish champion in running, I redefined my situation into being a *victim*.

Upon further scrutiny of my personal history I have been able to remember a few cases of stolen bikes, one of someone breaking and entering into my apartment, a child carrier was once stolen, a cottage broken into. But it was not important. It is the blue night in Finland that I do remember.

My preliminary reflections are two: Firstly, being a victim is not a thing, an objective phenomenon. It will not be the same to all people in situations externally described as being the "same." *It has to do with*

11

the participants' definition of the situation. Some will see victory (I dared to participate) where others see victims (I was cheated). Secondly, the phenomenon can be investigated both at the personality level and at the social system level. Some might have personalities that make them experience themselves as victims in most life situations while others tend to define life according to other dimensions. The tendency to see oneself as a victim might in the perspective be called a personality trait. At the level of social systems, some systems might be of the type where a lot of victimization is seen as taking place, while others are seen as being without victims. In what follows, I will concentrate on the sociology of the phenomena.

The ideal victim

Doing so, I will raise the question: what characterizes — at the social level — the ideal victim? With the term "ideal victim" I do not think of the person or category most perceiving herself or himself as a victim. Nor do I think of those in the greatest danger of being victimized or most often victimized. These might or might not be included. *By "ideal victim" I have instead in mind a person or a category of individuals who — when hit by crime — most readily are given the complete and legitimate status of being a victim.* The ideal victim is, in my use of the term, a sort of public status of the same type and level of abstraction as that for example of a "hero" or a "traitor." It is difficult to count these ideal victims. Just as it is difficult to count heroes. But, they can be exemplified. Most of us will have some cases in mind. Let me give you one from my culture: the little old lady on her way home in the middle of the day after having cared for her sick sister. If she is hit on the head by a big man who thereafter grabs her bag and uses the money for liquor or drugs — in that case, we come in my country, close to the ideal victim. It is so by at least five attributes:

(1) The victim is weak. Sick, old or very young people are particularly well suited as ideal victims.
(2) The victim was carrying out a respectable project — caring for her sister.
(3) She was where she could not possibly be blamed for being — in the street during the daytime.
(4) The offender was big and bad.
(5) The offender was unknown and in no personal relationship to her.

A contrasting example of a far from ideal victim would be a young man hanging around in a bar, hit on the head by an acquaintance who took his money. His head might be more severely hurt than that of the old lady, his money more dear to him. Nonetheless, he could not compete with her for getting the status as an ideal victim.

- He was strong.
- He was not carrying out any respectable project.
- He could and should have protected himself by not being there.
- He was as big as the offender.
- And he was close to the offender.

The importance of these differences is illustrated in rape cases. The ideal case here is the young virgin on her way home from visiting sick relatives, severely beaten or threatened before she gives in. From this there are light-years in distance to the experienced lady on her way home from a restaurant, not to talk about the prostitute who attempts to activate the police in a rape case.

So far I have stated that the *ideal victim is weak compared to the unrelated offender*, as well as having put a *reasonable energy into protecting herself* (in rare cases himself) against becoming a victim. These are necessary conditions. But they are not always sufficient. This is illustrated if we move into the area of family-violence. In my country, husbands can be convicted for raping their wives. I do not need to emphasize that the sentenced males are few and far between, and that their raped wives do not exactly represent the ideal type of victims. Such is also the case with wife-beating and maltreatment of children within families. We have every reason to believe that this is a major area of violent crime in my country, but still it seems to have been, up to very recently, next to impossible to get the phenomena out in the open, that is to sentence the criminals and to convey upon the victims their legitimate status as suffering victims.

Why?

I think the feminists have given the right answers. It is in the interest of all parties, except that of a few isolated rapists, to protect females against foreign intruders. It is in everyone's interest to protect our children against deviant monsters lurking in the streets or parks. Such monsters ought to get a sentence for life and the victims every possible care and attention. But my home is my castle. Children might behave provocatively, also sexually. And wives have after all entered a contractually-based relationship, one of providing mutual services. There is more between heaven and earth than neighbors can understand, and – so it is said – the man might have some relatively good reasons for his behavior. The extended family has shrunk, the servants have disappeared, left are isolated nuclear families with a cultural heritage of male dominance. Rudely expressed: beaten wives are not such ideal victims because we – males – understand the phenomena so extraordinarily well, and because we can get our definition of the situation to be the valid one. It is according to males' "Weltanschaung" and interests not to see rough handling of cohabitants as creating victims. When the man beat up his wife in my culture, and the police are called in, they called it, until recently, a case of "husbråk." That means noise in the house. Noise does not create good victims. Noise is something that needs to be muffled.

But with these examples, we enter an area where recently great changes have taken place. Wives are not "ideal victims." Not yet. But they are approaching that status. They are more ideal today than yesterday. The explanation of this development is probably as simple as it is sad: the development has taken place *because we are now affluent enough*, and *not* because we have improved morally, *not* because we are becoming more kind. We are now so affluent that parties can divorce – leave. Wives do not have to take it anymore. With changed material conditions, women find it less "natural" to receive the beating or domestic raping. They are also closer to a position where they can claim that their definition of the situation is the valid one. They can make the political claim of being real victims. As ideal as the old ladies. Or as the virgins walking home from caring for the sick.

This is not quite the situation. Not quite, and not yet. But development is moving in that direction. There are no reasons to believe that violence within the family has increased. But the status of women has changed. Their material conditions have changed, so has their self-conception. Beaten wives have thus come several steps closer to being ideal victims, that is – to be seen and to see themselves as such a species.

A condition, number six, for being an ideal victim, is thus that you are powerful enough to make your case known and successfully claim the status of an ideal victim. Or alternatively, that you are not opposed by so strong counter-powers that you can not be heard.

★★★

Could we conceive of a situation where ordinary women, wives or cohabitants, received, so to say, complete status as ideal victims if they were physically maltreated by their partners? I am, out of pure theory, far from certain that this ever could happen. I am even in doubt if it *ought* to happen. My reasoning above was that females got their definition of being victims of their cohabitants to stick when they got a material base for independence. But as (if) that base improves further, a new problem will arise. *Females can protect themselves by leaving. Why not then just leave if violence seems to come up?* Through independence they become similar to the man in the bar. He should have known before and left. And so should she. The more females attain an independent status, the more useful it is for them to claim victim-status, and the more they are listened to. But at the same time: the more they gain independence, materially, the less credibility is given to any claim of victim-status as a result of weakness or lack of possibilities for self-protection. I am well aware that my reasoning here is almost like discussing the dangers of too much rain in the Sahara. Equal rights for females are equally far away. When I nevertheless bring up the point, I do it out of pure theoretical concerns. The reasoning brings to the surface another important element in being an ideal victim: she (or sometimes he) must be strong enough to be listened to, or dare to talk. But she (he) must at the very same time be *weak enough not to become a threat to other important interests*. A minimum of strength is a precondition to being listened to, but sufficient strength to threaten others would not be a good base for creating the type of general and public sympathy that is associated with the status of being a victim.

Let me illustrate the importance of weakness through a description of some ladies who never made it as authorized victims.

The non-ideal victim

Just a few weeks ago, I spent an evening with a person who in Medieval times never would have achieved the status as an ideal victim. It was a lady in her late forties. Her face is what I remember best. It expressed, continually, such an unusual range of variation, a one-dimensional change, but wide and enormously fast. In the one second she had stars in her eyes and happiness expressed in every little wrinkle. In the next, her eyes were filled with sorrow, and her face with despair, bordering on hatred. I came to learn that this was a hate directed towards herself. But what if I had not come to know? And what if I had lived in a cultural framework which led me into alternative interpretations? The lady had a problem which might have complicated both her and my life if she had lived in another century, and I had met her at that time. She had a problem with small devils. Sometimes they crawled all over her. They represented a great nuisance to her. And they also indicated that she was a bad person. To me, she typified the "Arch-sinner." But she had good luck. She lives now. And she lives with people who are more influenced by the glittering stars in her eyes, than by her hatred. They relieve her with what I would call an arch-healing process. They make a little performance where they pick up all the small devils from her body, kick them out of the house and lock the door behind.

Four centuries earlier, we would have burned her. She confesses to having devils all over. She looks, in her bad moments, like a witch. She claims to be one. I have very seldom met such a clear case of a witch. And she is talkative. Maybe we even did not need to torture her to get information on other witches in the district. She could trigger off a big witch-hunt. We might be able to clean up the whole country, to the protection of our souls and to the glory of God.

My point is a simple one: ladies, weak or old, have not always been "ideal victims" mobilizing our sympathy. Today we can see the old witches as victims of oppression. But that is four hundred years too late. At the time of the witch-hunt, their torture was a matter of course and their burning a part of the public entertainment. Why were they not seen as victims, then?

There are, as we know, several theories on the forces behind the great witch-hunts of Medieval Europe.[2] For our purpose, it suffices to point to two striking contrasts between that time and ours. First: the role of females, particularly the older ones, have changed. In general, they seem to have had more power at that time than today. They had important functions, at birth, in cases of sickness, and in cases of death. And they had secrets. People with secrets do also have power, or potentialities for power. While our feelings toward our old ladies of today might be characterized by guilt due to the lack of attention we give them, our predecessors' feelings seem to have been more of respect and fear. This point must, however, not be stretched too far. By and large witches were recruited from the lower social strata. A great amount of power meant you were at least better protected against being forced into the status. A small amount of power was more suitable for witches.

The second contrasting element between that time and ours has to do with the general belief-system. Hell was a reality in Medieval times. The Devil was a King, small devils were his servants, witches his sub-servants – and his concubines. The Medieval times had also explanatory systems when it came to sickness and misfortune which made witches useful. People could bring it upon each other, with witches as intermediators. In that time, sickness was caused by human motives like envy or greed, where we today think of germs and too great a quota of cholesterol. The little old lady of today is stripped of power and important social functions in a culture with other beliefs. That makes her, in contrast to the ladies of the witch-age, particularly well suited for the role of the ideal victim in criminal cases. We are already swamped with guilt in our relationships to her. A crime against her gives us a most welcome opportunity to turn our attention – and emotions and anger – to the criminal.

★★★

But maybe Medieval thinking also had *some strengths* exactly because of its *personification of the source of unwanted conditions*. Personification makes action possible. This we find illustrated if we turn our attention to another type of non-ideal victim, one that is prevalent in our type of society. What I here have in mind is the ignorant victim, the one victimized without knowing. Or rather, the many victimized without knowing, neither that they are victimized, nor the source.

Sickness might again serve as an illustration. While I write this paper, the news reaches me that workers will have to pay more for their life insurance than functionaries. They have to pay higher premiums to their *own* insurance company, the one owned and run by the Labour Movement of my country. We are so sorry, say the representatives of the company, but the simple fact is that workers die earlier than functionaries. In the competitive market situation workers will therefore have to pay more, or the firm will go broke. Even though most of us in Scandinavia have become immensely more wealthy than before, class differences remain. People die unnecessarily early by belonging to the wrong class. They are victims of structural violence.

I lost the running-competition in that Finnish summer night. But later I got the information that enabled me to see myself as a victim, not just a loser or a failure. Furthermore, I got information that enabled me to find the offender. Instead of wasting my energies on improving my speed, a hopeless task in competition with a champion, or instead of brooding over one more failure in life, I was able to scold my competitor for unsporting behavior (and thereby initiate a lasting friendship) and thereafter choose an arena for life expressions more suited to my strengths than my weaknesses.

The working class child in the school system does not know that she or he is taking part in a competition designed by and for children from classes above. The working class child will take the defeat, as documented again and again in the studies of education, as a personal failure. It will be one more of the long row of signals that build up to the stable pattern of accepting rewards not so good as those at the top of society. Not victims, but losers become their self-definition. And most important: there are no particular culprits in this game. No specific person had laid down the rules that make class background essential for the outcome of the educational process. No particular individual is – more than others in his class – responsible for the shorter life-expectancy among workers. Workers become victims without offenders. Such victims are badly suited.

Witches and workers are non-ideal victims – victims in the meaning of seeing themselves or getting others to see them as such – because they have important, but not sufficient strengths, because other people have contrary interests, and because they lived or live in cultures with personalized responsibilities for sickness (witches), but with depersonalized responsibilities for living and working conditions (workers).

The ideal and the not-so-ideal offender

Ideal victims need – and create – ideal offenders. The two are interdependent. An old lady who breaks her hip after a fall on an icy pathway gets sympathy, but no headlines. If her fall were due to a pursesnatcher, she would have been well suited for at least a notice in the local newspaper. The more ideal a victim is, the more ideal becomes the offender. The more ideal the offender, the more ideal is the victim.

The point might be illustrated through the not-so-ideal offender. I have three types in mind. One is the drug-pusher. In Norwegian we call him "narkohai," that means "narco-shark." It is the big operator, the man who imports large quantities of dangerous drugs, the man who cynically and just for profit, causes enormous sufferings in the population. He does not use drugs himself. He does it only for the money. To punish him, we have increased the penal tariffs enormously. Our Parliament, the "Storting," has just received a proposal from our Cabinet to increase the tariff to 21 years for such dealers. In practice, it will be a harsher punishment than that for murder. The only problem left is the lack of such dealers. As Bødal (1982) had proven: with some few exceptions, the situation is one where the big sharks do not exist. Importers do of course exist. But they are nearly always users themselves. They are victims of their own trade. Probably they were victims before they engaged in the trade. Offenders that merge with the victims make for bad offenders, just as victims that merge with offenders make for bad victims. For the social pedagogical task of building up strong negative attitudes against drugs and drug dealers – getting acceptance for a penal tariff far in excess of all usual standards, the image of the shark was – and is – extremely much better suited than the offender who in reality is a suffering victim.

Most violent offenders are in reality not so ideal either. Most are known by the victim, many are intimately close to him or her. When it comes to violence between men, a great amount of it takes place in public places, while both offender and victim are intoxicated, and in situations where it is rather unclear who initiated the violent action. Statistically, this is the typical pattern. But as it is clear to us now, this gives a most unsuitable image of the perpetrator. The ideal offender differs from the victim. He is, morally speaking, black against the white victim. He is a dangerous man coming from far away. He is a human being close to not being one. Not surprisingly, this is to a large extent also the public image of the offender.

This brings me to my third case of an unsuitable criminal. As some of you will know from some very early publications of mine (Christie, 1952 and 1953) I once made a study of guards in concentration camps. But I did not study the guards of the enemy, I did not study German SS troops in Buchenwald or Sachsenhausen. I studied Norwegian guards, working for the Germans, but killing and torturing in Norway. I will not report the findings, but only the reactions to the findings. In great oversimplification, I found that the killers and torturers were quite ordinary Norwegians. They were like us, and we would have behaved as they did had we, with their age and educational background, been placed into their situation. The reaction to this finding was a non-reaction. No denial, but neither were there any comments. My article was published in a journal which was usually heavily quoted in the mass media. But not in this case. Twenty years later I was asked to publish the total manuscript as a book, and so I did (Christie, 1972). This time the findings were received with some attention. My interpretation is that the first reports in 1952 and 1953 appeared too close to the war. It was just too much – it became unbearable – to see the worst of the enemies, the torturers and killers, as people like ourselves. In the public mind they were Quislings, traitors, psychopaths, mad, evil. To survive in an occupied country, we need a de-humanized picture of the enemy, a real and distant offender. In 1972 new generations of readers had arrived. Their need for understanding was greater than their need for ideal offenders. In the meantime Milgram (1963) had published, the Vietnam war had taken place, the banality of atrocity was well established. Maybe I had good luck to be allowed to publish my first results already in 1952. Several years later I had a long conversation with professor Batawia of Warsaw University. After the war, he made a very thorough study of one of the major German war criminals, the director of one of the concentration camps, a man responsible for an unbelievable amount of sufferings and death among the prisoners. Batawia's results were similar to mine. They were never made public. I do in a way understand it, in a society as haunted as the Polish.

Ideal victims, real victims and scared victims

Let me make a short detour to the relationship between ideal victims, real victims and the scared ones. As already hinted at: ideal victims do not necessarily have much to do with the prevalence of *real victims*. Most ideal victims are *not* most frequently represented as real victims. The real victims are so to say the negation of those who are most frequently represented. In all official counts, the man in the bar is a much more common victim than the little old lady. Ideal victims are, however, very much *afraid* of being victimized. Study after study (in Scandinavia represented by Balvig 1979 and Olaussen 1983) show a very high connection between the qualities that qualify for becoming an ideal victim, and having a particular fear of being the victim of crime, particularly the crime of violence.

Many among the real victims do not fear. Probably they do not fear because they have more *correct information regarding the real risks*. They hang around in crime-exposed areas, but do at the same time know, by personal observation, that crime after all is only a minor phenomenon in these areas, minor compared to all other life-activities that go on. The old ladies get their information through mass media. They have no personal control of the information conveyed. They get a picture of an area – an existence – where crime is the major activity.

Victims and social conditions

Are victims wanted?

Yes. And no. But first: yes. Yes when it improves the situation of suffering individuals. Victims who are not seen as victims ought often to be seen as such. Wife-beating will not continuously be defined as noise when feminists cry out. It is a great improvement that material conditions and personal courage have allowed them to do so. Wives or cohabitants as an officially accepted and important category of victims is a necessary first step. The second step, however, would be to bring females even closer to equals. And that step would undermine their position as ideal victims. The ideal victim is in a subordinated, weak position. If females opted for a status as ideal victims, they would have to accept a lasting subordination. Not so total they were not listened to, but sufficient to enlist sympathy for the weak. With equality, they get reduced claims to the status of being a good classical victim.

Again the little old ladies can illustrate my point. They can be protected in two principally different ways. The one is more police, more severe punishments, still more public sympathy. But this is a solution with considerable costs, even for the old women. The costs are derived from the excessive attention given to their potential status as victims. This attention does also produce anxiety. This fear of crime is a life-handicapping feature of old people's existence. The more attention we give them as victims, the more they fear.

The other alternative would be to make old ladies once more eligible for witch-status. That means – adapted to modern times – not to give them such a dependent status as in our societies, not to let them live a life so stripped of important social functions. The old and often highly derogatory jokes about mothers-in-law do not exist any more in my culture. They are not needed. Mothers-in-law are not of any social importance any longer. Old people are placed outside of most important tasks in society. They are mostly well fed, comfortable, warm and often – in contrast to old-beliefs – visited by their relatives. But they are receivers, consumers, clients – not producers. No one is dependent on them. With more power, and a more active social life three things would have happened. They would probably more often become real victims of crime, they would receive less attention when they were victimized, and they would have less fear of becoming victims.

***

The ideal criminal can be seen in the same perspective. In certain stages of a social process it might be of the utmost importance to get certain acts defined as crime, and certain actors as criminals. Wife beaters are typical examples, as are also persons responsible for the breaking of laws against handling poisonous industrial products or laws on the protection of workers. But again, there are two roads to heaven. When the evil character of the acts has been clearly established, when wife-beating and sloppy disposal of poison and maltreatment of workers are well established as crimes, then comes the question of further measures.

And here we get in trouble with the concept of the ideal offender. The ideal offender is a distant being. The more foreign, the better. The less humane, also the better. Again a person, or rather a non-person, who creates anxiety. And also that calls for actions that might have counter-effects. By being that extremely bad, other acts, not quite that bad, can escape attention as well as evaluation. By having an oversimplified picture of the ideal offender, business for the rest of us can go on as usual. My morality is not improved by information about bad acts carried out by monsters.

As scientists, our major obligation is clear; we have to tell the truth. But if so, we can very seldom hope to be useful – and highly rewarded – in helping society to establish pictures of ideal offenders. There are too few monsters around. Most offenders are non-ideal. They are in most of their relationships and in most of their attributes like other people. This message would block attempts to externalize the problem. Consequently, criminologists are not listened to. The lesson I have learned, is that people have to find out for themselves. This means they must be brought into situations where they cannot escape the conclusion. Such situations are where they come close to the offender, where they get to know him personally. Fragmented societies with isolated individuals are ideal for creating ideal victims and ideal offenders. Knowledge makes for realistic and multidimensional evaluation – and sanctions directed against those deserving sanctions.

One important method to let people find out for themselves is to do our utmost to let victims and offenders get a realistic chance to get to know each other. I have in an article on "Conflicts as property" (Christie, 1977) emphasized the need for giving the victim a more important role to play in the criminal process. In my book *"Limits to pain"* (Christie, 1981) I try to be slightly more concrete, particularly in outlining the need for a civilization of the legal process. Acts *are* not. They become. The definitions of acts and actors are results of particular forms of social organizations. To me it seems an important ideal to help to create social systems where people are so close to each other that concepts as crime and criminals are seen by everybody as being of very limited usefulness. Blame and guilt are essential in social life. But I doubt if offenders and victims are.

Notes

[1] The author acknowledges the valuable comments he received from Vigdis Christie, Tove Stang Dahl, Sturla Falck, Ezzat Fattah and Anglika Schafft.

[2] Trevor-Roper (1956) and Lea (1888). For Norwegian conditions: Alver (1971).

References

Alver, Bente (1971) *Heksetro og trolldom* (Oslo).

Balvig, Flemming (1982) "Ungdomskriminalitet – med særlig henblick på retssystemets utvelgelsesmekanismer", *Arsberetning 1981 Kriminalistisk Institut*, Københavns Universitet, Stencilserie, no. 18, pp 33–49.

Bødal, Kåre (1982) *350 narkoselgere* (Universitetsforlaget).

Christie, Nils (1952) "Fangevoktere i konsentrasjonsleire", *Nordisk Tidsskrift for kriminalvidenskab vol. 41*, pp 439–58.

Christie, Nils (1953) ibid., vol. 42, pp 44–60.

Christie, Nils (1972) As a book (Oslo).

Christie, Nils (1977) "Conflicts as Property", *British Journal of Criminology*, vol. 17, pp 1–15.

Christie, Nils (1981) *Limits to Pain* (Oslo/Oxford).

Dahl, Tove Stang (1980) "Kvinner som ofre", *Nordisk tidsskrift for kriminalvidenskab*, vol. 70, pp 56–77.

Lea, Henry Charles (1888) *A History of the Inquisition of the Middle Ages* (London).

Milgram, S. (1963) "Behavioral Study of obedience", The Journal of Abnormal and Social Psychology, 67(4): 371-378.

Olaussen, Leif Petter (1983) "Om angst for vold og alvorlig sjikane." *Lov og Rett*, vol. 23, pp 115–34 (ph).

Trevor-Roper (1956) *Witches and Witchcraft* (Great Britain).

PART I

Exploring the 'Ideal Victim'

ONE

The ideal victim through other(s') eyes

Alice Bosma, Eva Mulder and Antony Pemberton

Nils Christie's legendary article on the ideal victim is firmly placed within the victimological canon. Christie drew our attention to the mechanisms underlying the extent to which we grant individuals victim status. As Daly (2014: 378) summarised: 'A victim status is not fixed, but socially constructed, mobilized and malleable'.

However, what factors influence this construction? Christie (1986) assumed that the most important reasons for perceiving a victim as legitimate and blameless are the specific character traits of the victim and of the relation between victim and offender. Substantiation on the reasons for this had no place in his brief chapter, but has only occurred in subsequent research and theorising. The first aim of this chapter is to expand on these two arguments using more contemporary theories that are important in (experimental and critical) victimology, namely, the Stereotype Content Model (SCM) (Fiske et al, 2002) and the Moral Typecasting Theory (MTT) (Gray and Wegner, 2009). The SCM can expand our insights into Christie's criteria of weakness, blamelessness and femaleness, while the MTT can shed more light on the big and bad offender and the (non-)relationship between offender and victim. These two theories provide more insight into the role of stereotypes in the perception of the victim and the dynamics of the relation between victim and offender.

They not only further Christie's (1986: 18) argument that 'being a victim is not a thing, an objective phenomenon', but also, in combination with the second half of our chapter, emphasise the redundancy of absolute victim(isation) characteristics as a factor in societal or individual constructions of the victim status. Indeed, where the first half of our chapter provides retrospective theoretical support of Christie's views, the second half adopts a more critical stance. Again, we confront Christie's perspective with more recent bodies of (theoretical) literature that go beyond the specific character traits of the victim and the relation between victim and offender, this time by emphasising the role of the observers of the victim, both individually and collectively, in determining whether the victim is seen as legitimate and blameless. We do this, first, through an analysis of the ideal victim against the backdrop of the work on the justice motive (Lerner, 1980; Hafer and Bègue, 2005). The justice motive – observers' need to believe in a just world – opens up the possibility to critically examine the extent to which the victim's *innocence* in fact makes her more or less ideal. This is a good deal more complicated matter than Christie made it out to be. The second analysis relates to the ongoing work on *framing*, which, in its initial conception, pre-dates Christie's ideal victim. However, the work in communication and social movement studies following the path-breaking work of Erving Goffman in 1973 has blossomed over the past 20 years. It suggests that the way in which the ideal victim is put to use in political and public discourse is an example of a more general phenomenon, which at once opens up the possibility for other 'ideal victim' stereotypes, while at the same time restricting the extent to which the use of such stereotypes can be overcome.

Stereotypes and moral typecasting

Stereotype Content Model

The SCM describes what emotions and behavioural tendencies people are expected to display towards a certain group, depending on the interaction between two broad continuous dimensions of stereotypicality that can be applied to any group. These two dimensions entail warmth on one of the axes, and competence on the other, and they are generally considered the two universal dimensions of social cognition (Fiske et al, 2007; for analogous concepts, see also Bakan, 1966; Spence and Helmreich, 1980). Groups and their members who are perceived as both warm and competent, which frequently means members of one's own in-group, are hypothesised to trigger feelings of admiration, and to invite both passive and active helping behaviour from the perceiver. Groups who are perceived as neither warm nor competent (such as homeless people or drug addicts) generally elicit feelings of disgust or contempt, as well as both active and passive harming behaviour from the perceiver. Different combinations of the two dimensions may elicit either envious prejudice (high competence but low warmth) or, most relevant for the current chapter, paternalistic prejudice (low competence but high warmth). Paternalistic prejudice reflects the seemingly benevolent attitudes towards a non-dominant group that simultaneously functions to justify and facilitate differences

Figure 1: Stereotype Content Model

Higher warmth ↑	**Paternalistic prejudice** Emotional reaction: Pity, sympathy Behavioural reaction: Active facilitation, passive harm Groups: Elderly, disabled, housewives	**Admiration** Emotional reaction: Pride, admiration Behavioural reaction: Active and passive facilitation Groups: Ingroup, close allies
	Contemptuous prejudice Emotional reaction: Contempt, disgust Behavioural reaction: Active and passive harm Groups: Poor, homeless, drug addicts	**Envious prejudice** Emotional reaction: Envy, jealousy Behavioural reaction: Passive facilitation, active harm Groups: Rich, Asians

→ Higher competence

Source: Adapted from Cuddy, Fiske and Glick (2008).

in status and power in favour of the dominant group (Glick and Fiske, 2001).

We expect that someone who has been victimised is generally perceived as non-threatening and easy to sympathise with, but is at the same time ascribed lower competence due to the fact that he or she 'was unable to stand up for him- or herself'. The perception of high competence in addition to high warmth is a particularly incompatible combination for being an ideal victim because, as Christie (1986: 23) states, 'sufficient strength to threaten others would not be a good base for creating the type of general and public sympathy that is associated with the status of being a victim'. This places the stereotypical and non-specified 'ideal victim' in the upper-left category of Figure 1, as the recipient of paternalistic prejudice. Behaviour that this group may expect from the social surroundings comprises active helping behaviour, but also neglect (Cuddy et al, 2008), depending on the convenience of either one action. Christie's criterion that the ideal victim is generally *weak in relation to the offender* (ie scores relatively low on the dimension of competence) is reflected in findings which show that a person who has been victimised is particularly likely to be derogated on those character traits that relate to competence (Kay et al, 2005). It is perhaps also reflected in the notion that the groups that Cuddy et al place in the upper-left category are those *thought* to be the most vulnerable to victimisation. Although very few studies have so far incorporated both theories, the model helps to explain why members of certain groups, for example, businessmen or feminists (people who are perceived as highly agentic/competent but rather less warm or communal), would, in relation to most crimes, have a hard time being accepted as ideal victims. Christie mentions 'the witch' as a related example. Specifically, persons initially considered competent but not warm who are victimised, thereby losing much of their competent status, are particularly likely to find themselves shifting towards the contemptuous prejudice category, and hence to be met by contempt or disgust rather than sympathy. It goes against our intuition that someone competent becomes dominated or victimised, particularly by interpersonal (sexual) violence, and thus this type of person is unlikely to be considered as a wholly *legitimate* or *blameless* victim.

In turn, the concept of the ideal victim is helpful in explaining why it is so difficult for victims to get rid of their 'victim status' and stop being viewed with pity by the social surroundings. Considering the SCM, one might expect that an exertion of competence, for example, as shown by the emotion of anger or actions of rational profit making (as displayed by Natascha Kampusch after her escape; see Van Dijk, 2009), assists in redirecting the perception of the victim as placed in the paternalistic prejudice category towards the admiration (high warmth and high competence) category. However, this change in category would entail a change in label from 'victim' to 'survivor' because inherent to the definition of (ideal) victim is precisely a notion of weakness or vulnerability (Lamb, 1999).

Moral Typecasting Theory

The MTT (Gray and Wegner, 2009) taps into the relational aspect of moral situations and portrays 'the idea that all moral perception is dyadic in nature' (Arico, 2012). Moral situations, as we perceive them, are situations in which we can identify an act of wrongfulness or an act of goodness. The MTT states that a moral situation is rarely perceived as one in which a victim is wronged in the absence of a wrongdoer, or as one in which an offender does wrong in the absence of a victim. Rather, the act of wrongfulness or goodness creates the necessity to (albeit often unconsciously) identify two moral parties: one who acts, and one who is acted upon. According to the MTT, a moral patient cannot at the same time be a moral agent. The moral agent is the party capable of either helping or harming, while the moral patient is the one who experiences the deed. The MTT contributes to the notion of the ideal victim as someone who is essentially blameless. Indeed, Gray and Wegner (2011) found that the portrayal of someone as a victim, as compared to a 'hero', led to a decrease in assigned blame to that person. They conclude that the status of victim leads to a perception of moral patiency, and hence to a perceived inability to act or be held responsible for acts. In some moral situations, the distribution of roles is clear enough: 'It is in everyone's interest to protect our children against deviant monsters lurking in the streets and parks' (Christie, 1986: 20). On the other hand, other situations speak to our moral senses but objectively lack offender and/or victim, asking of the observer a vast amount of effort to label each party (Gray et al, 2012). Christie (1986: 23) suitably describes that in Medieval times, sickness and misfortune were still unanimously accorded a moral status, meaning 'People could bring it [sickness and misfortune] upon each other, with witches as intermediators'.

In cases of crime victimisation, it is simple to speak of a moral situation in which a wrongful act occurs. The offender, then, ought not only be perceived as *big and bad*, but also as the one who *does* a big and bad thing *to* the victim. Indeed, in reality, we see a strong correlation between these features of the actor and the act, and hence between the notion of the ideal *offender* and the MTT. In an ongoing study by Pemberton and colleagues, life stories are collected from (indirect) victims of severe crimes, including homicide and physical and sexual violence. In one of the interviews, a victim of attempted manslaughter by her mentally ill husband recalls a conversation with a police officer during which she is repeatedly told that 'her husband is ill'. She shares her frustration about her own position and exclaims 'yes, I know by now that he is ill, *but then what am I?*'. This telling example hints at how the less morally agentic a 'big and bad' offender becomes in the eyes of the beholder, in this case due to mental illness, the less a victim is perceived as a moral patient. An example on a larger scale is given by Christie when he talks about the second type of non-ideal victim, who is the 'worker'. As it is practically complex and, moreover, largely undesirable for (governmental) institutions and the ruling classes to pinpoint themselves down as the agents, the situation of the 'working class *heroes*' remains morally unsaturated: 'Workers become victims without offenders. Such victims are badly suited' (Christie, 1986: 25).

The MTT finally serves as a valuable supplement to Christie's criterion of the ideal victim as someone who has no relation with the offender. In fact, the MTT poses that a perceived relation between victim and offender is of the utmost importance, but that it needs to be an unequal and inversed relation between patient and agent. The unequal relationship entails that the agent needs to be perceived as more powerful than the patient/victim. If the agent is big and bad, then the victim needs to be weak and innocent, which is, indeed, the inverse relationship also touched upon by Christie. In his words, 'Ideal victims need – and create – ideal offenders. The two are interdependent' (Christie, 1986: 25). Allowing for a broad interpretation of the word, we suggest that a relation is created between victim and offender as soon as victimisation becomes a possibility. The existence of a relation between offender and victim need not problematise the status of ideal victim as long as it is a relation of opposites and opposition (or clear oppression), rather than of perceived compliance. This may serve to explain why (futile) resistance during sexual victimisation is found to be such a significant factor in the establishment of the blamelessness of the victim (Davies et al, 2008; Van der Bruggen and Grubb, 2014), although not a criterion expanded upon by Christie. Failed resistance shows that a victim was far from compliant in his or her victimisation, but still a moral patient who could not help being acted upon. No resistance endangers the desired simplicity of the moral dyad, whereas successful resistance does the same and virtually changes a moral situation into a non-issue.

To conclude, the SCM and MTT contribute to a more in-depth analysis and nuanced view of the ideal victim criteria that have been proposed by Christie. They also, respectively, provide more empirical evidence as to why the witch and the worker are two particularly informative examples of non-ideal victims.

The justice motive and framing

The justice motive

The previous theories emphasised and supported several of Christie's key arguments. However, they also form a starting point for our main point of criticism, namely, that the criteria listed by Christie are neither necessary nor sufficient for someone to be granted the status of ideal victim.

When answering the question 'Who is the ideal victim?', one seems to be stuck in a catch-22. The approach that Christie takes is that the ideal victim is characterised by innocence. However, as we will see in this paragraph, the especially blameless and innocent might trigger observer reactions that include blame and derogation. We could also argue that the ideal victim is the victim who is *treated as if* (s)he is blameless and innocent, as a reward for being victimised

(Rock, 2002). We are hence left with a chicken-or-egg question: is it the extent to which the victim is ideal that influences reactions to them, or do reactions to the victim establish to what extent they are ideal? In the following paragraphs, we will explore the (ideal) victim through others' eyes and see that these eyes are necessary for the idea of the ideal victim.

First, the form of the ideal victim can change significantly depending on the situational context. Van Dijk (2009) points out that the ideal victim of restorative justice differs greatly from the ideal victim of retributive justice. Similarly, it has been pointed out that to be perceived as a legitimate/blameless (rape) victim *in court*, a victim needs to display certain qualities that are unspecified in Christie's listed criteria, such as sincerity and a thoughtful demeanour. As suggested by Larcombe (2002: 145):

> the point to emphasize is that the attributes of a 'successful rape complainant' are likely to be subtly but significantly different from the moral qualities of the chaste, middle-class, married woman at home – the figure normally identified as the 'ideal' rape victim.

Second, a victim may be accepted or rejected as legitimate not only on the basis of (context-dependent) victim characteristics, but also depending on the (implicit) needs or motives of the observer. An important motive that shapes people's attitudes towards victims is the *belief in a just world* (Lerner, 1980). According to the theory of the belief in a just world, people inherently believe – or, better, are motivated to think and behave *as if they believe* (Pemberton, 2012) – that the world is a just place where people get what they deserve. Being confronted with a victim, of course, is not in accordance with the view that the world is a just place – especially when this victim is blameless and innocent. However, despite this type of counter-evidence, research has shown that people (implicitly) defend this world view – in which good people deserve good outcomes and bad people deserve bad outcomes – because it has a positive influence on their well-being (Hafer and Rubel, 2015).

Defending this world view can be done in different ways. Often, it happens in accordance with what one might intuitively expect and what Christie describes about the ideal victim: when an observer encounters a legitimate and blameless victim, meaning a *good* person or *deserving* victim, the observer will react in a way that leads to 'granting the complete and legitimate status of being a victim'. More concretely, the observer will initiate positive actions towards the victim, such as compensating the victim or empathising with the victim. Additionally, the observer could predominantly focus on the *bad* nature of the offender. Believing that bad people deserve bad outcomes, the observer might punish the offender as a way to inflict this bad outcome upon the (big and) bad offender.

However, the same motive of believing that the world is a place in which good people deserve good things and bad people deserve bad things might lead to opposite reactions. In particular, when observers feel sceptical about their possibilities to help the victim, they may react negatively towards the victim (Sutton et al, 2008). When people react in a negative way to the victim, the maxim of the justice motive seems to be reversed. Instead of thinking 'bad people deserve bad outcomes', it becomes 'bad outcomes (victimisation) must be deserved', showing the victim in a bad light. Both types of reactions, positive and negative, are the result of being uneasy with the idea that injustice might befall any of us, including the blameless.

We could, with Christie, conclude that a victim should be neither too strong nor too weak in order to remain the ideal victim:

> The reasoning brings to the surface another important element in being an ideal victim: she (or sometimes he) must be strong enough to be listened to, dare to talk. But she (he) must at the very same time be *weak enough not to become a threat to other important interests*. (Christie, 1986: 21, emphasis in original)

However, the theoretical framework described earlier sheds light on this idea from a different angle. Christie refers to threatening the public culture while we can see from the perspective of the justice motive that threats to individual world views may also warrant this conclusion.

Insight into people's motives about maintaining the belief that the world is just teaches us some important lessons with regard to the idea of the ideal victim. First, and most clearly, it is not just the (perceived) characteristics of the victim that may be important in determining whether this victim will be readily given the complete and legitimate status of a victim; the implicit motives of observers also shape the reaction towards the victim. Second, it problematises the idea that a black-and-white dyadic portrayal of victim and offender (weak versus strong, respectable versus big and bad) leads to a more favourable position of the victim than a situation in which the victim is portrayed as closer to the offender. The more innocent the victim seems, the bigger a threat this victim forms to the view that the world is a just place and the more difficult it is to reach out to this victim. However, situations that are dyadically clear in nature facilitate proper reactions towards the perpetrator. The notion of the ideal victim might therefore be more important in determining this reaction than the reaction to the victim itself, as Christie essentially writes when he states the following:

> That makes [the little old lady], in contrast to the ladies of the witch-age, particularly well suited for the role of the ideal victim in criminal cases. We are already swamped with guilt in our relationships to her. A crime against her gives us a most welcome opportunity to turn our attention – and emotions and anger – towards the criminal. (Christie, 1986: 23)

Framing the victim

The justice motive is not the only more general phenomenon that can leave victims in the lurch, in a double bind or even in a catch-22. This is also true of the mechanisms underlying the manner in which victims and their plights tend to be portrayed, even by social movements that champion their plight. The nature of the ideal victim as a social construction has often been used as a cudgel to criticise such victims' movements for denying the reality of victimisation, including by Christie himself (Christie, 2010). Much of this echoes the manner in which Robert Elias (1993) viewed the way in which victims' needs are addressed in law-and-order campaigns: as political manipulation. The individual features of a small number of high-profile cases with ideal victims are used as a means to frame crime problems and the correct criminal justice response in a far wider range of situations. The fact that these extreme, but rare, cases are used as an exemplar for problems of victims in general, while this generalisation is questionable at best and most likely to be erroneous, is correctly viewed with much concern in the academic literature (see also Scheingold et al, 1994). This is all the more so because the net result of these campaigns is not an outpouring of actual and useful support for crime victims, but instead a deterioration of the position of suspects and/or offenders, in line with Christie's worries. It is unclear whether the sex offender registration and notification schemes of Megan's Law have benefited any victims or prevented any new cases of sexual offences against minors, but it is clear that the consequences for either those sentenced or merely suspected of these crimes resembles that of a witch-hunt.

However, we have also already noted the difficulty of overcoming the adoption of such stereotypes *tout corte*. The issue is that the ideal victim is an example of the type of shorthand for which Erving Goffman (1973) coined the term 'frame', which has subsequently become a mainstay of the communication (Entman, 1993, 2007) and social movement (Gamson, 1992; Benford and Snow, 2000) literature. As Robert Entman (1993, 2007) shows, a successful frame offers a problem definition, a causal analysis, a moral judgement and a remedy, preferably in one go. The simple and neat example of the ideal victim does so, but it is not the only generic description of victimisation that has this quality (Pemberton, 2014). The gendered violence movement, for instance, has a different stereotype, in which the offender is no stranger and the victim is not weak, but a *survivor*. This has not prevented the clear-cut framing quality of the battered woman being a regular feature of our media landscape over the past decades. Even emerging movements like those focusing on the plight of victims of environmental harm appear hell-bent on finding a similar stereotype of their own (Pemberton, 2014).

This is understandable as a matter of social movement strategy (Benford and Snow, 2000). Victim stereotypes serve as the frame that allows the communication of victims' movements' messages to a wider audience, while focusing the movements' own actions. The adoption of frames in social movements as a means to communicate messages, but also to maintain coherence within the group, already speaks to the extent to which counter-examples will be met with resistance and even hostility. In turn, the extent to which the frame is bandied about in media outlets can also convey a persuasive and/or normative message to individuals experiencing the phenomenon that the frame intends to describe (Entman, 2007). Frames also offer material for people to socially construct their own individual experience (Best, 2008). This is so in general, but is reinforced by the explicitly moral nature of victimisation. Much of the work of victims' movements has been to help victims understand that what they are going through should not be tolerated and that there are remedies available.

However, it is also not hard to see the difficulties that this may cause for victims whose experience in one way or another does not conform to that of the stereotype (Polletta, 2006). The gendered violence movement, for instance, rebelled against the notion of the ideal victim, in particular, the element that the offender and the victim are strangers to each other: most cases of gendered violence occur between acquaintances, family and/or intimate (ex-)partners. Moreover, the stereotype draws upon characteristics like wholesomeness and blamelessness to which many victims, in reality, do not comply. In all cases, framing invites stereotypes of which one feature is the clear-cut black-and-white distinction between victims and offenders (see also Best, 1999), which is at odds with the reality of victims who have a history of prior offences or were in one way or another involved in deviant behaviour themselves (see Corteen, this volume).

Beyond the lack of connection between the stereotypical narrative and the actual experience of large groups of individual victims, the frame might readily transform from a shorthand depiction of social reality to a normative demand (Pemberton, 2014). Frames also serve to establish boundaries against experience and, indeed, people, excluding them from membership of the movement. The extent to which victims live up to the stereotype's demands then forms the touchstone upon which acknowledgement and recognition becomes contingent. The justice motive already supplies the impetus for scrutinising the victims' behaviour for signs of blameworthiness, and/or at least for distances to the observer. The normative deployment of a frame expands upon this to include additional features of the victim's behaviour and character that may be judged.

The catch-22 here is that, on the one hand, a frame limits the extent to which real-life victims are or feel represented by the movements purporting to represent their best interests. Moreover, the frame imposes normative limits on victims' experience and behaviour. This can be an implicit demand in the sense that victims might grapple to fit their own experiences into the movement's frame. It might also be more explicit, where the movement uses the frame as a heuristic rule to demarcate its membership. This is in line with the way in which Christie understood the ideal victim. However, the other part of the double bind is at odds with his views. The frame is a necessary component of the identity of the movement advancing the position of victims, while it is also a key element of the manner through which the movement communicates with victims and also helps victims understand their own experience and the potential avenues to see that their needs are met. Unlike Christie's views, the literature on frames suggests that a frame's social construction of reality is not something that can be overcome, but instead a necessary component of the struggle to improve the position of victims. In addition, the literature on framing suggests that the exact characteristics of the frame deployed may vary as long as they fulfil the function of the frame in connecting the social movement's objective with individual experience.

Conclusion

More than 30 years after the publication of Christie's influential chapter, victims still seem to be in need of ideal characteristics in order to receive full acknowledgement of their victimhood. However, what these ideal characteristics are depend not only on the victim and the relation between the victim and offender, but also on the context and on the motives of the observers of the victim that provide acknowledgement.

Much of our analysis in this chapter supports Christie's observations of the form and the function of the ideal victim. The SCM and MTT offer support for the way in which he understood the characteristics of the ideal victim, and the manner in which he juxtaposed societal reactions to ideal victims, versus other possible victim schematas, such as the worker and the witch. Indeed, the axis of warmth and competence in the SCM proves helpful in understanding the complexity of victims shedding their 'victim status' and continuing to receive sympathy from their social surroundings. The MTT offers support for the central position Christie afforded to the relationship between victim and offender, and for the manner in which he described this relationship, while it expands on this by showing the need for this relationship to be an unequal and inversed relation between patient and agent.

The work on the justice motive and the body of literature on the phenomenon of framing have a more ambiguous relationship to Christie's ideas. The justice motive can help understand third parties' interests in the characteristics and behaviour of the victim, while the ideal victim can be viewed as a particular instance of a frame. However, the justice motive also calls into question whether the characteristics of the ideal victim, particularly innocence, are in fact 'ideal' from the viewpoint of observers, or instead serve to increase their distress. There is a contradiction in the manner in which the degree of suffering and innocence increases a sympathetic reaction to victims' plights and, at the same time, increases avoidance of their situation due to the distress that it provokes. This contradiction does not occur with regard to the reaction to the offender: the more innocent the victim is, and the more suffering he or she displays, the more negative and, indeed, punitive the reaction to the offender will be. In turn, the literature on framing confirms the difficulties that such stereotypical shorthands might have for the real-life experience of victims. However, it also shows the manner in which frames contribute to improving their plight and suggests that frames are an inevitable component of the struggle to improve the position of victims of crime.

References

Arico, A.J. (2012) 'Breaking out of moral typecasting', *Review of Philosophy and Psychology*, 3(3): 425–38.

Bakan, D. (1966) *The Duality of Human Existence: An Essay on Psychology and Religion*, Chicago, IL: Rand McNally.

Benford, R.D. and Snow, D.A. (2000) 'Framing process and social movements: an overview and assessment', *Annual Review of Sociology*, 26: 611–39.

Best, J. (1999) *Random Violence. How We Talk About New Crimes and New Victims*, Berkeley, CA: University of California Press.

Best, J. (2008) *Social Problems*, London and New York, NY: Norton.

Christie, N. (1986) 'The ideal victim', in E.A. Fattah (ed) *From Crime Policy to Victim Policy: Reorienting the Justice System*, Basingstoke: Macmillan, pp 17–30.

Christie, N. (2010) 'Victim movements at a crossroad', *Punishment and Society*, 12(2): 115–22.

Cuddy, A.J., Fiske, S.T. and Glick, P. (2008) 'Warmth and competence as universal dimensions of social perception: the stereotype content model and the BIAS map', *Advances in Experimental Social Psychology*, 40: 61–149.

Daly, K. (2014) 'Reconceptualizing sexual victimization and justice', in I. Vanfraechem, A. Pemberton and F.M. Ndahinda (eds) *Justice for Victims*, New York, NY: Routledge, pp 378–95.

Davies, M., Rogers, P. and Bates, J. (2008) 'Blame towards male rape victims as a function of victim sexuality and degree of resistance', *Journal of Homosexuality*, 55(3): 533–44.

Elias, R. (1993) *Victims Still. The Political Manipulation of Crime Victims*, London: Sage.

Entman, R.M. (1993) 'Framing: toward clarification of a fractured paradigm', *Journal of Communication*, 43(4): 51–8.

Entman, R.M. (2007) 'Framing bias: media distribution in the distribution of power', *Journal of Communication*, 57(1): 163–73.

Fiske, S.T., Cuddy, A.J., Glick, P. and Xu, J. (2002) 'A model of (often mixed) stereotype content: competence and warmth respectively follow from perceived status and competition', *Journal of Personality and Social Psychology*, 82(6): 878–902.

Fiske, S.T., Cuddy, A.J. and Glick, P. (2007) 'Universal dimensions of social cognition: warmth and competence', *Trends in Cognitive Sciences*, 11(2): 77–83.

Gamson, W.A. (1992) *Talking Politics*, New York, NY: Cambridge University Press.

Glick, P. and Fiske, S.T. (2001) 'Ambivalent stereotypes as legitimizing ideologies: differentiating paternalistic and envious prejudice', in J. Jost and B. Major (eds) *The Psychology of Legitimacy: Emerging Perspectives on Ideology, Justice, and Intergroup Relations*, New York, NY: Cambridge University Press, pp 278–306.

Goffman, E. (1973) *Frame Analysis: An Essay on the Organization of Experience*, New York, NY: Harper & Row.

Gray, K. and Wegner, D.M. (2009) 'Moral typecasting: divergent perceptions of moral agents and moral patients', *Journal of Personality and Social Psychology*, 96(3): 505–20.

Gray, K. and Wegner, D.M. (2011) 'To escape blame, don't be a hero – be a victim', *Journal of Experimental Social Psychology*, 47(2): 516–19.

Gray, K., Young, L. and Waytz, A. (2012) 'Mind perception is the essence of morality', *Psychological Inquiry*, 23(2): 101–24.

Hafer, C.L. and Bègue, L. (2005) 'Experimental research on just-world theory: problems, developments, and future challenges', *Psychological Bulletin*, 131: 128–67.

Hafer, C.L. and Rubel, A.N. (2015) 'Chapter Two – The why and how of defending belief in a just world', in J.M. Olson and M.P. Zanna (eds) *Advances in Experimental Social Psychology* (vol 51), London: Academic Press, pp 41–96.

Kay, A.C., Jost, J.T. and Young, S. (2005) 'Victim derogation and victim enhancement as alternate routes to system justification', *Psychological Science*, 16(3): 240–6.

Lamb, S. (1999) 'Constructing the victim: popular images and lasting labels', in S. Lamb (ed) *New Versions of Victims: Feminists Struggle with the Concept*, New York, NY: NYU Press.

Larcombe, W. (2002) 'The "ideal" victim v successful rape complainants: not what you might expect', *Feminist Legal Studies*, 10(2): 131–48.

Lerner, M.J. (1980) *The Belief in a Just World: A Fundamental Delusion*, New York, NY: Plenum Press.

Pemberton, A. (2012) 'Just-world victimology: revisiting Lerner in the study of victims of crime', in H. Morosawa, J.J.P. Dussich and G.F. Kirchhoff (eds) *Victimology and Human Security: New Horizons. Selection of Papers Presented at the 13th International Symposium on Victimology, 2009, Mito, Japan*, Nijmegen, NL: Wolf Legal Publishers, pp 45–67.

Pemberton, A. (2014) 'Environmental victims and criminal justice: proceed with caution', in A.C. Spapens, R. White and M. KLuin (eds) *Environmental Crime and its Victims*, Farnham: Ashgate.

Polletta, F. (2006) *It Was Like a Fever. Storytelling in Protest and Politics*, Chicago, IL: University of Chicago Press.

Rock, P. (2002) 'On becoming a victim', in C. Hoyle and R. Young (eds) *New Visions of Crime Victims*, Oxford: Hart Publishing, pp 1–22.

Scheingold, S.A., Olson, T. and Pershing, J. (1994) 'Sexual violence, victim advocacy, and republican criminology: Washington State's Community Protection Act', *Law & Society Review*, 28(4): 729–64.

Spence, J.T. and Helmreich, R.L. (1980) 'Masculine instrumentality and feminine expressiveness: their relationships with sex role attitudes and behaviors', *Psychology of Women Quarterly*, 5(2): 147–63.

Sutton, R.M., Douglas, K.M., Wilkin, K., Elder, T.J., Cole, J.M. and Stathi, S. (2008) 'Justice for whom, exactly? Beliefs in justice for the self and various others', *Personality and Social Psychology Bulletin*, 34(4): 528–41.

Van der Bruggen, M. and Grubb, A. (2014) 'A review of the literature relating to rape victim blaming: an analysis of the impact of observer and victim characteristics on attribution of blame in rape cases', *Aggression and Violent Behavior*, 19(5): 523–31.

Van Dijk, J. (2009) 'Free the victim: a critique of the Western conception of victimhood', *International Review of Victimology*, 16(1): 1–33.

TWO

Creating ideal victims in hate crime policy

Hannah Mason-Bish

Introduction

In July 2013, Bijan Ebrahimi was brutally murdered in Bristol, UK. The 44-year-old mentally disabled man, who had come to Britain as a refugee from Iran, had sought help from the police on a number of occasions because of the escalating harassment that he was receiving from neighbours. Members of the local community had accused him of being a paedophile after finding him taking photographs of young people who he had thought were vandalising his hanging baskets. He was arrested but quickly released due to a lack of evidence. Ebrahimi telephoned the police the day after his release from arrest, saying: 'My life is in danger. Right now a few of my neighbours are outside and shouting and calling me a paedophile. I need to see PC Duffy' (Peachey, 2015). However, PC Duffy did not attend, or even speak to Bijan, characterising him as an inconvenience and a nuisance. The next day, Lee James, a local neighbour, dragged Ebrahimi from his home and kicked him until he was unconscious. James was then joined by another neighbour who poured white spirit over Ebrahimi and set him on fire. James was eventually convicted of murder and sentenced to life in prison while Stephen Norley, who set Ebrahimi alight, received a four-year custodial sentence. As a result of failings leading up to the murder, 18 police officers involved in the case also faced disciplinary proceedings; two officers were given prison sentences for failing to protect Bijan.

The case presents a complex mix of factors that point towards the difficulties faced by victims of disablist hate crime, particularly those with mental disabilities or learning difficulties. In the previously discussed instance, we see a criminal justice response that criminalises the victim (in that Ebrahimi was arrested on suspicion of paedophilic offences) and, once exonerated, fails to take the required action to protect a vulnerable person. Despite the repeated acts of hostility directed towards him, no prosecutions – including for his eventual murder – were brought under the disability hate crime provisions. This case, as with others outlined in this chapter, illustrates a key area of concern to (disability) hate crime theorists: the arbitrary nature of criminal justice responses discerning between 'disability hate crime' and disabled persons being victims of (hate) crime. It would appear that the preference is to adopt the latter approach in a manner not fitting with other recognised forms of hate crime (in the UK, at least). In this chapter, an analysis of this differentiation invokes Christie's (1986) 'ideal victim' framework to assess how the construction of the victim is key to the ensuing response granted to them. In order not to conflate the two approaches, the terminology 'victims of disablist hate crime' will be adopted rather than 'disabled victims of hate crime'. This is to highlight that it is the disablism of the hate crime perpetrator rather than the disability of the victim that is to blame for the crime.

The extent to which victims of disablist hate crime – that is, people who have been targeted for victimisation as a result of disablism – are victimised, overlooked and under-protected is subject to a growing body of literature and research. There is wide-ranging evidence of the scale of the problem of disablist hate crime. The Crime Survey for England and Wales indicated that the 2015/16 rate of 3,629 was a 44% increase on the previous year (Home Office, 2016). Qualitative research demonstrates the dehumanising features of disablist hate crime, with victims often experiencing degrading treatment by perpetrators but also so-called 'low level' abuse, which can continue over months and years (Roulstone and Sadique, 2013; Sin, 2015). Reports such as Scope's (2008) *Getting Away with Murder* or the Equality and Human Rights Commission's (2011) *Hidden in Plain Sight* point towards how victims are ignored by the criminal justice system as well as by wider society. The common theme is that such violence is hidden but also subject to systemic failures and institutional disablism. These barriers have real consequences for victims, who then tend to normalise their experiences and thus not seek legal redress (Roulstone and Sadique, 2013; Thorneycroft and Asquith, 2017). This also has an international commonality in that jurisdictions with hate crime provisions find that disability is one of the categories least likely to be reported to police (Sherry, 2010; Levin, 2013).

Yet, when using Nils Christie's typology of the ideal victim, victims of disablist hate crime would appear to be a perfect fit for gaining policy and societal attention. In his seminal piece, he details particular attributes necessary for the construction of ideal victim status. These include: (1) the victim being weak; (2) the victim carrying out a respectable project; (3) the victim being without blame; (4) the offender being big and bad; (5) the offender being unknown to the victim; and (6) the victim being powerful enough to be heard but not so powerful as to threaten 'countervailing interests' (Christie, 1986: 19–21). Such a typology speaks to original conceptions of victimology in terms of victim precipitation and proneness. However, Christie is not making a moral judgement on the validity of the victim status; instead, he is just pointing towards a particular social construction. Importantly, this is not a static notion because people can become ideal victims as they (or society) change. In this brief synopsis, the predicament of victims of disablist hate crime appears to be a good fit for his ideal victim thesis. They represent members of society who are perceived as being weaker (generally, and in comparison to their perpetrators), blameless (for their state of being and victim status) and for whom the offender might be unknown in many cases. Similarly, they lack the power to be a threat to the established order.

However, this surface-level analysis belies a deeper structural problem in the recognition of victims of disablist hate crime as legitimate hate crime victims; this will be examined in this chapter, which expands upon Christie's piece by looking at the specific problems faced by victims who are not perceived as 'ideal' in several respects. By using the example of disability as a case study, I illustrate how 'ideal victims' need to be understood in the context of specific policy domains. In this regard, the hate crime discourse presents a useful example of the ways in which ideal victim groups are constructed through the process of policy formation. 'Hate crime' is the ultimate 'ideal victim' crime in that legislative approaches have specified very particular groups of victims as worthy of the enhanced protection that such laws afford. However, within this construction, there are more complicated attributes than Christie could have envisaged. Through an analysis of these, I aim to demonstrate that victims of disablist hate crime are perceived as inherently vulnerable and prone to victimisation, thereby ironically rendering them invisible in hate crime approaches (which prove redundant in attempting to enhance this construction of vulnerability further). Therefore, the chapter discusses the benefits and limitations of 'ideal victim' status for victims of disablist hate crime, and the sacrifices that must be made in this quest for recognition.

Constructing hate crime policy

Hate crime policies have become a common feature of many Western governments in recent decades. They have enabled states to send a positive message about values of tolerance and diversity to society generally and to minority groups specifically, particularly those who have been subject to victimisation. Although the exact wording and definitions of these policies differ in scope (both across strands and the jurisdictions where they exist), they do share some features of note. First, they stipulate which forms of *criminality* will be recognised, for example, assault, murder or criminal damage. Second, they tend to attach an *enhanced criminal sanction* in the form of an extended punishment. This is the declaratory function of hate crime laws and allows governments to demonstrate their tougher stance on certain crimes. Third, and the main focus of this chapter, they determine *which groups of victims* will be afforded said protections. The decision over which groups are included in hate crime laws can be understood in the context of the rising significance of identity politics and the mobilisation of different social movements seeking legal recognition. This has been informed by various civil rights campaigns, feminist efforts and other victims' rights groups; as a result, hate crime policy generally includes groups who have experienced a history of oppression and have gathered empirical evidence to demonstrate and document their experiences. Gail Mason (2013: 79) adds that they also need to have made a moral or emotional claim as regards a consideration of 'what these victim groups can do for the moral force of the law'. This, in turn, has led to claims of a victim 'hierarchy', where groups excluded from hate crime policy – or to whom hate crime resources are not appropriately utilised – feel disenfranchised. For example, groups such as the homeless are routinely targeted as victims of violence and prejudice but not afforded the protection of hate crime policy (see Duggan, 2013). Therefore, in order to be included in hate crime policy, not only must victims possess particular identity attributes for inclusion in recognised groups, but such groups need to be sufficiently cared about or influential to win over relevant policymakers.

The rolling implementation of hate crime laws in Great Britain evidences this hierarchy somewhat. The UK has seen the steady advent and expansion of hate crime policy over the last 20 years. Mirroring developments in the US, the initial legislative developments were framed with race as the first category enshrined in law. In Britain, this came about as a result of the racist murder of black teenager Stephen Lawrence in 1993, which prompted the New Labour government to enact a manifesto commitment to make racist violence a specific offence attracting an enhanced punishment (which they later did in 1997 after winning the general election). Religion was subsequently added as another category in 2001 after concerns about rising levels of Islamophobia in the UK following the '9/11' terror attacks in the US.

In this early formation, it is noteworthy that cases of 'stranger danger' came to be predominantly associated with notions and definitions of hate crime, in that it was possible to determine the motive as the perpetrator did not have any other reason for the attack (Mason, 2005). The prejudicial motive – the 'hate' for a person's identity – was determined to be what had caused the crime and thus warranted harsher than usual punishment. As such, key cases, such as that of Stephen Lawrence (and, in 2005, Anthony Walker – a black teenager murdered in Liverpool), came to be seen as archetypal hate crimes as a result of the attacks being committed by strangers to the victims. The connections here with Christie's ideal victim typology – in that the image of the stranger is a key tenet – appear evident. However, if race and religion formed the foundation of hate crime categories, and stranger violence the style in which this occurred, then the place of disability within provisions has been much more precarious.

Writing ahead of changes to include other forms of identity within hate crime frameworks, Jenness and Grattet (2001) described disability as part of a 'second tier' of provisions that, at the time, was seen to potentially include sexual orientation, gender and age as similar categories. Unlike racially and religiously motivated offences, evidencing prejudice in crimes against these groups warranted harder work to gather the required empirical evidence needed to convince policymakers that hate crime definitions should extend to include them. Disability has now been included in the US, UK (since 2003) and eight other Organization for Security and Co-operation in Europe (OSCE) countries. Inclusion in law is a start, but there is evidence to suggest that it has not been embraced to the fullest extent in terms of implementation. In 2015/16, the Crown Prosecution Service (CPS) in England and Wales completed 15,442 hate crime prosecutions. Of those, 941 were for disability hate crime; 75% resulted in a conviction, which was around 8% lower than for other forms of hate crime. A further disparity was the extent to which judges imposed a sentence uplift for cases of disability hate crime. This was only used in 11.9% of cases, compared with 37.8% for homophobic/transphobic crimes and 34.8% in cases of racially or religiously aggravated crimes (CPS, 2016). Recent policy reviews admit that disability lags behind other hate crime victim groups in terms of reporting, service provision and appropriate protection (Justice Inspectorate, 2015). Despite policy attention now being paid to disablist hate crimes, they remain 'cellophane crimes', in that 'people walk right through them, look right through them, and never know they are there' (Sherry, 2002: 1).

A key theme running throughout the literature on victims of disablist hate crime is the extent to which they are viewed not as victims of hostility, but as victims of their inherent *vulnerability*. As Roulstone and Sadique (2013) note, there exists an assumption that disabled people are easy targets. This is born partly from a history of medical models around disability but also from previous policy that has sought to utilise a social care rather than criminal justice response. Disabled people have needed to be 'protected' from themselves, from society and from the dangerous criminal 'other'. This means that – within a hate crimes framework – rather than being embraced within the identity politics-informed demand for a greater legal recognition of prejudice-motivated crimes, disabled people have instead been included as a result of wider social policies seeking enhanced safeguarding measures. In other words, the rhetoric surrounding disablist hate crime was more about promoting victim protection than punishing offender prejudice. Relating disablist hate crime to Christie's model, the 'ideal victim' relies upon understanding how the victim is constructed in relation to particular policies. Hate crime policy has developed in a specific way: around key 'figurehead cases' (those that tend to attract a high level of media attention), relating to 'stranger danger', reflecting campaigners' efforts, demarcating groups worthy of protection and so on. While an initial viewing of disabled hate crime *victims* might see them fit within the typology that Christie puts forward, considering this in conjunction with hate crime *policy* paints a much more complex picture. The chapter now moves on to a more detailed analysis of each attribute that Christie details in order to demonstrate this complexity.

The victim's weakness

Christie's first attribute is that the victim is weak. He stipulates that the 'sick, old or very young are particularly well suited as ideal victims' (Christie, 1986: 19). Furthermore, this weakness is particularly relative to the strength of the offender. Christie is not more specific about why this weakness is significant, but one might infer that this is because: (1) there might be increased harm and fear caused when a victim is weaker; and (2) it makes the criminal act more serious because they are selecting an easy target. Victims of disablist hate crime might appear to be ideal victims in this regard, potentially lacking the physical or mental strength to defend themselves. As Hughes (2009: 400) notes, this perception is based on an immediate visual appearance whereby the 'strong, well-formed, non-disabled, masculine body is the benchmark and against this benchmark a woman is found wanting and a disabled person – man or woman – is weak and vulnerable'. Popular discourse around disabled people has often portrayed them as having a 'spoiled identity' and as facing stigma and abuse relating to their disability (Simcock and Castle, 2016: 19). As such, they might be viewed as being weaker than the 'normal' (non-disabled) population. However, when examining the hate crime domain, there are further complicating factors. Although disabled people might experience prejudice related to perceptions of their weakness, this is somewhat different from other hate crime victims. It is somewhat unusual for hate crime victims to be seen as inherently *weaker* than (their) perpetrators. If we examine the case of Stephen Lawrence, who was murdered in a racist attack, he was not portrayed as being weak. Instead, the focus is on the perpetrator's motive, which, in turn, is about hostility towards the victim's identity.

In 2006, James Wheatley was jailed for 23 years for murdering Lee Irving, a mentally disabled man with learning difficulties. Wheatley repeatedly kicked and stamped on Lee in a number of attacks over nine days, eventually killing him. Three others were convicted for their role of helping to cover up the murder. Yet, despite the police and CPS submitting evidence that it was a disablist hate crime, the judge dismissed this in his sentencing remarks: 'In my judgement you were motivated in this offence not by hostility towards those with disability but by your vicious and bullying nature which particularly takes advantage of those who are unable to or less able to resist' (Kennedy, 2016).

Irving's family disputed this perspective, arguing that it was a hate crime because of the dehumanising language that they used during the attack, which was demonstrative of hostility based on disability. It appears that for 'ideal victims' of disability hate crime, being seen as weak suggests a crime of a different nature, one where victimisation has occurred as a result of being seen as an easy target rather than due to hostility towards the victim's identity. As such, this negates the complexity of (the offender's) motive, which the ideal victim framework does not allow for in hate crime cases.

Engagement in a respectable project

The second attribute that Christie describes is arguably rather opaque. He states that ideal victims should be carrying out a respectable project and gives the example of a woman caring for her sister. As a counter to this, he suggests the case of a young man who gets attacked while 'hanging around' in a bar and says that he is 'far from ideal' (Christie, 1986: 19). Van Wijk (2013: 163) suggests that, in reality, the young man in the bar would be viewed rather neutrally in contemporary society and that a man about to commit a crime might be a more useful interpretation of someone doing a disrespectful project. Many hate crime victims – particularly those who receive public attention and sympathy – are described as being engaged in neutral or respectful activities either before or at the time of their attack. For example, much attention was paid to the Christian background of Stephen Lawrence's family and that he wanted to become an architect (Cottle, 2004). Similarly, Jody Dobrowski was a young gay man for whom 'life was good' and 'had everything to live for' when he was brutally murdered in a homophobic attack in London in 2005 (Foufas, 2015). Jody had been walking home from work and was set upon by two men who beat him so severely that he had to be identified by his fingerprints. Sentencing his killers to 28 years in prison, Judge Brian Barker noted that they had only one motive and that it was 'Jody's tragic misfortune to cross [their] path' (BBC, 2006). This interpretation of Christie's 'respectable project' suggests that the victims – who were going about their daily activities when attacked – would have otherwise had the potential to make a contribution to wider society.

For victims of disablist hate crime, there are unique factors linked to this aspect of the ideal victim typology that make its application more complex. For a start, there is a long history of stereotyping the disabled and viewing their mere existence as problematic, wounded or monstrous (Hughes, 2009). As Anne Novis (2013: 121) notes, 'negative stereotypes towards disabled people start before birth, via segregation into day centres, residential homes, special schools and specialist employment'. As such, their lives do not exist; they are devalued or seen as burdensome. The label of 'vulnerability', so readily applied in policy contexts, is also emblematic of the burden that disabled people place on local services. Roulstone and Sadique (2013: 32) point towards the various safeguarding schemes that could risk 'disabled people losing, rather than gaining independence'. Negatively perceiving disabled people as 'abject' in terms of societal norms and values, in turn, impacts on their being able to engage in 'respectable projects' (Thorneycroft and Asquith, 2017). Furthermore, recent popular discourse in the UK around 'Fit for Work' schemes, coupled with cuts to Disability Living Allowance, fuel prejudices about disabled people being a drain on resources and therefore unlikely to be seen as carrying out any sort of respectable or worthwhile endeavours. The little old lady in Christie's example is depicted as caring for her sister, thereby making a contribution to society. In disability hate crimes, the victims are more likely to be considered the 'sister', in that they are being cared for. This means that within Christie's framework, their value as *contributors* is questioned.

Blamelessness

Christie suggests that to be granted ideal victim status, victims must be blameless in what happened to them. If individuals have a more ambiguous status, then they are less likely to be seen as victims (Bouris, 2007). Van Wijk (2013: 164) invokes the 'just deserts' theory to explain why people need to believe that bad things only happen to bad people (see Bosma, Mulder and Pemberton, this volume). This, in turn, generates empathy towards the innocent victim, who we care about and can see as deserving of our concern. Cases with these qualities tend to attract a high level of media attention, which Thorneycroft and Asquith (2017) refer to as 'figurehead crimes'. Often, the reporting emphasises the victim's 'innocence' and 'normality', which renders them a sympathetic figure. The homophobic murder of Mathew Shepard in the US is one such example that they invoke to demonstrate the power of a figurehead crime. In this case, a cultural shift towards increasing equality for gay people's rights, meant that Mathew's murder was afforded a lot of attention, both in policy terms (resulting in legislative changes) and in the press.

For victims of disability hate crime, their liability for being victimised sometimes lies in their gullibility. In 2006, Kevin Davies, a young man with epilepsy, was murdered by three people who called themselves his friends. They had taken advantage of Kevin, forcing him to wear a dog collar and leash, stealing from him, and abusing him over a period of time. Kevin was imprisoned by the group for four months before they killed him; yet, when the perpetrators were convicted, the judge described Kevin as being 'vulnerable, gullible and naïve' (Quarmby, 2011: 182). Similar themes have emerged in other cases. Brent Martin, who had learning difficulties, was killed by a group of young people who had befriended him in order to have him carry out petty crimes on their behalf over a sustained period of time. On the night he was murdered, the group chased him through the streets, periodically assaulting Brent before finally beating him unconscious. The final blow was delivered to his prone body, whereupon they stripped him from the waist down to further humiliate Brent. At the trial, his family talked about how he had often been 'blamed for the misdeeds of others' as the judge again pointed out his gullibility at having been taken advantage of (Quarmby, 2011: 182).

Katharine Quarmby's analysis of disablist hate crime provides a detailed assessment of the many ways in which targeted violence against disabled people has been ignored. She points out that disabled people have long been criminalised by the criminal justice system, so it is unsurprising that blame is apportioned to them. Aside from being naive, Quarmby also notes the number of disabled people who are accused of being paedophiles and sex offenders, as in the aforementioned case of Bijam Ebrahimi. This pattern of false accusations for some disabled people creates an obscured image of them as potentially to blame for their victimisation and thus not able to embody Christie's required notion of 'blamelessness'.

The big and bad offender

In Christie's typology, aspects of the offender's identity are stipulated that contribute towards perceptions of the victim's status. The (masculinised) offender is described as 'big and bad' in relation to the (feminised) weak and blameless victim. For hate crimes, the most exceptional and potentially straightforward cases tend to attract more attention in the popular media. This is because they play into the storyline narrative of an ideal crime, where there is no ambiguity about the offender's culpability. In addition, the idea that a person could be attacked purely because of a prejudice towards their identity underscores the offence as a particularly heinous and evil form of crime. Van Wijk (2013: 165) notes that 'we have an intrinsic willingness to believe that people who commit such acts differ fundamentally from us', and Christie asserts that an ideal offender is 'a human being close to not being one' (Christie, 1986: 26). It is this 'evil' element – the intent – that hate crime legislation specifically recognises: perpetrators are considered to require harsher punishments as victims suffer more harm (Iganski, 2001).

For disablist hate crime, there are complicating factors surrounding the majority of offenders that make it difficult to conceive of them as 'big and bad'. First, evidence suggests that the age profile of perpetrators is younger than for other forms of hate crime. CPS data from 2015/16 showed that 19.6% of defendants were aged 18–24 years old and 9.6% were aged 14–17 years old. Most defendants in disablist hate crime cases were men (75.3%), but there was a significantly higher proportion of women (24.5%) compared to other strands of hate crime

(17.1% in racially and religiously aggravated hate crime and 16.5% in homophobic and transphobic hate crime) (CPS, 2016). In cases of disablist hate crime, while the actions taken may be particularly heinous, the offender(s) may not come across as such. Therefore, it is harder to discern a specific 'big and bad' offender who can be seen as evil and different from everyone else.

The case of Fiona Pilkington and her daughter Francecca Hardwick is an example of the difficulty in discerning offenders in disablist hate crime cases. Fiona and her daughter had endured years of abuse, much of which was directed towards Francecca, who had a learning disability, from people described mostly as 'yobs' and 'youths' in media depictions of the case. Despite the police being called on no fewer than 38 occasions, no further action was taken, thus the harassment continued. Eventually, in 2007, Fiona drove herself and her daughter to a secluded area and set fire to the car, killing them both. The sustained nature and multitude of offenders involved in this case made discerning a clear motivation difficult. Nonetheless, a jury in the inquest found that the lack of police action and failure of local authorities to act had had a significant impact on Fiona's decision to take such drastic action (Quarmby, 2011). The failure of various institutions to respond appropriately to victims of hate crime means that they are effectively victimised again by the support services that let them down.

The unknown offender

Christie (1986: 19) argues that an absence of any familiarity between the victim and offender is a key attribute in granting ideal victim status. Specifically, there should be no prior personal relationship between the victim and offender. Christie does not specify why this is such a key attribute, but given his other definitions, one could infer that it is about the simplicity of motivation and ability not to assign any blame to the victim. Furthermore, the absence of information about the offender allows for the construction of a 'dehumanized picture … the more foreign the better' (Christie, 1986: 29). This is in keeping with the early victimology literature, which takes a positivist stance and looks to the image of the stranger as being the ultimate 'baddy'. Similarly, a key criticism of hate crime as a concept has been that it has too readily relied upon images of the stranger that have perpetuated the idea that offences are rare and extraordinary. Kielinger and Stanko (2002: 5) suggested that this 'places the responsibility for the violence on strangers and therefore on individuals rather than society as a whole'. In fact, for many victims, experiences of hate crime are a daily, normal occurrence but when 'hatred intersects with the known we prefer to blame the social relationships of the known for fuelling the individual act of violence' (Stanko, 2001: 327). Nevertheless, high-profile cases of hate crimes committed by offenders who were strangers to the victim have come to characterise everyday understandings about the nature of victimisation.

The relationship between victim and offender might therefore present a problem in attributing ideal victim status for many forms of hate crime. However, for victims of disablist hate crime, research suggests that this problem is more acute. Aside from the high proportion of victims who know the offender, either as a neighbour or friend, they might also be a carer. In 2001, an undercover documentary broadcast by the BBC exposed a shocking regime of abuse of disabled residents in a private hospital called Winterbourne View. Secret footage had been captured of people being taunted, jeered at, dragged across the floor and abused. In his analysis, Chih Hoong Sin (2015: 108) noted the shock that was expressed by politicians and the public alike and that, in this case, the criminal justice system did respond and prosecute the offenders for disablist hate crime. However, critics have argued that much of this abuse never reaches the courts because it happens in an institutional setting. This, combined with a perception that being a carer is a difficult and unskilled job with few rewards, sometimes leads to a level of sympathy more directed towards the perpetrators. The isolation of a disabled person who relies upon their carer leads to a level of complexity that is difficult to square with the ideal victim concept.

A further particular phenomenon related to disabled victims is that of so-called 'mate crime'. Described by Pam Thomas (2013: 136) as 'hostile incidents carried out by one or more people the disabled person considers to be their friends or relatives', it is a particular feature of this strand of hate crime victims. Interpersonal relationships are often deliberately cultivated by the offenders to exploit the vulnerability that they see in the victim and also a lack of support structures in place to assist the disabled person (Thomas, 2013: 139). Raymond Atherton is an example of a disabled man who was 'befriended' in this way by a group of teenagers who would steal from him, eat his food and take his money. He had few people to tell about what was happening and said that he would rather have the company of someone than no one (Thomas, 2013: 143). It later emerged that many agencies with whom Raymond was in contact knew of the abuse; despite him moving house, the abuse continued up until the point of his eventual murder. His two young killers, aged 17 and 15 at the time, were sentenced to three-and-a-half years and three years in prison, respectively (Quarmby,

2011: 103). In sum, the relationship between the victim and offender in cases of disablist hate crime is seen as a complex mix of institutional and societal failings. The deliberate targeting is somehow different from the random attack that Christie envisages and one to which a level of understanding has to be extended to the perpetrators, who might also have been failed by the system. Although this does not necessarily mean that offenders go unpunished, it does mean that disabled victims are less likely to be seen as 'ideal' and for sentence enhancements to be used.

Power and influence

The final attribute that Christie (1986: 21) puts forward relates to the power and influence of victim groups in gaining ideal victim status. This is balanced by being weak enough not to be a threat to other interests. In their examination of the construction of policy design, Schneider, Ingram and deLeon note that some groups have the access and resources to influence and shape policy, which allows them to be seen as worthy recipients of protection. This is about how groups are seen as having the right amount of sympathy and pity:

> lack of political power sharply curtails their receipt of benefits ... they do not have a strong role in the creation of national wealth, dependents are viewed as 'good' people but considerably less deserving of actual investments than advantaged people. (Schneider et al, 2014: 112)

This is of particular relevance to hate crime policy, where critics have argued that a victim hierarchy has been created precisely because of the reliance on campaign group activists in the construction of legislation. As I have argued in previous research, a frustration for campaigners has been the extent to which policymakers rely upon them to gather evidence and push for legal recognition (Mason-Bish, 2010). The costs and manpower involved with this means that smaller and less well-funded organisations struggle to have a role in the construction of hate crime policy and, therefore, what ideal victims might look like.

As with the other victim attributes that Christie notes, research has demonstrated the difficulties for victims of disablist hate crime in establishing themselves as important enough to count. Similarly, less well-resourced disabled people's organisations do not necessarily have direct access to government officials, but have often relied upon larger charities who (arguably) had less involvement with victims themselves (Mason-Bish, 2010). In an age of budget cuts and with so many other social problems to deal with, it is unsurprising that disabled people's organisations have found it difficult to push for the adequate implementation of hate crime provisions. Anne Novis (2013: 119) notes that this struggle is partly about being included in policy discussions but also in ensuring that these catered adequately for the needs of disabled people.

A further point is the extent to which disabled victims evoke sufficient compassion and sympathy as to warrant a response (see Ibanez, this volume). In her examination of emotions and hate crime law, Gail Mason (2013: 85) suggests that this is essential because people must feel an obligation to resist prejudice against that group because 'familiarity breeds compassion'. They need to possess the 'right amount of vulnerability, blamelessness and proximity to engender compassionate thinking' (Mason, 2013: 86). This can be about not having empirical credibility, being blameworthy or simply being too different and strange to 'invite concern'. Disabled victims might therefore not meet the criteria of being viewed with enough sympathy because, as we have seen, they might be considered as partly to blame due to their gullibility, or people may disbelieve the scale of the abuse they suffer. However, most potent is the claim that they are too strange, an argument supported by Thorneycroft and Asquith (2017). In their recent piece, they query why so few cases of disablist hate crime achieve 'figurehead status', despite the undisputed horrors that disabled people have suffered. They suggest that it is because the victims are 'abject' in that their existence and bodies are deemed less than human. The narrative of social policy has been about detecting and treating disabled people for their conditions, proposing abortions or mercy killings for people deemed defective. Anne Novis (2013: 119) argues that these messages are endorsed by government policies on benefit cuts that perpetuate a narrative that disabled people are a burden on the state. The nature of hate crimes against disabled people often shows elements of this dehumanisation in the way that they are enslaved and tortured as being less than human (Quarmby, 2011).

Constructing deserving victims

This chapter has so far demonstrated the problems for victims of disablist hate crime in terms of gaining recognition using Christie's 'ideal victim' typology. I would now like to take this analysis further by discussing the advantages of being an 'ideal victim' of hate crime. This is something about which Christie is rather ambiguous and he only implies what type of benefits a victim can expect to receive and that they may lead to calls for 'further measures' (Christie, 1986: 28). For hate crime, these measures include additional victim support and the potential to punish a perpetrator more harshly. However, as I have demonstrated, not all groups are treated equally, and victims of disablist hate crime have struggled to be seen as 'ideal' in this context. Despite this, there are potential benefits for focusing on hate crime as a way to challenge perceptions of disability. As Chih Hoong Sin (2015: 101) notes, there has been a historic tendency to view disabled people as being at risk of violence because of their disability. This creates an inertia in policy responses which assume that the best outcome is to protect disabled people from the abuse that their disability causes. This notion of inherent vulnerability evokes negative and paternalistic assumptions that point towards a need to care for or treat disabled people instead of giving them full access to criminal justice responses. So, although not seen as 'ideal' in Christie's formation, it is worth challenging and contesting what could be described as the 'dominant culture's demeaning picture of the group' (Fraser, 2000: 109). This speaks to how in the construction of social problems, identity politics has often sought to have forms of violence recognised in very particular ways; as Barbara Perry (2002: 488) has noted, 'rights claims embedded in hate crime legislation can be powerfully transformative discourses'.

Furthermore, the ideas of vulnerability and presumed weakness are connected to medical models of disability tied to notions of biological pathology. Instead, being recognised as victims of hate crime rather than victims of disability offer a greater connection with issues of discrimination and structural inequality. As Tom Shakespeare (1992: 40) notes: 'The achievement of the disability movement has been to break the link between our bodies and our social situation and to focus on the real cause of disability, i.e. discrimination and prejudice'. So, to be seen as worthy of protection in hate crime policy is to counter the fixation on inherent vulnerability, which could lead to suggestions that disabled people are less than full human beings and so less worthy of full citizenship rights (Hughes, 2009). In the politics of recognition, it is better to be seen as an ideal victim of hate crime than an ideal victim of disability. This is why campaigners have been so vociferous in their assertion that disablism must be recognised 'correctly'.

Concluding thoughts

Christie's classic typology draws upon notions of weakness, blame, evil and stranger danger in order to demonstrate which groups of people are most likely to be given the legitimate status of 'ideal victim'. In this

57

chapter, I have applied the typology to victims of disablist hate crime. In doing so, I have demonstrated that it is necessary to understand his work within a particular policy context as legislation is framed around constructions of crime that might have their own attributes. In itself, the case study of hate crime is an interesting one. It takes a particular policy response to victimisation and, through social movement campaigns and policymaking efforts, has created a specific set of deserving and undeserving victims. Many groups – older people, the homeless, sex workers – have not fitted with the general ideal victim typology and so have been left outside of policy efforts. Others – such as disabled people – have been included but have had problems having policy implemented. I argue here that this is because of the clash of ideal victims generally and the construction of ideal victims in specific policy. For hate crime, we have seen a concept emerge that has often relied upon notions of stranger danger, of simple motivations and of victim blamelessness. These have been relayed to the public through the media to garner support. However, disability has had a more difficult journey, in that victims are seen as less sympathetic and more complicated than 'true' hate crime victims. This has meant that the benefits of being an ideal victim in terms of sentence enhancement and victim support have often been lacking. Worse than this, it has meant that 'endemic low aspirations for such groups lead to fatalistic acceptance that disabled people cannot expect anything different' (Sin, 2015: 101).

The examination of disabled victims also leads us towards some unpalatable truths. The historic treatment of disabled people has focused on medical concerns around the pathological body. Policy has tended to see the *disability* as the offender – the 'thing' that causes the problems and limitations. Disabled people are victims of their disability rather than attitudes and discrimination. As such, issues of gullibility have often been used to excuse victimisation, with often a reliance on blaming a lack of treatment or appropriate care rather than encouraging access to justice. This 'diagnostic overshadowing' (Sin, 2015) is further complicated by the 'abject' nature of disabled people, which renders them invisible to the criminal justice system. The ideal victim typology reminds us of the need to challenge popular discourse around victims of crime. The justice system is slowly acknowledging the specific nature of the victim experience and has published guidance that recognises the phenomenon of 'mate crime', the problems of assumed vulnerability and the role of society in challenging this. Campaigners feel that they are being heard more by policymakers (Brookes, 2013; Novis, 2013). However, we have to acknowledge our own role in the construction of ideal victims and the extent to which we accept or challenge these ideas.

References

BBC News (online) (2006) 'Men jailed for gay barman murder', 16 June. Available at http://news.bbc.co.uk/1/hi/england/london/5087286.stm (accessed 10 April 2018).

Bouris, E. (2007) *Complex Political Victims*, Bloomfield: Kumarian Press.

Brookes, S. (2013) 'A case for engagement: the role of the UK Disability Hate Crime Network', in A. Roulstone and H. Mason-Bish (eds) *Disability, Hate Crime and Violence*, London: Routledge, pp 126–34.

Christie, N. (1986) 'The ideal victim', in E.A. Fattah (ed) *From Crime Policy to Victim Policy: Reorienting the Justice System*, Basingstoke: Macmillan, pp 17–30.

Cottle, S. (2004) *The Racist Murder of Stephen Lawrence: Media Performance and Public Transformation*, Westport, CT: Praeger.

CPS (Crown Prosecution Service) (2016) *CPS Hate Crime Report*, London: Crown.

Duggan, M. (2013) 'Working with victims: values and validations', in M. Cowburn, M. Duggan, A. Robinson and P. Senior (eds) *The Values of Criminology and Community Justice*, Bristol: Policy Press.

Equality and Human Rights Commission (2011) *Hidden in Plain Sight*, London: EHRC.

Foufas, C. (2015) 'Why Jody Dobrowski is a name we must never forget', *Telegraph*, 16 October. Available at: http://www.telegraph.co.uk/men/thinking-man/11934107/Why-Jody-Dobrowski-is-a-name-we-must-never-forget.html (accessed 9 May 2017).

Fraser, N. (2000) 'Rethinking recognition', *New Left Review*, 3(May–June): 107–20.

Home Office (2016) *Hate Crime, England and Wales, 2015/16*, Statistical Bulletin, London: Crown.

Hughes, B. (2009) 'Wounded/monstrous/abject: a critique of the disabled body in the sociological imaginary', *Disability and Society*, 24(4): 399–410.

Iganski, P. (2001) 'Hate crimes hurt more', *American Behavioral Scientist*, 45(4): 626–38.

Jenness, V. and Grattet, R. (2001) 'Examining the boundaries of hate crime law: disabilities and the "dilemma of difference"', *Journal of Criminal Law and Criminology*, 91(3): 653–98.

Justice Inspectorate (2015) *Joint Review of Disability Hate Crime*, London: Crown.

Kennedy, R. (2016) 'Lee Irving murder: judge brands killer a "vicious bully and a coward" as he is jailed for life', *Chronicle Live*, 2 December. Available at: http://www.chroniclelive.co.uk/news/north-east-news/lee-irving-murderer-james-wheatley-12264798 (accessed 9 May 2017).

Kielinger, V. and Stanko, E. (2002) 'What can we learn from people's use of the police?', *Criminal Justice Matters*, 48: 4–5.

Levin, J. (2013) 'Disablist violence in the US: unacknowledged crime', in A. Roulstone and H. Mason-Bish (eds) *Disability, Hate Crime and Violence*, London: Routledge, pp 95–105.

Mason, G. (2005) 'Hate crime and the image of the stranger', *British Journal of Criminology*, 45(6): 837–59.

Mason, G. (2013) 'The symbolic purpose of hate crime law: ideal victims and emotion', *Theoretical Criminology*, 18(1): 75–92.

Mason-Bish, H. (2010) 'Future challenges for hate crime policy: lessons from the past', in N. Chakraborti (ed) *Hate Crime: Concepts, Policy, Future Directions*, Cullompton: Willan, pp 58–77.

Novis, A. (2013) 'Disability hate crime: a campaign perspective', in A. Roulstone and H. Mason-Bish (eds) *Disability, Hate Crime and Violence*, London: Routledge, pp 118–25.

Peachey, P. (2015) 'Bijan Embrahimi murder: man killed by lynch mob pleaded with police for help', *Independent*, 21 December. Available at: http://www.independent.co.uk/news/uk/crime/bijan-ebrahimi-murder-man-killed-by-lynch-mob-pleaded-with-police-for-help-a6782266.html (accessed 9 May 2017).

Perry, B. (2002) 'Hate crimes and identity politics', *Theoretical Criminology*, 6(4): 485–502.

Quarmby, K. (2011) *Scapegoat: Why We are Failing Disabled People*, London: Portobello.

Roulstone, A. and Sadique, K. (2013) 'Vulnerable to misinterpretation: disabled people, "vulnerability", hate crime and the fight for legal recognition', in A. Roulstone and H. Mason-Bish (eds) *Disability, Hate Crime and Violence*, London: Routledge, pp 25–39.

Schneider, A., Ingram, H. and DeLeon, P. (2014) 'Democratic policy design: social constructions of target populations', in P. Sabatier and C. Weible (eds) *Theories of the Policy Process* (3rd edn), Boulder, CO: Westview Press, pp 105–50.

Scope (2008) *Getting Away With Murder*, London: Scope.

Shakespeare, T. (1992) 'A response to Liz Crow', *Coalition* (September).

Sherry, M. (2002) 'Don't ask, tell or respond: silent acceptance of disability hate crimes', paper presented at the Ed Roberts Post Doctoral Fellowship in Disability Studies at the University of California at Berkley Public Lecture Series, 21 November.

Sherry, M. (2010) *Disability Hate Crimes: Does Anyone Really Hate the Disabled?*, London: Routledge.

Simcock, P. and Castle, R. (2016) *Social Work and Disability*, Cambridge: Polity Press.

Sin, C.H. (2015) 'Using a layers of influence model to understand the interaction of research, policy and practice in relation to disablist hate crime', in N. Chakraborti and J. Garland (eds) *Responding to Hate Crime: The Case for Connecting Policy and Research*, London: Policy Press.

Stanko, E. (2001) 'Re-conceptualising the policing of hatred: confessions and worrying dilemmas of a consultant', *Law and Critique* (Special Edition, 'Hate crimes: critical reflections', ed L. Moran), 12(13): 309–29.

Thomas, P. (2013) 'Hate crime or mate crime? Disability hostility, contempt and ridicule', in A. Roulstone and H. Mason-Bish (eds) *Disability, Hate Crime and Violence*, London: Routledge, pp 135–46.

Thorneycroft, R. and Asquith, N. (2017) '"Figurehead" hate crime cases: developing a framework for understanding and exposing the "problem" with "disability"', *Continuum: Journal of Media and Cultural Studies*, 31(3): 482–94.

Van Wijk, J. (2013) 'Who is the "little old lady" of international crimes? Nils Christie's concept of the ideal victim reinterpreted', *International Review of Victimology*, 19(2): 159–79.

THREE

The lived experiences of veiled Muslim women as 'undeserving' victims of Islamophobia

Irene Zempi

Introduction

Following the 2001 terrorist attacks on 9/11 in the US, and 7/7 in the UK four years later, and, more recently, the Islamic State of Iraq and Syria (ISIS) directed attacks in France, Germany and Belgium, the religion of Islam is associated with violence, religious fundamentalism and the global 'war on terror'. In this context, the wearing of the niqab (face covering; hereafter called the 'veil') is often perceived as *the* key visual symbol of Islam in the West. Typically, media discourses about Islamist extremism are illustrated by the image of a Muslim woman in full veil. Through her clothing, this female figure is used to illustrate the 'abnormal', a 'stranger among us', as well as an extreme belief system, embodying the potential threat of terrorist attacks (Meer et al, 2010). The wearing of the veil is also seen as a 'threat' to notions of integration and national cohesion, as well as a visual embodiment of gender oppression and gender inequality.

According to Perry (2014), the controlling images of veiled Muslim women render them especially attractive and available targets for hate crime. Indeed, the research literature demonstrates that veiled Muslim women are particularly vulnerable as targets of Islamophobic attacks (see, eg, Wing and Smith, 2006; Githens-Mazer and Lambert, 2010; Allen et al, 2013; Zempi and Chakraborti, 2014; Awan and Zempi, 2016). The underpinnings of Islamophobic violence are the invocation of negative images and stereotypes associated with veiled Muslim women. At the same time, their dress code identifies them from non-Muslims and, to this end, marks them as visible targets of Islamophobic hate crime (Haddad, 2007).

Despite their vulnerability to Islamophobic hate crimes, veiled Muslim women are unlikely to be perceived as innocent victims worthy of our sympathy and support; rather, they are less valued and thus less protected in comparison to 'ideal victims' (Jiwani, 2005). Veiled Muslim women might be denied the ideal victim identity due to the criminalisation of the veil, especially in light of the banning of the veil in European countries such as France and Belgium. Additionally, they might be denied an ideal victim identity in light of national and international events whereby Islam and Muslims are demonised by political rhetoric and state policies. Against this background, veiled Muslim women are seen as hate crime victims on the margins. Mason (2014) states that such victims of hate crime struggle to engender compassionate emotion for their plight and, hence, fail to convince others that they are undeserved targets of harm that is sufficiently serious to warrant collective concern. Hate crime victims on the margins are branded as 'illegitimate' due to insufficient empirical credibility and their subsequent unheard claims of vulnerability, their extra-marginal position or ambiguous moral status (Williams and Tregidga, 2014). Drawing on empirical research, this chapter demonstrates the implications of the label of 'undeserving victims' for veiled Muslim women who experience Islamophobic hate crime.

Stigmatisation of veiled Muslim women

As Carrabine et al (2009) observe, some victims enjoy a higher status in the crime discourse and their victimisation experiences are taken more seriously than others. According to Christie (1986), in order to be given complete and legitimate status, victims must be judged to be weak, vulnerable, innocent, respectable and blameless. In contrast, victims who are judged to be troublesome, distasteful, trivial or engaged in risky behaviour are generally considered to be 'non-ideal victims' (Mason, 2014).

Carrabine et al (2009) point out that this hierarchy of victimhood stems from notions of 'deserving' and 'undeserving' victims. In this regard, there is a nexus between sympathy and the ideal victim. The literature (Baier, 1994; Nussbaum, 2001; Aradau, 2004; Walklate, 2011) demonstrates that deserving victims are those who are capable of generating sentimental emotions such as feelings of sympathy, compassion or pity for the harm inflicted upon them. In other words, deserving victims appear to generate public sympathy for their victimisation. They are seen as innocent victims who deserve help, care and compassion. In contrast, undeserving victims do not generate such sentimental emotions as they are seen as blameworthy for their victimisation; to this end, they deserve the suffering since they have brought the suffering on themselves.

This illustrates a dichotomy between 'innocent' and 'blameworthy' victims. Typically, non-ideal victims are judged to be blameworthy because they were somehow 'asking for it' by engaging in risky or immoral behaviour. From this perspective, the characteristics or behaviour of individual victims can act as precipitating factors in a crime event. In this case, the notion of victim precipitation becomes shorthand for 'victim blaming' (Carrabine et al, 2009). Veiled Muslim women who experience hate crime are often seen to be blameworthy. In this regard, it is important to consider the common stereotypes surrounding the wearing of the veil in the West. Bullock and Jafri (2002: 36) highlight three 'personas' that Muslim women are thought to occupy in the popular imagination, and that thus define what Muslim women 'are supposed to be and do': the first is the harem belly-dancer character, the mysterious and sexualised woman of the 'Orient'; the second is the oppressed Muslim woman; and, finally, there is the militant Muslim woman.

Veiled Muslim women are constructed as racialised, exotic 'Others' who do not fit the Western ideal of womanhood (Perry, 2014). At the same time, they are likely to be stigmatised due to their affiliation with Muslims, a group that is often associated (in the West) with negative stereotypes, attitudes and perceptions (Poynting and Mason, 2007). Moreover, the wearing of the veil signals Muslim women as docile, oppressed, submissive and passive. From this perspective, the wearing of the veil is understood as an oppressive and subordinating practice, which is not welcome in the West (Chakraborti and Zempi, 2012). Mahmud and Swami (2010) found that veiled Muslim women are considered unattractive and less intelligent, while Unkelbach et al (2008, 2009) found that Muslim women wearing the hijab (headscarf) were subjected to more aggressive behaviour in a shooter bias paradigm than non-hijabi targets.

While the veil is taken as a sign of gender inequality and oppression, it is also seen as a sign of Islamist terrorism. Even though Muslim females are stereotypically inferred to be oppressed (while Muslim males are stereotypically seen as being aggressive, belligerent and hostile), it should be noted that Muslim women are not free from the common Muslim stereotypes as Muslims in general are portrayed as evil, barbaric, backwards, terrorists, religious fundamentalists and uncivilised (Cole and Ahmadi, 2003; Haddad, 2007). As Perry (2014) points out, if veiled Muslim women are not characterised as exotic or as oppressed, they are represented as dangerous and threatening; this is fuelled by the controlling image of the 'Muslim as terrorist'. To this end, veiled Muslim women are represented as agents of terrorism or as the tools of Islamist terrorism aiming to infiltrate the West (Jiwani, 2005). From this perspective, Muslim women are not seen as real women or mothers like Western women; rather, they are seen as 'mothers of suicide bombers' (Perry, 2014). Moreover, veiled Muslim women might be seen as terrorist bodies on the basis that their face is covered and, to this end, the veil could be used as a camouflage for a terrorist (Zempi and Chakraborti, 2014).

Finally, veiled Muslim women are feared and reviled on the same basis as all Muslims but they are also 'othered' because of the visibility of the veil. Indeed, it is well established in the literature that there is a significant relationship between being visible as a Muslim and experiencing Islamophobic hate crime (Allen, 2010). If the markers of Islam (eg a Muslim dress or a Muslim name) are absent, 'passing' as a non-Muslim is possible for who do not 'look like' a Muslim (Garner and Selod, 2015). As such, being visually identifiable as a Muslim has been found to be the most powerful antecedent to negative behaviours against Muslims (Allen and Nielson, 2002). According to Goffman (1963), individuals whose stigma is visible experience more hostility than individuals with concealable stigmas. Given that the majority of Muslim women do not wear the veil, those Muslim women who do wear it are likely to be perceived as having a controllable stigma for actively choosing to wear it (Ghumman and Ryan, 2013). Based on Goffman's (1963) approach, individuals who have such controllable stigmas are more likely to be subjected to stigmatisation based on the premise that they are perceived as being responsible for their own condition. In this respect, when Muslim women choose to wear the veil, they are seen as purposefully isolating themselves and rejecting Western values. From this perspective, the wearing of the veil is seen as a sign of self-segregation; it is thought to hinder face-to-face communication, which is necessary in an open society as well as broader engagement with non-Muslims. As such, veiled Muslim women 'deserve' to be punished for choosing to isolate themselves from wider society but do not 'deserve' our sympathy or support.

Taken in isolation or collectively, these stereotypes are commonly presented as justification for expressions and acts of hostility towards veiled Muslim women as a means of responding to the multiple perceived threats of the veil as a symbol of gender oppression, self-segregation and Islamist terrorism. These stereotypes also mark Muslim women as blameworthy victims of Islamophobic hate crime.

State policies criminalising the wearing of the veil

The construction of the veil exclusively through the lens of Islamist terrorism, gender oppression and self-segregation has triggered a spate of national and international reforms focused on the criminal law, which are used to justify state restrictions on the wearing of the veil in public places (Fredette, 2015). In 2010, France became the first European country to ban the wearing of the veil in public, while in 2011, Belgium followed suit. Nicolas Sarkozy, then president of France, stated that veils oppress women and were 'not welcome' in France. In 2014, the European Court of Human Rights (ECtHR) upheld the veil ban in France, declaring that the idea of 'living together' was the 'legitimate aim' of the French authorities, thereby lending support to perceptions of the veil as a 'threat' to national cohesion and integration. In 2016, French Riviera mayors introduced a ban on burkinis (full-body Islamic swimsuits). French Prime Minister Manuel Valls stated that burkinis were 'the affirmation of political Islam in the public space'. Although the 'burkini ban' has now been lifted (after France's highest administrative court overruled the law), some mayors refuse to lift the restrictions. In some parts of Italy, local authorities have also banned burkinis.

Germany has no national law restricting the wearing of Muslim veils, but half of Germany's 16 state governments have outlawed the wearing of both headscarves and veils by teachers. In December 2016, German Chancellor Angela Merkel called for a veil ban wherever legally possible for the 'good of Germany'. She stated: 'Show your face. The full covering is not permissible and should be banned'. Several parts of Catalonia in Spain have laws against the wearing of the veil in public. Although Spain's Supreme Court has overturned the ban, ruling that it 'limits religious freedom', certain areas continue to enforce the veil ban. In this case, they use the 2014 ECtHR ruling that banning the veil does not breach human rights. In January 2017, the ruling coalition in Austria agreed to prohibit the wearing of the veil in public spaces as well as a general ban on state employees wearing the headscarf. In the Netherlands, there is a partial ban on the veil, which means that Muslim women cannot have their faces covered in schools, hospitals and on public transport.

The UK does not have a ban on Islamic dress, but schools can decide their own dress code and prevent students from wearing veils. In January 2016, the chief inspector for the Office for Standards in Education (Ofsted) instructed other inspectors to downgrade institutions where they believed that the wearing of the veil – by students or teachers –

hindered 'positive social interaction'. At the same time, a number of British politicians have expressed strong feelings of antipathy towards the wearing of the veil in public in the UK. For example, in September 2013, the then Home Office Minister Jeremy Browne called for a national debate about banning the veil in schools. Nick Clegg, then Deputy Prime Minister, suggested that he may support banning the veil in classrooms, while the then Prime Minister David Cameron stated that Muslim women could be banned from wearing veils in schools, courts and other institutions. The UK Independence Party (UKIP) has systematically argued for banning the veil on the basis that it is a symbol of an increasingly divided Britain, gender oppression and a security threat. In July 2010, a YouGov survey found that 67% of the public supported a veil ban in public in the UK. A further YouGov survey, in August 2016, found that banning the veil continued to be a popular policy in the UK. Specifically, a majority of the public (57%) supported a veil ban in public in the UK.

Chakraborti and Zempi (2013) argue that by making the wearing of the veil a criminal offence, this law promotes a climate of intolerance, even hostility, thereby legitimising violence targeted at veiled Muslim women – be it in terms of the violation of human rights, discrimination, harassment on the street or victim-blaming attitudes. The veil ban promotes this negative discourse not only in those countries where the ban has been enforced, but also in other European countries, such as the UK, where it is still legal to wear the veil. This finding is illustrative of the domino effect of European policy, whereby events in one European country can influence public opinion in its neighbouring states (Chakraborti and Zempi, 2013). From this perspective, the veil ban justifies and rationalises a negative discourse that makes Muslim women blameworthy as victims of Islamophobic hate crime, both nationally and internationally.

As we see in what follows, the stereotyping of the veil has serious implications on the lived experiences of veiled Muslim women as victims of Islamophobic hate crime and the ways in which they are dealt with by the criminal justice system. This, in turn, has led to unwillingness among some victims to engage with the police and courts.

The research study

The aim of this study was to examine the lived experiences of Muslim women who wear the niqab in the UK. Specifically, this was a qualitative study that included 60 in-depth interviews and 20 focus groups with niqab-wearing women in Leicester between 2011 and 2012. All the participants wore full-length jilbabs (long robes) accompanied with hijabs (headscarves) and niqabs (face veils), mostly in black, and they were thus visibly identifiable as Muslim women in their public encounters. Participation in the study was voluntary. Prospective participants were identified through local Muslim organisations, including mosques, Muslim schools and Islamic centres, as well as local Muslim university student societies and Muslim women's groups. Participants unaffiliated to any local Muslim organisations or groups were also recruited through snowball sampling. Participants' real names have been replaced by pseudonyms in order to maintain their anonymity.

Experiences of Islamophobia

Throughout individual and focus group interviews, participants reported that suffering Islamophobic hate crime was 'part and parcel' of being a veiled Muslim woman in the UK. They described incidents of attempted and/or actual physical assaults (including taking the veil off), pushing, shoving and being spat at, and even incidents where passing vehicles had attempted to run them over. They also described incidents where people on the street or from moving cars had thrown eggs, stones, alcohol, water bombs, bottles, takeaway food and rubbish at them. In addition, verbal abuse from strangers in public (including streets, parks, shopping centres and public transport) was a common experience among participants. They also reported experiencing intimidation and harassment on social networking sites such as Facebook, Twitter and MySpace, as well as blogs and chat rooms. Underlying these incidents of intimidation, violence and abuse was a clear sense of Islamophobic sentiments, and this was made apparent through the language used by the perpetrators that signified their motivations for the attacks. For example, participants had been called names such as 'Muslim terrorists', 'Muslim bombers' and 'Suicide bombers', which indicate the perpetrators' perceptions of veiled Muslim women as a security or terrorist 'threat'.

Moreover, participants reported being used as a form of 'entertainment'. For example, they were called names like: ninja, Catwoman, Batman, Darth Vader, ghost woman, bin bag, letterbox, postbox, witch and walking coffin. They were also subjected to swearing, such as 'fucking freak', 'Muslim bitch' and 'Muslim whore'. So-called 'low-level' incidents, such as persistent staring, being ignored and/or avoided by people, being laughed at, being monitored at shops and being stalked by strangers on the street, were common themes that underpinned participants' accounts as they described their experiences of Islamophobic hate incidents in public.

Ultimately, these manifestations of Islamophobic hate crime were not isolated incidents; rather, there was always the reality, the fear and the expectation of another attack. This paints a picture of an everyday phenomenon, which can be better understood as a process rather than as incidental occurrences. Further qualitative research into the experiences of Muslim women who wear the veil has been conducted in five European countries: Belgium, Denmark, France, the Netherlands and the UK (Brems, 2014). The data show very strong similarities, such as the harassment and abuse of veiled Muslim women by strangers in public places. For example, veiled Muslim women in the Netherlands reported regularly being confronted with people who scolded, insulted or spat at them (Moors, 2009, 2014). Some women also mentioned being physically threatened, with cars attempting to hit them and people throwing things at them or trying to pull off the niqab (Moors, 2009, 2014). Echoing these experiences, veiled Muslim women in the UK and France described a stream of violent insults in public places, including being violently pushed, spat at and having their veils pulled off (Boutelja, 2011).

In the present study, participants argued that the typical perpetrator was a white male; however, it was evident that the perpetrator could be anyone, such as women, members of ethnic and racial minorities (including European Union [EU] nationals), and children:

> "For me, it can be anybody. At the beginning, it was mostly men but now I get a lot of abuse from women as well. Women can be very offensive and they will say and do horrible things to us." (Raja)

> "I was coming here [the mosque where the focus group interview took place] and I heard children, they were not all white children, shouting 'There is a ninja in this car' and then they threw snow at my car." (Nisha)

> "I don't know how other sisters feel, but for me, Asians are racist as well. I have come across that, the specific comment was 'Bitch take that off your face' and that wasn't from a white person." (Focus group participant)

> "We have a tough time with Eastern Europeans. Blatant mocking and laughing in our face and all in another language has left us bewildered as well as hurt." (Focus group participant)

Moreover, participants revealed that they had suffered abuse from fellow Muslims. In this context, the abuse came from members of the Muslim community who saw themselves as Westernised or non-practising Muslims:

> "It's not just about Islamophobia coming from non-Muslims. There are also Muslims who don't like the niqab. They say to me that we shouldn't wear it because we give them a bad name. We have it from both sides, Muslims and non-Muslims." (Focus group participant)

In some cases, the abuse came from participants' Muslim family members. Participants explained that some Muslim parents accept and encourage their daughters to wear the *hijab* but do not like the *niqab*, viewing the latter as an extreme form of practising Islam. Other Muslim parents were not necessarily opposed to the wearing of the veil itself, but fear for their daughters' safety: "How can I blame a person on the street when I've had problems from my own [Muslim] family? How do I have the right to wear it in public when my whole family doesn't agree with it?" (focus group participant).

For those participants who had converted to Islam, family members objected vehemently to their becoming Muslim, let alone supporting their decision to wear the veil. Throughout interviews and focus group discussions, it was clear that those participants who had converted to Islam often felt obliged to hide the fact that they wore the veil in order to avoid conflict with family members, while others were sometimes forced to cut off communication with their family due to intense disagreements about their decision to convert to Islam and/or wear the veil:

> "When I visit my [non-Muslim] parents, I take my niqab off and I keep the hijab on, but even with the hijab, they are not happy." (Zoe)

> "My parents don't like the fact that I'm wearing a niqab. My mum especially, she finds it hard to deal with it, so when I go to meet them, I take it off out of respect so that

they don't feel uncomfortable with me in public." (Focus group participant)

With respect to the relationship between perpetrators and victims, participants explained that they were usually targeted by strangers on the street. This is consistent with the views of Githens-Mazer and Lambert (2010), who found that manifestations of Islamophobia are invariably random in nature on the basis that veiled Muslim women are randomly targeted when they are seen in public. According to Chakraborti and Garland (2015), hate crimes are often committed by relatively 'ordinary' people in the context of their everyday lives. Iganski and Levin (2004) found that hate crime is often perpetrated by 'ordinary' members of the community rather than right-wing extremists.

Participants argued that their confidence had been severely affected as a result of their recurring experiences of targeted hostility, with many stating that they felt worthless, unwanted and that they did not belong. Participants also reported feeling unwelcome in the UK:

> "Everyone thinks we are the enemy. I feel that I don't have the right to be here. It crushes my self-esteem." (Parveen)

> "We feel like social lepers that no one wants to engage with." (Maryam)

> "We've been made to feel that we are totally unwanted. It's like we are a virus to the community." (Focus group participant)

> "We don't belong anywhere. We have no place. It's like we are not wanted anywhere." (Focus group participant)

Participants also described feelings of shame, self-doubt and guilt. They referred to incidents of Islamophobic victimisation as humiliating and embarrassing. The following comments help to convey the sense of humiliation and embarrassment that veiled Muslim women might feel when experiencing Islamophobic victimisation in public, often in view of people passing by who do not intervene to help them:

> "I feel humiliated and I feel totally alone even though there are so many people around. If somebody would speak up and say 'Leave her alone, it is up to her how she dresses' but nobody has ever come to my defence." (Kalila)

"It is awful because when they do it, they all do it publicly. There are witnesses all over the place. People are looking but nobody does anything. Nobody says 'It is wrong'." (Karima)

"When people abuse me, I feel intimidated because I don't know where to go and there's no one actually there to help me." (Aliyah)

Relatedly, the fact that no one would intervene to help them had culminated in many feeling a sense of blame. Participants were made to feel responsible and guilty for being attacked on the basis that they were different and Muslim. Concurrently, self-blaming was a way of making sense of their victimisation. The notion of self-blame is illustrated in the following comments:

"When you have someone abusing you like that, you automatically feel 'It's my fault because I'm wearing this'." (Huda)

"We feel we are causing a crime and we are not. We are just covering ourselves; that is not criminal. Well now it is criminal in France but it's not in this country." (Focus group participant)

Participants reported that nobody cared about their victimisation and, as such, they were shocked that this study was interested in their experiences:

"Nobody takes any action about it, nobody really cares. I am surprised you do. We didn't know that there was support until you mentioned it to us." (Samina)

"We feel nobody wants to listen to us. I was shocked that you'd come to hear us. We feel that nobody wants to hear us, to see us, people don't look at us as humans anymore, they treat us like we are subhuman." (Focus group participant)

In some cases, bystanders joined in and started abusing them as well:

"I got on the bus and a woman with a pushchair called me a 'Dirty Muslim' and spat at me, and then other people on the bus started calling me names too. The bus driver did not intervene." (Sabirah)

"Once, I was in town [Leicester city centre] and somebody pulled my niqab off. He did it on purpose. Nobody stepped in to help me. People tend to look away. But I've had incidents where other people joined in the abuse. I was verbally abused by a group of white men, I was told 'You're a terrorist, go back to your own country!' and then someone walking past said 'I will slit your throat, you Bin Laden bitch'." (Anisa)

Secondary victimisation in the criminal justice system

The majority of participants revealed that they would not normally disclose their experiences of Islamophobic victimisation to anyone, including family, friends or the police. They felt stigmatised by such incidents and this feeling was reinforced by previous experiences of being treated insensitively by others. There was also a sense of resignation on the part of participants, who had accepted that incidents of Islamophobic victimisation were going to happen as long as they wore the veil. This fact, in combination with feelings of shame and the fear of being blamed, had resulted in this victimisation not being disclosed to anyone:

"Other veiled sisters that I know don't really talk about it. I don't tell anyone, and same with everyone else I think. It is embarrassing, so I just forget about it." (Jamilah)

"Sisters feel helpless and in a state of despair, and then having to report to the police or give evidence to court, this only exacerbates our plight. We keep quiet to avoid further abuse." (Rehana)

Disclosure of victimisation can make veiled Muslim women vulnerable on the basis that they may encounter hostility, disbelief or judgemental attitudes, and this can have a harmful effect upon them to the extent of re-victimising them. Indeed, a barrier to reporting their experiences of Islamophobic victimisation to the authorities was the fact that participants feared victim-blaming attitudes, insensitive questioning and hostile responses from criminal justice agents, particularly the police and the courts. Specifically, some participants feared that they would become the ones under investigation or on trial on the basis of wearing the veil. In some cases, they feared that they would be seen as blameworthy for their victimisation for wearing the veil. According to Wolhuter et al (2009), in addition to the suffering caused by Islamophobic incidents, there is the possibility of further suffering caused by the way in which veiled Muslim women are treated within the criminal justice system. Victim-blaming attitudes, as well as discriminatory policies and practices that result in additional trauma and further violation of victims' rights, could be understood as 're-victimisation' or 'secondary victimisation' (Cambell and Raja, 2005). Williams (1999) highlights the added impact of secondary victimisation through the police investigation and court processes. Along similar lines, Dunn and Shepherd (2006) observe that the emotional impact of giving evidence is likely to be particularly difficult for witnesses who may be vulnerable or intimidated. Certainly, the way in which the police conduct the initial interview appears to be significant. Questions which suggest that victims provoked the attack by wearing the veil can evoke feelings of guilt and self-blame that impair the victim's recovery process and discourage disclosure. Likewise, a lack of respect for veiled Muslim women's cultural and religious needs, such as failing to provide a female officer or Muslim women being forced to take the veil off in court, could also cause the victim further suffering that amounts to secondary victimisation:

> "It wasn't easy giving a statement to a male officer. It really made me understand why other sisters don't report it." (Hadiqa)

> "As victims, we feel frightened and intimidated to go through the criminal justice system because we know that the veil will be a problem in court. A lot of sisters are hoping they can live their lives without ever having to contact the police about anything." (Focus group participant)

Most participants were adamant that the police would fail to understand the seriousness of the case, empathise with them and accommodate their religious and cultural needs. The following comments help to illustrate some of the key concerns raised by participants in relation to victim-blaming attitudes and a lack of understanding/empathy within the police service:

"The police won't help us. They think we are some kind of monsters." (Nabeeha)

"We feel that the police will not take it seriously. They don't understand women in veil anyway, so how are they going to deal with this crime? They probably think we shouldn't cover our face anyway." (Focus group participant)

"We feel misunderstood by the police. I've got stares from the police as well. I walked past the police and the police officer looked at me thinking 'You are one of the terrorists'. I could tell." (Focus group participant)

As can be seen in the quotations, there was a lack of confidence in the police, particularly in terms of being treated as a 'suspect community'. The 'low-status, powerless groups' (Reiner, 2010: 93) that the dominant majority in society see as distasteful occupy the lower end of the hierarchy of victimisation (Carrabine et al, 2009). When members of such groups report a crime to the police, they have to engage in a struggle to have their experiences taken seriously. This has led to complaints from these social groups that they are being 'over-policed' as problem populations but 'under-policed' as victims (Carrabine et al, 2009). Allen et al (2013) found that for many Muslim women, there is a very real sense of fear and mistrust in dealing with the police and state agencies, while, at the same time, cultural and religious factors combine with that mistrust to create additional obstacles to reporting their experiences to the police.

Conclusion

Typically, veiled Muslim women are perceived as constituting a 'threat' to society. They are viewed as dangerous in terms of public safety, community cohesion and gender equality, and they are defined as a group of individuals who are distinctly different from 'us'. Bauman (1997) argues that societies have a need to set 'the others' apart – those individuals who do not fit in. This contributes to a polarisation of people into the categories of 'us' and 'them'. The 'ideal victim' is described inclusively as one of 'us', symbolising the good, innocent citizen. Since all law-abiding citizens can be exposed to crime, 'victims R us' (Stanko, 2000: 13). A crime victim who lives up to the expected victim role is a deserving victim (Goodey, 2005). In this regard, the fundamental requirement for an individual to be seen as the ideal victim is that they are innocent and blameless – prudent citizens (Garland, 2001). As such, ideal victims are perceived as blameless in relation to their victimisation. This also produces an inclusive victimhood as a result of the underlying assumption that 'it could have been me' (Heber, 2014). However, veiled Muslim women who experience hate crime do not fall into the ideal victim category as people who can be blamed for being victimised are unlikely to be granted ideal victim status. When individuals have a potentially ambiguous status, the audience is unlikely to empathise with them and view them as deserving victims (Heber, 2014). Veiled Muslim women are blamed for their victimisation: had they not wore the veil, they would not have taken the risk of being attacked.

Many scholars have used the analogy of the little old lady as the ideal victim. Van Wijk (2013: 160) explains that 'Christie's archetypal ideal victim is the "little old lady", who after having cared for her sick sister, gets robbed by a big and hooded drug addict in clear daylight'. Benefiting from ideal victim status may help to improve the situation of suffering individuals. The little old lady might benefit in different ways: while she is being victimised, bystanders may intervene and chase off the offender, while after being victimised, she could receive support and justice from criminal justice agencies (Van Wijk, 2013). Drawing on individual and focus group interviews conducted with veiled Muslim women, this chapter has demonstrated the implications of the label of 'undeserving victims' for veiled Muslim women who experience Islamophobic hate crime. The data showed that participants sometimes suffered in silence, concealing their experiences of Islamophobic abuse from family and friends, as well as the authorities. Participants described feelings of shame, self-doubt, guilt, humiliation and embarrassment; these feelings were exacerbated by the fact that no one would intervene to help them. In some cases, bystanders joined in and started abusing them as well. Based on previous encounters with criminal justice agencies, participants feared that they would encounter hostility, disbelief or judgemental attitudes from the police and/or courts. The perceptions captured by the participants in this study have implications for not only tackling hate crime towards veiled Muslim women, but also providing them with support mechanisms and criminal justice responses that eliminate feelings of guilt, shame and self-doubt.

References

Allen, C. (2010) *Islamophobia*, Surrey: Ashgate.

Allen, C. and Nielsen, J. (2002) *Summary Report on Islamophobia in the EU after 11 September 2001*, Vienna: European Monitoring Centre on Racism and Xenophobia.

Allen, C., Isakjee, A. and Young, O. (2013) *Understanding the Impact of Anti-Muslim Hate on Muslim Women*, Birmingham: University of Birmingham.

Aradau, C. (2004) 'The perverse politics of four-letter words: risk and pity in the securitisation of human trafficking', *Journal of International Studies*, 33(2): 251–77.

Awan, I. and Zempi, I. (2016) 'The affinity between online and offline anti-Muslim hate crime: dynamics and impacts', *Aggression and Violent Behaviour*, 27: 1–8.

Baier, A. (1994) *Moral Prejudices: Essays on Ethics*, Cambridge, MA: Harvard University Press.

Bauman, Z. (1997) *Postmodernity and Its Discontents*, Cambridge: Polity Press.

Bouteldja, N. (2011) *Unveiling the Truth: Why 32 Muslim Women Wear the Full Face Veil in France*, London: Open Society Foundations.

Brems, E. (2014) 'Introduction to the volume', in E. Brems (ed) *The Experiences of Face Veil Wearers in Europe and the Law*, Cambridge: Cambridge University Press, pp 1–17.

Bullock, K. and Jafri, G.J. (2002) 'Media (mis)representations: Muslim women in the Canadian nation', *Canadian Women's Studies*, 20(2): 35–40.

Campbell, R. and Raja, S. (2005) 'The sexual assault and secondary victimization of female veterans: help-seeking experiences with military and civilian social systems, *Psychology of Women Quarterly*, 29: 97–106.

Carrabine, E., Cox, P., Lee, M., Plummer, K. and South, N. (2009) *Criminology: A Sociological Introduction*, Oxon: Routledge.

Chakraborti, N. and Garland, J. (2015) *Hate Crime: Impact, Causes and Responses*, London: Sage.

Chakraborti, N. and Zempi, I. (2012) 'The veil under attack: gendered dimensions of Islamophobic victimisation', *International Review of Victimology*, 18(3): 269–84.

Chakraborti, N. and Zempi, I. (2013) 'Criminalising oppression or reinforcing oppression? The implications of veil ban laws for Muslim women in the West', *Northern Ireland Legal Quarterly*, 64(1): 63–74.

Christie, N. (1986) 'The ideal victim', in E. Fattah (ed) *From Crime Policy to Victim Policy: Reorienting the Justice System*, London: Macmillan, pp 17–30.

Cole, D. and Ahmadi, S. (2003) 'Perceptions and experiences of Muslim women who veil on college campuses', *Journal of College Student Development*, 44(1): 47–66.

Dunn, P. and Shepherd, E. (2006) 'Oral testimony from the witness's perspective – psychological and forensic considerations', in A. Heaton-Armstrong, E. Shephard, G. Gudjonsson and D. Wolchover (eds) *Witness Testimony: Psychological, Investigative and Evidential Perspectives*, Oxford: Oxford University Press.

Fredette, J. (2015) 'Becoming a threat: the burqa and the contestation over public morality law in France', *Law & Social Inquiry*, 40(3): 585–610.

Garland, D. (2001) *The Culture of Control: Crime and Social Order in Contemporary Society*, Oxford: Oxford University Press.

Garner, S. and Selod, S. (2015) 'The racialization of Muslims: empirical studies of Islamophobia', *Critical Sociology*, 41(1): 9–19.

Ghumman, S. and Ryan, A.M. (2013) 'Not welcome here: discrimination towards women who wear the Muslim headscarf', *Human Relations*, 66(5): 671–98.

Githens-Mazer, J. and Lambert, R. (2010) *Islamophobia and Anti-Muslim Hate Crime: A London Case Study*, London: European Muslim Research Centre.

Goffman, E. (1963) *Stigma: Notes on the Management of Spoiled Identity*, Englewood Cliffs, NJ: Prentice Hall.

Goodey, J. (2005) *Victims and Victimology: Research, Policy and Practice*, Harlow: Pearson Education Limited.

Haddad, Y. (2007) 'The post 9/11 hijab as icon', *Sociology of Religion*, 68(3): 252–67.

Heber, A. (2014) 'Good versus bad? Victims, offenders and victim-offenders in Swedish crime policy', *European Journal of Criminology*, 11(4): 410–28.

Iganski, P. and Levin, J. (2004) 'Cultures of hate in the urban and the rural: assessing the impact of extremist organisations', in N. Chakraborti and J. Garland (eds) *Rural Racism*, Cullompton: Willan, pp 108–21.

Jiwani, Y. (2005) '"War talk" engendering terror: race, gender and representation in Canadian print media', *International Journal of Media and Cultural Politics*, 1(1): 15–22.

Mahmud, Y. and Swami, V. (2010) 'The influence of the hijab (Islamic head-cover) on perceptions of women's attractiveness and intelligence', *Body Image*, 7(1): 90–3.

Mason, G. (2014) 'The symbolic purpose of hate crime law: ideal victims and emotion', *Theoretical Criminology*, 18(1): 75–92.

Meer, N., Dwyer, C. and Modood, T. (2010) 'Embodying nationhood? Conceptions of British national identity, citizenship and gender in the "veil affair"', *The Sociological Review*, 58(1): 84–111.

Moors, A. (2009) 'The Dutch and the face-veil: the politics of discomfort', *Social Anthropology*, 17(4): 393–408.

Moors, A. (2014) 'Face veiling in the Netherlands: public debates and women's narratives', in E. Brems (ed) *The Experiences of Face Veil Wearers in Europe and the Law*, Cambridge: Cambridge University Press, pp 19–41.

Nussbaum, M. (2001) *Upheavals of Thought: The Intelligence of Emotion*, Cambridge: Cambridge University Press.

Perry, B. (2014) 'Gendered Islamophobia: hate crime against Muslim women', *Social Identities*, 20(1): 74–89.

Poynting, S. and Mason, V. (2007) 'The resistible rise of Islamophobia: anti-Muslim racism in the UK and Australia before 11 September 2001', *Journal of Sociology*, 43(1): 61–86.

Reiner, R. (2010) *The Politics of the Police* (4th edn), Oxford: Clarendon Press.

Stanko, E. (2000) 'Victims R us', in T. Hope and R. Sparks (eds) *Crime, Risk and Insecurity*, London: Routledge, pp 13–31.

Unkelbach, C., Forgas, J.P. and Denson, T.F. (2008) 'The turban effect: the influence of Muslim headgear and induced affect on aggressive responses in the shooter bias paradigm', *Journal of Experimental Social Psychology*, 44(5): 1409–13.

Unkelbach, C., Goldenberg, L., Müller, N., Sobbe, G. and Spannaus, N. (2009) 'A shooter bias against people wearing Muslim headgear in Germany', *International Review of Social Psychology*, 22(3/4): 181–201.

Van Wijk, J. (2013) 'Who is the "little old lady" of international crime? Nils Christie's concept of the idea victim reinterpreted', *International Review of Victimology*, 19(2): 159–79.

Walklate, S. (2011) 'Reframing criminal victimization: finding a place for vulnerability and resilience', *Theoretical Criminology*, 15(2): 179–94.

Williams, B. (1999) *Working with Victims of Crime: Policies, Politics and Practice*, London: Jessica Kingsley Publishers.

Williams, M. and Tregidga, J. (2014) 'Hate crime victimisation in Wales: psychological and physical impacts across seven hate crime victim-types', *British Journal of Criminology*, 54(4): 946–67.

Wing, A. and Smith, M. (2006) 'Critical race feminism lifts the veil? Muslim women, France, and the headscarf ban', *U.C. Davis Law Review*, 39: 743–86.

Wolhuter, L., Olley, N. and Denham, D. (2009) *Victimology: Victimisation and Victims' Rights*, Abingdon: Routledge-Cavendish.

Zempi, I. and Chakraborti, N. (2014) *Islamophobia, Victimisation and the Veil*, Basingstoke: Palgrave Macmillan.

FOUR

Being 'ideal' or falling short? The legitimacy of lesbian, gay, bisexual and/or transgender victims of domestic violence and hate crime

Catherine Donovan and Rebecca Barnes

Introduction

In October 2009, Stephen Gately, a member of the boy band Boyzone, died at his home in Spain, aged 33 years old. Gately was openly gay and in a civil partnership. Jan Moir, a columnist for the *Daily Mail*, a national newspaper in the UK, dedicated part of her column to speculating on Gately's death, initially connecting Gately to the 'dozens of household names [she named Heath Ledger, Michael Jackson, Amy Winehouse, among others] … idols [who] live a life that is shadowed by dark appetites or fractured by private vice' (Moir, 2009a). However, she outlined her shock, which she imagined others would share, that Gately was one of these names given that he seemed to be 'charming, cute, polite and funny'. Moir then undermined Gately's career, saying that 'he could barely carry a tune … [h]e was the Posh Spice of Boyzone, a popular but largely decorous addition'. Finally, Moir reaches her main point that Gately, being gay, was therefore implicated in his own death. He had come out – or, as Moir puts it, had been 'smoked out' – because of the threat from a newspaper to out him. The fact of his sexuality, for Moir, is enough to cast serious doubts over his death:

> Whatever the cause of death is, it is not, by any yardstick, a natural one. Let us be absolutely clear about this. All that has been established so far is that Stephen Gately was not murdered. And I think if we are going to be honest, we would have to admit that the circumstances surrounding his death are more than a little sleazy.… Another real sadness about Gately's death is that it strikes another blow to the

> happy-ever-after myth of civil partnerships.... For once
> again, under the carapace of glittering, hedonistic celebrity,
> the ooze of a very different and more dangerous lifestyle
> has seeped out for all to see. (Moir, 2009a)

The response to this column clearly took Moir and the *Daily Mail* unawares. The following week, Moir issued an almost but not quite unreserved apology. Moir explained how her original column was neither homophobic, nor anti-civil partnerships, nor anti-gay lifestyles: 'I have never thought, or suggested, that what happened that night represented a so-called gay lifestyle; this is not how most gay people live' (Moir, 2009b). Instead, Moir insisted that she would have raised the same questions about somebody heterosexual, and suggested that there might now be a 'compulsion' to see homophobia where it is not.

In discussions about 'ideal victims', there is very little focus on how lesbian, gay, bisexual and/or transgender (LGB and/or T)[1] people make sense of experiences of victimisation. While this chapter focuses on criminal victimisation, Moir's account of Stephen Gately's death illustrates that being LGB and/or T can provide opportunities, for those who so wish, to ascribe both culpability and agency to any misfortunes that they might experience. Moir's words exemplify the ways in which the lives of LGB and/or T people – and gay men particularly – are socially constructed to point to hidden deficiencies, of morality typically, but also of more essentialised personality flaws, which explain not only their outsider status in society, but also their liability in any circumstances of their being victimised. In this chapter, we will explore the implications of this further by focusing on two examples of crimes that LGB and/or T people might experience that are both related to the broad field of violence: domestic violence and abuse (DVA) and hate crime. Through this discussion, we want to show not only how being an ideal victim is dependent on the ways in which apparently inherent, structural and experiential factors are interpreted (by those victimised as well as by those being asked to respond to those victimised) (see Walklate, 2011) in the process of considering ideal victim status, but also how the construction of behaviours deemed criminal can also shape ideas about who can be victimised. We will argue that many barriers remain to recognising LGB and/or T people as either victims or perpetrators of DVA, but with regard to hate crime, we argue that, conversely, legal recognition of hate crime concerning sexuality and/or transgender identity has given LGB and/or T victims greater legitimacy than was previously accessible to them. Before developing this discussion, we first turn to Christie's (1986) work to unpack who the ideal victim and ideal offender are.

Christie's ideal victims and offenders: binaries and blind spots

Crucially, recognising and naming the ideal victim is a social process undertaken by different stakeholders within society with an interest in not only how behaviours are defined as problematic and criminal, but also what response there needs to be to them. Stakeholders include those experiencing the behaviours as well as those enacting them, those approached for help (both informally and formally) and broader institutions, organisations and movements in society that have a role to play in debates about such behaviours and societal responses, for example, the media (regarding the impacts of reality crime television programmes on constructions of the ideal victim, see, eg, Cavender et al, 1999), faith leaders, politicians, academics, campaigning groups for victims and feminists. This sociological approach is important to counteract the growing trend within the broad field of violence to simultaneously, and yet somewhat contradictorily, frame the problem of violence as socially constructed and draw on individualistic, psychological frameworks to address it (see also Walklate, 2011). Martinez and Casado-Neira (2016) suggest that a social-constructionist approach to violence against women, which locates its aetiology around gender inequality, can ignite self-blame among women, for whom the social-structural framework does not answer the 'Why me?' question. Psychological approaches to trauma plug this gap with a focus on individuals' personality traits that have led to their victimisation, 'bringing the ghost of blame and responsibility closer instead of pushing it away' (Martinez and Casado-Neira, 2016: 45). In this chapter, we wish to foreground the social conditions that can lead to the violence experienced by LGB and/or T people and consider the implications for society rather than individuals in attending to those conditions.

In his discussion of the ideal victim and ideal offender, Christie (1986) conceptualises victimhood as not only a social process, but also an interactive one between those experiencing victimisation and those responding to it as providers of formal or informal help and, more broadly, society. Thus, what has happened to an individual (or individuals) is only one aspect taken account of in the evaluation of whether the individual is an ideal victim. Other aspects include the conditions under which the victimisation happened (eg location or time of day), to whom it happened, who enacted the victimising behaviour and whether there was a prior relationship between those two parties. In considering to whom the victimising behaviour occurred, demographic factors are central to the process of evaluation that can take place; Christie's work focuses on gender and age, but to update this list, we can add, not exhaustively, social class, 'race' and ethnicity, sexuality, whether they are disabled, and what their immigration status is. In addition to these structural factors, Christie suggests that questions (literally or rhetorically) are also asked about the victimised person's conformity to acceptable social roles, which might be 'read' from their dress, appearance, behaviours, the location of the behaviours and the time of day or night that the behaviours took place. Such evaluation is necessarily social, relying on broader beliefs, understandings, expectations and assumptions about how members of different social groups should probably behave. It becomes apparent how this process has influenced Moir's evaluation of Gately's death. Questions we might ask at this stage are why and in whose interests any of this might be important when somebody has experienced victimisation. We return to this question later.

The six attributes of Christie's 'ideal victim' have several binaried assumptions underpinning them and reflect the different ways in which power – structural, personal and/or experiential – might impact on the recognition and legitimacy of victim status. The first assumption, reflected in the gendered pronouns used, is that the ideal victim is not only female, but inhabits a particular mode of femininity: weakness and respectability within, and conformity to, a female gender role. Several studies confirm that ideas about ideal victims exist and that a particular, passive, weak, non-agentic femininity is central to its constructions (Madriz, 1997; Anderson, 2008; Carbin, 2014; Wilson and O'Brien, 2016). Studies also suggest that the ideal victim is a young *white* woman (Madriz, 1997; Wilson and O'Brien, 2016) or sometimes an *older* white woman (Jagervi, 2014; Zayokowski et al, 2014). Studies with young men confirm this as findings suggest that they resist any attempt to position themselves as victims because, as Burca (2013) puts it, they associate victimhood with 'whining' and the opposite of masculinity (see also Anderson, 2008; Dunn, 2012). However, rejecting the status of victim is not only the preserve of men or, indeed, heterosexual men, and we return to this later.

Conversely, the ideal offender is assumed to be male, inhabiting a particular mode of masculinity that is oppositional to feminine victimhood: being 'big', 'bad' and predatory (Christie, 1986; see also Madriz, 1997; Wilson and O'Brien, 2016). Being predatory assumes that the offender acts with randomness in the targeting of 'obvious' weak/vulnerable victims. Other binaries overlay and reinforce these gendered binaries: the ideal victim is 'weak' while the ideal offender is 'strong'; the ideal victim is blameless while the ideal offender is to blame; and the ideal victim is respectable while the ideal offender is 'bad'. Implicit in the latter binary are constructions of social class, and evidence suggests that being middle class and 'respectable' are core attributes of the ideal victim (Madriz, 1997; Jagervi, 2014; Zaykowski et al, 2014). These binaries speak to the immediate relationship context existing between the ideal victim and offender: the location, the existence of a prior relationship between them, the activities being carried out by each and the time of day in which those activities occur.

The sixth binary, also gendered, speaks to the structural power inhabited and exercised by the ideal victim and offender in relationship to each other, as well as in the relationship between each and broader society. As Christie (1986: 21) argues, the conditions for being an ideal victim must also include the extent to which 'you are powerful enough to make your case known and successfully claim the status of victim'. In a parallel discussion, Walklate (2011) rightly critiques Green's axis of vulnerability as a tool for establishing those who are most/least at risk of harm. This axis turns on harm and risk to achieve a measure that equates vulnerability to crime with the risk from crime and the harm done by crime. Walklate argues that the measurements are informed by crime victimisation surveys, which are problematic insofar as they are limited by the narrow focus on particular kinds of crimes, and because of the focus on an assumed deficit in those victimised that providers of help position themselves to address. Instead, Walklate (2011: 190) offers an axis of resilience in an attempt to take the focus away from vulnerability as the core definition of the victim in order to better resist the ways in which 'the capability of individuals to resolve their own personal troubles that belong to them has been increasingly eroded'. This is a radical argument in the face of other commentators critiquing neoliberal trends to responsibilisation and self-care in crime prevention (Garland, 1996; Rose, 2000). Yet, this approach also facilitates the possibility of ideal victims being understood as agentic rather than passive and broadens the scope for those victimised to accept the status temporarily in order to attempt redress.

While we do not have space to fully debate these matters here, we are keen to emphasise – with particular reference to LGB and/or T people – that 'victim' status is not so readily available to all who experience victimisation. Critically, dominant constructions of ideal victims and ideal offenders shape the extent to which those victimised by crime can articulate their experience and victim status, and whether their voice will be heard by 'the authorities', as well as the extent to which the ideal victim challenges existing power relationships between women and men, as represented by and through the state, society and the criminal justice system (Christie, 1986). Next, we discuss how these circumstances affect LGB and/or T people who experience DVA, whereby their victimisation runs counter to dominant understandings of, and responses to, ideal victims and ideal offenders of DVA.

Less-than-ideal victims: LGB and/or T people experiencing DVA

Recognising the tenuous eligibility of LGB and/or T people to be ideal victims underlines how constructions of ideal victims and ideal offenders typically reinforce particular political or other interests. In their work – the most detailed, mixed-methods UK study of DVA in same-sex relationships to date – Donovan and Hester (2011, 2014) argue that there exists a public story about DVA. Drawing on Jamieson's (1998) concept of public stories, they argue that, since the 1970s, feminist activism, scholarship and political allies have successfully worked to change the status of DVA from it being a private trouble – a 'domestic' – to being a public issue (Mills, 1959). However, they argue that an unintended consequence of the success of the feminist movement is that the public story of DVA makes it difficult for other stories of DVA to be told or heard. Public stories, Jamieson argues, can act as templates, providing resources from which people draw to make sense of their own lives, as well as to inform the future living of their lives. They can be aspirational, cautionary and educative, but are necessarily often pared back to enable simple messages to be recognised and digested. They are also rarely neutral but instead 'invariably have an interest in telling a particular version of events' (Jamieson, 1998: 10–11). The public story of DVA depicts it as a problem of heterosexual men for heterosexual women, a problem of primarily physical violence and a problem of a particular presentation of gender – the bigger 'stronger' embodied man being physically violent towards the smaller, 'weaker' embodied woman (Donovan and Hester, 2010, 2014). Christie's binary of the ideal victim and the ideal offender can be seen plotted in this public story, where a passive femininity and aggressive masculinity are pitched in opposition in the abusive relationship dynamic.

While the empirical evidence supports the construction of those typically victimised through DVA as heterosexual women (Walby et al, 2017), the limitations of this public story are many, not least because this story makes it difficult for women who do not experience physical violence (Eckstein, 2011), heterosexual men and LGB and/or T people being victimised in their intimate relationships to recognise their experience and name it as DVA, seek help and receive validation from others. Indeed, studies in the US have found that police, refuge workers and psychology students, respectively, assess heterosexual women as at higher risk than those victimised in same-sex male or female relationships and believe: that escalation is more likely in a heterosexual relationship than same-sex relationships; that violence between men is less serious than in other relationships; and that violence between women is perceived as more serious than that between men but is dependent on the appearance of the perpetrator (Pattavina et al, 2007; Brown and Groscup, 2009; Little and Terrance, 2010).

In their mixed-methods UK study exploring the use of abusive behaviours in LGB and/or T relationships, Donovan et al (2014) also found evidence of the impact of the public story of DVA. Marcus, a young trans man, reflects on the first relationship he had as a lesbian when he was in his mid-teens:

> I'm not going to say it was, you know, violent or abusive but I think it had very dangerous elements to it…. Like it wasn't easy for her to be with me, and I kind of don't blame her for being the way she was [pause] and … I was never like a battered wife, you know. (Marcus, white trans man, aged 21, quoted in Donovan et al, 2014: 28)

In his account, Marcus acknowledges that his relationship was dangerous but compares his experience with what he believes is 'real' DVA: battered wives. He finds his experience wanting and, in addition, suggests that he might have been to blame for at least some of the violence and abuse he experienced, in contrast to the battered wife, who is assumed to be blameless for her fate.

However, the difficulty is not only in the structural composition of an abusive relationship as heterosexual, but also in the associations made between gender and victim binaries: the public story reinforces expectations that neither women can be perpetrators nor men victimised. In his account of an abusive first gay relationship entered into when he was in his early 30s, Colin explains that he was 'more the physical aggressor' because he was most likely to become physically violent in the regular conflict he and his partner had. A focus only on the physical violence enacted in this relationship, however, fails to understand the impacts of the emotional abuse Colin was regularly subject to:

he would kind of know which buttons to press? And be very kind of nasty and vindictive and, you know, calling me … things like a dirty old pervert and, you know, not good enough and not worthy and, desperate and all these kind of things. All the things that would really kind of upset me and, 'I will ruin you. I'll ruin your career', all that kind of thing. (Colin, white gay man, late 30s, quoted in Donovan et al, 2014: 26)

Finally, the presentation of gender in the public story can also be a barrier to decision-making about help-seeking because of a realisation about non-conformity. In her account, Sarah recalibrated her evaluation of the DVA she experienced as 'mild' when she reflected on the fact that she had been abducted, physically assaulted and dumped miles from home without any money by her ex-partner, again in her first same-sex relationship:

[Y]eah, I'd put that in as a serious incident. But even then I didn't report it. You know, at the end of the day, (laughing) I was sort of four or five inches taller than her. She was a tiny wee thing, and I thought people are never going to believe me. They're just gonna go, 'Oh, look, she couldn't beat you up!'. (Sarah, white lesbian, early 30s, quoted in Donovan and Hester, 2014: 163)

So far, our argument has been that the public story of DVA is heternormatively gendered and that this has an impact on how LGB and/or T people might be able to recognise their experiences as DVA – that the very way in which social problems are constructed involves the construction of stories about ideal victims and offenders. However, we also suggest that other kinds of public stories exist that influence how individuals make sense of their opportunities for living and that these stories might also impact on whether they identify victimisation. For example, Donovan and Hester (2014) and Donovan et al (2014) found that some of those victimised had somewhat low expectations of same-sex relationships; the impacts of homophobia being that some LGB people expected that their relationships might be difficult, unhappy, even abusive. William explains:

I think at the time I thought that was just the way a same sex male relationship was … Obviously since then I've sort of grown up, become more mature, more worldly wise.…

And again, there wasn't the emphasis on it [DVA] that there is in today's society. And it was a lot more covered up. (William, white gay man, early 40s, quoted in Donovan and Hester, 2014: 80)

Being LGB and/or T can therefore result in difficulties in recognising relationship experiences as abusive and naming experiences as DVA because of the public story and accompanying legacies of homo/bi/transphobic constructions of LGB and/or T lives as abnormal and deviant, leading to unhappy, possibly violent, relationships. Conversely, Barnes (2011) found that for women in lesbian relationships, prevalent community knowledges about women's relationships being the most 'feminist' (most equal and non-violent) of any kind of relationship also made it difficult for some women to realise that their relationship was a domestically violent one and to talk about (see also Ristock, 2002; Irwin, 2008). Understanding the self as a victim of DVA is therefore complex to navigate as an LGB and/or T person because the problem is constructed as a heterosexual problem and because LGB and/or T identities and lives are either sometimes understood as deeply problematic in themselves or, conversely, within some, particularly lesbian, communities, constructed as idealistically egalitarian.

Recognising and naming the problem are part of the process of decision-making about help-seeking; deciding to do something and deciding where to go for help are other aspects in this – non-linear – process (see Liang et al, 2005). Constructions of the ideal victim of DVA that fix it as a heterosexual woman's problem can also impact on the choices about seeking formal and/or informal sources of support. At the most basic level, there are extremely few refuges for men in the UK (Baker-Jordan, 2017). It is not clear that refuges are the best response for male victims of DVA because not enough is known about what their needs are in a UK context. However, we use refuges as symbolic of the visibility of services for heterosexual women experiencing DVA. Most empirical work suggests that the places that LGB and/or T people go for help with DVA are individualistic and privatised: the majority of those who seek formal help go to counselling and therapeutic services in the National Health Service and the private and the third sectors (LGBT Domestic Abuse Forum and Stonewall Housing London, 2013; Donovan and Hester, 2014; Donovan et al, 2014). There are several readings of this, one of which includes the suggestion that those victimised are constructing their experiences as 'relationship problems' and perhaps the result of their own behaviour. Self-blame is typical, not least because it is encouraged by abusive partners among those victimised through DVA regardless of gender and sexuality (Donovan and Hester, 2014). This might be exacerbated among those whose expectations of their intimate relationships are low as a result of generalised homo/bi/transphobia, which constructs LGB and/or T lives as deviant or damaged.

Moreover, some LGB and/or T people have suggested that they would not seek help from formal services for fear of reinforcing such perceptions. As Clare explained:

> And at some points it was like 'well I, I need a bit of support through this' and did consider contacting [company counselling service], but actually wasn't quite sure about the confidentiality of it.... I perceived that it would be seen negatively if it got out that I was having problems in my gay relationship and I think there's, there's a, a reluctance actually for a lot of gay people to admit that there are problems, because you don't want to give gay relationships (short laugh) a bad press, you know. (Clare, white bisexual woman, 35, quoted in Donovan et al, 2014: 23)

What Clare's and other accounts show is that rather than LGB and/or T people being uniformly shaped by neoliberal trends to responsibilisation (Rose, 2000) and self-care, and therapeutic responses to domestically violent experiences, there are those among these communities who are also engaged in a more collective, reputational, self-care. Stanko and Curry (1997) have previously argued that while neoliberal trends have encouraged self-care in crime prevention; certain social groups have long realised that the state's services, particularly within the criminal justice system, have constructed an ideal victim and ideal offender that automatically excludes them from unquestioning state protection. Women, black and minority ethnic women and men, and lesbians and gay men have historically been constructed not only as unreliable witnesses, but also, especially those who are black or belong to other minority ethnic groups, as well as gay men, as potential criminals to be the subject of surveillance rather than as potential victims of crime.

Problematising a femininity predicated on victimhood

That ideal victims are female – and conventionally feminine – is explicit in Christie's (1986) analysis, while their heterosexuality is implicit. Yet, it is problematic to construct the ideal victim as defenceless and blameless and therefore, apparently necessarily, feminine. Such a construction can prevent men from identifying their need for help for fear of being emasculated (Davies and Rogers, 2006; Anderson, 2008; Dunn, 2012). For gay men, the navigation of victim and masculine identities can be further complicated (Davies and Rogers, 2006; Dunn, 2012), as we consider later. However, there is evidence that women also reject constructions of victimhood that are predicted on passivity, weakness and lack of agency (Jagervi, 2014). In her analysis of so-called honour-based violence in Sweden, Carbin (2014) also argues that the dominant construction of victims does not allow for accounts of young women's resistance to any notion of them being victims of their culture and/or families, but points to evidence of some young women doing so outside the mainstream.

Donovan and Hester (2014) argue that in domestically violent and abusive relationships, there are two relationship rules: first, the relationship is for the abusive partner and on their terms; and, second, the victim/survivor is responsible for the abusive partner, the relationship, any children and the household if they cohabit. Being responsible for the abusive partner and relationship requires those being victimised to undertake relationship work to manage and placate the abusive partner. Donovan and Hester also found that practices of love provide a 'glue' keeping the abusive relationship together. Abusive partners reveal their need/neediness when their behaviour has brought about a crisis in the relationship and the victim/survivor might consider leaving. Their need/neediness typically relates to stories of their difficult or abusive pasts and personal struggles. Such revelations elicit loving care from victims/survivors, who position the abusive partner as needy and dependent on the love, care, protection and loyalty of the victim/survivor. They found that women especially talked about wanting to or believing that they could 'fix' their abusive partner. Such practices of love, however, leave victims/survivors not identifying their status as an ideal victim: they are not passive, weak or without agency. On the contrary, they often feel that they are 'stronger' and responsible for looking after their abusive partner. Amy explains:

> the nice side of her outweighed the ugly side of her, for want of a better word. Yeah, and I felt like it wouldn't be fair for me to say, 'Oh, right, I've seen this behaviour, it's really ugly, I'm going, bye,' after a couple of years or something. It wasn't fair at all. So I did feel responsible to try and help her out and try and look after her and try and support her.... But also I think I felt a greater responsibility because it was the first time in all of that time that she'd ever

disclosed the alcohol use and the events which led to the alcohol use. You know, and a lot of that stuff was around abuse. So it was very difficult. (Amy, white lesbian, early 30s, quoted in Donovan and Hester, 2014: 140)

Christie (1986) agrees with feminists who argue that the relationship context in DVA prevents (heterosexual) women from being perceived as ideal victims because of patriarchy – that men in general have a vested interest in shoring up the patriarchal authority of individual men in their intimate relationships. The critique of this power structure has (albeit unintentionally) resulted in the public story of DVA that precludes other accounts of DVA being told and heard, including the accounts of LGB and/or T people. We now turn to hate crime to reflect on the extent to which the ideal victim and ideal offender are helpful in making sense of this crime and the help-seeking practices of those victimised.

LGB and/or T hate crime victimisation

In his work on gay men as victims of hate crime, Dunn (2012) argues that if masculinities are necessarily tenuous and fragile, they are almost certainly seen as incompatible with being gay. When gay men in his study talked about hate crime victimisation, they struggled to accept the term 'victim' because of it 'having wholly negative connotations and for some it was unhelpfully gendered' (Dunn, 2012: 3447). For those who have been called a 'cissy' at school, they have learned that to be 'like a girl' is the worst possible thing that they can be because it simultaneously undermines and reveals their (gay) masculinity and (gay) sexuality as non-(hetero)normative. Once they are adults, those associations might be revisited if they are victimised, impacting on their ability to make sense of their constructed sexuality and gender identities. This construction, albeit one of subordinate gay masculinity (see Connell, 2005), is more in line with hegemonic masculinity: self-reliance, being able to look after oneself and being physically able to fight off an attacker. These constructions are further shaped by 'race' and social class (Dunn, 2012) but the use of the word 'victim' can be counterproductive, regardless of gender and sexuality, in empowering those who are victimised by violence (or other crimes).

Yet, Dunn also points to some of those victimised by hate crime/incidents who were able to accept the label 'victim' as a transitory moment in their journey to achieving redress or 'fighting back'. Jagervi (2014) similarly found that young men who had reported victimisation to the police found ways to distance themselves from any association with the ideal victim and instead focused on their following parents' advice to report and of pitching their decision as the right thing to do. The role of help providers in facilitating the maintenance of self-identities as agentic rather than passive or weak is also important (Dunn, 2012; Jagervi, 2014). It is perhaps in the matter of hate crime that there are the possibilities for challenging the construction of the ideal victim as defenceless and blameless.

What Christie's analysis does not deal with in any depth is those who are victimised because of the social group to which they belong, or because of the social group to which they are believed/perceived to belong. Hate-motivated crime, as it has come to be known, is understood in this way. In England and Wales, legislation exists for enhanced sentences for hate crimes with regard to 'race', faith, sexuality, transgender identity and disability (Clayton et al, 2016). The police are also expected to record hate incidents – those experiences of hate that are below the threshold of any crime. Hate crimes affect groups who are marginalised because of their race, faith, disability, sexuality or transgender identity; these are the group memberships, or 'protected strands', recognised in law but there are other groups that might claim being victimised by hate (on the basis of their age, gender or being sex workers or Goths) (Chakraborti and Garland, 2015). LGB and/or T individuals might also be targeted for their intersecting identities, such as the case of the killing of 49, mainly African and Hispanic, people in a gay club in Orlando, US, in 2016 (*Guardian*, 2016). What can Christie's analysis offer us here? Those victimised are not victimised for what they have to take – money, property – but for being who they are. Therefore, Donovan et al (forthcoming) have suggested that hate crime legislation can be seen as evidence of a state atoning for its previous discriminatory practices and oppression of minoritised groups, in part, by criminalising discriminatory practices that lead to actual violence and or abuse targeting minoritised groups (see also Gruenewald and Kelley, 2014).

There has been growing evidence that hate crime/incidents have far-reaching negative impacts for those targeted (Chakraborti and Garland, 2015), including those relating to mental health and those impacting on material living conditions and employment (Williams and Tregidga, 2014). The evidence suggests that most of those experiencing hate crime/incidents do not report their experiences to the police or any third-party reporting agency, for many of the same reasons that many people do not report DVA (regardless of sexuality and gender): because they do not think that they will be taken seriously, they think the incidents are too insignificant or they fear retaliation (Chakrobarti and Garland, 2015). Again, there are parallels with the reporting of DVA, where Donovan and Hester (2011) argue that there is a gap of trust between LGB and/or T people and the police. However, Gruenewald and Kelley (2014) point to the evidence that hate-motivated homicide is increasing in the US; thus, hate crime cannot be assumed to only include the so-called 'everyday' violence that many LGB and/or T people report in hate crime surveys (Kielinger and Stanko, cited in Ardley, 2005). The evidence also suggests that those committing hate crime/incidents are often not strangers, but people known to LGB and/or T people: their neighbours, family members or school or college peers. In their work, Donovan et al (2014) found that 42% of survey respondents (*n* = 872) reported experiencing homo/bi/transphobia from family members.

Within the paradigm of victimology and the ideal victim, those victimised by hate crime are a contradiction. With hate crime, the individual targeted is representative of the group to which they (are assumed to) belong. We have already discussed the ways in which LGB and/or T people have been constructed as already deviant, dangerous and/or morally suspect, which has impacts for their own self-identities as well as their abilities to recognise their experiences in intimate relationships as DVA. Hate crime/incidents could be and often are accepted as 'normal' and to be expected (Browne et al, 2011), while reporting is understood as not possible given the negative reactions expected from the authorities. Yet, through the passing and implementation of hate crime legislation, the very groups that are constructed in the rest of the criminal justice system as suspect victims of crime and are more expected to be offenders become (potential) ideal victims of tailor-made laws created to protect them. Given these contradictions, it is not very surprising that reporting rates are low, and much still needs to be done to build trust between LGB and/or T people and mainstream agencies, especially the police.

These issues notwithstanding, the fact that some people do report hate crime/incidents on the grounds of sexuality and/or transgender identity to the police or third-party reporting agencies (Clayton et al, 2016; Macdonald et al, 2017) suggests a shift in the construction of the ideal victim. While the infancy of this process of recognising and responding to LGB and/or T victimisation should not be understated, the hate crime paradigm arguably opens up a new landscape in which LGB and/or T identities can be understood as ideal victim identities through which individuals might expect a serious, respectful response on reporting. The evidence suggests that this is not always the case

(Dunn, 2012; Williams and Tregidga, 2014); yet, some individuals still seem determined to exercise their right as an active citizen to take action against the hate crime/incidents targeting them. In so doing, these individuals are also engaged in a process of challenging their suspect identity and, instead, pointing to those committing hate crime/incidents as criminal (see Donovan et al, forthcoming). The fact that they do suggests that there are ways of reshaping dominant constructs of the ideal victim and ideal offender to elicit an empowered, agentic individual who has been victimised.

Conclusion

Christie's ideal victim and offender provide a framework for understanding how social processes are involved in the construction of legitimate victims and demonised offenders. However, by discussing DVA and hate crime, we have shown that Christie's analysis is itself implicated in the construction of an ideal victim and offender that, because of their heteronormativity, make it difficult for those LGB and/or T individuals to make sense of situations in which they are victimised. With DVA, we first argued that the ideal victim and ideal offender are constructed in heteronormative ways, precluding the possibility that LGB and/or T people could be ideal victims or offenders. Second, within the field of violence, the ways in which particular behaviours are constructed in the problem of DVA has also been done through a heteronormative public story that reifies physical violence. Third, existing homo/bi/transphobia that constructs LGB and/or T lives as in deficit can lead some individual LGB and/or T people to have low expectations about what their intimate relationships might be like, normalising unhappiness and abuse – especially so in a first relationship (Donovan and Hester, 2014). Homo/bi/transphobia might also influence individuals' decision-making about where to seek help. Reporting rates of DVA by LGB and/or T people to mainstream agencies are disproportionately low. Instead, they are most likely to seek (formal) help from individualistic and privatised sources, namely, mental health and therapeutic services.

We have also problematised the construction of the ideal victim as blameless, defenceless and associated with femininity. The evidence we have presented suggests that this construction of the victim is rejected by most people, regardless of gender and sexuality, who instead present as competent and agentic. We agree with Walklate (2011) that focusing on vulnerability and risk reinforces a passive construction of the ideal victim but disagree that a focus merely on resilience will address the broader contextual factors that shape how and who is legitimised as having been victimised.

In exploring the paradigm of hate crime alongside the paradigm of the ideal victim, we suggest that there are contradictions: hate crime legislation attempts to construct LGB and/or T people as legitimate victims, whereas elsewhere in the criminal justice system, they have been constructed as potential criminals and unreliable witnesses. However, we have also pointed to the possibilities of hate crime legislation in challenging the construction of the ideal victim as heteronormative and passive – if not of being blameless – since the law encourages an active challenge by LGB and/or T people to the behaviour of those who would enact hate crime/incidents. Such legislation can be seen as encouraging a different construction of both a victim and offender that challenges structural inequalities in society.

Note

[1]   The authors acknowledge that there are other identities relating to gender and sexuality that are emerging in countries across the world, such as Two-Spirited, pansexual, non-binary, genderqueer, intersex and so on. In this chapter, we refer to LGB and/or T people as an umbrella term for all of these identities, partly for brevity and partly for accuracy, since most current literature focuses on those identifying as LGB and/or T people/communities.

References

Anderson, K. (2008) 'Constructing young masculinity: a case study of heroic discourse on violence', *Discourse and Society*, 19(2): 139–61.

Ardley, J. (2005) 'Hate crimes: a brief review', *International Journal of Sociology and Social Policy*, 25(12): 54–66.

Baker-Jordan, S. (2017) 'Male victims of domestic violence are being failed by the system', *Independent*, 13 March.

Barnes, R. (2011) '"Suffering in a silent vacuum": woman-to-woman partner abuse as a challenge to the lesbian feminist vision', *Feminism & Psychology*, 21(2): 233–9.

Brown, M.J. and Groscup, J. (2009) 'Perceptions of same-sex domestic violence among crisis center staff', *Journal of Family Violence*, 24(2): 87–93.

Browne, K., Bakshi, L. and Lim, J. (2011) '"It's something you just have to ignore": understanding and addressing contemporary lesbian, gay, bisexual and trans safety beyond hate crime paradigms', *Journal of Social Policy*, 40(4): 739–56.

Burcar, V. (2013) 'Doing masculinity in narratives about reporting violent crime: young male victims talk about contacting and encountering the police', *Journal of Youth Studies*, 16(2): 172–90.

Carbin, M. (2014) 'The requirement to speak: victim stories in Swedish policies against honour-related violence', *Women's Studies International Forum*, 46: 107–14.

Cavender, G., Bond-Maupin, L. and Jurik, N.C. (1999) 'The construction of gender in reality crime TV', *Gender & Society*, 13(5): 643–63.

Chakraborti, N. and Garland, J. (2015) *Hate Crime* (2nd edn), London: Sage.

Christie, N. (1986) 'The ideal victim', in E. Fattah (ed) *From Crime Policy to Victim Policy: Reorienting the Justice System*, Basingstoke: Macmillan, pp 17–30.

Clayton, J., Donovan, C. and Macdonald, S. (2016) 'A critical portrait of hate crime/incident reporting in North East England: the value of statistical data and the politics of recording in an age of austerity', *Geoforum*, 75: 64–74.

Connell, R.W. (2005) *Masculinities*, Cambridge: Polity Press.

Davies, M. and Rogers, P. (2006) 'Perceptions of male victims in depicted sexual assaults: a review of the literature', *Aggression and Violence Behaviour*, 11(4): 367–77.

Donovan, C. and Hester, M. (2010) '"I hate the word 'victim'": an exploration of recognition of domestic violence in same sex relationships', *Social Policy and Society*, 9(2): 279–89.

Donovan, C. and Hester, M. (2011) 'Seeking help from the enemy: help-seeking strategies of those in same sex relationships who have experienced domestic abuse', *Child and Family Law Quarterly*, 23(1): 26–40.

Donovan, C. and Hester, M. (2014) *Domestic Violence and Sexuality: What's Love Got to Do with It?*, Bristol: Policy Press.

Donovan, C., Barnes, R. and Nixon, C. (2014) *The Coral Project: Exploring Abusive Behaviours in Lesbian, Gay, Bisexual and/or Transgender Relationships, Interim Report*, Sunderland and Leicester: University of Sunderland and University of Leicester. Available at: https://www2.le.ac.uk/departments/criminology/documents/coral-project-interim-report

Donovan, C., Clayton, J. and Macdonald, S. (forthcoming) 'New directions in hate reporting research: heterogeneity, agency and relationality', *Sociological Research Online*.

Dunn, P. (2012) 'Men as victims: "victim" identities, gay identities, and masculinities', *Journal of Interpersonal Violence*, 27(17): 3442–67.

Eckstein, J.J. (2011) 'Reasons for staying in intimately violent relationships: comparisons of men and women and messages communicated to self and others', *Journal of Family Violence*, 26(1): 21–30.

Garland, D. (1996) 'The limits of the sovereign state: strategies of crime control in contemporary society', *British Journal of Criminology*, 36(4): 445–71.

Gruenewald, J. and Kelley, K. (2014) 'Exploring anti-LGBT homicide by mode of victim selection', *Criminal Justice and Behaviour*, 41(9): 1130–52.

Guardian (2016) 'Orlando shooting as it happened', 13 June. Available at: https://www.theguardian.com/world/live/2016/jun/12/florida-nightclub-shooting-terrorism-suspect-updates

Irwin, J. (2008) '(Dis)Counted stories: domestic violence and lesbians', *Qualitative Social Work*, 7(2): 199–215.

Jagervi, L. (2014) 'Who wants to be an ideal victim? A narrative analysis of crime victims' self-presentation', *Journal of Scandinavian Studies in Criminology and Crime Prevention*, 15(1): 73–88.

Jamieson, L. (1998) *Intimacy and Personal Relationships in Modern Society*, Cambridge: Polity Press.

LGBT Domestic Abuse Forum and Stonewall Housing London (2013) *Roar Because Silence is Deadly*, London: LGBT Domestic Abuse Forum and Stonewall Housing.

Liang, B., Goodman, L., Tummala-Narra, P. and Weintraub, S. (2005) 'A theoretical framework for understanding help-seeking processes among survivors of intimate partner violence', *American Journal of Community Psychology*, 36(1): 71–84.

Little, B. and Terrance, C. (2010) 'Perceptions of domestic violence in lesbian relationships: stereotypes and gender role expectations', *Journal of Homosexuality*, 57(3): 429–40.

Macdonald, S., Donovan, C. and Clayton, J. (2017) 'The disability bias: understanding the context of hate in comparison with other minority populations', *Disability & Society*, 32(4): 483–99.

Madriz, E. (1997) 'Images of criminals and victims: a study on women's fear and social control', *Gender & Society*, 11(3): 342–56.

Martinez, M. and Casado-Neira, D. (2016) 'Fragmented victims: women victims of gender-based violence in the face of expert discourses and practices in Spain', *Women's Studies International Forum*, 59: 39–47.

Mills, C.W. (1959) *The Sociological Imagination*, New York, NY: Oxford University Press.

Moir, J. (2009a) 'Why there was nothing "natural" about Stephen Gately's death', *Daily Mail*, 16 October (updated version of 16 November 2009 titled 'A strange, lonely and troubling death …'). Available at: http://www.dailymail.co.uk/debate/article-1220756/A-strange-lonely-troubling-death--.html

Moir, J. (2009b) 'The truth about my views on the tragic death of Stephen Gately', *Daily Mail*, 23 October (updated 16 November 2009). Available at: http://www.dailymail.co.uk/debate/article-1222246/The-truth-views-tragic-death-Stephen-Gately.html

Pattavina, A., Hirschel, D., Buzawa, E. and Bentley, H. (2007) 'A comparison of the police response to heterosexual versus same sex intimate partner violence', *Violence Against Women*, 13(4): 374–94.

Ristock, J. (2002) *No More Secrets: Violence in Lesbian Relationships*, London: Routledge.

Rose, N. (2000) 'Government and control', *British Journal of Criminology*, 40: 321–9.

Stanko, B. and Curry, P. (1997) 'Homophobic violence and the self "at risk": interrogating the boundaries', *Social and Legal Studies*, 6(4): 513–32.

Walby, S., Towers, J., Balderston, S., Corradi, C., Francis, B., Heiskanen, M., Helweg-Larsen, K., Mergaert, L., Olive, P., Palmer, E., Stockl, H. and Strid, S. (2017) *The Concept and Measurement of Violence Against Women and Men*, Bristol: Policy Press.

Walklate, S. (2011) 'Reframing criminal victimization: finding a place for vulnerability and resilience', *Theoretical Criminology*, 15(2): 179–94.

Williams, M.L. and Tregidga, J. (2014) 'Hate crime victimization in Wales: psychological and physical impacts across seven hate crime victim types', *British Journal of Criminology*, 54(5): 946–67.

Wilson, M. and O'Brien, E. (2016) 'Constructing the ideal victim in the United States of America's annual trafficking in persons reports', *Crime, Law and Social Change*, 65(1): 29–45.

Zaykowski, H., Kleinstuber, R. and McDonough, C. (2014) 'Judicial narratives of ideal and deviant victims in judges' capital sentencing decisions', *American Journal of Criminal Justice*, 39(4): 716–31.

FIVE

New victimisations: female sex worker hate crime and the 'ideal victim'

Karen Corteen

New victimisations and the inclusion of the non-ideal victim into the criminal justice process

> Due to resistance on the part of sex workers and sex work projects, some progress is being made in some quarters of the criminal justice process. This can be seen in the recognition of crimes and harms perpetrated against sex workers as a form of hate crime. (Stoops, 2016: 209–10)

Although the concept of hate crime and hate crime laws is contested, hate crime 'has become embedded within law, criminal justice systems, academia, politics and society' (Corteen, 2014: 175). Hate crime legislation was introduced in the UK and the US in the 1980s and 1990s. Contemporarily, in some quarters, female sex workers have been included in criminal justice hate crime policy and practice (Campbell and Stoops, 2010; College of Policing, 2014; Campbell, 2015). Legislative hate crime measures enable certain members of some identifiable groups to draw on the violences of the law and/ or the violences of the criminal justice process. This is because hate crime legislation encourages and facilitates the infliction of harsher punishments in cases of crimes motivated by hate, bias or prejudice; it 'creates a sentencing enhancement to already-existing criminal statutes' (Contreras, 2016: 182). The recognition of the victimisation of female sex workers does not enable the violences of the law to be triggered in that it does not enable tougher sentences. However, hate crime laws and hate crime policy and practice are symbolically important in the messages that they convey to perpetrators, victims, institutions and society (Dixon and Gadd, 2006; Mason, 2013). They strongly censure crimes and victimisation motivated by bias and/or hatred and they acknowledge the actual, and signal, harms experienced by the victim and the group to which they belong (Dixon and Gadd, 2006; OSCE and ODIHR, 2009; Mason, 2013). Finally, they observe and express that such victims warrant protection and redress from the criminal justice system and access to victim services (OSCE and ODIHR, 2009; Mason, 2013). All of which have significant implications for criminal justice responses to perpetrators and victims – in this case, female sex workers and 'their' victimisers. Christie (1986: 18) asserts that 'being a victim is not a thing' or 'an objective phenomenon'; rather, 'victims' are socially constructed. In this ongoing process, victims' characteristics and their ostensive culpability or otherwise are significant. Female sex worker victim characteristics and their social, situational and interactive contexts have not necessarily changed. However, the manner in which female sex workers and sex worker victimisation are currently understood and interpreted has changed in some quarters, in that they are constructed and responded to as victims of hate crime.

The concept or label of 'victim', 'rather than being something that can be taken for granted or assumed', can be considered to be 'a meaning that gets attached to people' (Dunn, 2016: 49). The media play a pivotal role in constructing and shaping such meanings. Fuelled by the media, 'popular discourse about crime and criminal justice … is dominated by polarized perceptions of criminal and victim, of good and bad, innocent and guilty' (Edwards, 2004: 969). In Christie's (1986) terms, with regard to crime victims, there are 'ideal', 'less than ideal' and 'non-ideal' victims and perpetrators. Given that female sex workers comprise a non-ideal victim identity, the introduction and acceptance of female sex worker hate crime victimisation in Merseyside (England), including by Merseyside Police, is unusual (and unique).

The chapter begins with a discussion of defining victims. It highlights that in keeping with Christie's conceptualisation of prostitutes, female sex workers constitute non-idealised victims. Building on the notion of non-ideal victims, the concept of 'deviant victim' is explained and the manner in which female sex workers are constructed in criminal justice responses to female street sex work is outlined. A discussion of new victimisations in the form of hate crime and criminal justice hate crime measures is provided, followed by an overview of female sex worker hate crime. The final section of this chapter examines what the inclusion of female sex workers in police hate crime policy and practice may mean for Christie's central historical and contemporaneous 'ideal victim' thesis. In so doing, Mason's (2013) discussion of hate crime law, ideal victims, emotion and compassion will be drawn upon.

Defining victims – the multiple identities of female sex workers

> The policing of prostitution continues to present difficult challenges for those involved.... It is understandable because society as a whole has an equivocal attitude towards prostitution and those involved. Some regard prostitution as a moral rather than criminal issue, some an anti-social behaviour problem, some as a crime of abuse and exploitation, others as an issue of social care and welfare. And some may even regard it as a career choice. (ACPO, 2011: 4)

Focusing on crime, early victimologists, such as Von Hentig and Mendlesohn, sought to make a distinction between victims and non-victims, the consequences of which was the production of victim typologies (see Mawby and Walklate, 1994; Walklate, 2007). This may have created the opportunity to glean insights into the victim–offender relationship and the intricacies and complexities of victimisation; however, it also created 'an impression of a hierarchy of victimisation, with some victims achieving victim status more easily than others' (Davies, 2016: 18). As Karmen (2016: 2) explains: 'Some individuals who sustain terrible injuries and devastating losses might be memorialized, honored, and even idolized, while others might be mocked, discredited, defamed, demeaned, socially stigmatized, and even condemned for bringing about their own misfortunes'.

For Walklate (2016: 251), '[w]ho is included and excluded from understandings of victimhood is important for understanding the nature and extent of criminal victimisation and what might be done about it'. Thus, within and outside victimology, defining victims, especially crime victims, has been an ongoing endeavour. Some victims can achieve victim status more 'readily and easily' than others (Walklate, 2007: 28) on the proviso that they constitute the 'perfect', 'model' or 'true' victim of crime. Regarding this, a good and appropriate starting point given the focus of this book is Christie's (1986) 'ideal victim' concept. As Duggan and Heap (2016: 243) note that the 'discrepancy in treatment' of victims 'was first critiqued' by Christie in his recognition that 'some victims were deemed more "deserving" than others in the statutory and social imagery'. Christie (1986) is frank and adamant that his identification of the ideal victim is not concerned with an individual's subjective self-application of victim status, or those who are regularly victimised or at the greatest risk of victimisation. Individuals who perceive themselves to be victims, who are victimised the most often or who are at utmost risk of victimisation might or might not be included in Christie's conceptualisation of the ideal victim – but they are not *it*.

The ideal victim and their legitimate status as an ideal victim is a social construction, yet the ideal victim can be exemplified in that they can be typified and demonstrated. This demonstration of the ideal victim is pivotal to the conceptualisation of the expected and accepted attributes of the prototypical victim. Such attributes comprise: innocence and vulnerability; no criminal history of their own; no culpability; not being out of place and, moreover, doing some kind of good; and having a lack of capacity to fight back or resist a big and bad perpetrator with whom they have no acquaintance. Walklate (2007: 28) states that, '[i]ndeed, this "ideal victim" fits all the common-sense stereotypes of the "legitimate" victim of rape'. Also, as Duggan and Heap (2016: 243) point out, the '"stranger" element also implies that it is a person, not an organisation', who has perpetrated the offence and that the offence 'is likely to be a single incident'. The non-ideal victim flip-side attributes encompass: some aspect of blame and a lack of vulnerability; some hint of deviant status and/or an element of culpability; being somewhere and doing something that they should not be; being acquainted with the perpetrator; and possibly having some capacity to defend oneself. It is clear within this distinction between the ideal and non-ideal victim that female sex workers, especially female street sex workers, would not be located favourably on this hierarchy.

The acknowledgement of female gender-based victimisation by predominantly male perpetrators on the part of second-wave feminists in the 1970s tied 'femininity with victimhood and risk consolidating women and girls as the ideal victim' (Bricknell, 2016: 86). However, not all women and girls are automatically bequeathed with the ideal victim status. This can be clearly seen in Christie's work, wherein a woman's sexual virtue (or lack of) impacts on their positioning on the continuum as either an 'ideal', 'less than ideal' or 'non-ideal' victim; his discussion of rape illustrates the difference between these 'ideal' types. At the top is the severely beaten, physically resistant 'young virgin on her way home from visiting sick relatives', in the middle is 'the experienced lady on her way home from a restaurant' and at the bottom of the victim hierarchy is the 'prostitute who attempts to activate the police in a rape case' (Christie, 1986: 19). The prostitute (and hence the female sex worker) thus serves as a contrast – two steps removed from the ideal victim and one step removed from the less than ideal, thus embodying the status of a non-ideal victim.

Christie is not the only theorist to locate prostitutes outside of the acquisition of ideal and legitimate victim status. Walklate (2007: 28), drawing on Carrabine et al's 'hierarchy of victimisation', comments that at 'the bottom of the hierarchy would be the homeless, the drug addict, the street prostitute'. Importantly, Walklate (2007: 28) continues to state, 'all those groups of people for whom it is presumed that victimization is endemic to their lifestyle, thus rendering any claim to victim status a highly problematic one'.

The status of the female sex worker as a non-ideal victim is predicated on notions of 'victim precipitation', 'victim provocation' and 'victim culpability', and subsequently 'victim blaming'. As Davies (2016: 17) explains, these concepts are 'emotive and controversial' as they imply that the victim has played a role in the offence and their victimisation. In addition, if the victim was thought to be acting in a way that could be considered risky, in that 'they were taking part in activities that are likely to bring forth harm or increase their own vulnerability', they may be viewed and construed as 'the author of their own misfortune, having brought the suffering on themselves' (Davies, 2016: 18). In sum, 'provocative' and 'risky' victims are 'guilty victims' and, as such, they are 'less deserving of the label "victim" due to their own role in the process' (Davies, 2016: 18). In addition, if an individual does not meet the cultural or spatial 'normative expectations for a victim identity', they may be considered to be a *deviant victim* (Davies, 2016: 18, emphasis in original). For Dunn (2016: 50), the more blameworthy the victim, 'the more deviant the label and the less sympathy society imagines they deserve'; this process can be envisaged as a continuum in that when an incidence of victimisation becomes 'more ambiguous, the label moves towards the "blame" (and "deviant victim") pole'.

Bequeathing an individual with the label of non-ideal victim or deviant victim is not a harmless act devoid of consequences. Being labelled as such can result in a lack of reporting, recording, prosecution and guilty outcomes of prosecutions (Dunn, 2016), and it can mean a lack of justice and redress for victims. Furthermore, the attribution of victim status from the 'ideal' victim to the 'non-ideal' and 'deviant' victim is often highly gendered and this is significant 'in a culture in which women's virtue is more highly policed than the behaviours of sexual predators' (Dunn, 2016: 50). Female sex workers comprise the deviant victim as they are blameworthy. The sexual behaviours of female sex workers 'do not fit the dominant scripts for what constitutes "appropriate" citizenship' (Sanders and Campbell, 2014: 535). Female sex workers' behaviours and lifestyles are deemed to be victimisation-prone due to female sex workers engaging in risky activities and hence increasing their own vulnerability and precipitating their victimisation. Their lack of virtue and respectability and their deviation from normative gender expectations results in little, if any, social and cultural sympathy for the endemic victimisation that they encounter as part of their working life.

There is an array of literature which contends that the legislative framework in England and Wales exacerbates sex workers' vulnerability to violence, distances them from support services and is connected to and influences the violences to which sex workers are subject (see Sanders and Campbell, 2014). Driven by an abolitionist agenda, 'with the primary utopian goal of eradicating sex work', responses to sex work across Europe and beyond favour criminalisation – especially of the demand and purchasing of sex (Sanders and Campbell, 2014: 537). Governing sex work via criminalisation increases the 'discourse of disposability' (Lowman, quoted in Sanders and Campbell, 2014: 539) and the victimisation and murder of sex workers. In contemporary criminal justice strategies and responses in England and Wales, female sex workers are simultaneously conceptualised as victims of exploitation and violence in need of therapy/support/saving and agentic subjects who are blamed for anti-social behaviour, public nuisance and a moral and safety threat to communities. Current strategies and responses to female sex workers try to be compassionate towards their plights, including the victimisation that they experience when at work. Yet, they are simultaneously tough on street sex workers and on clients (Scoular and Carline, 2014). For example, the Policing and Crime Act 2009 increased criminal interventions against clients and subjected on-street sex workers to Engage and Support Orders that comprise compulsory rehabilitation (Scoular and Carline, 2014). Female sex workers therefore occupy multiple identities that provoke multiple responses – they are victims of exploitation and violence who are in need of support, anti-social, a public nuisance, and threatening to communities. Culturally and institutionally, female sex workers are deemed undesirable and they are stigmatised and discriminated against. Subsequently, with regard to being crime victims, they are non-ideal victims; perhaps worse than this, they are blameworthy, culpable, deviant victims.

New victimisations – hate crime and hate crime laws

minority groups that remain distant, unknowable or foreign will struggle for public sympathy. As a consequence, we might expect such groups to be among the least protected under hate crime legislation. (Mason, 2013: 11)

Walklate (2007: 77) points out that it is 'important to remember that recognising the process of victimization, of who may become a victim of what kind of behaviour, is not a static one', and thus '[n]ew "victimisations" can be recognised and responded to'. Hate crime is an example of this. In a nutshell, '[h]ate crime law governs criminal conduct that involves an element of prejudice or bias on the part of the perpetrator towards a presumed attribute of the victim' (Mason, 2013: 3). Hate crime has to be contextualised in relation to the aftermath of the Holocaust and concerns regarding civil rights and non-discrimination from the 1960s onwards (Goodey, 2016). It also has to be understood in relation to 'a convergence of several social forces, including the emergence of identity politics, the rise of victims' rights movement and the return of retributivism to penal policy and practice' (Mason, 2013: 3). In the UK since 1997, when the Labour Party were elected into power, the 'recourse to law' in the context of crime targeted against minority groups 'has become more acute' (Walklate, 2007: 148).

The term 'hate crime' refers to a 'type of crime, rather than a specific offence within a legal code', or, put another way, it 'describes a concept, rather than a legal definition' (OSCE and ODIHR, 2009: 16). While '[p]rotected groups can be added to hate crime legislation ... determining the elements and actions of a hate crime and associated victimisation can be challenging' (Contreras, 2016: 161). Notwithstanding that overall target characteristics must account for the harm, and hate crime 'warrants recognition and action as a particularly damaging form of crime' due to its divisive nature and ripple effect of 'intimidating entire groups in society' (Goodey, 2016: 92). Hate crime is aimed at 'prejudicial or biased criminal acts against a person or property that are motivated by a victim's actual or perceived sexuality, race, ethnicity, disability, religion and gender' (Corteen, 2014: 175). In the approach to hate crime in Merseyside, this definition has been extended to sex workers (Campbell and Stoops, 2010; College of Policing, 2014; Campbell, 2015). Gender-based crimes are mainly or exclusively aimed at women and girls, and are encapsulated in the phrase 'gender-based violence' (Bricknell, 2016). Female sex workers are victimised because they are female and because they are sex workers. Female sex workers challenge and threaten patriarchal cultural norms and gendered expectations with regard to: female virtues; female sexuality; female respectability and domesticity; female behaviour in public; sexually exclusive compulsory coupledom; and hegemonic patriarchal familialism. As such, they are subject to cultural and institutional marginalisation, stigmatisation, discrimination and criminalisation.

Due to the historical trajectories in the development of hate crime laws, policies and practices, their content and application differs between countries (Mason, 2013; Goodey, 2016). In England and Wales, the precursor to the introduction of hate crime laws regarding racial hatred, bias and prejudice was the Macpherson inquiry into the investigation of the murder of Stephen Lawrence. Hate crime legislation permits harsher sentences on the grounds that 'the goal of the sentence is to serve as a specific and general deterrent' (Contreras, 2016: 182). The appeal to the law as a symbolic referent and 'as a vehicle for change is not impossible but is fraught with difficulties' (Walklate, 2007: 154). Such difficulties include: the unintended consequences of resorting to the law; state co-option for its own interests; and benefits to the victim at the expense of the offender (see Walklate, 2007). In addition, when discussing hate crime legislation Ray and Smith (2001: 213) state, 'there is considerable uncertainty as to its appropriateness and effectiveness'. Also, Corteen (2014: 177) when discussing homophobic hate crime laws, concludes that drawing on the violences of the law in the form of tougher punishments for acts of homophobic hate crime is 'counter-intuitive', possibly 'counter-productive', and that 'institutional and cultural homophobia remains intact'. However, despite such concerns, one of the repeated and stronger arguments for hate crime legislation is its legal symbolic and expressive power. Mason (2013: 1) states that the 'symbolic purpose' of hate crime laws 'is well recognized' in that they 'make a public statement' that 'prejudice-related crime ... will not be tolerated and that serious penalties will apply'. Indeed, '[t]hey implicitly claim that prejudice itself, not just its criminal manifestation, is wrong' (Mason, 2013: 1–2).

In sum, '[h]ate crime laws are important in three ways' (OSCE and ODIHR, 2009: 7): first, they explicitly condemn the bias and/or hatred on the part of the offender; second, they acknowledge the depth of harm caused to a direct victim, to 'the group with which that victim identifies herself or himself' and to communities (OSCE and ODIHR, 2009: 11); and, third, they carry and convey the message that the protection of the law and criminal justice system should be afforded to those affected and that those who are affected are worthy of such protections. As discussed previously, sex workers are culturally and institutionally 'othered'. Therefore, hate crime laws and the inclusion of female sex worker victimisation into Merseyside Police responses to hate crime are especially important with regard to violence against female sex workers. To date, they are the first and only police force in England and Wales to do this.

New victimisations – female sex workers and hate crime

> Sex workers share the out-group status of the 'other' central to discrimination faced by other groups who experience hate crime. (Campbell, 2015: 58)

> they [hate crime laws] aim to help reconfigure perceptions of such [traditionally underprivileged] groups as deviant, dangerous or illegitimate Others. (Mason, 2013: 5).

'Everyday, a proportion of sex workers go to work and do what they have to do to survive' (Stoops, 2016: 209). Yet, sex work is an emotive and controversial area that creates divides with regard to how it is conceptualised and experienced, and how it should be responded to. On the one hand, it is an activity comprising a lack of choice, exploitation and coercion that should be abolished (Gall, 2006; Marshall, 2016). On the other hand, it is a career choice that warrants a rights-based approach. As Stoops (2016: 208) notes, sex work is not, in and of itself, inherently dangerous; however, some sections can be. In the UK, while street sex workers comprise approximately 25% of all sex workers, they account for 95% of sex worker homicides. The '"othering", marginalisation and criminalisation' of sex workers cultivates in a climate in which the victimisation of sex workers 'can flourish' (Campbell, 2015: 58). Corteen and Stoops (2016: 211) stress that '[a]mid the various manifestations of sex work, sex workers are at a greater risk of, and have a greater actual experience of harassment, victimisation and harm than the general public'. This is particularly so if the sex worker is working on the streets and if they are female (College of Policing, 2014; Campbell, 2015).

The kinds of victimisation that sex workers in the UK are subject to include 'murder, rape, violence and a range of other crimes', and perpetrators include 'residents who do not want sex workers in their area; passers-by; and police officers' (Stoops, 2016: 208). Drawing on the work of Kinnell (2009), Stoops explains the classification of three perpetrator types. These include non-clients, namely, general passers-by, vigilantes, partners, family members, muggers, robbers, drug dealers and pimps. This is the biggest group of perpetrators, who may victimise sex workers when working or not. This can include attacking sex workers, throwing objects at them or entering premises under false pretences. Stoops comments that only some of the violence committed against sex workers 'is likely to be reported to outreach workers, let alone the police' (Stoops, 2016: 208). Keeping with the same group of perpetrators, Stoops (2016: 208) asserts that '[t]he continuum of abuse by passers-by, residents, young people and so forth is endemic in many street-working areas, and ranges from insults to assaults, robbery and, in some cases, murder'. The next group of perpetrators are the 'pseudo-clients' – individuals who pretend to be clients in order to steal from or attack sex workers. At the outset, pseudo-clients behave as clients, 'they pay or offer to pay, but then turn violent and force repayment, force acts that have not been paid for, refuse to use condoms and frequently rob the sex worker of all her money' (Stoops, 2016: 208). The third and final category is the bad clients – those that believe that as part of their payment, they have the right to commit violence.

It can be seen, then, that sex work is a 'risky business' (Saunders, 2004, cited in Stoops, 2016). In addition to sex work being a risky business, sex workers are 'also subject to cultural issues of stigma, discrimination and the law' (Stoops, 2016). However, Stoops (2016: 209) is rightly keen to point out that although the stigmatisation of, and discrimination towards, sex workers is harmful, and that while the commission of crime and harm against sex workers from an assortment of perpetrators is a certainty, 'sex workers are not passive victims allowing such victimisation to happen to them'. There is worldwide resistance to victimisation on the part of sex workers through a variety of schemes that identify problematic clients or those pretending to be clients – '[t]his is true resistance by sex workers for sex workers and has solved many crimes' (Stoops, 2016: 209). Such resistance is important, especially given that sex workers are 'practice victims', in that men who kill sex workers often go on to commit murders of non-sex workers (Stoops, 2017).

Sex workers comprise 'a group whose experiences of victimisation fit within a number of established definitions of hate crime but who have sat outside the established hate crime groups' (Campbell, 2015: 55). The predominant absence of sex worker victimisation from discussions of hate crime within academia and within criminal justice police policy and practice is at least in part due to the 'positioning of victimised sex workers as "deviant victims", "risky victims" and the "victimological other"' (Corteen and Stoops, 2016: 211). Within and outside the criminal justice system, they have been overwhelmingly constructed as 'a deviant, undesirable public nuisance unworthy of criminal justice protection' (Corteen and Stoops, 2016: 211). They fail to meet that which is required to be bestowed the status of 'ideal victim' (Christie, 1986), and their victim status is repudiated.

Research in the city of Liverpool (Merseyside) documented that 80% of sex workers had experienced violence during the course of their work and there was vast under-reporting of such crimes of violence to the police (Campbell and Stoops, 2010). Under-reporting occurs due to 'a lack of trust, and a belief the police will not treat it seriously or will treat it as an occupational hazard' (Campbell, 2015: 57). Also, sex workers are concerned that they will: be judged negatively; be arrested; face prosecution; be publicly identified; and have their premises closed down (Campbell, 2015). This results in some offenders believing that a lack of reporting means that they will not get caught. In the UK and elsewhere, police policy and practice concerned with hate crime and hate victimisation exclude sex workers (Campbell, 2015). However, in Merseyside, it became clear to sex work project workers and to sex workers themselves that crimes committed against sex workers were indicative of something more than regular crimes. Both believed that 'sex workers were being attacked *because* they were sex workers' and thus that 'these crimes fitted the "hate crime" mantel' (Stoops, 2016: 209, emphasis in original). Sex worker partnerships maintained that violent attacks on street sex workers 'were fuelled by gender hostility' and that 'there were similarities with other types of hate crime' (College of Policing, 2014: 9). Merseyside Police concurred with this assessment of (hate) crimes against sex workers. Subsequently, a policy memorandum was signed off on 15 December 2006 by Merseyside Police. It 'included that incidents motivated by the victims sex worker status "should be recorded as a hate crime and follow the areas strategy in dealing with such cases"' (Campbell, 2015: 60). The declaration of the victimisation of sex workers as a hate crime happened at a time wherein 'one of the most famous sex worker murder sprees that the UK had ever seen' was taking place (Stoops, 2016: 209). In 2006, the then Chief Constable Bernard Hogan-Howe declared:

> Merseyside Police are determined to bring all perpetrators of Hate Crime to justice.... We were the first force in the country to recognise and respond to attacks against sex workers as a form of hate crime. The challenge is to build the trust of those vulnerable to attack to report offences and information to us. (Quoted in Stoops, 2016: 209)

On another occasion, the same former Chief Constable made a public video statement in the promotion of the police force policy, in which he stated: 'Sex workers are members of the community who are vulnerable to attack ... we will not tolerate violence against sex workers.... Merseyside Police are determined to bring all perpetrators of hate crime to justice' (Chief Constable Bernard Hogan-Howe, quoted in Campbell, 2015: 60).

Concerns regarding the non-reporting of prevalent violent crimes against sex workers and a number of sex workers being murdered, together with positive partnerships in Liverpool, were the backdrop to the unprecedented decision on the part of Merseyside Police in 2006 regarding treating violence against female sex workers as a hate crime. Campbell (2015) was a manager of a sex work project in Liverpool between 2005 and 2008. The first time that Campbell (2015: 59) became aware that 'a hate crime procedure could be applied to a sex work matter' was in 2005, when the police and council identified a piece of graffiti as hate crime graffiti. The graffiti entailed an image of the serial murderer Peter Sutcliffe with the text 'Warning: Sutcliffe Operates in this Area'. Campbell and Stoops (2010: 9) state that police policy at that time encompassed an 'enhanced response with more attention and police resources being allocated to it'. According to Campbell (2015: 55–60), since 'the inclusion of sex workers in hate crime policing policy', this predominantly unprotected and criminalised group have derived 'real advantages' and it has 'resulted in a range of positive outcomes'. Such advantages, positive outcomes and progressive changes include the comparable unprecedented increases in the reporting, prosecution and conviction of crimes against sex workers in Merseyside (College of Policing 2014; Campbell, 2015). For example, there was a 400% increase in the proportion of sex workers reporting to the Ugly Mugs scheme making formal reports to police between 2005 and 2009. Also, 'the conviction rate for crimes against sex workers in Merseyside that made it to court between 2007 and 2011 was 83%' (Campbell, 2015: 60). For cases involving rape and sexual offences, the national 'generic' rate was 58% compared to the rate for Merseyside of 75%. Campbell (2015: 60) asserts that '[a]s of the end of 2011, 32 victims were known to have received justice, with 25 offenders convicted, an unprecedented number in the UK'.

'Laws – especially – criminal laws ... are an expression of society's values', and if enforced, hate crime laws 'express the social value of equality' and advocate 'the development of those values' (OSCE and ODIHR, 2009: 7). In relation to violence against sex workers, responding to such violences as a hate crime challenges institutional and cultural bias and discrimination towards, and hatred of, female sex workers on the grounds that they are sex workers. The College of

Policing (2014) document that research reports a change of attitude among police officers in Merseyside, namely, that they demonstrate greater respect towards sex workers, that they have an increased understanding of the crimes committed against them and that Merseyside Police officers finally take the reporting of crime on the part of sex workers more seriously while dealing with them 'sensitively and in a victim-centred manner'. Three crucial lessons can be learnt from the progress that has been made in Liverpool as a result of responding to female sex worker victimisation as hate crime. One is that 'investigating and prosecuting crimes against sex workers *and* preventing victimisation and protecting potential and actual victims can be done' (Corteen and Stoops, 2016: 212, emphasis in original). Second, in order for this to done, there needs to be 'commitment and resources … dedicated to do this' (Campbell and Stoops, 2010: 10). Third, 'the longer-term goal of changing cultural and institutional stigma that, at best enables and, at worst, encourages sex work hate crime, harm and victimisation in the first instance can be addressed' (Corteen and Stoops, 2016: 212). However, the focus of the final section of this chapter is not whether sex worker hate crime is desirable or not, or the extent to which it is put into practice or not, or the extent to which it is successful or not. The focus here is what the inclusion or exclusion of female sex worker hate crime into criminal justice policy and practice means for Christie's (1986) 'ideal victim' concept. It is to this point that the discussion will now turn.

The ideal victim concept

> becoming a victim is neither simple nor straightforward. Victim status is something that has to be achieved and involves a process from the individual recognizing that they have been victimized and thus may claim the label, through to being socially and/or in policy terms being recognized as a victim. (Walklate, 2007: 28)

Gaining recognition as a victim is a complex process but one that can be demonstrated and typified by drawing on Christie's ideal victim concept. Therefore, many theorists have understandably drawn and continue to draw on this when discussing victims and victim status. At the deserving end of the victim hierarchy, Christie highlights 'the weak, vulnerable and disempowered victim'; at the less or non-deserving end sits 'victims who belong to socially marginalised groups – such as street-sleeping homeless people, drug addicts or alcoholics, and street sex workers' (Duggan and Heap, 2016: 244). Thus, as a result of 'victim-blaming prejudice', victims of crime may find their 'victim status invalidated' and, indeed, 'may also even be implicated or deemed culpable for the harm that they have incurred' (Duggan and Heap, 2016: 244).

However, the recognition and inclusion of female sex worker victimisation into police hate crime policy and practice both *challenges* and *upholds* Christie's ideal victim concept. It has been established that female sex worker identities are othered, and that their victim status is that of a non-idealised identity as they constitute the deviant victim. This is due to their socially constructed and ill-perceived immorality and culpability, as well as their 'chosen' victimisation-prone occupation. However, the incorporation of female sex workers into police hate crime policy and practice disrupts the symbolic certainty of sex workers' non-idealised identity and comprises a symbolic reversal as female sex workers have been reconstructed from that of a threat to that of being threatened. However, this reconstruction is confined to female sex workers in Liverpool, Merseyside sex worker projects and the criminal justice system in Merseyside. Thus, the inclusion of female sex worker victimisation in police hate crime policy and practice is an exception, albeit an important one. With regard to other forces in the UK, the ideal victim concept maybe, and more than probably, explains why crimes against sex workers and sex worker victimisation are not perceived or responded to as hate crimes.

For Mason (2013: 1), hate crime laws comprise 'moral work' and this 'is dependent on the capacity of victim groups to engender compassionate thinking that helps reconfigure perceptions of them as dangerous, illegitimate or inferior Others'. Therefore, in order for minority groups to embody the 'moral claim embedded in hate crime law', they must not 'fall short of the image of ideal victims' (Mason, 2013: 1). Also, in order for minority or particular groups to draw on hate crime legislation for their protection, they must do so not just on their 'degree of political influence, but also by a hierarchy of victimhood' that evokes 'compassionate emotion and thinking towards them' (Mason, 2013: 2). Female sex workers do fall massively short of ideal victim imagery and they have little, if any, political influence or compassionate emotion and thinking towards them at the cultural and institutional level. Yet, despite this, in Merseyside, they are included in that which is considered hate crime and hate crime victimisation. This poses a challenge to the centrality of the ideal victim and the cultural and institutional role at the national level in ascertaining victim status. It challenges the ideal victim framework in that victims do not necessarily have to be weak and respectable to be given if not the status of an ideal victim, then some kind of victim status. Securing victim status alone can bring legitimate legal protections. At the local level, the culmination of the recognition of increased sex worker victimisation, including murder, and the recognition of the nature of such violence as biased, prejudiced and motivated by hatred, together with positive partnership working between sex workers, sex worker projects and Merseyside Police, resulted in the recognition of sex worker victimisation as a hate crime in this geographical area. Sex worker victimisation is not only constructed and conceived of as a criminal offence; it is deemed worthy of additional denunciation. This highlights that with regard to notions of the ideal victim, important and significant anomalies or exceptions can occur and the hierarchy of victimhood can be challenged in criminal justice policy and practice.

The inclusion of non-ideal victims or, moreover, deviant victims in police hate crime policy and practice illustrates that responses to victims that fall short of the ideal can be predominantly based on that which is within the legal remit and does not necessitate cultural, emotional and compassionate thinking towards a particular group. Indeed, a response underpinned by a legal and professional framework may cultivate the latter. While tougher punishments can only be afforded 'towards a communal attribute that is specified in legislation' (Mason, 2013: 5), the additional denunciation afforded to sex worker victimisation has brought 'real advantages' with regard to reporting, prosecuting, punishing and preventing such crimes, as well as achieving justice and redress for victims (Campbell, 2015: 55).

For Mason (2013: 6), the 'nexus between sympathy and the ideal victim … is important but understated in Christie's work'. Mason also notes that there is a body of literature which suggests that 'feelings of sympathy, compassion or pity' – in other words, 'sentimental emotions' – are required to evoke state protection from crime, harm and victimisation and to evoke the moral force of the law. However, as can be seen in this example of a new victimisation, 'sentimental education' (Garland, 1990, quoted in Mason, 2013: 6) is not always a precursor to or facet of the challenge to the 'bigoted norms and values' that may hinder victim status and victims' access to the criminal justice system. The prejudiced perceptions of female sex workers are symbolically and practically challenged by their inclusion in responses to hate crime in Merseyside.

The capacity or not to engender emotional and compassionate thinking plays an important role in the construction and conception of the ideal and non-ideal victim (Mason, 2013). Also, it does go some way to explain discrepancies between those who are harmed and injured and afforded victim status and those who are not. This may go some way to explain why the unprecedented step on the part of Merseyside Police has not been taken by any other police force in England and Wales (and beyond). This may be evidence that the ideal victim concept still has contemporary relevance, in that victims that are deemed immoral, non-respectable and blameworthy are denied victim status. Furthermore, female sex workers are culturally and institutionally marginalised, stigmatised, discriminated against and criminalised. Indeed, due to the threat that female sex workers pose to 'the dominant scripts for what constitutes "appropriate" citizenship' (Sanders and Campbell, 2014: 535), patriarchal gender expectations and hegemonic familialism, they may well be construed as nearer to Christie's unsympathetic ideal offender. However, the inclusion of female sex worker victimisation in Merseyside hate crime policy and practice, while unique, does illustrate that this process is not universal and exceptions are possible.

To conclude, contemporarily, victims and victimisation have been re-imagined 'along the lines of demarcated identities' (Duggan and Heap, 2016: 244). Thus, while some crime victims' experiences of the criminal justice process may be enhanced, others 'remain overlooked entirely if they do not fit the re-imagined, politically prioritised, "ideal victim" typology' (Duggan and Heap, 2016: 244). This is evidenced with regard to new victimisations such as hate crime. Therefore, Christie's rubric remains contemporarily relevant and largely intact, as evidenced by the fact that, '[f]or symbolic purposes … the ideal victims of hate crime law are those who have the right amount of vulnerability, blamelessness and proximity to engender compassionate thinking' (Mason, 2013: 12) in order to reverse their negative cultural and institutional construction of 'Otherness'. Female sex workers do not have this and, at present, they lack the capacity to reconfigure their non-ideal and deviant victim status to that of a suffering, sympathetic, legitimate victim deserving of protection, justice and redress.

Female sex workers are no more ideal today than they were in the past and they do not appear to be any nearer to claiming that they are real victims – as real '[a]s the old ladies. Or the virgins walking home from caring for the sick' (Christie, 1986: 20). Hence, female sex workers remain overwhelmingly excluded from hate crime legislation and criminal justice hate crime policy and practice. Strong cultural and institutional 'counter-powers' (Christie, 1986: 21) outweigh or overshadow the plight of female sex workers when victimised, harmed and injured. Mason (2013: 12) notes how 'legislative protection itself might produce a sense of legitimacy that generates feelings of compassion'. It is doubtful that the inclusion of female sex workers in the response of Merseyside Police to hate crime has achieved this within or outside criminal justice. However, it does demonstrate that the notion of the ideal victim can be challenged symbolically and practically and that non-ideal and deviant victims can be bequeathed institutional victim status even though they are far from ideal. 'New' harms therefore – such as hate crime victimisation – can be explored to re-examine the extent to which the ideal victim thesis holds true in contemporary society. It can be used to evaluate the hierarchy of victimisation that rests upon notions of ideal, less than ideal and non-ideal victim imagery with regard to who is and who is not included in hate crime legislation and criminal justice hate crime policy and practice.

References

ACPO (Association of Chief Police Officers) (2011) 'ACPO strategy for policing prostitution and sexual exploitation'. Available at: http://www.npcc.police.uk/documents/crime/2011/20111102%20 CBA%20Policing%20Prostitution%20and%20%20Sexual%20 Exploitation%20Strategy_Website_October%202011.pdf

Bricknell, S. (2016) 'Gender and victimisation', in K. Corteen, S. Morley, P. Taylor and J. Turner (eds) *A Companion to Crime, Harm & Victimisation*, Bristol: Policy Press, pp 85–7.

Campbell, R. (2015) 'Not getting away with it: linking sex work and hate crime in Merseyside', in N. Chakraborti and J. Garland (eds) *Responding to Hate Crime: The Case for Connecting Policy and Research*, Bristol: Policy Press, pp 55–70.

Campbell, R. and Stoops, M. (2010) 'Taking sex workers seriously: treating violence as hate crime in Liverpool', *Research for Sex Work*, 12 December, pp 9–10.

Christie, N. (1986) 'The ideal victim', in E.A. Fattah (ed) *From Crime Policy to Victim Policy: Reorienting the Justice System*, Basingstoke: Macmillan Press, pp 17–30.

College of Policing (2014) *Hate Crime Operational Guidance.* Coventry: College of Policing. Available at: http://www.college.police. uk/What-we-do/Support/Equality/Documents/Hate-Crime-Operational-Guidance.pdf

Contreras, N. (2016) 'Racist hate crime', in K. Corteen, S. Morley, P. Taylor and J. Turner (eds) *A Companion to Crime, Harm & Victimisation*, Bristol: Policy Press, pp 181–3.

Corteen, K. (2014) 'Homophobic hate crime', in R. Atkinson (ed) *Shades of Deviance: A Primer on Crime, Deviance and Social Harm*, London: Routledge, pp 175–8.

Corteen, K. and Stoops, M. (2016) 'Sex work, hate crime and victimisation', in K. Corteen, S. Morley, P. Taylor and J. Turner (eds) *A Companion to Crime, Harm & Victimisation*, Bristol: Policy Press, pp 210–13.

Davies, P. (2016) 'Blame and victims', in K. Corteen, S. Morley, P. Taylor and J. Turner (eds) *A Companion to Crime, Harm & Victimisation*, Bristol: Policy Press, pp 17–19.

Dixon, B. and Gadd, D. (2006) 'Getting the message? 'New' Labour and the criminalization of hate', *Criminology and Criminal Justice*, 6(3): 309–28.

Duggan, M. and Heap, V. (2016) 'Victim hierarchy', in K. Corteen, S. Morley, P. Taylor and J. Turner (eds) *A Companion to Crime, Harm & Victimisation*, Bristol: Policy Press, pp 243–5.

Dunn, J. (2016) 'Deviant victims', in K. Corteen, S. Morley, P. Taylor and J. Turner (eds) *A Companion to Crime, Harm & Victimisation*, Bristol: Policy Press, pp 49–51.

Edwards, I. (2004) 'An ambiguous participant: the crime victim and criminal justice decision-making', *British Journal of Criminology*, 44(6): 967–82.

Gall, G. (2006) *Sex Work Union Organising: An International Study*, Basingstoke: Palgrave Macmillan.

Goodey, J. (2016) 'Hate crime and victimisation', in K. Corteen, S. Morley, P. Taylor and J. Turner (eds) *A Companion to Crime, Harm & Victimisation*, Bristol: Policy Press, pp 91–3.

Karmen, A. (2016) *Crime Victims: An Introduction to Victimology* (9th edn), Boston, MA: Cengage Learning.

Kinnell, H. (2009) *Violence and Sex Work in Britain*, Cullompton: Willan Publishing.

Marshall, R. (2016) 'Sex workers and human rights: a critical analysis of laws regarding sex work', *William & Mary Journal of Women and the Law*, 23(1): 47–77.

Mason, G. (2013) 'The symbolic purpose of hate crime law: ideal victims and emotion', *Theoretical Criminology*, 18(1): 1–18.

Mawby, R.I. and Walklate, S. (1994) *Critical Victimology: International Perspectives*, London: Sage.

OSCE (Organisation for Security and Cooperation in Europe) and ODIHR (Office for Democratic Institutions and Human Rights) (2009) *Hate Crime Laws: A Practical Guide*, Poland: OSCE/ODIHR. Available at: http://www.osce.org/odihr/36426?download=true

Ray, L. and Smith, D. (2001) 'Racist offenders and the politics of hate crime', *Law and Critique*, 12(3): 203–21.

Sanders, T. and Campbell, R. (2014) 'Criminalization, protection and rights: global tensions in the governance of commercial sex', *Criminology and Criminal Justice*, 14(5): 535–48.

Scoular, J. and Carline, A. (2014) 'A critical account of a "creeping abolitionism": regulating prostitution in England and Wales', *Criminology and Criminal Justice*, 14(5): 608–26.

Stoops, M. (2016) 'Sex workers and victimisation', in K. Corteen, S. Morley, P. Taylor and J. Turner (eds) *A Companion to Crime, Harm & Victimisation*, Bristol: Policy Press, pp 208–10.

Stoops, M. (2017) Conversation with Shelly Stoops, Operational Manager at SAFE Place Merseyside, 10 February.

Walklate, S. (2007) *Imagining the Victim of Crime*, Maidenhead: Open University Press.

Walklate, S. (2016) 'Victimological other', in K. Corteen, S. Morley, P. Taylor and J. Turner (eds) *A Companion to Crime, Harm & Victimisation*, Bristol: Policy Press, pp 251–3.

SIX

The 'ideal migrant victim' in human rights courts: between vulnerability and otherness

Carolina Yoko Furusho

Who are the vulnerable migrants?

In light of the polarised debate surrounding the limits of ethical state responses to migration, two radical discourses can be identified. On the one hand, it is deeply worrisome how the notion of the deviant and dangerous migrant 'other' in the societal imagination bears an intimate link to the 'moral panics' underlying national security discourses and increasingly stricter 'crimmigration' laws (Aas, 2010). The ascension of this derogatory stereotype resonates with Nils Christie's (1986) assessment that the more foreign and less human a perpetrator is, the closer they are to the notion of the 'ideal offender'. On the other hand, I suggest that an expansion of globalised networks of solidarity has propelled a powerful albeit double-edged discourse on migrant vulnerability in human rights advocacy, framing 'vulnerable migrants' as ideal victims of human rights violations and thus taking a diametrically opposed stance to the anti-migrant discourse.

Against this backdrop, I attempt to analyse how the notion of the ideal victim can help explicate promising achievements, as well as uncover potentially exclusionary dimensions, of human rights discourse on migrant vulnerability, leading to the normalisation of invisible harms. To fulfil this purpose, Christie's 'ideal victim' theory underpins a critical analysis of the recognition of human rights victims in the context of migration, focusing on how regional human rights courts adopt the notion of vulnerability as a legal heuristic. My argument is threefold. First, I adopt the ideal victim as a conceptual framework to build a critical assessment of how vulnerable migrants are framed as such in human rights decision-making. Second, I discuss the potential effects of vulnerability by showing through illustrative cases that whereas some migrant groups are categorised as vulnerable, others might have their vulnerability selectively recognised depending on intersecting factors, for instance, age, gender or ethnic and national affiliation, creating a doubly exclusionary mechanism. Third, I suggest that these exclusions reveal the power dynamics underlying the complex intertwinement between legal and political discourses on vulnerability, indicating not only the promise, but also the potential pitfalls, of human rights courts' practice of identifying vulnerable migrant victims. To conclude, I argue that the vulnerable migrant is often labelled as such by virtue of association with the characteristics of an ideal victim, such as weakness, frailty and passivity. I further argue that this may prove problematic for two reasons: first, it relies on eliciting societal compassion to seek recognition, enabling political manipulation; and, second, it might entail stigmatising and paternalistic responses that are palliative, rather than enabling long-term structural changes.

Idealising a vulnerable migrant victim

Globalisation has taken place alongside the strengthening of border controls and the securitisation of migration (Bosworth and Guild, 2008). The conservative discourse on migration relies on the ascription of the status of 'folk devils' (Cohen, 2002) in the collective conferring of deviance to asylum-seekers, refugees and undocumented migrants. This negative image, which links migration and the stigma of illegality, often propels audiences to feelings of anxiety and fear, paving the way for misrecognition, exclusion, othering and even racism (O'Neill, 2012). Aas (2010) reminds us that irregular immigrants might be considered as the 'global others'. Global mobility is shaping novel labels of outsiders and new 'others' in the globalised arena, in that some populations are caught up in 'non-spaces', exemplified by refugee camps and detention facilities (Hannah-Moffat et al, 2012). In Garland's (2001) 'criminology of the other', those who commit offences, such as illegal immigrants, are considered as another 'kind' of human, intrinsically different from law-abiding citizens and presenting threats to the existing social order. Aas (2010: 437) argues that this is a relevant notion in understanding how the public eye interprets and expresses concern over the prejudiced perception of foreigners 'contaminating the local', especially when concerning issues of human trafficking, terrorism and transnational organised crime.

Moral boundaries are presently drawn not only through discourse, but also through exclusionary practices against migrants. Judith Butler (2013: 167) inscribes immigration law in a biopolitical regulatory framework, 'one that does not have to sentence a life, or a set of lives, to death in order to let them die'. Butler (2004) brings the issue of inequality to the heart of the discussion when conceptualising precarity as the unequal allocation of politically induced modes of, on the one hand, perishing and dying, and, on the other hand, thriving and flourishing. Legal and political arrangements allow for some lives to be recognised as precarious and worthy of receiving life-sustaining resources while others do not enjoy the same normative recognition. In this regard, the Inter-American Court of Human Rights (IACtHR) summarises reasons for migrant vulnerability in the following terms:

> Migrants are generally in a vulnerable situation as subjects of human rights; they are in an individual situation of absence or difference of power with regard to non-migrants (nationals or residents). This situation of vulnerability has an ideological dimension and occurs in a historical context that is distinct for each State and is maintained by de jure (inequalities between nationals and aliens in the laws) and de facto (structural inequalities) situations. This leads to the establishment of differences in their access to the public resources administered by the State.... Cultural prejudices about migrants also exist that lead to reproduction of the situation of vulnerability; these include ethnic prejudices, xenophobia and racism, which make it difficult for migrants to integrate into society and lead to their human rights being violated with impunity.[1]

For Peroni and Timmer (2013), the recognition of vulnerable groups by the European Court of Human Rights (ECtHR) has been a noticeable and welcome development, a commentary that was mirrored by Clerico and Beloff (2014) with regards to the IACtHR. In the European context, the Roma minority, children, women, persons with disabilities, refugees and asylum-seekers, and HIV-positive persons are among those who have been recognised as vulnerable; for its IACtHR counterpart, some examples are indigenous populations, women, undocumented migrants, children and persons deprived of their liberty.

Praising vulnerability in human rights courts

Peroni and Timmer (2013) argue that the deployment of vulnerability by the ECtHR entails positive changes in the way human rights courts decide cases, presenting three characteristics: first, it is relational, focusing on wider social circumstances; second, it is particular, mindful of how shared group-specific experiences might raise distinct concerns; and, third, it is harm-based, pointing to the harms of misrecognition in cases of discrimination and maldistribution, as well as in situations of material dispossession. In the case of migrants, for instance, asymmetrical relationships and disadvantage can be identified and, as a result, remedies tackling structural inequalities can be set out. Moreover, the recognition of vulnerability could arguably pave the way for transforming the detrimental connotations associated with illegal migratory status that underlie the prejudice against migrants and result in discriminatory practices and violence.[2]

With respect to the concrete implications of recognising a vulnerable applicant in the ECtHR, Timmer (2013: 165) explains that if the applicant is considered vulnerable, the state is given a narrower margin to justify the alleged breach on the applicant's right; it is hence more likely to be considered as having committed a human rights violation. Moreover, when applying proportionality and balancing state actions against the applicant's rights, not only does vulnerability tilt the scales towards a favourable decision for the presumed victim's claim, increasing his or her odds of being considered as a victim, but it also extends the victim's rights once their victim status is established, ascribing stronger positive obligations to the state, including in the socio-economic realm.[3]

Interpretation is thereby affected in a way that bolsters additional or enhanced obligations from the state towards a vulnerable individual in a context-sensitive manner. As a result, changes in legislation and policymaking are expected from the state in order to comply with the judicial rationale of the court, potentially having a wider impact in changing structures that sustain vulnerability-enabling patterns, that is, predictably victimising environments. In an optimistic endorsement of this conceptual innovation, Timmer argues that vulnerability could be considered a 'quiet revolution' in the Strasbourg court. The extent of this argument can be further scrutinised by theoretically engaging with both vulnerability and the ideal victim as analytical concepts.

Christie's theory: a brief explanation

Christie (1986) explains that being a victim cannot be apprehended as an objective fact; rather, it is a societal or group definition of a particular situation – whereas some emphasise it, others choose to deem it less relevant. In this context, the ideal victim would be a category of individuals to whom the victim status is more readily and completely attributed, without any question regarding its legitimacy. An ideal victim has certain identifiable attributes. First of all, the victim is weak, helpless and female. Second, she is careful and respectable, neither exposing herself to risk nor doing something morally reprehensible. Third, although disempowered in her archetypical frailty, she must be empowered enough to make her case known and claim victim status, not having counter-powers to silence her claims. Last but not least, an ideal victim must have as a counterpoint an ideal offender, whose main features consist in being 'big', 'bad' and a stranger to the victim. According to Christie, the more foreign and the less human, the more ideal the offender, that is, this archetype is shored up by social anxiety and fear in relation to the idea of a monster from far away who can be differentiated from common and dignified citizens. Thus, the ideal offender plays an important role in creating the ideal victim: the more ideal the offender, the more ideal the victim, and the reverse logic also applies. What ensues is that when offenders are victimised, they are far from being ideal victims, for example, when drug traffickers become addicts, victims of their own trade (Christie, 1986: 21–5).

One insightful contribution of Christie's concept is the conclusion that individuals who want to have their plights heard and their victim status recognised have better odds at achieving their goal if they have the right amount of power: neither too much to threaten established societal interests of dominant classes, nor too little that their voices are completely unheard. Hence, ideal victims must be strong enough to be listened to but also weak enough not to become a threat to other important interests and undermine public sympathy associated with being a victim (Christie, 1986: 27). In an interesting example, he cites the case of domestic abuse laws until the 1980s in Finland, which were handled as noise complaints; he correctly suggests that reducing violence to noise is a way to narrow down the problem as a nuisance that must be silenced, rather than a serious issue to be resolved and tackled. He argues that with the empowerment of women in male-dominated societies, domestic rape and beating became denaturalised as women gradually attained positions of power that allowed them to raise concerns and change previous definitions; they hence became closer to the ideal victim than in the past. He continues on to assert that when gender equality is achieved, though, their credibility as victims will be compromised due to the reduced amount of sympathy that they will elicit when making a claim as weakness and subordination are necessary criteria to fit within the ideal victim archetype.

Power to be a victim versus power of being a victim

In this respect, Miers (1990) suggests that complex interacting processes unfold whereby individuals are either categorised as victims or excluded from this category altogether. Drawing on his account, Walklate (2007) places the following question at the heart of a feminist-informed critical victimology: how is the victim label created and who has the power to place that label? It is important to factor into the equation the uncertainty of emotions, such as public sympathy and compassion, and the asymmetrical strength of the political actors who play a key role. These influential elements might be decisive in the assignment of the victim label. Conversely, Miers argues that creating a victim could also be a powerful way to harness emotions from the public, such as public sympathy, towards political goals. Concerning the latter, Miers warns about the potential danger that ensues from constructing a victim, since focusing on a specific kind of victimisation may be a political strategy to naturalise even more hazardous harms: 'The presence, or the possible identification, of a victim is routinely used to emphasise other people's deviance, diverting attention from other (worse) forms, or reiterating traditionally accepted forms' (Miers, 1990: 220). It is interesting to note how this indicates that the legal and political realms are entwined in a mutually reinforcing relationship, in that the power to be a victim, which is affected by public emotions in the political arena, can be used to achieve the position of victim in the legal sphere, and the power of being labelled as a victim by a court of law may concomitantly affect the capacity to harness sympathy from the public and tilt the scales of political struggles in favour of certain agendas.

Vulnerability as a measurement for ideal victimhood

Drawing on Christie's provocative framework, some points can be raised regarding how migrants are framed in the interpretation of human rights courts. First of all, the identification of vulnerable applicants and the assignment of the vulnerable label seem to point to a quasi-legal categorisation, indicating proximity to the ideal victim archetype. On the basis of a need for special protection, it follows that vulnerable applicants should be treated differently, that is, with a higher level of protective obligations by states, which is often a rationale premised upon care, dependence and compassion, reconciling the apprehension of social contexts of vulnerability with individual narratives of victimisation. I argue that vulnerability can thus be seen as increasing the odds of an applicant being acknowledged as a victim of a human rights violation, constituting a measurement for 'ideal victimhood'.[4]

Since the obligations of the state are increased from merely protecting to providing 'special protection', recognition of vulnerability entails a higher degree of accountability by the state with regard to the vulnerable subject. This enhanced protection translates into incremental duties, which arguably increases the applicant's odds of being considered as a victim. Revisiting Christie's ideal victim, the more vulnerable the applicant, the more readily and easily the victim status is assigned to her. Hence, vulnerability can be considered as a measurement of a person's proximity to embodying what the ideal victim should be. In the social imaginary, images linger of those who could 'deservingly' merit to have their suffering deemed relevant and be recognised as a victim, that is, archetypes of ideal victims, as well as of ideal offenders to be placed opposite to them and further highlight their vulnerable situation. Vulnerability provides a reason to bolster the idea of a 'deserving' ideal victim. For instance, the vulnerability of a migrant child, a seemingly uncontroversial assumption, brings her close to the top of the ideal victim pyramid, making her case from the outset much stronger when claiming a human rights violation, as shall be further discussed in the next section.

In other words, I suggest that vulnerability may be a proxy for measuring how ideal a prospective victim may be. In this context, structural inequalities may be tackled and inclusion may be fostered through the recognition of vulnerability and victimisation. Shedding light on the invisible victimisation of marginalised groups by highlighting their vulnerable status thus triggers legal responses to pre-existing inequalities and power imbalances, reshaping the very content of what it means to be a human rights victim and what a human rights violation requires and entails. The ideal victim concept helps delineate the extent to which vulnerability is capable of bolstering inclusion and social justice and, as a consequence, allows for critical conjectures about its conceptual limits within law.

Challenging vulnerability: a doubly exclusionary mechanism?

Having established that vulnerability can be a measurement of how ideal a victim is, it seems logical to assume that individuals or groups whose vulnerability is conspicuous and recognisable are better off than those who are not. In other words, applicants who are successful in their claims before human rights courts and are assigned the victim label would have legal validation of their narrative and could benefit from compensation and other forms of redress from the state in question, whereas the ones whose victim status had not been recognised due to an inability of the court to take into consideration their vulnerability would not benefit from ensuing material reparations and guarantees of non-repetition.

A pertinent reflection posited by Christie in relation to the ideal victim is that real victims rarely possess all these features, thereby not fitting the archetype and encountering more hindrances in gaining societal validation as victims. Although vulnerability allows for the inclusion of individuals who are disadvantaged or marginalised in extant social and institutional structures by altering and expanding the scope of human rights victimhood, it is reasonable to assume that many real-life victims exist and not all of them meet the threshold for recognition of vulnerability, which consequently means that their victimisation is not recognisable as such. One must be wary of the power relations underlying human rights institutions in order to determine how assigning vulnerability and victimisation is likely to engender exclusionary mechanisms.

Intersectionality (Crenshaw, 1989) seems to be a good start to disrupting preconceived notions of an ideal victim by problematising existing categories as it investigates interlocking and simultaneous structural oppressions that strike a particular context, operating in specific forms of power and affective relationships (Cooper, 2015). This constitutes a relevant tool to deconstruct essentialised categories and reveal how power relations operate to create multiple identities, and sheds light on how the law succeeds or fails to take this into account. An intersectional reading will permeate the following sections in an attempt to reveal in which ways vulnerability may or may not destabilise the juridical framing of 'victim' by the courts.

Exclusion by misrecognition

Regarding the punitive tendency of states against migrants, 'crimmigration law' is the depiction of a phenomenon that blurs the boundaries between criminal justice and immigration policy, with increasing reliance of immigration procedures in criminal law processes and crime control through immigration processes (Stumpf, 2006). Immigration detention illustrates how immigration has borrowed criminal punitiveness (Hannah-Moffat et al, 2012). This stigmatising depiction of migrants as dangerous others leads to increased forms of lawful violence and coercion aiming at detaining, excluding, imprisoning and marginalising migrants. At the margins, other structures, such as racism, sexism and other forms of discrimination, encounter a breeding ground (Calavita, 2005). Against this backdrop, migrants are a priori seen as dangerous threats, increasing their potential to be ideal offenders, and hence farther away from being considered as ideal victims. Christie's depiction of the ideal offender as the 'big', 'bad', foreign man from far away and not acquainted to the victim is an attempt to explain how the social imaginary conceives of migrant others. The evilness and physical strength of the ideal offender chime with the prejudices assembled in the image of the 'non-civilised' and often racialised foreigner, who is unconstrained by norms of propriety and civility and does not hesitate to use physical force following erratic and irrational behaviour.

Beduschi (2015: 46) claims that there exists a problem of perception of undocumented migrants as 'individuals who are appropriately deprived – or less entitled to – human rights', and asserts the importance of human rights courts and international instruments in shoring up these rights and defining their content. On the other hand, asylum-seekers and refugees rely upon a robust set of judicial decisions,[5] institutions and norms in international law, in addition to widespread media coverage, which countenance the idea of this particular group as worthy of compassion due to their hyper-precarity (Waite et al, 2014). By contrast, undocumented migrants do not easily escape 'othering' strategies, especially due to the ascription of illegal or even criminal status, often embodying the imagined idea of the dangerous other, who 'autonomously' chose to migrate, rather than being forced to flee in order to survive, hence incurring a blameworthiness and being a threat to the security of citizens. If migrants, especially those who live in illegality, incarnate the ideal offender, it stands to reason that less sympathetic responses will arise, casting a shadow upon their vulnerability and victimisation. The vulnerability of the ideal migrant offender is hardly recognisable due to the fact that he or she is seen as the one aggravating or even creating the vulnerability of others, unless there are other elements to highlight their vulnerability.

Migration and age: selective recognition?

It does not come as a surprise that both the ECtHR and the IACtHR have vehemently expressed their concern with the vulnerability of migrant children, even illegal ones. In Advisory Opinion OC-21,[6] the IACtHR asserts that migrant children are particularly vulnerable. It imposes on states a special commitment to guarantee and protect their human rights, focusing on the transversal criterion of age, but urging them to take into account:

> other personal factors, such as disability, being a member of an ethnic minority group, or living with HIV/AIDS, as well as the particular characteristics of the situation of vulnerability of the child, such as a victim of trafficking, or separated or unaccompanied, for the purpose of determining the need for specific additional positive measures.[7]

Furthermore, the court continues on to affirm that children who are unaccompanied by their families and female children may be more vulnerable to human trafficking for labour and sexual exploitation, calling upon states to fight trafficking with investigations, victim protection and media campaigns.[8]

In the ECtHR case of *Mubilanzila vs. Belgium*,[9] for example, the case where an illegal migrant child was placed in a detention centre led the court to rule that the migrant was a victim of human rights violations, namely, the right not to suffer inhuman and degrading treatment and the right to security and liberty, due to the fact that her vulnerability as a child should prevail over her illegal status. Hence, the applicant's age was a decisive factor in acknowledging her victim status; had she not been a minor, it stands to reason that the court would have ruled it differently, not recognising her victimisation and, hence, not assigning her the status of human rights victim and establishing corresponding obligations on the state. This case instantiates how vulnerability can bring someone one step closer to being recognised as a victim.

One the one hand, the recognition by the courts of illegal migrant children as vulnerable may make a dent in the othering scheme, bringing hope with regard to the possibilities of resisting oppressive state practices against illegal migrants such as crimmigration. Conversely, should any breach of immigration rules be punishable with detention? Although this merits deeper scrutiny, crimmigration practices have already established an answer: whatever harms that arise from this systematic legal practice to the human rights of migrants will be naturalised harms inasmuch as detention centres are not contested on an overarching normative level, bar few exceptions made to those labelled as vulnerable. If human rights courts adopt a 'pick-and-choose' approach steered by public sympathy, vulnerability can only get us so far in terms of combating this abominable practice. In this regard, an underlying politics of compassion, or a politics of pity (Walklate, 2011), may place the spotlight on some types of victims to the detriment of others, even if they are all subjected to harmful practices that should be tackled and addressed by states.

Selective recognition of vulnerable migrants by courts points to two conclusions. First, the court maintains its reputation of looking after those thought to be the most vulnerable, in consonance with public emotions of sympathy towards refugees and those who seek asylum, migrant children or victims of trafficking, while 'non-ideal', 'non-vulnerable' or 'deviant victims' whose vulnerability is not recognisable are excluded from the material reparations that such recognition may entail (Miers, 1990: 221). This exclusion operates not only on a material level, but also on a symbolic and legal level, as non-ideal vulnerable victims are not recognised as victims and neither is their suffering recognised as a human rights violation. Second, the court fails to address how systemic power imbalances between the state and migrants who are illegal or whose legal status is unstable profoundly affect the recognition and protection of migrants' freedoms and rights, being conducive to vulnerabilities with the overspilling effect of worsening victimising environments. In this way, it establishes a threshold of recognisability that forecloses the reality of undocumented migrants, disregarding their position of vulnerability and disadvantage in the web of power relations that renders them susceptible to victimisation. In other words, to be more precise, it applies selective sensitivity to their disadvantage, rendering it normatively salient in certain cases and being oblivious to it in others.

Under a vulnerability analysis, it follows that certain migrants might be considered 'victimological others' (Walklate, 2011, 2016), in that this particular focus renders only certain vulnerable migrants more visible to the detriment of others, a visibility that is dependent upon their capacity to elicit public sympathy. The problem that arises is twofold: first, certain individuals are excluded from being considered as vulnerable even though the arguments posited for vulnerability can be rationally applied to them as well, although not capable of attracting the same amount of compassion or sympathy; second, the structural patterns that engender these victimisations, which may perpetuate systemic forms of harm, remain virtually unchallenged as only small concessions to certain kinds of vulnerable groups are put forward. Thus, it seems like discrepancies in recognising vulnerability might implicitly entail condoning the juridical invisibility of certain individuals. In addition to perpetuating selective inequality, wider social and cultural frameworks supporting oppressive power dynamics towards migrants remain untouched, unwittingly advancing reform-mongering in a larger harm-producing framework that has been gradually consolidated and naturalised.

Exclusion by recognition

Another kind of exclusion should be highlighted: exclusion by recognition itself. This suggestion goes to the heart of Christie's idea that the victim must have just enough power to be recognised as a victim but not so much as to undermine the credibility of her victim status. The symbolic power of the embedded archetypical victim in the societal imaginary implies a 'hierarchy of victimisation' that places groups of individuals as 'deserving' of the victim label and others as 'unworthy' of being categorised as victims due to their high-risk lifestyle (Carrabine et al, 2014: 117). The hierarchy of victimisation shows how the suffering of some victims may be overlooked whereas the plight of others may be recognisable. An 'ideal migrant victim' further reveals the essentialising and exclusionary logic of labelling victims by setting the criteria for those who 'merit' the victim label and those who do not.

In the following cases, the framing of vulnerability in these sentences will serve to demonstrate that recognising a vulnerable victim might also bring about undesired results that reinforce social exclusion and hinder transformative solutions to patterns of human rights violations, particularly the stigmatisation of both victims and offenders.

Migration and gender: essentialisation and stigmatisation?

Jurisprudential developments in the ambit of the ECtHR with respect to illegal migrant workers in saliently gendered labour activities have gained scholarly attention and praise (Mantouvalou, 2013). In *Siliadin v France*,[10] a Togolese 15-year-old girl who was lured into France by her employer under the false promise that she would be able to work and study ended up becoming an undocumented migrant domestic worker and was recognised by the ECtHR as a victim of servitude. In *C.N. v United Kingdom*,[11] the applicant was a Ugandan woman who worked under exploitative conditions as a live-in carer. Similarly to the reasoning in *Siliadin*, the Strasbourg court recognised C.N.'s vulnerability, linking her vulnerable situation to subtler forms of coercion and control enabled by her undocumented status. In these cases, underlying power inequalities between workers and employers were, to some extent, identified and teased out by reference to irregular status as a source of aggravated vulnerability. Moreover, in addition to their recognition as victims on the grounds of their right not to be subjected to servitude, the court declared the failure of the state to conduct proper investigations, imposing a duty to provide monetary compensation. In both sentences, the court attempted to address victimising structures by setting out the need to consider domestic servitude as a specific criminal offence in order to afford effective protection to victims. Furthermore, a concern with the gendered nature of servitude and slavery can be found in the court's assertion that contemporary slaves are migrant women who are domestic workers.[12]

Intriguingly, in both cases, the offenders were compatriots: in *C.N.*, P.S. was a relative who helped her get into the country and was in control of all of the wages she earned; in *Siliadin*, Mrs D. was a French national of Togolese origin who had promised her both employment and education opportunities in France, but did not fulfil her promise, making her work in the house she shared with Mr D. and months later 'lending' her[13] to another couple of friends, Mr and Mrs B., to perform years of unpaid labour under abusive conditions that, according to the ECtHR's ruling, amounted to servitude. In both cases, their passports were withheld by the offenders. The 'innocence' of these victims with respect to their irregularity was demonstrated by the fact that someone else was in control, rendering them blameless for their illegal status and, hence, placing them closer to the ideal victim. Moreover, offenders are characterised as sharing a national background with the victims, partially embodying the mythical foreign aura of the ideal offender. Although the national background of Mr and Mrs B. were not informed, the judgement mentioned that Siliadin's father had consented to the work arrangement at their house and that when she escaped, she went back in obedience to her paternal uncle's advice.[14]

Doezema (1999: 38) points out how Western discourses on trafficking may place traffickers as evil foreign villains. In this regard, the geographical origin of the offenders should be noted as bringing them closer to the notion of ideal offenders, which according to Christie, makes victims even more ideal. Although the harmful nature of the actions perpetrated by both offenders is undeniable, merely stating the need for a state's positive obligations to have adequate criminal provisions seems to strike a chord, albeit imperfectly, with Spivak's (1993: 92) famous postcolonial critique of 'white men saving brown women from brown men'. In these cases, the understanding of harm is narrowly circumscribed within the reach of the colonial eyesight, producing the vulnerable victim as a subject in her subaltern position of weak, deceivable, exploitable and 'innocent' insofar as her illegal status was not a direct result of her own actions, but the result of an evil offender, whose recurrent portrayal forms the ideal offender and shores up crimmigration practices and racist assumptions.

Moreover, stigmatising may also occur by means of essentialising migrant women as the process of identifying vulnerability does not seem to follow clear guidelines and it is not consistently applied across all cases. For instance, in *R.H. vs Sweden*,[15] a Somali asylum-seeker whose asylum application had been rejected claimed that she had fled a forced marriage and was at risk of sexual assault if deported. Despite recognising the widespread nature of violence against women in Somalia, the court based its decision on evidentiary inconsistencies, arguing that the victim's statements were contradictory and inferring that she had 'access to both family support and a male protection network',[16] which thwarted her claim that she was vulnerable. By dismissing her vulnerability and deciding that deportation did not constitute a violation of her right not to suffer inhuman and degrading treatment, the court regrettably disregarded underlying patriarchal elements that aggravated rather than mitigated her vulnerability, not to mention that it corroborated gender stereotypes that associate female vulnerability with male protection.

To further illustrate, in another case cherished for its intersectional approach (Yoshida, 2013) of a Nigerian sex worker legally resident in Spain who was repeatedly a victim of physical and verbal abuse by police officers, the court recognised the 'particular vulnerability inherent in her position as an African woman working as a prostitute'.[17] Although the accumulation of different grounds of discrimination was identified, referring to her vulnerability as inherent to her identity as an African female prostitute harbours underlying deterministic assumptions about gender, race and line of work that might have hindered transformative responses. Despite the court's awareness of intersecting systems of power, this awareness did not seem to have much impact in shaping additional state duties.

Although these cases may be seen as important advancements in protecting vulnerable migrant women (Mantouvalou, 2013), a deeper critique of the power mechanisms underlying these contexts of vulnerability and subsequent victimisation can only be achieved by critically deconstructing references to women, or minority women undertaking precarious forms of labour, as monolithic categories. The ideal victim, imagined as the helpless female victim in need of protection, can reinforce stigmatising patriarchal notions and block agency-fostering alternatives. In this regard, the racial element also plays a role in widespread depictions of victims 'deserving' of compassion, corroborating assumptions of passivity in a politics of pity that may privilege victim-targeted services that focus on the trauma of victimisation rather than concentrating, for instance, on the victim's ability to actively partake in the resolution of her personal experience of victimhood (Walklate, 2011). A narrow conceptualisation of vulnerability that stigmatises and essentialises victims as weak, helpless and disempowered may lead to strictly paternalistic and insufficiently progressive responses to deal with the wider structures of power in which victimisation takes place.

Conclusion: rescuing vulnerability?

Despite a priori suspicions that may be elicited of migrants as ideal offenders, certain migrant groups that are recognised as vulnerable by the courts have taken a step towards becoming closer to the ideal victim, in that their suffering has become cognisable and their claims for victim status have been increasingly successful. The rise of certain migrant groups demonstrates that some have gained sufficient power to be heard, but not enough to threaten the prevalent interests of dominant classes. Nonetheless, both the power to be a victim and the power of being a victim indicate less than ideal power imbalances in society, in that empowered individuals rely upon eliciting compassion and sympathy to gain access to justice and fight oppression, a mechanism that might selectively include some to the detriment of others.

Similarly to patriarchy as the dominant structure against which domestic violence laws came about, the colonial legacy underlying legal and institutional arrangements that naturalise victimisations connected to migratory fluxes and impelled by global neoliberal inequalities can be identified as hegemonic interests. One must be wary that legal reforms and progressive judicial judgements may be palliative measures that empower only a small portion of those affected by violence and marginalisation to be recognised as victims, perpetuating and reproducing, rather than dismantling, oppressive power structures of exclusion and subordination. Moreover, being recognised as a victim still remains a far cry from overcoming such structures and advancing progressive pathways towards social justice and equality.

Notwithstanding, vulnerability reasoning still offers promise as a critical and interpretive tool, disrupting, to some extent, ideal notions of victim and offender. Victims are constructed through the interpretation of victimising events, which take place in a specific place in a particular time; vulnerability spreads throughout different periods and geographies, revealing wider contextual structures. Rather than abandoning concepts such as vulnerability, I suggest that we take note of the ways in which human rights discourse unveils how vulnerability and victimisation feed into each other across time, often intersecting, either in mutual reinforcement or instead in clashing antagonism, sustaining and breaking conceptual boundaries in law and politics. This requires going beyond ideal archetypes and into the force field where individuals are entrenched in power struggles, resisting and at times even surviving; it also entails critiquing hidden agendas underneath a politics of pity and contesting the unwitting creation of victimological others.

Notes

[1] Advisory Opinion 18/2003, IACtHR.

[2] See IACtHR, *Expelled Dominican and Haitian Persons from the Dominican Republic*, Judgment of 28 August 2014.

[3] *M.S.S. v. Belgium and Greece*, no. 30696/09, ECtHR 2011.

[4] For the purposes of this chapter, I am focusing mainly on human rights victimisation connected to 'core rights', namely, torture or inhuman and degrading treatment and slavery and servitude. That being said, a striking caveat is how recognition of vulnerability may produce the exact opposite effect in claims of right to privacy and family life, for example, when a person with disability wishes to exercise autonomy and counter a state-mandated action, such as being institutionalised, or a terminally ill patient with disability wishes to be euthanised. Albeit important, this will not be discussed herein for it does not have direct relevance to the scope of this chapter.

[5] See *Tarakhel v. Switzerland*, no. 29217/12, paras 99, 118 and 132, ECHR 2011.

[6] Advisory Opinion 21/2014, para 114, IACtHR.

[7] Advisory Opinion 21/2014, para 114, IACtHR.

[8] Advisory Opinion 21/2014, para 156, IACtHR.

[9] *Mubilanzila Mayeka and Kaniki Mitunga v. Belgium*, no. 13178/03, ECHR 2007.

[10] *Siliadin v France*, no. 73316/01, ECHR 2005.

[11] *C.N. v UK*, no. 4239/08, ECHR 2012.

[12] *Siliadin*, para 88.

[13] 'Prêter', the French verb for 'to lend', was used with quotation marks in the description of this fact of the ECtHR's original judgement (para 12).

[14] *Siliadin*, para 34.

[15] *R.H. v. Sweden*, no. 4601/14, ECHR 2015.

[16] *R.H. v. Sweden*, no. 4601/14, ECHR 2015, para 72. Admittedly, the expression 'male protection network' was used by the applicant; however, it is regretful that the court uncritically adopted it, especially under a reasoning that utterly disregarded the applicant's account of the facts.

[17] *B.S. v. Spain*, no. 47159/08, para 62, ECHR 2012.

References

Aas, K.F. (2010) 'Global criminology', in E. McLaughlin and T. Newburn (eds) *The Sage Handbook of Criminological Theory* (1st edn), London: SAGE, pp 427–46.

Beduschi, A. (2015) 'The contribution of the Inter-American Court of Human Rights to the protection of irregular immigrants' rights: opportunities and challenges', *Refugee Survey Quarterly*, 34(4): 45–74.

Bosworth, M. and Guild, M. (2008) 'Governing through migration control', *The British Journal of Criminology*, 48(6): 703–19.

Butler, J. (2004) *Precarious Life: The Powers of Mourning and Violence*, London: Verso.

Butler, J. (2013) *Dispossession: The Performative in the Political*, Oxford and Cambridge: Oxford Wiley.

Calavita, K. (2005) *Immigrants at the Margins: Law, Race, and Exclusion in Southern Europe*, Cambridge: Cambridge University Press.

Carrabine, E., Cox, P., Fussey, P., Hobbs, D., South, N. and Thiel, D. (eds) (2014) *Criminology: A Sociological Introduction*, London: Routledge.

Christie, N. (1986) 'The ideal victim', in E.A. Fattah (ed) *From Crime Policy to Victim Policy: Reorienting the Justice System*, Basingstoke: Macmillan, pp 17–30.

Clerico, L. and Bellof, M. (2014) 'Derecho a condiciones de existencia digna y situación de vulnerabilidad en la jurisprudencia de la Corte Interamericana', Seminario de Latinoamérica de Teoría Constitucional y Política SELA, 21 June.

Cohen, S. (2002) *Folk Devils and Moral Panics* (3rd edn), London: Routledge.

Cooper, B. (2015) 'Intersectionality', in L. Disch and M. Hawkesworth (eds) *The Oxford Handbook of Feminist Theory*, Oxford: Oxford University Press.

Crenshaw, K. (1989) 'Demarginalizing the intersection of race and sex: a black feminist critique of antidiscrimination doctrine, feminist theory, and antiracist politics', *University of Chicago Legal Forum*, 1: 139–67.

Doezema, J. (1999) 'Loose women or lost women? The re-emergence of the myth of white slavery in contemporary discourses of trafficking in women', *Journal of Gender Issues*, 18(1): 23–50.

Garland, D. (2001) *The Culture of Control: Crime and Social Order in Contemporary Society*, Oxford: Oxford University Press.

Hannah-Moffat, K., Lynch, M. and Bosworth, M. (2012) 'Subjectivity and identity in detention: punishment and society in a global age', *Theoretical Criminology*, 16(2): 123–40.

Mantouvalou, V. (2013) 'Workers without rights as citizens at the margins', *Critical Review of International Social and Political Philosophy*, 16(3): 366–82.

Miers, D. (1990) 'Positivist victimology: a critique part 2: critical victimology', *International Review of Victimology*, 1(3): 219–30.

O'Neill, M. (2012) *Transgressive Imaginations: Crime, Deviance and Culture*, Basingstoke: Palgrave Macmillan.

Peroni, L. and Timmer, A. (2013) 'Vulnerable groups: the promise of an emerging concept in European Human Rights Convention law', *International Journal of Constitutional Law*, 11(4): 1056–85.

Spivak, G.C. (1993) 'Can the subaltern speak?', in L. Chrisman and P. Williams (eds) *Colonial Discourse and Post-Colonial Theory: A Reader*, London: Routledge, pp 66–111.

Stumpf, J. (2006) 'The crimmigration crisis: immigrants, crime and sovereign power', *American University Law Review*, 56(2): 367–419.

Timmer, A. (2013) 'A quiet revolution: vulnerability in the European Court of Human Rights', in M. Fineman and A. Grear (eds) *Vulnerability: Reflections on a New Ethical Foundation for Law and Politics*, Farnham: Ashgate.

Waite, L., Valentine, G. and Lewis, H. (2014) 'Multiply vulnerable populations: mobilising a politics of compassion from the "capacity to hurt"', *Social & Cultural Geography*, 15(3): 313–31.

Walklate, S. (2007) *Imagining the Victim of Crime*, Maidenhead: McGraw Hill, Open University Press.

Walklate, S. (2011) 'Reframing criminal victimization: finding a place for vulnerability and resilience', *Theoretical Criminology*, 15(2): 179–94.

Walklate, S. (2016) 'Victimological other', in K. Corteen, S. Morley, P. Taylor and J. Turner (eds) *A Companion to Crime, Harm and Victimisation*, Bristol: Policy Press, pp 251–3.

Yoshida, K. (2013) 'Towards intersectionality in the European Court of Human Rights: the case of B.S. v Spain', *Feminist Legal Studies*, 21(2): 195–204.

SEVEN

'Our most precious possession of all'[1]: the survivor of non-recent childhood sexual abuse as the ideal victim?

Sinéad Ring

Introduction

A key contribution of Christie's has been to show that the category of the ideal victim is an expression of societal attitudes and values. In order to qualify as an ideal victim, a person's characteristics and 'their' crime must resonate with established social norms and values. They cannot threaten established social hierarchies. Examining the details of who can(not) be an ideal victim in a particular society and for a specific crime illuminates the hidden values, assumptions and norms of a society that underpin these categories.

This chapter examines the relevance of the ideal victim to understanding the discursive construction of the figure of the non-recent childhood sexual abuse survivor in Ireland.[2] Since Ireland 'discovered' non-recent childhood sexual abuse as a problem in the 1990s, child abuse survivors have succeeded in gaining public sympathy and societal responses in the form of criminal prosecutions, changes to civil law and official inquiries. The chapter argues that while the categorisation is helpful in exposing the operation of power in relation to how some people come to gain legitimate victim status, to focus exclusively on the ideal victim as an explanatory framework is to omit an important part of the story. The notion of an ideal victim is of limited applicability because it fails to account for the threat posed by such people to the established order of Church and state, and the entrenched culture of denial around sexual violence against children. The ideal victim trope erases from analysis the victim's agency in deciding to disclose the abuse after years of silence. Further, it ignores the importance of the context in which a victim's story is made audible

141

to the broader political community; in this case, the role of the broader violence against women and children movement in amplifying the voices of adults who were abused as children. Finally, it fails to account for the enduring ambivalence of the Irish state's response to survivors' claims for justice and commemoration.

The chapter first examines the ways in which Christie's typology of the 'ideal victim' helps to explain how the figure of the non-recent childhood sexual abuse survivor came to prominence in Ireland in the late 20th and early 21st centuries. In particular, the political and legal responses to survivors' claims for justice, as well as the media construction of the child abuser as a monster (the corollary of the ideal victim), are examined. The chapter then explores why the ideal victim trope does not adequately explain the figure of the non-recent childhood sexual abuse survivor. It is argued that the ideal victim category fails to account for the deeply shocking and controversial nature of these survivors' claims in the Irish context. Neither does it express the agency and courage of survivors in participating in documentaries and taking legal actions against abusers, the Church and the state, or the role of feminist activism in amplifying the voices of victims in public discourse. Finally, the chapter points to the ways in which the Irish state has failed to learn the lessons of the past 20 years, thus indicating that the non-recent childhood sexual abuse survivor remains an outsider of contemporary public discourse on victimhood.

The recognition of legitimate suffering

Perhaps the primary way in which non-recent childhood sexual abuse survivors may be understood as ideal victims is the way in which their stories and their victimhood became part of the public imaginary and the nation's sense of itself. In the early to mid-1990s, Ireland, like many other Western countries (see John Jay College of Criminal Justice, 2004; Adriaenssens, 2010; Deetman et al, 2011; Independent Inquiry into Child Sexual Abuse, 2017; Royal Commission into Institutional Responses to Child Sexual Abuse, 2017; Scottish Child Abuse Inquiry, 2017) experienced a surge in the number of people talking about and reporting the sexual abuse that happened to them as children many years earlier (Pine, 2010; Holohan, 2011; O'Sullivan, 2002; Ring, 2017a). Adult reports of childhood sexual abuse continue in the present (One in Four, 2016). Irish society was forced to recognise the harm of sexual abuse and to reckon with its history of widespread child abuse in institutions. This recognition was reflected in a striking political response, indicating that these survivors were considered 'legitimate' victims. Taoiseach[3] Bertie Ahern issued a public apology to survivors of institutional abuse on behalf of the Irish state in 1999. This was followed by a further apology by Taoiseach Enda Kenny in 2011 (RTÉ, 2011) and an apology from the Garda Commissioner for failing to protect children from clerical child sexual abuse (O'Brien, 2009).

The sheer scale of the state's legal response further exemplifies the social legitimacy and power of non-recent childhood sexual abuse survivors. Official inquiries were established to discover the truth of the recent past. The Commission to Inquire into Child Abuse was established to investigate abuse in industrial and reformatory schools.[4] The Residential Institutions Redress Board (RIRB) was created to provide monetary redress to survivors of institutional abuse.[5] Judge-led inquiries were established to investigate clerical abuse in individual archdioceses (Department of Justice, Equality and Law Reform, 2005; Commission of Investigation, 2009, 2010).[6] Alongside but separate to the work of these inquiries, the courts grappled with the demands for justice of survivors. The numerous reports to police of non-recent childhood sexual abuse resulted in criminal investigations and prosecutions (Ring, 2009). The periods within which personal injury actions for past sexual abuse may be taken were extended (Gallen, forthcoming).

The state's legal responses also embraced future-oriented reforms. A new statutory basis for child protection was introduced (Dukelow and Considine, 2017: 309–10). The criminal law on sexual violence against children was amended and extended: new criminal offences relating to child pornography[7] and the withholding of information about child abuse were created.[8] The maximum penalty for sexual assault on a child was increased.[9] Disparities in the law's treatment of abuse of males and females were addressed.[10] Procedural changes were made to facilitate the giving of testimony in trials by children (O'Malley, 2013).

In addition to the multifaceted political and legal responses to the claims of non-recent childhood sexual abuse survivors, there are other reasons to consider these survivors as ideal victims. First, their victimisation happened decades earlier, so their claims for recognition and redress could arguably be seen as something capable of being resolved without any threat to the status quo. More importantly, however, they had suffered the worst form of abuse of power, involving violations of their bodily autonomy and traumatic effects on their mental health. By the final decades of the 20th century, the outdated attitudes that blamed child victims for the abuse they suffered (Stevenson, 2000) had been replaced with a culture that was more receptive to children as victims. Therefore, in keeping with Christie's typology, these survivors were seen as weak and blameless, and could thus elicit public sympathy that translated into legal and political action. According to Christie, a further condition of ideal victim status is that the offender must be 'big and bad', or the symbolic converse of the innocent victim. In the Ireland of the late 1990s and early 21st century, those identified as possible or confirmed abusers were constructed by the media as 'monsters', or the embodiment of absolute evil. This discursive construction of abusers as evil is examined next.

The monstrous abuser

Criminologists have used Christie's work to explore the idea that in order to have an ideal victim, there must always be an ideal offender. Both victim and offender are two sides of a binary construct (Rock, 1998: 195). The young, 'innocent' unsuspecting target represents the opposite of the adult predatory male 'monster' who was previously unknown to them (McAlinden, 2014: 182). The official and popular discourses surrounding two high-profile criminal prosecutions of alleged child sexual abusers illustrate elements of Christie's 'ideal offender' typology. These are the cases of Brendan Smyth and Nora Wall.[11]

Brendan Smyth is the most notorious child sexual abuser in Irish history. Smyth was a Catholic priest who pleaded guilty in 1993 to 74 charges of indecent and sexual assault, involving the sexual abuse of 20 young people over a period of 36 years. He had previously served four years in a Northern Ireland prison for similar offences. The Church authorities had known of his activities for many years and simply moved him around the island of Ireland, north and south of the border. His crimes eventually came to public attention in a report by Chris Moore on Ulster Television's *Counterpoint* programme entitled 'Suffer little children', which was broadcast in October 1994 (Moore, 1995). The broadcast had a profound effect on Irish public life. The Taoiseach Albert Reynolds was forced to resign as a result of the political fallout following revelations that the Attorney General delayed processing requests for Smyth's extradition to Northern Ireland, where he faced more abuse charges, and accusations that ministers had misled the Dáil[12] about their knowledge of such cases in the Attorney General's office. The Attorney General, who had since been appointed President of the High Court, also resigned. The black-and-white close-up image of Smyth leering into a camera lens as he was lead out of the Central Criminal Court in July 1997 became an iconic image, one that summed up the national crisis around child sexual abuse. More than 20 years later, Smyth's impact continues to be felt by survivors and by society (Kelly, 2015; Collins, 2017). The recently concluded Historical Institutional Abuse Inquiry in Northern Ireland dedicated a module to his activities.[13] Two of Smyth's victims are currently taking a civil action following their discovery that the Church authorities had been informed of Smyth's abuse of another child some years prior to his abuse of them (*The Irish Times*, 2017).

The case of Nora Wall demonstrates the extreme media 'monstrification' that happens in relation to certain people who are accused of child sexual abuse. In 1999, Nora Wall, a former nun, was convicted of the rape and sexual assault of a 10-year-old girl on charges dating back to 1987/88. She was the first woman in the state to be convicted of rape and one of very few people to receive a life sentence for the crime (Newman, 2002). Wall was tried shortly after the transmission of the three-part documentary *States of Fear*, which had detailed the abuse and exploitation of children in the nation's residential institutions. Wall was alleged to have held the child's ankles while her co-accused, Paul McCabe, raped her. In the print and television media, she was portrayed as the 'evil nun', as a 'lesbian nun' and as 'sister Anti-Christ' (O'Sullivan, 2008: 310–11). Although Wall had left the Sisters of Mercy in 1994, the press insisted on referring to her as 'Sr Dominic', her ordained name (O'Sullivan, 2008: 316). However, Wall's conviction was overturned just four days later when it transpired that a witness had testified for the prosecution who should not have done so because of concerns about her reliability. In November 1999, the Director of Public Prosecutions accepted that Wall and her co-accused were entitled to be presumed innocent of all charges. Wall successfully sued the Irish state for a miscarriage of justice certificate (Carolan, 2016).

Although very different in substance, the cases of Brendan Smyth and Nora Wall point up the ways in which certain alleged abusers could be made to fit a particular mould of an ideal offender. This further underscores the energy invested in maintaining a strict division in the public's mind between evil offenders, on the one hand, and innocent ideal victims, on the other.

Christie (1986: 29) warned that the focus on the ideal offender means that crimes perpetrated by less abhorrent offenders, or crimes that are not as easily classified as 'evil', become more hidden from public attention. Victims of violence in the home do not make ideal victims because they are victims of the culturally accepted male dominance of families. Therefore, while it is in everyone's interest to identify and eliminate offending perpetrated by strangers lurking down dark alleys, the same does not apply to offending in the home. In the case of Ireland, the focus on clerical abuse and abuse in state-run institutions worked to the detriment of a sustained scrutiny of less visible forms of sexual violence against children, such as sexual violence within the home, for example. Harry Ferguson (1995: 249), a renowned social worker with expertise in the area of child sexual abuse, put it thus: 'The most common single occupational group represented in these cases has in fact been farmers. Yet we have not begun to talk routinely about "paedophile farmers"'.[14] The effect of all this is that it is more difficult for victims of abuse within families, and those being abused in other, newer institutions, such as the refugee and asylum system (McMahon, 2015), to speak up and have their voices heard.

So far, this chapter has set out the ways in which the ideal victim trope illuminates the figure of the non-recent childhood sexual abuse survivor in Ireland. However, there are many indications that the category of ideal victim does not fully express the complexity of these survivors' experiences. The next section examines the ways in which non-recent childhood sexual abuse survivors are non-ideal victims.

Contesting the 'ideal' status of victims of non-recent childhood sexual abuse

A key condition of ideal victim status is that they must not threaten any established social order (Christie, 1986: 21–3). The ideal victim is passive in that they achieve their legitimacy through their (pre-existing) characteristics, such as weakness, rather than their actions after the crime. Non-recent childhood sexual abuse survivors, however, threatened the established position of the Catholic Church in Irish society, and, by extension, the idea of Irishness itself. For reasons that had much to do with the traumatic experiences of colonialism, famine and civil war, the Church was at the heart of Irish society and oversaw the political and social aspects of post-independence Ireland. It controlled most of the hospitals and schools, and, most importantly, it imposed repressive and patriarchal attitudes to sex and sexuality (Smith, 2004; Inglis, 1998). The notion that sex is the greatest sin was 'inculcated deeper and lasted longer in the bodies and souls of the Irish than among the rest of the West' (Smith, 2004: 122). The patriarchal and repressive attitudes towards sex were connected to broader ideals around what it meant to be Irish (Howes, 2002: 925). In this climate, it is not surprising that sexual violence against children was not taken seriously. A journalist's comment indicates a society where the discussion of sexual violence was taboo: 'Of course children were slow to talk about [abuse]. They didn't have the language. Even women who suffered from breast cancer didn't talk about it because you couldn't talk about breasts' (O'Leary, 2006: 228).

The abuse of children in institutions was effectively tolerated by the community; the Ryan Commission also showed that the broader community, including the Gardaí (police), facilitated the Church's incarceration of vulnerable women and children and inaction over reports of abuse. Furthermore, the strategies of denial and culture of silencing were not confined to the institutional setting; survivors' testimonies to the courts indicated that silencing and denial extended into the community, including into police stations and family homes (Ring, 2017a).[15] Indeed, some children did, in fact, report to adults but they were ignored or actively humiliated for having done so (Ring, 2017a).

In short, therefore, the possibility of reporting sexual abuse in state-run institutions or in the community, *and being believed*, was extremely narrow indeed. Those who came forward and went public in the mid-1990s with their experiences of abuse threatened not only the position of the Church, but the fabric of the nation. Their courage and resilience in coming forward cannot be overestimated. As such, it is inaccurate to term these survivors as 'ideal' because the category fails to capture their resilience and intersectional complexity. In order to highlight just how controversial and difficult it was for survivors, the next section highlights some examples of people who fought to have their voices heard, demonstrating a courage and a resilience that is not reflected in the 'ideal victim' label.

An age of witnesses

The public awakening around the phenomenon of non-recent childhood sexual abuse was triggered by reports into familial abuse (South Eastern Health Board, 1993), as well as excellent journalism highlighting clerical abuse and abuse in residential institutions. However, at the heart of the documentaries and newspaper articles were the voices of individual survivors speaking publicly about their experiences. This testimony came from survivors not only of sexual abuse, but also of other kinds of harm, such as emotional, physical and mental abuse. A prime example is the groundbreaking *States of Fear* series of documentaries (Raftery, 1999), which featured women and men survivors of mental, physical and emotional torture, neglect and sexual abuse in residential and industrial institutions. In November 1992, Christine Buckley spoke on the leading current affairs and chat show, *The Late Late Show*, of the abuse she suffered as a child at the hands of the Sisters of Mercy at the St Vincent's Industrial School, Goldenbridge. She worked with Louis Lentin on the documentary *Dear Daughter* (Lentin, 1996), which dealt with her experiences and those of other inmates at Goldenbridge.

In 1994, *The Sunday Times* newspaper broke the story of how Andrew Madden had been paid IR£27,500 by the Catholic Church to cover up three years of sexual abuse by one of its priests. Forcing him to sign a letter of confidentiality, officials believed that the crimes of Madden's abuser, Father Ivan Payne, would never come to light and a few thousand pounds would put a stop to the publicity. Following denials by the Church, Madden took the courageous step of revealing his identity and the documents outlining the transaction. Eventually, this led to the Gardaí investigating, which resulted in Payne being charged with the sexual abuse of Madden and others.[16]

As Payne was investigated, dozens of other abuse cases emerged, including some that had been perpetrated in state institutions. These included Mannix Flynn, whose experiences at Letterfrack Industrial School run by the Christian Brothers were reported in a national newspaper in 2002 (McLaughlin, 2002). The same year, the BBC broadcast *Suing the Pope* presented a series of testimonies from young men who had been abused as children by Fr Sean Fortune.[17] Some explained how they had tried to have him removed but that nothing had happened until one young man, Colm O'Gorman, went to the Gardaí in the mid-1990s.[18] Monica Fitzpatrick spoke publicly about her fears that her son Peter's death by suicide was linked to Fr Fortune (Donnelly, 2002). These personal stories elicited an outpouring of public anger and sympathy and led to the establishment of an official inquiry (Department of Justice, Equality and Law Reform, 2005).

Alison Cooper was the young woman at the centre of a notorious case of familial sexual abuse. In 1993, she appeared on television and gave interviews to a journalist for a book, thereby allowing her voice to personalise and contextualise the reports of the criminal trial and the government's official report into the health board's failings in the case (Cooper, 1993; O'Faoláin, 1993; South Eastern Health Board, 1993). Marie Collins went public in the late 1990s about the abuse she suffered as a 13-year-old girl at the hands of Fr Paul McGennis during a stay in hospital. In 1998, Sophia McColgan's story of enduring years of rape and torture at the hands of her father was published (McKay, 1998). McColgan had given evidence against her father, who was jailed for life, and then went on to successfully sue the state for failing to protect her and her siblings from the abuse (Sgroi, 1999).

In speaking up about the abuse they suffered, adults who disclosed their trauma were breaking not only their own silence, but also the silence and denial of a nation. This was an enormous task that took multiple acts of courage and resilience. By participating in television documentaries, by taking legal actions against the Church and the state, and by speaking in public or writing about their experiences, these individuals were much more than ideal victims; they were agents of political change. The ideal victim trope is also an inappropriate descriptor of non-recent childhood sexual abuse survivors in Ireland because it denies the role of the broader cultural context and of feminist activism in facilitating the emergence of survivors' stories into public discourse.

The role of feminist activism

The public disclosures of sexual abuse happened in a context in which feminist activists working with survivors of sexual violence had been campaigning and drawing attention to the issue of child sexual abuse for years. The first rape crisis centre, the Dublin Rape Crisis Centre (DRCC), opened its doors in 1979. In 1984, its Director stated that the centre was seeing many young women who needed to talk about childhood abuse that had gone on for years: 'We can't say rape or incest is increasing. What we can say is that the more talk there is, the more the veil of silence is lifted, the more comfortable women are about coming forward' (McKay, 2005: 81). A report by the Irish Council for Civil Liberties working party on child sexual abuse in 1986 found that one in four girls and one in four boys had been sexually abused, and that it was a problem that was being ignored because most cases take place within the family and the vast majority go unreported (Magill, July 1986, cited in Ferriter, 2009: 451).

In 1989, therapists from the DRCC published *Surviving Sexual Abuse* (Walsh and Liddy, 1989), a handbook based on the counselling models developed at the centre (McKay, 2005: 147). Other strategies involved campaigning to reform the legal process (Fennell, 1993). Feminists from rape crisis centres around the country, children's rights charities and feminist academics provided feedback to the Law Reform Commission of Ireland (1990: 100–12) on its consultation on reforming the law on child sexual abuse. In 1998, the DRCC and Trinity College Dublin published a report examining the legal process and victims of rape in European Union member states (Bacik et al, 1998).

The public outrage caused by the facts of a particularly controversial legal case in 1992 focused public attention on the problem of child abuse in a unique way. The so-called 'X case' involved a 14-year-old girl who was suicidal. Upon discovering that she had been raped and was pregnant, the girl's parents took her to a sexual assault treatment unit, reported the rape to the Gardaí and arranged for her to have an abortion in England.[19] When the girl's father inquired whether they should have DNA tests done on the foetus to provide evidence for a trial, the Gardaí passed the question to the Director for Public Prosecutions, who informed the Attorney General Harry Whelehan. Whelehan invoked the Irish Constitution to obtain an injunction to stop the girl leaving the country. The High Court ruled that the girl was not permitted to leave the country for nine months and if she did so, she could be imprisoned. This caused a national outcry. President Mary Robinson said that the Irish people were experiencing 'a very deep crisis in ourselves' (*The Irish Times*, 1992). Ten thousand people took to the streets of Dublin in protest and there were similar protests nationwide. The singer Sinéad O'Connor called the High Court decision 'an invasion of the civil rights of all Irish women' (RTÉ, 1992). Importantly, feminists linked the case to the brutal reality of life for many women and girls in the country. Dr Mary Henry, Chairwoman of the Friends of the Rape Crisis Centre, highlighted that this was not an unusual case, but part of a culture of patriarchy and widespread sexual violence (*Evening Herald*, cited in McKay, 2005: 180). The case was ultimately resolved by the Supreme Court, which held that the girl had a right to an abortion in Ireland (*AG v X* [1992] 1 IR 1),[20] but its impact in highlighting the problem of child sexual abuse as an appropriate subject for public discussion and examination was considerable.

Through the 1990s and early 2000s, feminist activists and commentators persevered in highlighting the 'ordinariness' of sexual violence whenever a high-profile case was featured in the media, and in communicating the significance of documentaries such as *States of Fear* (McKay, 2005: 241). In this way, the voices of survivors were amplified in the national discourse and feminists resisted attempts to allow the significance of disclosures of non-recent childhood sexual abuse to be lost in an urge to move on from the past.

Problems of remembrance and representation

In addition to the agency of survivors and the importance of feminist solidarity in amplifying survivors' voices, perhaps the clearest indication that non-recent childhood sexual abuse survivors are not ideal victims is the state's continued ambivalence towards them. No national memorial to survivors of child sexual abuse exists (despite the recommendation of the Commission to Inquire into Child Abuse [2009] to this effect). People who received redress payments are subject to criminalisation and the threat of imprisonment if they speak about their settlement,[21] and plans have been mooted to hold their records for 75 years, without any access for researchers.[22] This means that anyone wishing to delve into the past to search for survivors' and offenders' stories would be severely hampered. These approaches to the aftermath of disclosure demonstrate how institutionalised and entrenched active silencing mechanisms can be.

Furthermore, the Irish state seems not to have learned any of the lessons of the past 20 years of revelations of abuse. There continue to be grave failings in child protection: a recently published independent audit of more than 5,400 cases dealt with by the Gardaí over an eight-year period found serious failures in recording, a dearth of child-protection training for Gardaí and poor and limited communication, cooperation and coordination between Gardaí and Tusla (the Child and Family Agency). It also uncovered evidence of the repeated removal of some children by Gardaí from the same family circumstances, which suggested systemic failings of child protection (Gartland, 2017a). Lack of funding is a further problem; the Gardaí record between 17,000 and 20,000 suspected child abuse cases each year, yet there are only six social workers trained in joint interviewing (with Gardaí) of children for the entire country and there are fewer than 10 trained specialist Gardaí (Cusack, 2017; Gartland, 2017b). There is an urgent need for a more trauma-informed approach to how the criminal justice system deals with survivors of sexual violence (Ring, 2017b).

Conclusion

Using the notion of the ideal victim to explore the emergence of the survivors of non-recent childhood sexual abuse and the subsequent treatment of the justice claims of these survivors is revealing. In many ways, they may be understood as fitting the ideal victim trope: they achieved legitimate victim status because of their easily established innocence and the awfulness of the crimes perpetrated against them, along with the monstrification of those accused of abuse.

On closer examination, however, it appears that non-recent childhood sexual abuse survivors were far from ideal. In order for their claims for justice to be finally heard by the community, they had to expose their experiences to the court of public opinion. In doing so, they demonstrated great courage, resilience and agency. They also had the support of feminists, who prepared a space in public discourse in which their accounts could be heard and amplified their voices when they did speak. Therefore, the notion of the ideal victim is inadequate to describe the full complexity of the emergence of these stories because it ignores the agency and courage of survivors, as well as the role of feminist solidarity.

An ideal victim analysis also provides important insights into how Irish society views the phenomenon of child abuse, both in the present and in the past. The continued ambivalence and inadequate response to the suffering of survivors is indicative of a society that views them as being far from ideal and more like outsiders of a political community who are not full subjects of law (Lacey, 1998). Therefore, despite the seemingly profound political and legal responses to the revelations of non-recent childhood sexual abuse, strategies of denial and silencing continue to shape the construction of non-recent childhood sexual abuse survivors in Ireland.

Notes

[1] The quote is taken from Enda Kenny's speech in the wake of the report into abuse and the cover-up of abuse in the Cloyne Archdiocese (see RTE, 2011).

[2] Although Christie's article was written before the surge in interest in victims of non-recent childhood sexual abuse survivor, his work is very helpful in exploring the connections between victimhood as a political status and broader societal values and anxieties surrounding sexual violence against children.

[3] Ireland's equivalent to a prime minister.

[4] Implemented via the Commission to Inquire into Child Abuse Act 2000. The Commission found that abuse was endemic in both school systems.

[5] Under the Residential Institutions Redress Act 2002.

[6] In addition, reviews of child safeguarding practices were conducted by the Catholic Church (see National Board for Safeguarding Children in the Catholic Church in Ireland reviews and overview reports, available at: https://www.safeguarding.ie/publications).

[7] Under the Child Trafficking and Pornography Act 1998.

[8] Under the Criminal Justice (Withholding of Information on Offences against Children and Vulnerable Persons) Act 2012.

[9] Under the Sex Offenders Act 2001 and Criminal Law (Sexual Offences) Act 2006.

[10] Under the Criminal Law (Rape) (Amendment) Act 1990 (see also O'Malley, 2013).

[11] Others that might be mentioned are Ivan Payne, whose activities are examined in Commission of Investigation into Catholic Archdiocese of Dublin (Commission of Investigation, 2009: ch 24) and Joseph McColgan (see McKay, 1998).

[12] The Irish lower house of Parliament.

[13] Available at: https://www.hiainquiry.org/modules-0

[14] Harry Ferguson also gave expert evidence on the subject to the Supreme Court in 2006 in the case of *SH v DPP* 2006 IESC 575.

15 For a discussion about how hegemonic understandings of legitimate victim behaviour influenced the courts' decisions in applications brought by defendants in criminal prosecutions to halt the trial on account of the delay, see Ring (2017a).

16 Payne served four-and-a-half years of a six-year prison sentence and was released in 2002.

17 Several young men gave powerful and convincing testimony of having being abused by Fr Fortune: Colm O'Gorman, Pat Jackman, Damien McAleen and Donnacha MacGloinn (Crowe, 2006).

18 Mr O'Gorman is now the Director of Amnesty International (Ireland).

19 Ireland has one of the most restrictive abortion regimes in the world. Abortion is only available in Ireland when there is a real and substantial risk to the woman's life. Lack of clarity in the law as to when these circumstances pertain means that many women and girls in need of an abortion, for whatever reason, must travel to the UK (see Quilty et al, 2015). The law on abortion in Ireland is currently the subject of renewed public debate (see Bardon, 2017).

20 However, the constitutional lack of clarity about the rights of pregnant women in need of an abortion, and the rights of the foetus, continue to plague Irish women and Irish medical practice (see Enright et al, 2015; Quilty et al, 2015).

21 Sections 28(1) and 28(6) of the Residential Institutions Redress Act 2002.

22 Under the General Scheme of a Retention of Records Bill 2015.

References

Adriaenssens, P. (2010) *Rapport des activités de la Commission pour le traitement des plaintes pour abus sexuels dans une relation pastorale Commission pour le traitement, des plaints pour abus sexuel au cours d'une relation pastorale.*

Bacik, I., Maunsell, C. and Gogan, S. (1998) *The Legal Process and Victims of Rape*, Dublin: Dublin Rape Crisis Centre.

Bardon, S. (2017) 'Abortion committee members warn of long road to remove Eighth Amendment', *The Irish Times*, 20 December.

Carolan, M. (2016) 'Ex-nun Nora Wall settles damages case for miscarriage of justice', *The Irish Times*, 12 May.

Christie, N (1986) 'The ideal victim', in E.A. Fattah (ed), *From Crime Policy to Victim Policy. Reorienting the Justice System*, Basingstoke: Macmillan: 17–30.

Collins, L. (2017) 'Brendan Smyth's evil deeds can never be forgotten', *The Irish Independent*, 23 July.

Commission of Investigation (2009) *Report in the Catholic Archdiocese of Dublin*, Dublin: The Stationery Office. Available at: http://www.justice.ie/en/JELR/Pages/PB09000504 (accessed 30 July 2017).

Commission of Investigation (2010) *Report into Cloyne Archdiocese*, Dublin: The Stationery Office. Available at: http://www.justice.ie/en/JELR/Pages/Cloyne-Rpt (accessed 19 December 2017).

Commission to Inquire into Child Abuse (2009) *Final Report*, Dublin: Stationery Office.

Cooper, A. (1993) *The Kilkenny Incest Case, as Told to Kieron Wood*, Dublin: Poolbeg.

Crowe, C. (2006) 'On the Ferns Report', *Dublin Review*, 22: 5–26.

Cusack, J. (2017) 'Gardai given training in abuse victim interviews', *The Sunday Independent*, 12 May.

Deetman, W., Daijer, N., Kalbfleisch, P., Merckelbach, H., Monteiro, M. and De Vries, G. (2011) *Sexual Abuse of Minors in the Roman Catholic Church* [*Seksueel Misbruik van Minderjarigen in de Rooms Katholieke Kerk*], Amsterdam: Balans.

Department of Justice, Equality and Law Reform (2005) *Report of the Ferns Inquiry*, Dublin: The Stationery Office.

Donelly, A. (2002) 'Mother believes son's suicide linked to Fr. Fortune Unanswered questions', *Irish Independent*, 29 March.

Dukelow, F. and Considine, M. (2017) *Irish Social Policy* (2nd edition), Bristol: Policy Press.

Enright, M., Conway, V., de Londras, F., Donnelly, M., Fletcher, F. et al (2015) 'Abortion law reform in Ireland: a model for change', *feminists@law*, 5(1).

Fennell, C. (1993) 'Criminal law & the criminal justice system: women as victim (criminal law & the criminal justice system: women as accused)', in A. Connolly (ed) *Gender and the Law in Ireland*, Dublin: Oak Tree Press, pp 151–71.

Ferguson, H. (1995) 'The paedophile priest: a deconstruction', *Studies*, 84(334): 247–57.

Ferriter, D. (2009) *Occasions of Sin*, Dublin: Profile Books.

Gallen, J. (forthcoming) 'Historical abuse and the statute of limitations', *Statute Law Review*,. Available at: https://doi.org/10.1093/slr/hmw045

Gartland, F. (2017a) 'Child-protection audit "a wake-up call" for society, report author says', *The Irish Times*, 29 May.

Gartland, F. (2017b) 'Therapy units criticise Garda handling of child interviews', *The Irish Times*, 28 June.

Holohan, C. (2011) *In Plain Sight. Responding to the Ferns, Ryan, Murphy, and Cloyne Reports*, Dublin: Amnesty International.

Howes, M. (2002) 'Public discourse, private reflection: 1916–1970', in A. Bourke (ed) *The Field Day Anthology of Irish Writing* (vol 4), Cork: Cork University Press, pp 923–30.

Independent Inquiry into Child Sexual Abuse (2017) 'About us'. Available at: https://www.iicsa.org.uk/about-us (accessed 30 July 2017).

Inglis, T. (1998) *Moral Monopoly: The Rise and Fall of the Catholic Church in Ireland*, Dublin: University College Dublin Press.

John Jay College of Criminal Justice (2004) *The Nature and Scope of the Problem of Sexual Abuse of Minors by Catholic Priests and Deacons in the United States*, New York, NY: United States Conference of Catholic Bishops, City University of New York.

Kelly, L. (2015) 'Victim of paedophile Brendan Smyth: "I still don't know where the pictures are that he took of my body"', *The Irish Independent*, 23 June. Available at: https://www.independent.ie/irish-news/news/victim-of-paedophile-brendan-smyth-i-still-dont-know-where-the-pictures-are-that-he-took-of-my-body-31323251.html

Lacey, N. (1998) *Unspeakable Subjects. Feminist Essays in Legal and Social Theory*, Oxford: Hart.

Law Reform Commission of Ireland (1990) *Report on Child Sexual Abuse* (LRC 32-1990), Dublin: Stationery Office.

Lentin, L. (1996) *Dear Daughter* (documentary-drama), Dublin: Radio and Television of Ireland (RTE) and The Irish Film Board.

McAlinden, A.-M. (2014) 'Deconstructing victim and offender identities in discourses on child sexual abuse: hierarchies, blame and the good/evil dialectic', *British Journal of Criminology*, 54(2): 180–98.

McKay, S. (1998) *Sophia's Story*, Dublin: Gill and Macmillan.

McKay, S. (2005) *Without Fear. 25 Years of the Dublin Rape Crisis Centre*, Dublin: New Island Books.

McLaughlin, B. (2002) 'To hell in Connaught', *The Sunday Independent*, 22 December.

McMahon, B. (2015) *Report of the Working Group to Report to Government on Improvements to the Protection Process, Including Direct Provision and Supports to Asylum Seekers*, Dublin: Stationery Office. Available at: http://www.justice.ie/en/JELR (accessed 31 July 2017).

Moore, C. (1995) *Betrayal of Trust: The Father Brendan Smyth Affair and the Catholic Church*, Dublin: Marino.

Newman, C (2002) 'Imposing a life sentence for the crime of rape is extremely rare', *The Irish Times*, 12 October, p 4.

O'Brien, C. (2009) 'Garda apologises for failure', *The Irish Times*, 26 November.

O'Faoláin, N. (1993) 'Next time there has to be someone who can say "Well, I tried. I did my best"', *The Irish Times*, 3 June.

O'Leary, O. (2006) *Party Animals*, Dublin: O'Brien Press.

O'Malley, T. (2013) *Sexual Offences. Law Policy and Punishment* (2nd edn), Dublin: Round Hall.

One in Four (2016) 'Annual Report 2015', Dublin. Available at: http://www.oneinfour.ie/content/resources/One_in_Four_Annual_Report_2015.pdf (accessed 31 July 2017).

O'Sullivan, E. (2002) '"This otherwise delicate subject": child sexual abuse in early twentieth-century Ireland', in P. O'Mahony (ed) *Criminal Justice in Ireland*, Dublin: Institute of Public Administration, pp 176–202.

O'Sullivan, C. (2008) 'The nun, the rape charge and the miscarriage of justice', *Northern Ireland Legal Quarterly*, 59(3): 305–25.

Pine, E. (2010) *The Politics of Irish Memory: Performing Remembrance in Contemporary Irish Culture*, Basingstoke: Palgrave Macmillan.

Quilty, A., Kennedy, S. and Conlon, C. (2015) *The Abortion Papers Volume 2*, Cork: Cork University Press.

Raftery, M. (1999) *States of Fear* (documentary television series), Dublin: Raidió Teilifís Éireann (RTÉ).

Ring, S. (2009) 'Beyond the reach of justice? Complainant delay in historic child sexual abuse cases and the right to a fair trial', *Judicial Studies Institute Journal*, 2: 162–203.

Ring, S. (2017a) 'The victim of historical child sexual abuse in the Irish courts 1999–2006', *Social and Legal Studies*, 26(5): 562–80.

Ring, S. (2017b) 'Trauma and the construction of suffering in Irish historical child sexual abuse prosecutions', *International Journal for Crime, Justice and Social Democracy*, 6(3): 88–103.

Rock, P. (1998) 'Murderers, victims and "survivors"', *British Journal of Criminology*, 38(2): 185–200.

Royal Commission into Institutional Responses to Child Sexual Abuse (2017) 'About us'. Available at: https://www.childabuseroyalcommission.gov.au/about-us

RTÉ (Raidió Teilifís Éireann) (1992) 'An internment camp for pregnant young women', television news report. Available at: http://www.rte.ie/archives/exhibitions/1666-women-and-society/459005-x-case-protest-march/

RTÉ (2011) 'Enda Kenny speech on Cloyne Report'. Available at: https://www.rte.ie/news/2011/0720/303965-cloyne1/

Scottish Child Abuse Inquiry (2017) 'About the inquiry'. Available at: https://www.childabuseinquiry.scot/about-the-inquiry/

Sgroi, S. (1999) 'The McColgan case: increasing public awareness of professional responsibility for protecting children from physical and sexual abuse in the Republic of Ireland', *Journal of Child Sexual Abuse*, 8(1): 113–27.

Smith, J.M. (2004) 'The politics of sexual knowledge: the origins of Ireland's containment culture and the Carrigan Report (1931)', *Journal of the History of Sexuality*, 13(2): 208–33.

South Eastern Health Board (1993) *Kilkenny Incest Investigation Report*, Dublin: The Stationery Office. Available at: http://www.lenus.ie/hse/bitstream/10147/46278/4/zkilkennyincestinvestigation.pdf (accessed 7 July 2017).

Stevenson, K. (2000) 'Unequivocal victims: the historical roots of the mystification of the female complainant in rape cases', *Feminist Legal Studies*, 8: 343–66.

The Irish Times, (1992) 'Text of President's statement', 20 February, p 6.

The Irish Times (2017) 'Victims of paedophile priest Brendan Smyth to get new court hearing', 23 March. Available at: https://www.irishtimes.com/news/crime-and-law/courts/high-court/victims-of-paedophile-priest-brendan-smyth-to-get-new-court-hearing-1.3022127

Walsh, D. and Liddy, R. (1989) *Surviving Sexual Abuse*, Dublin: Attic.

EIGHT

'Idealising' domestic violence victims

Marian Duggan

Introduction

Understanding and responding to domestic violence victimisation has long been a contested issue for feminist sociologists, legal theorists, criminologists and victimologists alike. A large part of the discussion has focused on enacting legal protections and redress for victims, which, in turn, has required that dominant myths and stereotypes be challenged in order for victims to be deemed worthy of criminal justice recognition and intervention in the first place. Socio-political rhetoric around domestic violence and abuse has traditionally posed one fundamental question: *'Why didn't she leave?'*. Much is rendered evident in this short sentence: that the onus is on the victim to act; that the victim is perceived to be female; that the victim had the opportunity and ability to leave; that the victim had somewhere to go; and that the victim is the only one who would (or should) be leaving. Rarely do we hear sentiments querying why the perpetrator acted as they did, or continued in this vein. Perhaps the most worrying element of this question is the implication that by leaving, the victim would be in a better – *safer* – position. Decades of feminist research has indicated otherwise: for many women, leaving a violent partner increases their vulnerability and may result in the perpetrator's violence towards them becoming fatal (Lees, 2000; Humphries and Thiara, 2002; Krug et al, 2002).

This was certainly the case for Clare Wood, who was murdered by her ex-partner, George Appleton, in 2009. Like a growing number of modern couples, Clare had met George online; they dated for about 18 months before she ended the relationship on account of his serial unfaithfulness. George had also been abusive towards Clare on several occasions while they were together. As is the case with many domestically abusive situations, this violence escalated following their split. During the short time in which they were separated, Clare contacted Greater Manchester Police at least five times with allegations that indicated George's increasingly violent behaviour. She reported a variety of instances, from criminal damage and harassment, through to sexual assault and making threats to kill. In the final, fatal incident, George strangled Clare and set her body alight before taking his own life.

Despite her repeated contact with the police, Clare remained unaware of George's history of violence against women. This included three previous convictions under the Protection from Harassment Act 1997 and a prison sentence for one particularly brutal assault on a former partner. Like many victims of domestic abuse, the only evidence Clare had to go on about his potentiality for increased harm was the escalation in victimisation that she herself was experiencing. This case was a key catalyst for the implementation of the Domestic Violence Disclosure Scheme (DVDS), known colloquially as 'Clare's Law' in her memory. It is one of several efforts to reduce domestic violence in the UK that adopt an early intervention approach. The DVDS addresses a gap highlighted in Clare's case, in that it permits members of the public to apply to the police for information if they have concerns about a person's propensity for domestic violence. It is a policy that, according to Clare's father, Michael, might have saved her life (*The Telegraph*, 2012).

While it is difficult (and relatively early) to know whether or not this scheme is, indeed, reducing domestic violence, concerns have been raised about targeting a 'background-checking' policy such as this at *domestic violence* victims specifically (Duggan, 2012). Drawing on Christie's (1986) exploration of an ideal victim concept, this chapter demonstrates how the DVDS may be putting applicants at greater risk of harm as a result of several key factors. The analysis presented in this chapter provides a critical review of how the domestic violence victim's status is (re-)conceptualised through the policy's prioritisation of the 'active and engaged applicant' – a status that contrasts decades of feminist research suggesting that the nature and impact of domestic violence *lessens* a victim's ability to seek help. Notions of responsibility, blame and risk are evaluated in relation to Christie's 'ideal victim' framework to explore the potential 'idealisation' of the compliant domestic violence victim and the exclusionary impact that this policy has on 'non-ideal' victims.

Domestic violence victimisation and prevention

At present, domestic violence per se is not explicitly criminalised in English criminal law (Platek, 2009); indeed, a common definition of this concept was only agreed upon in 2004, though has been subject to revision since. As it currently stands, the UK government's definition of domestic violence includes a range of interpersonal relationships, recognising familial abuse as well as romantic relationships. It is outlined on the Home Office website as:

> any incident or pattern of incidents of controlling, coercive, threatening behaviour, violence or abuse between those aged 16 or over who are, or have been, intimate partners or family members regardless of gender or sexuality. The abuse can encompass, but is not limited to: psychological; physical; sexual; financial; emotional.[1]

Domestic violence victimisation has a contentious history in criminal justice practice and policy. For decades, victim-blaming discourses and ideologies sought to find fault with the (usually female) victim; this both negated and excused the actions of the (usually male) perpetrator while also illustrating the impunity with which such victimisation could take place. This links to the discussion of power (and 'counter-powers') highlighted by Christie; dominant discourses that function to silence the knowledge and truth professed by the otherwise powerless have both informed and reinforced cultural stereotypes about how, why, when and to whom domestic violence occurs (see Donovan and Barnes, this volume). Despite feminist efforts to highlight the experiences of those suffering from interpersonal abuse meted out by partners, changes to criminal justice responses proved to be a long and slow process. Reasons for this can be found in wider criminological research, which indicated that domestic violence was considered 'rubbish work' in policing circles, analogous to dealing with drug users, prostitutes and the homeless (Reiner, 1990). This, coupled with cultural stereotypes that victims had somehow provoked or deserved the abuse, meant that few investigations and even fewer prosecutions ensued, despite a growing awareness of the breadth of the problem (Walby and Allen, 2004).

Acknowledging the negativity surrounding domestic violence in particular, Christie (1986: 20) illustrates how such disturbances may be seen by some as both a literal and metaphorical 'noise in the house', adding that this noise 'does not create good victims. Noise is something that needs to be muffled'. In the UK, recent political developments, such as the expansion of the official definition of domestic violence to include coercive control and recognise that it can apply to younger people, have begun to reflect the need for development and change in the state's response to domestic violence. However, although substantial amounts of feminist research have succeeded in putting domestic violence on the legislative and socio-political map, the impact of this in actually reducing victimisation is perhaps less successful than desired. Little appears to have changed in terms of statistics: one in four women experience domestic violence in their lifetimes (Council of Europe, 2002); a third of domestic violence cases start during a woman's pregnancy (Lewis and Drife, 2001, 2005); women are significantly more likely than men to be killed by a current or former partner (Krug et al, 2002); and in the UK, domestic violence accounts for roughly a third of all recorded violent crime (ONS, 2017), with an average of two women a week being killed by a current or former partner (Povey, 2005).

What *has* changed is the incremental steps being taken towards improving the criminal justice response to domestic violence victims. Several significant developments in statutory approaches have occurred in recent years. These include: the establishment of multi-agency working; the establishment of specialist domestic violence courts; enhanced criminalisation for breaches of civil and criminal sanctions (such as non-molestation and occupation orders); enhanced victim status through demarcation as a 'vulnerable/intimidated witness'; and better recording of domestic violence offenders. Two key events can be seen as having informed these changes. First, the Beijing *Platform for Action* (UN Women, 1995) outlined several strategic objectives to promote the human rights of women, with which UK policies were aligned. Second, the UK general election manifesto upon which Labour won in 1997 focused heavily on addressing domestic violence (Matczak et al, 2011: 3). Importantly, a key focus was on prevention and support; this indicated that recommendations arising from (largely feminist) research into this area were being heeded and the need for interventions beyond enhanced criminalisation was being acknowledged.

Specialist support was also put in place through the creation of Independent Domestic Violence Advisers (IDVAs) to work with high-risk victims. IDVAs function as a primary point of contact; they work with clients (victims) from the point of crisis, assessing levels of risk, developing safety plans and overseeing practical short- and long-term solutions to safeguard clients and, where relevant, their children. These measures highlight the shift in focus towards the greater care of and engagement with victims, in addition to the traditional punitive focus that centred on the offender. Enhancing victim provisions was particularly necessary as it was increasingly recognised that many victims of domestic violence were reluctant to pursue justice through the courts for reasons that included the fear of retaliation or ostracism (from friends and/or family), or losing custody of their children (if the risk posed to them from the offender was deemed to extend to dependants) (Walby and Allen, 2004).

The Domestic Violence Disclosure Scheme

Clare Wood's case proved to be a catalyst for the implementation of the DVDS as a result of several factors. The Independent Police Complaints Commission (IPCC) investigation into Greater Manchester Police's handing of Clare's case deemed that there had been significant failings on their part (though these stopped short of causing her death). The coroner in Clare's case suggested in her report that a disclosure process ought to be established so that people could find out whether or not a person that they were in a relationship with had a history of violence towards previous partners, stating:

> subject to appropriate risk assessment and safeguard, I recommend that consideration should be given to the disclosure of such convictions and their circumstances to potential victims in order that they can make informed choices about matters affecting their safety and that of their children. (Home Office, 2013: 2)

This proposal was supported by Clare's father, who joined forces with a UK national newspaper (*The Daily Mail*) to lobby for the policy to be implemented. This relationship between high-profile, emotive cases and subsequent criminal justice developments has become more notable in recent years. Having a family member seek justice and the prevention of similar harm to others is not unusual, but it is usually done in a manner that reinforces the 'feminisation of victimisation' through an idealised notion of a victim figurehead (Duggan and Heap, 2014). In Clare's case, much like other 'named cases' such as Sarah's Law (the Sex Offender Register, named after murder victim Sarah Payne) and Megan's Law (the Sex Offender Register in the US, named after murder victim Megan Kanka), the female victim has paid the ultimate price at the hands of the male assailant while also demonstrating many characteristics of Christie's ideal victim typology at the point of their death.

The popularity of this national campaign was hard for the government to ignore; in 2011, they issued a 10-week consultation process whereby members of the public were invited to provide their views on the proposed DVDS. Of the 259 responses received, perhaps the most notable were from Refuge and Women's Aid, two key UK domestic abuse organisations. Both cited their opposition to the proposed policy on the grounds of perceived inefficiency and a significant deficit in the resourcing needed to match the likely enhanced demands that would be placed on both the police and domestic abuse organisations. Nevertheless, the government launched the DVDS as a 14-month pilot project during 2012–13 in four police force areas: Greater Manchester, Gwent, Wiltshire and Nottinghamshire. The Home Office evaluation of this pilot indicated a saving of £260 million per year: an estimated 500 requests for information under the DVDS would cost £0.39 million in police officer and IDVA time but would reduce domestic violence by 0.2% annually (Home Office, 2011: 12). This was an attractive prospect given that the Conservative–Liberal Democrat Coalition had promised a £28 million budget and a renewed focus on victims, prevention and localised responses to domestic violence. Therefore, from the government's perspective, there were clear economic benefits to press ahead with the policy on a national level.

On 8 March 2014, Theresa May (then Home Secretary) announced the national implementation of the DVDS across England and Wales. Her decision to choose International Women's Day as the launch date provided some indication of the target audience for this policy, as did the media's colloquial reference to it as 'Clare's Law'. Whereas previous disclosure routes were largely *reactive* (in that they responded to incidents of domestic violence that had already taken place), the DVDS proposed a more *proactive*, early interventionist mechanism designed to reduce the likelihood of incidents. To do this, the DVDS offers people 'the right to ask' about a person's history. The applicant, either the individual whose safety is in question (person 'A') or a concerned third party (person 'C'), can request relevant information about someone (person 'B', also known as the 'subject'). The information can include past allegations, arrests, charges, convictions and failed prosecutions for domestic violence-related behaviour, and can be disclosed only on the basis that doing so is to prevent future domestic (physical, sexual, psychological, etc) violence. Some parity exists across England and Wales (which are considered as a singular unit in legislative terms) and Scotland with regards to the DVDS, with the latter country implementing their version of the policy in 2015. At the time of writing (in 2017), Northern Ireland had not adopted any measures reminiscent of the DVDS, though calls for this to be considered have been made by those working with domestic violence victims in the region.

In 2016, the Home Office published an evaluation of the first year of the DVDS's national operation. All 43 police forces were represented, as were the findings from workshops undertaken with 29 practitioners (statutory and third sector) who had different levels of involvement with the policy. The report outlined its remit early on, stating that it was 'not designed to consider any impact DVDS may have had on domestic violence and abuse victims or estimate the "value for money", but rather to assess how it was operating and how it might be further developed' (Home Office, 2016: 3). A total of 4,724 applications had been received and 1,938 disclosures made during the period from 8 March to 31 December 2014. Findings from the practitioner workshops indicated that in dealing with these, there was evidence of 'good practice emerging', such as markers being placed on the Police National Computer following a disclosure in order to 'alert other officers to an individual potentially at high risk of domestic violence or abuse' (Home Office, 2016: 4). Enhancing front-line officers' knowledge and understanding of the DVDS was also identified as a good way of promoting it to the public in a way that may increase their access to it, suggesting that the policy was here to stay for the time being (Home Office, 2016: 4).

In sum, the Home Office evaluation saw clear benefits with the way in which the policy was operating in terms of data management, sharing and production. However, a key concern for feminist and domestic violence researchers is victim safety. The DVDS was designed and promoted as encouraging individuals 'to take responsibility for safety of the victim'; as will be demonstrated in this chapter, this safety can only be partially addressed and, in some cases, may be compromised as a result of a victim's attempts to access DVDS information. The remainder of this chapter draws on ongoing research into the DVDS, assessing elements of the policy through Christie's ideal victim framework. In doing so, it evidences issues of responsibility, blame and risk that underpin emerging concerns around the 'idealising' of domestic violence victims under this scheme.

Victim responsibilisation

One of the first things Christie (1986: 18) notes in his chapter is that 'being a victim is not a thing, an objective phenomenon. It will not be the same to all people in situations externally described as being the "same"'. Domestic violence excellently exemplifies this point; the subjective perspective of the victim as to the nature or seriousness of their situation may be impeded by a range of internal and external factors. Studies have indicated an association between the way in which female victims of domestic violence assess risk and their lived experiences of subsequent victimisation (Weisz et al, 2000; Cattaneo et al, 2007). A key factor is the level of restrictive social, economic and psychological monitoring by a partner during the relationship (what is now recognised in UK legislation as 'coercive control'). Women whose partners exercised greater control over broader aspects of their lives were more likely to experience ongoing repeat victimisation as a result of related issues, such as not recognising the abuse, not being able to challenge it or being fearful of doing so. This suggests that as the victim gradually realises that they are experiencing harmful and potentially dangerous behaviours, their capacity to act may simultaneously diminish as their ability to seek help is impeded by their partner. In other words, for some victims, the more certain they become that they need help, the less able they are to access it.

It could be argued that it is these same victims who are expected to proactively avail themselves of the information and safeguarding measures offered by the DVDS. The nature of the 'right to ask' aspect of the policy infers that an applicant will be alerted to the potential for an escalation in violence by virtue of their partner's concerning behaviour, or perhaps through being informed about their partner's violent past by someone else (possibly even their partner). The assumption here is that a person will recognise what they are experiencing as being a cause for concern. A further assumption is that they will take steps to do something about it, and in the case of the DVDS, that they will know that this particular policy exists. However, while it is possible that people with previous experiences of domestic violence victimisation may be more attuned to potentially worrying signals as a result of their familiarity with prior incidents, domestic violence varies considerably in its nature and scope, so the behaviours experienced in a past relationship may not necessarily be mirrored by a future partner. Similarly, their current partner's actions may be varied or inconsistent. The abuse may also involve directly addressing the victim's concerns by way of 'gaslighting': this is the psychological manipulation of a person that causes them to doubt their own sanity (and any potential suspicions they may have about a partner).

Not only is the nature, type and impact of domestic violence victimisation incredibly varied, but so too are the thresholds for tolerance of those subjected to it. Depending on a person's background, they may be alerted to potential dangers early on in a relationship or conversely may endure a higher level of abuse before addressing the problematic behaviour. This makes knowing *when* to access available information difficult. The applicant might decide to apply as soon as they feel that they have cause for concern; alternatively, they might adopt the 'wait and see' approach to assess changes in the frequency, severity or outcome of their partner's behaviour. Ultimately, the policy leaves the decision about if and when to apply for a disclosure up to the victim, but it is important to be aware that many victims do not report *actual* instances of domestic violence, never mind suspicions about it.

Attributing blame

The potential for enhanced victim blaming through the DVDS is also of concern. Christie's (1986: 18) suggestion that it may be possible to see victimisation or one's disposition towards being victimised as a 'personality trait' was similar to the (often critiqued) work of earlier victimologists (such as Von Hentig, 1940, 1948; Mendelsohn, 1947; Wolfgang, 1958; Amir, 1967, 1971). Applying such notions to domestic violence specifically, Lenore Walker's (1979) work on the 'battered woman syndrome' suggested that some people may have a predisposition to victimisation as a result of abused partners taking on a form of 'learned behaviour'. While this was useful in part to dispel myths around abused women 'liking' the violence that they experienced (often inferred through the woman's tendency to remain with the abuser or be subjected to repeat victimisation from subsequent partners), Walker's work was problematically influential in creating a disempowered victim identity that largely eradicated (or obstructed) the woman's autonomy. Not all women victims of domestic violence fit this 'learned helplessness' model; therefore, the potentiality for victim blaming for not seeking out help remains high.

Scholarly discussions around the 'feminisation of victimisation' have highlighted evidence of blame (rather than sympathy) being attributed to female victims of sexual and domestic interpersonal crimes (Bryant and Spencer, 2003; Valor-Segura et al, 2011). Unlike with other types of criminal victimisation, a level of culpability is often implied in the discourse towards women who are persecuted by an intimate (male) partner. Popular rhetoric already focuses on the perceived culpability of women who encounter a succession of violent partners (in a way not applied to men who repeatedly victimise), often suggesting that she should 'know better'. Not only is this unhelpful and stigmatising, but it also serves to deflect attention from the predatory or repeat abuser.

The volatile nature of domestically abusive relationships also accounts for the back-and-forth nature that a couple may go through with respect to being together. In cases where the perpetrator is particularly controlling or domineering, the victim may be convinced that they are better off with the abusive partner as they believe that no one else will want them, or they cannot function independently. For victims with traumatic backgrounds, or who have been through difficult situations, this form of emotional blackmail can be very persuasive in their decisions to remain with an abusive partner. Furthermore, the normalisation of interactions within the remit of what is expected (by the victim) or what is directed (by the perpetrator) means that many domestically abusive situations may not come to light without some form of third-party intervention as, in some cases, the victimised partner is often the last person to realise the situation that they are in.

Aside from inferred personality traits, there may be external factors impeding a person's ability to seek information, advice or escape. Upon closer scrutiny, the old adage of 'Why doesn't she just leave?' overlooks many hidden barriers to exiting an abusive or controlling relationship that may make the decision to leave a difficult one for a victimised partner. Depending on the housing arrangements, the partner who is being abused might be the person in whose name the tenancy or housing documents are registered. Part of the abuser's controlling nature may include having all of the utilities in the abused person's name, meaning that unless they are able to cancel contracts, they are still economically liable for these costs if they do flee the family home. Therefore, they might not be in a position to 'just leave' or leave on a permanent basis. If there are children involved, considerations about their schooling (if of school age) or friendship groups may preclude a person from exiting a volatile relationship. Economics also play a significant part; there are fewer emergency refuge beds (either for single people or those with children) available and not always in the locality, meaning that transport costs will be incurred. Being able to sustain oneself (and any dependants) is a consideration when fleeing abuse, as is the potential impact on any employment a person might have. Similarly, a person's social and family support network may be in the locality in which they live, making moving away from this more difficult.

All of the issues mentioned earlier indicate the hardships facing an abused person who is weighing up the decision to seek out information via the DVDS, to act on this or to leave. As funding for domestic violence refuges, services, organisations, support and so forth continues to diminish, it is perhaps more pertinent to ask 'Where can she go?'.

Yet, societal discourse remains focused on the abused person's decision (rather than *ability*) to stay or remain in the relationship. Rarely is the focus on the perpetrator to leave (or desist).

Risk enhancement

As Christie (1986: 21) cautions, increased independence and the ability to take control of a situation means that some may view victimisation as desired or provoked if such situations are not duly altered given the opportunity. However, people who request information about a partner under the DVDS may be put at greater risk of harm in a number of ways as a direct result of engaging with this policy.

Part of the DVDS decision-making process involves weighing up the applicant's risk of harm from the subject against the subject's breach of privacy as the result of a disclosure. Ordinarily, the applicant ('A') should be in an intimate relationship with the subject ('B') (or they should be a relevant third party, 'C') in order to be able to request information. The disclosure criteria states that applicants who are requesting information on a partner are required to notify the police if they separate from them in the interim period (as their request is being processed) as this may nullify their application.[2] Information cannot be disclosed if they have separated from their partner as this would undermine the risk threshold and render the breaching of the subject's privacy unlawful. As the DVDS decision-making process can take up to six weeks, this relationship status requirement may come at a cost to the safety of the applicant. Furthermore, technically, the subject should be told that an application has been made about them; however, if doing so is likely to escalate the risk of harm to the applicant, then they need not be consulted. If the subject *is* informed about the application, then owing to the intimacy clause, they will be able to identify who has requested the disclosure.

Upon receiving the disclosure information, the applicant is faced with a choice to either remain in the relationship or terminate it. A logical decision may be to separate from their partner, but they may be unaware that separation does not guarantee their safety. Indeed, Clare Wood was not in a relationship with George Appleton when he murdered her. Studies have long indicated that for some women, the risk of incurring violent (including fatal) victimisation from a male partner increases as a result of her attempts to seek a temporary separation or to exit the relationship entirely (Fleury et al, 2000; Dobash et al, 2007). News media claims along the lines that the DVDS is helping victims to 'escape' may contribute to this decision to leave, but these are misleading. At present, no record is kept (by the police or anyone else) of what – if any – actions a victim took following a disclosure. Therefore, it is currently unknown what – if any – impact this policy is having on victims' safety. Nonetheless, the idealised victim perhaps *would*, indeed, terminate the relationship; conversely, this would leave the perpetrator free to move on to a new partner, meaning that the risk of violence is not necessarily reduced, but rather deflected.

Regardless of whether the person leaves or stays, once they have the information, it is vital to ensure that safeguarding measures are not just focused on the short term, but consider the potential long-term implications on the applicant and their dependants. This usually means applicant involvement with domestic violence specialist support organisations. However, Grace (2015) highlights that the evaluation questionnaire used in the Home Office assessment report into the pilot study showed that out of 111 disclosures, only four recipients indicated that they had contacted support services following the disclosure. No reasons were given for such a low take-up, but it is important to recognise that the ongoing impact of austerity measures may be negatively impacting on engagement with the community voluntary sector. Reductions in services and the capacity to provide support may deter some applicants from accessing resources if they feel that their needs are less serious by comparison to others. Therefore, it is necessary to assess the availability and accessibility of support structures for victims who may seek out information via the DVDS but then find that they are in an impossible situation with regards to what to do next.

Conclusion: contradictions to the 'ideal victim' concept

It could be argued that the 'ideal victim' concept is not a helpful one in cases of domestic violence as the typology is undermined in almost every way. Victims are not necessarily weak in terms of physical or psychological fortitude; certainly, victims (or those at risk of victimisation) who engage with the DVDS are difficult to cast as weak given that they are proactively seeking out safeguarding measures. The notion of the 'weak' victim also might not resonate with male victims of domestic violence, who may already be dissuaded from interacting with the DVDS as a result of the term 'Clare's Law'. Victims may or may not be carrying out respectable projects; indeed, perhaps the very nature of checking up on a partner's past could be seen by some as undermining the respect needed for a trusting relationship. Victims are not necessarily viewed as being without blame given the historically patriarchal nature of seeking to attribute blame for domestic violence to the victim themselves. Furthermore, if there have been repeat incidents and the victim has remained in the relationship or living with the perpetrator, blame is often attributed more readily in such circumstances. If the premise of a policy such as the DVDS is to allow a person to make an 'informed decision' about the future of their relationship, then it is important that they are made aware that the abuse will not necessarily desist just because they are no longer in a relationship with the perpetrator.

Towards the end of his analysis, Christie (1986: 29) turns his attention to the notion of the 'ideal offender', indicating how most offenders are instead 'non-ideal', which causes problems for criminologists and the public alike. With regards to domestic violence offenders in particular, it is difficult to denote what would be an ideal situation; thus, most – if not all – instances are likely to be 'non-ideal' in Christie's terms. By the very nature of this type of violence, the offender is not a stranger to the victim. They are not always big and/or bad; indeed, physicality may be of little importance when emotional, financial or psychological abuse is a factor. People in the offender's social circle or workplace may not recognise them as being someone capable of inflicting such victimisation on a loved one as they have not been witness to this aspect of their personality. Such assumptions, coupled with the private setting in which much of the victimisation takes place, assisted in keeping domestic violence hidden from the public imagination for so long; therefore, it is important that knowledge of this feeds into policies that seek to effect positive, useful change with regards to reducing domestic violence.

Note
[1] See https://www.gov.uk/guidance/domestic-violence-and-abuse.
[2] At the point of writing, this separation stipulation appeared to be under review within the Home Office.

References

Amir, M. (1967) 'Victim precipitated forcible rape', *Journal of Criminal Law, Criminology and Police Science*, 58(4): 493–502.

Amir, M. (1971) *Patterns in Forcible Rape*, Chicago, IL: University of Chicago Press.

Bryant, S. and Spencer, G. (2003) 'University students' attitudes about attributing blame in domestic violence', *Journal of Family Violence*, 18(6): 369–76.

Cattaneo, L., Bell, M., Goodman, L. and Dutton M. (2007) 'Intimate partner violence victims' accuracy in assessing their risk of re-abuse', *Journal of Family Violence*, 22: 429–40.

Christie, N. (1986) 'The ideal victim', in E.A. Fattah (eds) *From Crime Policy to Victim Policy*, London: Macmillan.

Council of Europe (2002) *Recommendation of the Committee of Ministers to Member States on the Protection of Women against Violence*, Strasbourg: France Council of Europe.

Dobash, R., Dobash, R., Cavanagh, K. and Medina-Ariza, J. (2007) 'Lethal and nonlethal violence against an intimate female partner', *Violence Against Women*, 13: 329–53.

Duggan, M. (2012) 'Using victims' voices to prevent violence against women: a critique', *British Journal of Community Justice*, 10(2): 25–38.

Duggan, M. and Heap, V. (2014) *Administrating Victimization: The Politics of Anti-Social Behaviour and Hate Crime Policy*, Basingstoke: Palgrave Macmillan.

Fleury, R., Sullivan, C. and Bybee, D. (2000) 'When ending the relationships does not end the violence: women's experiences of violence by former partners', *Violence Against Women*, 6: 1363–83.

Grace, J. (2015) 'Clare's Law, or the national Domestic Violence Disclosure Scheme: the contested legalities of criminality information sharing', *The Journal of Criminal Law*, 79(1): 36–45.

Home Office (2011) 'Domestic Violence Disclosure Scheme Pilot Assessment'. Available at: https://www.gov.uk/government/uploads/system/uploads/attachment_data/file/260894/DVDS_assessment_report.pdf (accessed 10 March 2018).

Home Office (2013) *Domestic Violence Disclosure Scheme (DVDS) Pilot Assessment*, London: Home Office.

Home Office (2016) *Domestic Violence Disclosure Scheme (DVDS): One Year on – Home Office Assessment of National Roll Out*, London: Home Office.

Humphreys, C. and Thiara, R. (2002) *Routes to Safety: Protection Issues Facing Abused Women and Children and the Role of Outreach Services*, Bristol: Women's Aid Federation of England.

Krug, E., Dahlberg, L., Mercy, J., Zwi, A. and Lozano, R. (eds) (2002) *World Report on Violence and Health*, Geneva: World Health Organization.

Lees, S. (2000) 'Marital rape and marital murder', in J. Hanmer and N. Itzin (eds) *Home Truths about Domestic Violence: Feminist Influences on Policy and Practice: A Reader*, London: Routledge.

Lewis, G. and Drife, J. (2001) *Why Mothers Die: Report from the Confidential Enquiries into Maternal Deaths in the UK 1997–9; Commissioned by Department of Health from RCOG and NICE*, London: Royal College of Obstetricians and Gynaecologists Press.

Lewis, G. and Drife, J. (2005) *Why Mothers Die 2000–2002: Report on Confidential Enquiries into Maternal Deaths in the United Kingdom*, London: CEMACH.

Matczack, A., Hatzidimitriadou, E. and Lindsay, J. (2011) *Review of Domestic Violence Policies in England and Wales*, London: Kingston University and St George's University of London.

Mendelsohn, B. (1947) 'New biosocial horizons: victimology', *American Law Review*, 13: 649.

Office for National Statistics (ONS) (2017) 'Domestic Abuse in England and Wales: Year Ending March 2017'. Available at: https://www.ons.gov.uk/peoplepopulationandcommunity/crimeandjustice/bulletins/domesticabuseinenglandandwales/yearendingmarch2017 (accessed 10 March 2018).

Platek, M. (2009) 'Criminal law models of domestic violence prevention', *Archives of Criminology*, 601–61.

Povey, D. (ed) (2005) *Crime in England and Wales 2003/2004: Supplementary Volume 1: Homicide and Gun Crime*, Home Office Statistical Bulletin No. 02/05, London: Home Office.

Reiner, R. (1990) *The Politics of the Police*, Oxford: Oxford University Press.

The Telegraph (2012) 'Father of domestic killing victim: "Clare's Law" would have saved my daughter', 5 March. Available at: http://www.telegraph.co.uk/news/uknews/law-and-order/9122935/Father-of-domestic-killing-victim-Clares-Law-would-have-saved-my-daughter.html (accessed 1 May 2017).

Valour-Segura, I., Expósito, F. and Moya, M. (2011) 'Victim blaming and exoneration of the perpetrator in domestic violence: the role of beliefs in a just world and ambivalent sexism', *The Spanish Journal of Psychology*, 14(1): 195–206.

Von Hentig, H. (1940) 'Remarks on the interaction of perpetrator and victim', *Journal of Criminal Law and Criminology*, 31(3): 303–9.

Von Hentig, H. (1948) *The Criminal and His Victim*, New Haven, CT: Yale University Press.

Walby, S. and Allen, J. (2004) *Domestic Violence, Sexual Assault and Stalking: Findings from the British Crime Survey*, London: Home Office Research, Development and Statistics Directorate.

Walker, L. (1979) *The Battered Woman Syndrome*, New York, NY: Springer.

Weisz, A., Tolman, R. and Saunders, D. (2000) 'Assessing the risk of severe domestic violence: the importance of survivors' predictions', *Journal of Interpersonal Violence*, 15(1): 75–90.

Wolfgang, M. (1958) *Patterns in Criminal Homicide*, Philadelphia, PA: University of Pennsylvania Press.

NINE

Environmental crime, victimisation, and the ideal victim

Pamela Davies

Introduction

Christie's (1986: 17) seminal piece on 'The ideal victim' opens with remarks on being a victim: 'It is often useful within the social sciences to rely on personal experiences, or at least take this as our point of departure'. He goes on to make two preliminary reflections before stating that he will concentrate on the sociology of the phenomena:

> Firstly, being a victim is not a thing, an objective phenomenon.... Secondly, the phenomenon can be investigated both at the personality level and at the social system level.... At the level of social systems, some systems might be of the type where a lot of victimization is seen as taking place, while others are seen as being without victims. (Christie, 1986: 18)

In the same way that Christie chose to introduce his ideas about the concept of the ideal victim with a focus on the sociology of phenomena, this chapter, as, indeed, the book as a whole, does likewise. My exploration of the sociology of phenomena invokes a case study that draws on personal experience; by using this as my point of departure, I illustrate a number of issues surrounding victims and victimhood. The case study is of the closure of the Rio Tinto Alcan (RTA) aluminium plant at Lynemouth, Northumberland, in the north-east of England, where my husband worked for many years. I have already written about this closure from a feminist-influenced victimological perspective (Davies, 2014). Part of this chapter does likewise. However, the chapter as a whole gives a more sustained emphasis to the way in which Christie's work has impacted upon my own critical analysis of the closure. It dwells on the particular ways in which his insightful and highly original way of explaining his sophisticated theoretical propositions have steered my own thinking and victimological imagination. His work has impacted upon what I feel is important to write about. As a self-labelled feminist-influenced criminologist-cum-victimologist, I strive to make observations about my own position and relationship to what is happening in the social world. The case illustration that I have chosen to focus on in this chapter is personal but political, and it has been significant in terms of furthering my own understandings and conceptualisations of victim identity and experiences of harm and injustice, and of provoking me to be at pains to communicate the impacts of the global at the local and personal levels.

The remainder of this chapter revisits the ideal victim concept and explores how this has influenced my own thinking, in this case, about specific tensions between social and environmental justice and, indeed, victimisation from environmental governance. Before outlining the case study that forms the basis of my reflections, I first briefly explore the victim in the context of environmental justice. I then reflect upon the non-ideal victim and contemplate the theme of 'witches and workers' in Christie's thesis under the heading of 'Defining victimisation'. This reflection clearly illustrates the contested nature of victimisation and how there are alternative conceptualisations of victimisation that are at complete odds with the individualised concept of the 'ideal victim'. The section commencing 'Corporations as monsters' serves as the context for an examination of the non-ideal offender, and this is a segue into a broader discussion about green harms, victims and social conditions at local and global levels, social conditions being a topic that concerned Christie in the final section of his article.

The victim in the context of environmental justice

When Christie's article was published, a number of influences were seeping into the criminological agenda. The concept of globalisation took on huge significance in the 1980s and, among other global issues, concerns about conservation and the environment surfaced in the social sciences towards the end of that decade. Since then, such concerns have only intensified, with social, economic and political debates gathering momentum. During the 1980s, the 'feminist critique' (see Smart, 1976) of criminology was consolidated, with empirical inquiries mushrooming (Heidensohn, 1985, 1989, 1996) in its wake. Christie was well attuned to these feminist debates and ruminates on how these ideas impact upon victimhood and the bind that women may find themselves in should they tip the balance and become too independent and strong. His article famously refers to 'the little old lady' as the ideal victim of violent crime and to the young virgin as the ideal rape victim, as compared with the non-ideal rape scenario of husbands raping wives. He also discusses how 'the role of females, particularly the older ones, have changed' and the importance of power and culture in whether or not 'ladies, weak or old', are seen as 'ladies of the witch-age' or 'well suited for the role of the ideal victim' (Christie, 1986: 23). Interesting though this avenue is, several chapters in this volume follow up on the role that gender plays in determining victim status (see the Introduction and Chapter Eight by Duggan, as well as the contributions by Fohring, Corteen, Zempi, Rainbow, Bows, Cohen, Donovan and Barnes). This chapter is not insensitive to gender; indeed, it is feminist-influenced. However, it chooses to foreground the social tensions arising from green crime and victimisation, an area of crime and victimisation that Christie himself does not specifically exemplify.

In the early 1990s, something of a green critique happened after Lynch (1990) first suggested a 'green criminology'. Since this time, there has been a growing caucus of scholars variously writing about green criminality and environmental and ecological harms to human and non-human species. Green *criminology*, as Nurse (2016) has pointed out, requires embracing a range of different conceptions on what green criminology is, what is seeks to achieve and what perspectives and meanings of green are to be included. Broadly, however, it is concerned with environmental criminology, environmental justice and ecological – including species – justice. Some have extended their work to include analysis of environmental harms from a *victimological* perspective; indeed, as early as 1996, Williams suggested an environmental victimology (Williams, 1996). In relation to the latter, it is humans as victims that feature most prominently in the literature as objects of victimisation. Rather more recently, others have explored how victims are created and suffer as a result of harmful environmental activities, how environmental harms might be prevented, and how criminal damage and non-criminal harms might be responded to (see Skinnider, 2011; Hall, 2013a, 2013b; White, 2015) in order to complement the developing field of green criminology. Hall's contribution considered the scope of environmental harm and victimisation and concluded that, like other victim groups, environmental victims are far from homogeneous, a point worth remembering as we come to the case illustration in this chapter.

Contemporarily, green crime and victimisation are presenting some interesting moral and ethical challenges. Let us briefly explore three types of green or eco-justice: environmental justice; ecological justice;

and species justice. Environmental justice typically refers to people having equal access to a healthy environment and natural resources, as well as a voice in decision-making processes related to the environment. At the centre of this form of justice are human beings with social rights, and within this conceptualisation, eco-feminists have made a contribution to an understanding of how inequality and discrimination is mediated by gender (Nurse, 2016). Victims are human, though human victims of environmental harm are not widely recognised as victims of 'crime'. Ecological justice accords importance to nature, the land, rivers, mountains, flora, fauna and landscapes. Under this conceptualisation, the victim is the biosphere, specific ecosystems and environments. This conceptualisation of victim thus goes beyond the former conceptualisation of victim, which is largely anthropocentric in nature. Species justice, often subsumed within ecological justice, foregrounds the interests of non-human animals and species. In this conceptualisation, the victims are animals and plants. The category 'victim' can thus incorporate a wide variety of human and non-human species.

White (2015) suggests that there are three important dimensions to the study of environmental victims. First, much environmental harm has traditionally been ignored or condoned by governments and industry. Second, and in addition to the problem of disinterest, by taking into account both the human and the non-human and the varieties of victim noted earlier, the study of environmental harm is rendered complicated. Third, it is important to consider the physical location of harms within particular geographical contexts and he thus cautions that particular circumstances must be taken into account in the conceptualisation of victimisation: 'Varying types of environmental harm pertain to different geographical levels' (White, 2015: 36). Some issues are on a planetary scale (such as oceans and fisheries), while some are national in geographical location and others are local, with laws tending to be formulated in particular geographically defined jurisdictions. Furthermore, although environmental harm may originate in one specific location, due to natural processes of water and air movement and flow, it can spread to other regions, countries and continents. A localised source of a problem – such as the emission of toxic carbons into the atmosphere – can move across time and space, having a cumulative impact with major consequences on a global level. Along this continuum of green havoc, a range of different 'victims' are harmed and this illustrates how and why environmental harm and victimisation become complicated. Some victims are ignored, and where they are recognised, there are competing claims to victim status, with some laying claim to having more traditional status than others. Thus, there are inequalities in respect of good victim status. From a critical social harm perspective, this presents a case for particular circumstances being taken into account in the moral weighing up of interests and harms in any given situation, and this impacts upon the appropriateness of different regulatory strategies and how nation-states choose to implement and comply with these responsibilities.

As already noted, I have explored some of the nuances and dimensions of victimisation in a case study of the closure of the aluminium smelter at Lynemouth. While remaining sympathetic to green and environmental concerns and to the principles of green criminology, my assessment has a distinctly broader *victimological* starting point. After a brief outline of the case study of the closure of an aluminium plant, the discussion returns to some of the points made by green scholars around victim groups, ethical issues and justice. Although the history of green criminology is not lengthy, there is a strong connectivity to the second part of Christie's thesis around the not-so-ideal offender. Even more, recent green victimology scholarship connects well with the sub-theme that runs throughout Christie's thesis, the not-so-ideal victim. The latter points are all considered in the remainder of the chapter.

Case study

In 2014, my analysis of the sociology of the closure was published in an article in *Theoretical Criminology* entitled 'Green crime and victimization: tensions between social and environmental justice' (Davies, 2014). In that article, I use the closure of the aluminium plant in Lynemouth as a case study of tensions around social and environmental justices and victimisations. A summary of this is provided in Box 9.1.

Box 9.1: Rio Tinto Alcan and the aluminium smelter at Lynemouth

In 2011, Rio Tinto Alcan, one of the world's largest producers of aluminium, announced the closure of the smelter at Lynemouth in the north-east of England. The plant, a major local employer, closed in March 2013. This closure is a catalyst for examining global concerns about environmental emissions standards and the costs of compliance. I suggest that the plant's closure is a success in green terms. I argue that where closure is officially considered a compliance option, there are hidden but high costs of closure on already-deprived local and regional communities. My discussion focuses on these costs and how green crime and green compliance creates collateral damage, other types of victimisation that are not negligible. The social justice concerns that I elaborate upon relate to the physical, economic and social impact of industrial contraction upon employees and other workers whose livelihoods and disposable income depend upon the existence of the plant. These extend to concerns about the local and regional economy, as well as relationships and experiences in the aftermath of the closure, including the impact on work, gender relations, social networks, younger generations and family and social life. I underline the potential diffuse and negative impact that the closure of a single large employer has on people's lived experiences, with risks of a further spiralling degeneration of community. Thus, broader social concerns exist about the future of communities where closure happens. I represent these concerns as obscured costs that are rendered invisible on the global stage.

While remaining sympathetic to green and environmental concerns and to the principles of green criminology and social justice, as proposed by White (2008) and Beirne and South (2007), my assessment has a *victimological* rather than a *green* starting point. From this perspective, I conclude that where environmental policies and regulations are designed to prevent or minimise destructive or injurious practices into the future, based upon analysis and responses to harms identified in the present, there are moral and ethical challenges for a green criminology. As clearly headlined in the subtitle, my article explored 'Tensions between social and environmental justice' that appear to represent value conflicts between social and environmental justice.

In my case study of the closure, I use insights from victimology and from sociologists' studies of previously affected communities to portray a gloomy future for the workers and the wider community that relied on the plant's existence, predicting negative impacts on social networks and bleak prospects for younger generations. I suggest that the regressive impact of increased social inequality and poverty in the north-east of England is not likely to feel like sustainable development to grandparents, mothers, fathers and their children; families who have lost their livelihoods in and around Lynemouth.

The Lynemouth smelter closed in 2013. The power plant on which it depended for energy remains open, having converted to biomass to survive, sadly too late for the smelter at Lynemouth to do the same. Britain has since closed three giant coal power plants, Kingsnorth in Kent, Cockenzie in Scotland and Didcot A in Oxfordshire (Gosden, 2013). The closure of the smelter at Lynemouth and of other major industries, including our 'dirty' power stations, is a success story for green environmental policies. I maintain that this success comes at a very high price to those in already-impoverished communities who have been abandoned by major employers. In 2016, more than one in six workers in Britain's steel industry (most of whom are resident workers in the north-east of England or Scotland) faced unemployment. This followed 1,200 job losses affecting steel workers in Scunthorpe and Scotland and 2,200 jobs losses at Redcar. These closures, together with those of power stations, have taken an immense toll on already-impoverished and decimated communities and on the life chances of the populations that inhabit these bleak towns and cities (Davies, 2017).

Defining victimisation: workers and communities as non-ideal victims

A significant proportion of Christie's discussion focuses on the non-ideal victim and the not-so-ideal offender. Here, I draw on the case study introduced earlier to reflect upon the non-ideal victim and contemplate the worker aspect of the theme 'witches and workers' in Christie's thesis. This reflection clearly illustrates the diffuse nature of victimisation. It connects to the 'many victimized without knowing neither that they are victimized, nor the source' (Christie, 1986: 24). The contested and competing definitions of victimisation are also illustrated, showing how the conceptualisation of victimisation as proffered in the case example is at complete odds with the individualised concept of the 'ideal victim'.

According to Christie (1986: 24–5), workers are non-ideal victims because they have important, but not sufficient, strengths, because other people have contrary interests, and because they live in cultures with depersonalised responsibilities for living and working conditions. The area in which the closure occurred and from where the workforce were predominantly recruited was a traditional mining area. The demise of coal mining in the early 1980s had left thousands of men in the region unemployed. The local closures were, of course, part of the general contraction throughout the European Community of coal mining. In England and Wales, this ultimately resulted in the Miners' Strike of 1985 (Stead, 1987). Following deindustrialisation in geographically isolated areas and single occupational communities, scholars have explored the human consequences of immiseration (Stead, 1987; Waddington et al, 1994; Waddington, 2003; Waddington and Parry, 2003; Wray and Stephenson, 2012). According to these analyses, Marx's concept of immiseration is useful to any understanding of the consequences of post-industrialism. Such was the rate of social and economic degeneration following the pit closures in this particular region in the North-East that the British government granted £28 million to the Canadian-owned company Alcan to help reduce unemployment in the local authority area of Wansbeck. Since the decline of shipbuilding, the closure of the docks and the demise of the fishing industry in the North-East, the villages surrounding Ashington have long been isolated. The Wansbeck area generally has experienced deindustrialisation, and few alternative opportunities for employment of any description exist in the region.

Lynemouth and the towns in the south-east part of the county of Northumberland score poorly across a range of indicators of deprivation (employment, income, wages, benefits and allowances). In terms of education and health deprivation, the neighbourhood has one of the highest levels on both of these scores. Levels of children in need are often linked to levels of deprivation. Out of 12 local authority areas in the North-East, Northumberland had the fourth-highest proportion of children in need in 2011/12 (Warburton, 2013). Three of the eight characteristics belonging to pit communities identified by Bulmer in 1975 are physical isolation, the economic preponderance of a single industry and a working-class majority of the population (Bulmer, 1975). These applied to the communities around Lynemouth when the plant closed. Bulmer's remaining five characteristics (daily experience of arduous work pervading the community; endemic industrial conflict; segregated gender roles; public and male-dominated leisure; and close-knit, overlapping and supportive social networks) have been slipping away from this community since the closure of the pits. These defining characteristics of the local and regional communities might now be lost forever. They are additional costs, yet to be measured and quantified; the qualitative assessment of these invisible costs has yet to be exposed. These are the diffuse and invisible impacts of closure that have captured my own victimological conscience and imagination.

As Evans and Fraser (2004) have argued, there are several links between communities and victimisation. In the context of the case study drawn upon in this chapter, an appreciation of potentially negative impacts, such as job and disposable income losses as a consequence of closure, might be considered as victimological harms. The related economic and social connections and affective consequences of closure in an isolated and already-impoverished community, as described earlier, are potentially destructive to communities. In order to establish how this community can be framed as victimised, I have drawn on victimological concepts that are derived from Christie's inspired analysis of victimhood.

From a critical/harm-based social science perspective, victimologists (Davies et al, 1999, 2004, 2007, 2014) suggest that 'invisible' social harms and injustices take place within the global world that are worthy of examination. Such harms incur suffering akin to victimisation, yet are rendered invisible for a number of reasons, including their non-crime status. Such harms substantially impact the lives of their victims and the communities in which they occur, and, in turn, these injustices impact heavily on the work of social, health, welfare and criminal justice agencies and other regulatory bodies. It is not a crime to close an industrial plant, yet doing so in an area whose economic wealth is generated almost exclusively from a single industry causes significant further harms and losses that impact substantially in terms of costs to individuals, families and communities. Workers are rendered unemployed. They are among the many victimised, with the source of their victimisation hard to pin down.

The concepts of indirect, tertiary and re-victimisation, in part, explain suffering that does not meet the criteria of criminal victimisation. Essentially, these vocabularies are used to draw attention to the impact that crime has not on those directly involved in the particular event concerned, but on a wider circle of 'victims' who may have been affected by a particularly shocking event or life-changing experience. In the context of this case study, those vicariously victimised are those individuals and families in the local and regional community who bore the brunt of the closure. The ripple effect of closure has devastating consequences on individuals, families and communities. They have been disempowered, and a major plank of their social capital has been removed. They have experienced the equivalent of having been robbed of their jobs and financial resources, and their chances of replacing these losses by legitimate means in the aftermath of the closure are, as the deprivation data suggest, severely restricted. These impacts on plant workers, their families and local businesses are discounted. Those suffering have no claims to 'real' victimhood.

Building on critical and radical criminological perspectives, some green criminologists prefer to use the terminology 'environmental harm' rather than environmental crime. Looking beyond criminology, Hillyard et al (2004) argue that focusing on harm rather than crime has several advantages. It acknowledges the multitude of harms that affect people from birth to death, including mass harms and combinations of physical, financial/economic, emotional and psychological, sexual, and cultural atrocities. A harm-based approach acknowledges individual, group, corporate and collective harms and actions/non-actions. The weakness of radical and critical victimologies in this regard is evident.

As explored elsewhere, this has led to an expanded focus on undetected, under-reported, hidden and invisible crimes, including sexual crimes and victimisations, environmental harms (including climate change, air pollution, eco-terrorism and corporate bio-piracy), honour crimes, elder abuse, male sex work, war and crimes, health and safety crimes, and fraud (see Davies et al, 2014).

Returning to the idea of community victimisation, studies in the wake of the closure of the coal mines and demise of the pit communities have explored sociological questions about the effects of closure on family and social life, and the impact on family relations, including money problems, stress, illness, family disputes and young people's futures (Stead, 1987; Waddington et al, 1991). The gendered nature of the experiences and activism following closures is a key theme in such work, and my own case study of the closure explores the gendered nature of emotional responses linked to victimisation.

Since the turn of the century, others have developed the links between communities and victimisation. Particular experiences that collectives and groups suffer are increasingly being recognised. The scholarship on hate crimes and the emergent legislation and measures to protect special categories of vulnerable victims are testament to this. Victimological research is also emerging, with powerful testimonies of the suffering endured by communities (see, eg, McGarry and Walklate, 2015; Walklate et al, 2015; O'Leary, 2018). In this way, the cultural complexity of victimhood (Walklate et al, 2015; Arfman et al, 2016) is being constantly explored, further evidencing the changing nature of victimisation as envisaged by Christie. However, no matter how inspired these new *victimological* developments are, they sit in contradistinction to the obsession with the *criminological*, with crime and with the offending individual (Hillyard, 2005). I now turn to the corporation as the non-ideal offender.

Corporations as monsters and non-ideal offenders

As noted at the start of the previous section, a good deal of Christie's discussion attends to the not-so-ideal offender, and he explores the problems that emerge should we oversimplify the picture of the ideal offender. Here, I explore why and how this is, indeed, problematic; again, I do so in the context of the case study example. An overly simplistic representation of the corporation as monster is morally bankrupt. Christie's idea that morality is not improved by bad acts carried out by monsters captures the essence of my own assessment of the closure of the plant at Lynemouth. My own critical yet realist assessment of the tensions between social and environmental justice prompted a rather different analysis by Lynch (2015). Lynch's re-examination focuses more strongly on the corporation – Rio Tinto – as monster. In this assessment, the offender is a distant, foreign, non-person – an inhumane being. The corporation is literally inhumane, a non-entity in an individualised sense. The corporation does not therefore equate to an ideal offender. For Lynch, however, using Christie's conceptualisation of the ideal victim, the corporation is the extreme bad. However, this is unhelpful as corporations are not ideally suited to being criminalised by criminal justice systems that are framed around individualised conceptions of justice. Corporations are unsuitable criminals (Christie, 1986: 26) and, as Christie also points out, there are too few monsters around. The ideal-type offender suggests that bad acts are carried out by monsters. Corporations become distanced and depersonalised to the extent that the destructive attributes and activities that they engage in are let off the hook. Lynch reconstructs the offender to accommodate the corporation as monster. In a crude Marxist assessment, the corporation is entirely blameworthy. This leaves us in the Christie-like predicament in which our own morality is not improved. The inhumane capitalist monster is our scapegoat for environmental degradation and potentially for creating risks to health (Lynch, 2015). An assessment that is capable of capturing the multiplicity of harms and a range of blameworthy offenders is an assessment that concentrates, as does Christie, on the sociology of the phenomenon. Christie reminds us that the phenomenon can be investigated both at the personality level and at the social system level.

Victimisation from environmental governance

Here, I begin to tie together some of threads from the preceding sections. Under the conceptualisation of environmental justice, the victim is human. Humans are protected from injurious and harmful pollutants and emissions that have a negative impact on human health. Environmental harm is thus regulated by equality and rights-based protection laws and protection regimes. The UK uses judicial review procedures to ensure that the public can participate in decision-making. In April 2010, the European Court of Justice ruled that the power plant supplying the aluminium smelter at Lynemouth was subject to the emission limit values laid down in an environmental treaty in 2001 to fight global warming. This took the form of a directive – 2001/80/EC of the European Parliament on the limitation of emissions of certain pollutants into the air from large combustion plants – the Kyoto

Protocol. The UK government had been unable to succeed in court in challenging the categorising of the smelter at Lynemouth as a large combustion plant, and the fate of the plant was henceforth distinctly gloomy. Following the court case, the plant was given just a matter of weeks to comply with Directive 2010/75/EC on industrial emissions (a recast of various component directives, including 2001/80/EC on large combustion plants). If it did not, the government would be liable to pay fines to the European Commission for failing to implement the directive properly. The calculated projected costs to the business from compliance with the various strands of new or impending legislation totalled £105 million (Davies, 2014). The option taken to meet the costs of compliance within the broader context was of closure. The local impact of the closure has been speculated upon previously, and I suggest that, morally and ethically, the local and regional consequences of closure deserve weighing up against the injurious and harmful pollutants and emissions that have a negative impact on human health on a planetary scale.

To push the point about the weighing up of interests, I will labour the point about the import of particular circumstances and particular contexts. Corporations such a Rio Tinto have environmental responsibilities. International environmental law requires states to protect the environment and a growing body of European Commission legislation and European Court of Justice judgements demand compliance. However, it is too simplistic to offload full responsibility for closure on the Rio Tinto monster. If policies at very local levels are to be seen and experienced as fair and just, grass-roots understanding (Davies, 2008) of where the impacts of change would have the greatest emphasis – on families and sets of personal relationships, on local social dynamics, and on formal and informal networks in communities – is essential. Closures due to policy change emanating from Europe can be viewed and experienced as far removed, abstracted and damaging if broader and potentially destructive consequences are not adequately factored in and considered. Alongside the relevance of victimological concepts for understanding the predicament of residents in South-East Northumberland, equally important are their affective experiences. Within the social sciences, sociological perspectives are increasingly suggesting that human emotion is important generally in understanding social relations, and, increasingly, emotions are seen as a crucial link between micro- and macro-levels of social reality. Subjective, embodied and experiential aspects of social change are important (see Davies, 2011a, 2011b), and virtually all theories of emotions in society visualise emotions as mobilising and guiding behaviour (Turner and

Stets, 2005). While an ethics of sympathy and affective civilities more generally is difficult to achieve in the new 'civilised' barbarism inspired by neoliberalism, which makes empathy and compassionate sentiments difficult to expand past domestic sentimentalism, this does not justify a paucity of theoretical discussion and debate that brings emotion back in (Davies, 2011b). In drawing together these arguments around the concept of victimisation, together with an ethic of affective civility, to understand the predicament of those experiencing the aftermath of the closure, Lynemouth and its surrounding area emerges as a victimised community.

A final thread that I want to return to is the idea of multiple harms and victimisations. While there are various typologies of victims rendered more visible due to developments within green victimology, there are other victims created as a consequence, in part, of environmental governance. In the circumstances and context of Lynemouth, this begs the question: should the British government have worked harder to find a solution to the environmental challenges? In the circumstances and context of Lynemouth, many have found themselves falling short of the ideal victim stereotype: their experiences of victimisation are a collective form of victimisation that are the result of the victimisation of a collective set of circumstances, albeit, in large part, the corporate victimisation perpetrated by Rio Tinto Alcan (RTA) Ltd.

Conclusion

This chapter revisited the ideal victim concept and explored how this has influenced my own thinking about specific tensions between social and environmental justice. Furthermore, it developed the idea of victimisation from environmental governance, a distinctive sub-theme of environmental justice, and an, as yet, underdeveloped area of moral and ethical debate. I have drawn on a case-study illustration as the basis for my reflections about victim identity, experiences of harm and injustice. The chapter commenced with a brief exploration of the victim in the context of green crime and environmental justice. In reflecting on the non-ideal victim and with reference to Christie's theme of 'witches and workers' – and with a focus on the latter – I have problematised traditional definitions of the victim and have examined alternative conceptualisations of victimhood and victimisation. This reflection clearly illustrates the diffuse nature of victimisation and how a narrow, individualised, personified and idealised conceptualisation of victimisation is at complete odds with the experience of harm and injustice that communities can suffer. Such analysis further evidences the paucity and narrowness of traditional conceptions and perspectives in the positivist schools of victimology. However, in giving consideration to 'corporations as monsters', the chapter has also problematised the ideal offender. Despite huge efforts and a 13-year struggle to hold corporations legally accountable for the most serious of harms – workplace killing (Tombs, 2016) – there has been limited movement towards the legal demonisation of the corporate monster. This reflection may be illustrative of the lack of impact that radical, critical and social harm perspectives have had on the idea of state- and corporate-sponsored victimisation. Communities and collectives are still not perceived or treated as 'real victims' or 'real offenders'. Criminology and victimology are inadequate or not very good at dealing with collectives, both in terms of offenders and victims.

Since 1986, feminist-influenced thinking has continued apace and, in the context of the case study explored, it has prompted me to suggest that there is a gendered nature to the harms experienced by workers and their dependent families. Although this has not been the main feature of this chapter, it taps into a feminist theme that Christie was well attuned to. Also since 1986, new types of victimhood have emerged. If this is something that Christie did not exactly prophesise, his ideas were certainly sympathetic to the revealing of different types of victim: 'Victims who are not seen as victims ought often to be seen as such' (Christie, 1986: 27). Christie's ideal-type characterisations of the victim and of the offender and his problematised conceptualisations of these constructs endure the test of time and have lasting utility. They sit comfortably alongside the newly recognised need to, for example, attune to collective suffering, as well as with the key ideas evident in the growing body of work on the dynamic and culturally complex nature of victimhood. In this respect, Christie might be considered the founder of cultural victimology.

In summary, this chapter has explored the continued utility of Christie's 'ideal victim' concept at the same time as it has drawn to the fore the concerns of a feminist perspective, which, as noted previously, impacted upon criminology in the same period that he published this seminal thesis. I have shown that a sustained focus on green crime and victimisation has rendered visible new victims, as predicted by Christie (non-humans and species, and eco/biospheres). Similarly, global to local dimensions of victimisation remain important, as Christie's work implies (and as demonstrated in this chapter via environmental victimology and environmental governance). Among the interesting moral and ethical challenges outlined, it is important to note how some communities and collectives are not perceived or treated as 'real victims', and some corporations are not perceived or treated as 'real offenders'.

Acknowledgement

I am grateful to my friend and colleague Dr Tanya Wyatt for informally reviewing my draft of this chapter. I am a sympathetic visitor to the field of green crime and victimisation and I hope my revisions have done justice to her incisive comments and observations.

References

Arfman, W., Mutsaers, P., Van der Aa, J. and Hoondert, M. (2016) 'The cultural complexity of victimhood', Tilburg Papers in Culture Studies Paper 163, Tilburg University.

Beirne, P and South, N. (2007) *Issues in Green Criminology: Confronting Harms against Environments, Humanity and Other Animals*, Cullompton: Willan.

Bulmer, M. (1975) 'Sociological models of the mining community', *Sociological Review*, 23(1): 61–92.

Christie, N. (1986) 'The ideal victim', in E.A. Fattah (ed) *Crime Policy to Victim Policy: Reorienting the Justice System*, Basingstoke: Macmillan, pp 17–30.

Davies, P. (2008) 'Looking out a broken old window: community safety, gendered crimes and victimisations', *Crime Prevention and Community Safety: An International Journal*, 10(4): 207–25.

Davies, P. (2011a) 'The impact of a child protection investigation: a personal reflective account', *Child & Family Social Work*, 16(2): 201–9.

Davies, P. (2011b) 'Post-emotional man and a community safety with feeling', *Crime Prevention and Community Safety: An International Journal*, 13(1): 34–52.

Davies, P. (2014) 'Green crime and victimization: tensions between social and environmental justice', *Theoretical Criminology*, 18(3): 300–16.

Davies, P. (2017) 'Green crime, victimization and justice: a rejoinder', *Critical Sociology*, 43(3): 465–71.

Davies, P., Francis, P. and Jupp, V. (eds) (1999) *Invisible Crimes: Their Victims and Their Regulation*, Basingstoke: Macmillan Press.

Davies, P., Francis, P. and Jupp, V. (eds) (2004) *Victimisation: Theory, Research and Policy*, London: Palgrave/Macmillan.

Davies, P., Francis, P. and Greer, C. (eds) (2007) *Victims, Crime and Society*, London: Sage.

Davies, P., Francis, P. and Wyatt, T. (eds) (2014) *Invisible Crimes and Social Harms*, Critical Criminological Perspectives Series (eds R. Walters and D. Drake), Basingstoke: Palgrave Macmillan Press.

Evans, K. and Fraser, P. (2004) 'Communities and victimisation', in P. Davies, P. Francis and V. Jupp (eds) *Victimisation: Theory, Research and Policy*, London: Palgrave/Macmillan.

Gosden, E. (2013) 'Swansong of Old King Cole', *The Sunday Telegraph*, 31 March, p 7.

Hall, M. (2013a) 'Environmental harm and environmental victims: scoping out a "green victimology"', *International Review of Victimology*, 20(1): 129–43.

Hall, M. (2013b) *Victims of Environmental Harm: Rights, Recognition and Redress under National and International Law*, London: Routledge.

Heidensohn, F. (1985) *Women and Crime*, London: Macmillan.

Heidensohn, F. (1989) *Crime and Society*, London: Macmillan.

Heidensohn, F. (1996) *Women and Crime* (2nd edn), London: Macmillan.

Hillyard, P. (2005) 'Criminal obsessions: crime isn't the only harm', *Criminal Justice Matters*, 62(1): 26–46.

Hillyard, P., Pantazis, C., Tombs, S. and Gordon, D. (eds) (2004) *Beyond Criminology: Taking Harm Seriously*, London: Pluto Press.

Lynch, M.J. (1990) 'The greening of criminology: a perspective for the 1990s', *The Critical Criminologist*, 2(3): 3–4, 11–12.

Lynch, M.J. (2015) 'Green criminology and social justice: a re-examination of the Lynemouth plant closing and the political economic causes of environmental and social injustice', *Critical Sociology*, 43(3): 449–64.

McGarry, R. and Walklate, S. (2015) *Victims: Trauma, Testimony and Justice*, London: Routledge.

Nurse, A. (2016) *An Introduction to Green Criminology & Environmental Justice*, London: Sage.

O'Leary, N. (2018) *A Victim Community? Collective Stigma and the Legacy of the Media in High Profile Crime*, London: Palgrave Macmillan.

Skinnider, E. (2011) *Victims of Environmental Crime – Mapping the Issues*, Vancouver: The International Centre for Criminal Law Reform and Criminal Justice Policy.

Smart, C. (1976) *Women, Crime and Criminology: A Feminist Critique*, London: Routledge and Kegan Paul.

Stead, J. (1987) *Never the Same Again: Women and the Miners' Strike*, London: The Women's Press.

Tombs, S. (2016) *Social Protection After the Crisis: Regulation Without Enforcement*, Bristol: Policy Press.

Turner, J.H. and Stets, J.E. (2005) *The Sociology of Emotions*, Cambridge: Cambridge University Press.

Waddington, D. (2003) *Developing Coalfields Communities: Breathing New Life into Warsop Vale*, Bristol: Policy Press.

Waddington, D. and Parry, D. (2003) 'Managing industrial decline: the lessons of a decade of research on industrial contraction and regeneration in Britain and other EU coal producing countries', *Institute of Materials, Minerals and Mining. Transactions. Section A: Mining Technology*, 112(1): A47–A56.

Waddington, D., Wykes, M. and Critcher, C., with Hebron, S. (1991) *Split at the Seams? Community, Continuity and Change after the 1984–5 Coal Dispute*, Milton Keynes: Open University Press.

Waddington, D., Dicks, B. and Critcher, C. (1994) 'Community responses to pit closure in the poststrike era', *Community Development Journal*, 29(2): 141–50.

Walklate, S., Mythen, G. and McGarry, R. (2015) '"When you see the lipstick kisses …" – military repatriation, public mourning and the politics of respect', *Palgrave Communications*, 1: 15009.

Warburton, D. (2013) 'Children suffer as pressure builds on families', *The Journal*, 20 April, p 5.

White, R. (2008) *Crimes Against Nature: Environmental Criminology and Ecological Justice*, Cullompton: Willan.

White, R. (2015) 'Environmental victimology and ecological justice', in D. Wilson and S. Ross (eds) *Crime, Victims and Policy: International Contexts, Local Experiences*, Houndmills, Basingstoke: Palgrave Macmillan, pp 33–52.

Williams, C. (1996) 'An environmental victimology', *Social Science*, 23(1): 16–40. (Reprinted in: White, R. (2009) *Environmental Crime: A Reader*, Cullompton: Willan Publishing, pp 200–22.)

Wray, D. and Stephenson, C. (2012) 'Standing the gaff: immiseration and its consequences for the post industrial mining communities of Cape Breton Island', *Capital and Class*, 36(2): 323–38.

PART II

Exploring the 'Non-Ideal' Victim

TEN

Revisiting the non-ideal victim

Stephanie Fohring

Introduction

Ideal victims and real victims represent two very different groups. One is rooted in social stereotypes and falsehoods, holding a 'hero like public status', while the other, as the name would suggest, is what one finds in the real world. Real victims are more often young than old, more often men than women, more often known to their offender than not, and more often engaged in not entirely virtuous activities when victimised. In an ideal world, this would not affect the care and support received following victimisation, or the recognition of the harm and suffering that has been inflicted. Sadly, though, in our imperfect world, deviations from the fictional ideal may result in blaming, derogation, cruelty and injustice.

It is safe to say that most 'real' victims of crime would find it extremely difficult to meet the ideal victim requirements; thereby, they default into the category of the non-ideal. This chapter will first review Christie's discussion of the two types of non-ideal victim that he identifies: witches and workers. It will then go on to discuss how the expanded concept of the non-ideal victim now includes those who are deprived of the recognition of the harm done to them, potentially leading to further hardship and secondary victimisation. This chapter explores another category of non-ideal victim: the 'victim' who refuses this label and distances themselves from the identity. A brief review of survey-based research around this category of victim motivates a more qualitative exploration of victim identity and labels. Findings from qualitative research will be presented to support the suggestion that (some) victims have strong adverse feelings to the word 'victim' and actively work to avoid any association with it. Finally, a discussion of how social-psychological theory might help to explain the phenomenon provides new insight into this under-researched group of non-ideal victims.

Christie's (non-)ideal

In his relatively brief discussion of the non-ideal victim, Christie gives two examples of who might fall into such a category. The first example is of the medieval witch whose 'torture was a matter of course and their burning a part of the public entertainment' (Christie, 1986: 22). Why are witches non-ideal? The answer, Christie suggests, is because they had power. Elderly women in the middle ages were heavily involved in births, deaths and cases of sickness, and commanded much more respect, and even fear, that the elderly women of today (Christie, 1986: 23). Such power is incompatible with the ideal victim, who must be weak and innocent.

The workers and labourers of our society, who Christie (1986: 24) describes as victims of 'structural violence', are a second example of the non-ideal victim (see Davies, this volume). They are victims of a system, a competition, designed by and for the classes above. Their resulting failures are reorganised into a self-definition of losers rather than victims (Christie, 1986: 24). Also significant here is the absence of a specific offender. This again makes workers incompatible with the ideal victim, who must have a 'big and bad' offender. The ideal victim is often linked to the ideal offender, in that the general public's reactions to crime are directed at individual offenders and victims, so that in the aftermath of an event, the characteristics and behaviours of both are scrutinised and blame is directed at these agents rather than at any broader social or economic systems of injustice (Spalek, 2006: 31).

According to Christie, these 'witches and workers' are non-ideal victims because they have important, but not sufficient, strength, because other people have contrary interests, and because they lived or live in cultures with either personalised responsibilities for sickness (witches) or depersonalised responsibilities for living and working conditions (workers) (Christie, 1986: 24–5). This is the full extent of Christie's discussion of the non-ideal; limited essentially to those who do not quite meet the strict qualities associated with ideal victim status. The assumption here, of course, is that these victims are harmed by their failure to achieve victim status. The workers, for example, see themselves as losers and failures rather than as victims of an unfair system.

This depiction of the non-ideal as the disadvantaged victim has continued since Christie first described the problem, evolving into discourses around deserving and undeserving victims, hierarchies, and blame (Richardson and May, 1999; McEvoy and McConnachie, 2012). The most straightforward current example is, of course, the victim of sexual violence who is denied victim status (and likely blamed) due to failing to meet any of the requirements for the ideal. This is exemplified by the young woman (or, even less likely ideal, young man) out drinking with friends, and therefore engaged in a not-so-respectable activity, who is assaulted by a partner or acquaintance – an offender who is neither big nor bad, nor unknown to the victim. Contemporary discourse would also likely discuss the victim's level of intoxication, apparel, sexual history (Grubb and Turner, 2012) and failure to fight back as additional reasons to incite blame or withhold victim status.

Numerous other examples of situations where the denial of victim status can be harmful are available in the literature, for example: families and friends of victims of terrorist activities in Northern Ireland (Lynch and Argomaniz, 2015); men as victims of sexual assault (Smith et al, 1988; Coxell and King, 1996); elderly victims of rape (Lea et al, 2011); victims of marital rape (Whatley, 2005); victims of domestic violence (Bryant and Spencer, 2003); sex workers (Miller and Schwartz, 1995); or even victims of housebreaking who did not remember to lock the door (Maguire and Bennett, 1982). The denial of victim status may have severe and long-term consequences for victims in need of help and recognition. Returning to the example of the sexual assault victim, simply being believed when reporting an incident to the police is key to feeling supported, further engagement with the criminal justice system and longer-term mental health (Jordan, 2004). Acquiring legitimate victim status will be linked to receiving many benefits and resources, from legal aid and compensation, to access to justice, through to medical care and counselling. Additionally, the simple act of acknowledgement as a victim, as wronged, is often of significant importance to victims. Where and why acknowledgement is not readily given and the problems associated with the inability to achieve victim status are the primary focus of contemporary victimological research and literature. However, when considering the non-ideal, the major shortcoming of both Christie's original work and more recent work is that he assumes that all victims want to be recognised as such when, in fact, this is not the case.

Expanding the concept of the non-ideal

The idea that victims of crime may, in fact, be strongly opposed to being called 'victims' is growing in the victimological literature (Van Dijk, 2009; Rock, 2004; Fohring, 2015). In his work on the victim label, Van Dijk (2009) discusses observations by Spalek (2006) and van Tesseling (2001), suggesting that the prototypical characteristics of victims as weak and helpless are in stark contrast to the values of our modern Western society, where individualism, strength and power are highly valued. It is not surprising that victims may actively seek to distance themselves from victimhood; they are acutely aware of the negative connotations associated with the victim label. However, victims who deny or refute their status repudiate the entrenched social norms surrounding the ideal victim, thereby making them the epitome of the non-ideal and 'forsaking their entitlement to compassion and respect and provoking anger and moral indignation instead' (Van Dijk, 2009: 24).

There are many reasons, both social and personal, why one may want to avoid victim status (Taylor et al, 1983). Socially, although eliciting compassion for victims, the label assigns to them a social role of passivity and forgiveness that they may find to be increasingly restraining (Van Dijk, 2009). Further negatives are well documented and include such unfortunate phenomena as the victim blaming already discussed, but also the more general negative reactions encountered by victims, including hostility, derogation, isolation and rejection. More specifically, the challenges faced by victims in the criminal justice system are also not easily overcome. From intrusive physical exams, to cruel cross-examination, judgement by the media, retaliation and intimidation from the offender, and the airing of personal health issues, it is not hard to see why one may want to avoid such experiences (Herman, 2003).

Personally, victimisation is associated with loss and suffering, including loss of property, physical and or psychological well-being, one's sense of control, and self-esteem (Rock, 2004; Spalek, 2006). More recently, research has begun to recognise the personal factors associated with claiming or refusing victim status. For example, Weiss (2011: 458), in the context of studying victim rationales for not reporting to the police, discusses the 9% of her sample of National Crime and Victimisation Survey (NCVS) 'narratives' that neutralised their unwanted sexual experiences by rejecting a victim identity. The shortcomings of Weiss's analysis, however, result from the fact that she focuses solely on the physical experience of the would-be victim. The victim identity is rejected simply because the potential victim was able to physically resist an attempted assault. Specifically:

> the accounts work by emphasizing victims' resiliency, strength, and independence, while disavowing the helplessness, passivity, and vulnerability often associated with victimhood .... by depicting themselves as 'survivors'

who were able to take care of matters themselves, rather than as helpless victims in need of assistance and protection, reporting to police becomes a less relevant or appropriate response. (Weiss, 2011: 459)

This discussion of rejecting the victim identity, though valid, is incomplete. It does not discuss any psychological reasons for wanting to avoid the victim identity and assumes that the only victims able to do so are those who successfully fought off attackers. This is, however, not the only situation where a victim may try, and ultimately succeed, in rejecting the victim identity. Victims who did suffer through a completed attack may still reject the label.

In another attempt to explain the phenomenon of non-reporting, Brennan (2016) discusses crime labelling, and the subsequent discounting of crime as an alternative explanation for low reporting of violent crime. In this research, using three pooled sweeps of the Crime Survey England and Wales (CSEW) (to maximise the sample of relatively rare events), Brennan sought to identify the factors that both predict crime labelling and discounting. This was done by modelling a number of variables, such as the impact of the incident on the victim (harm, unjustness and feelings of vulnerability) and the extent to which the incident matches their prototype of a crime (legality and the victim–offender relational context), as well as neighbourhood characteristics predicted to affect either labelling or discounting (Brennan, 2016: 7).

Results showed that harm, the perceived unjustness of the incident and victim–offender relational distance played a fundamental role in the decision to label violence as a crime, whereas frequency of victimisation and victim initiation of the incident predicted discounting. Brennan (2016: 16) thereby concludes that 'when victims interpret violence against them, they appear to do so unencumbered by social norms'. These findings indicate that decisions about crime are informed by personal and context-specific factors rather than social or structural processes. Although this takes us considerably further to understanding the aversion to the victim label, the psychological processes at work that may also influence discounting and rejecting the victim label remain elusive.

In a slightly different approach, Fohring (2015) used the Scottish Crime and Justice Survey (SCJS) to model the impact of labelling and psychological distress on the reporting of both property and personal crimes. Labelling the incident as a crime was by far the strongest predictor of reporting for both property and personal crimes, increasing the odds of reporting both property and personal crimes by a factor of six and 14, respectively. Additionally, in both models, the effect of emotional responses to crime was profound: the odds of reporting a property crime increased substantially when the victim experienced anger, shock, fear, a loss of confidence or vulnerability, and had difficulty sleeping, whereas personal crimes were affected by fear and having difficulty sleeping.

Fohring explains this finding by suggesting that more severe psychological reactions are associated with higher rates of reporting, and are likely found in victims who have difficulty coping with the psychological impact of the crime. When the impact is so severe that it cannot be integrated with our existing world view, it is much more difficult to reject victimhood, hence the labelling of the traumatic incident as a crime and themselves as a victim. Since they are already victims, they are free to report the incident or seek support without further endangering their pre-existing beliefs (Fohring, 2015).

The quantitative research reviewed here goes some way in showing two important things: first, victims do regularly shun the label; and, second, rejection of the victim label and/or identity is linked with non-reporting, and may thus be considered a serious concern for the criminal justice system. That being said, it is not able to go so far as to discuss the reasoning behind the decision. Although each piece of research purports a slightly different explanation for the non-reporting, none can say why it is that victims find the label so aversive. Therefore, an alternative approach may be necessary to further investigate this phenomenon, namely, qualitative research.

Qualitative evidence

Qualitative research offers a means by which to address some of the shortcomings identified in the previous, survey-based work around victim labelling and identity. As such, we turn now to some examples of victims who would likely meet the criteria of the non-ideal victim, that is, although having experienced one or more incidents of crime, the participants refused to label themselves as victims.

The data reported here were collected via interviews with 45 victims of crime from across Scotland and Northern England. Incidents did not necessarily take place in Britain, although only two respondents reported either incidents or consequences of crime occurring outside Britain. The age range of participants varied from 16 to 65, with a range of crime types reported, including vandalism, assault, rape, murder (co-victims), racial harassment, housebreaking and child sexual assault. Participants were recruited through a variety of methods in order to reach a sample that had not necessarily reported crimes to the police. These included newspaper adverts and social media, with the assistance of Victim Support Scotland and the Crown Office of the Procurator Fiscal, as well as the Justice Analytics division of the Scottish government. During the interview, participants were asked, among other things, about their thoughts and feelings regarding the word 'victim', if they thought of themselves as victims, and if they thought what had happened to them was a crime.

The rejection of the victim label, although not ubiquitous, was startlingly common, even among those respondents who reported serious crimes such as sexual assault and rape. Additionally, an awareness of the negative social stigma surrounding victimisation was evidenced, as were a number of negative descriptors or words associated with victims and victimisation. For example:

> "I think, like I said earlier, it might have been different if I was more seriously injured but I can't really say I considered myself a victim, which is my own point of view, you know. Just, I consider it more as being unlucky, just an unlucky incident you know.... Yes I guess it's a word with a lot of negative connotations, I suppose it would make you feel vulnerable in a way ... that's maybe why I don't like to think of myself as a victim because it makes you feel a bit vulnerable." (P003, male)

The quotation from this man is particularly relevant for a number of reasons. First, this participant experienced childhood sexual assault, yet still insists on his non-victim status and rationalises it via the apparent lack of "serious injury". Physical injury aside, sexual abuse in childhood will likely be viewed as one of the most severe forms of crime by the layperson, clinician or academic; yet, this man obviously sees things differently as he was not physically injured as a result of the abuse. What is more, one could argue that masculinity is driving the dissociation as male victims generally, and male victims of sexual assault specifically, do not fit the image of the 'ideal' victim. Men as victims of sexual assault could be placed at the bottom of a hierarchy of victims, among those who must fight for recognition of their status as victims. Thus, this participant is 'non-deal' in the sense that he is male, but also in the sense that rather than fighting for recognition as a victim, he distances himself from the concept.

Reasons for desiring this distance are also apparent in the quotation. Not only does the man recognise the negative connotations associated with victimhood, but he also suggests that actively identifying as a victim may result in feelings of vulnerability, a feeling that he wishes to avoid. Vulnerability is a prototypical characteristic of the ideal victim, as well as victims more generally, which makes the way in which this discussion of vulnerability is worded interesting: the participant suggests that the label makes *you* feel vulnerable, is this because he even has difficulty admitting that it makes *me* feel vulnerable?

Similar to vulnerability is, of course, weakness:

> "I don't want to be a victim because that implies weakness, kind of long-term damage, and it also feels like it's giving the other party a victory, to me anyway. Yes, I think generally my conception of victim is I think of people who can't help themselves, so I think of, I think of alcoholics as victims of their illness, I think of like crack addicts as victims, I think of, I think of people who have been abused as victims and I just wouldn't put myself in that category, rightly or wrongly." (P030, female)

'Victim implies weakness' is a powerful statement, but one that fits with the concept of the ideal. All victims are certainly not weak, and the ones I have spoken to over the course of my career have amazed me with their strength and resilience, yet also their willingness to be vulnerable and admit that they are struggling, something that even the average person often finds difficult to do. The statement is bold in that it goes beyond saying that weakness *may* be a characteristic associated with victims, instead saying that victims *must* be weak. To this participant, 'victim' not only implies weakness, but also what she calls "long-term damage". Long-term damage, from a psychological sense, may indeed result from criminal victimisation. This goes beyond clinical diagnoses of post-traumatic stress, and relates to a more core, foundational functioning of the psyche that is difficult to repair. A self-image based around weakness and 'damaged goods' is not going to promote a healthy sense of self-confidence and will not do much to aid recovery from crime.

Also interesting in the earlier quotation is the neutrality that the participant uses when speaking of the offender. She says "the other party" rather than offender, suspect, defendant or any other arguably value-laden word when describing the person who harmed her. Why, then, should she not also have a neutral term to describe herself? Further, as she describes her conception of victims, which includes alcoholics and crack addicts, it adds weight to her reasoning to not want to be associated with the term. This also brings in a new element of weakness: here, this is not referring to a weakness as a result of victimisation, but a more general weakness of character, the inability to give up alcohol or drugs. When thinking of 'victim' in such a way, it makes sense that the participant would not 'put herself in that category' and raises interesting questions about similarities and differences between different subgroups of victims, such as our focus on victims of crime, but also victims of disease and illness, and/or victims of natural phenomena. Do they all carry the same negative connotations?

> "I really don't like that word 'victim'. I actually, I really have an issue with that word 'victim'.... I don't like thinking of that word. I don't, I think it's like ... I can't, it just, it does something to me inside my head every time I hear the word and I think because of that situation, the police kept referring to me as 'victim'. Victim Support, you were the victim and it's like you're saying all this to me and that sounds bad but you're not doing anything, nothing was there to make it better or he got off with it and I'm still left with all this carnage inside of me and I just really, I just don't like the word." (P026, female)

This participant describes a powerful dislike of the word 'victim', to the extent that "it does something inside my head". This suggests an element of anger, as she speaks of both the police and Victim Support referring to her as a victim, but never asking if this was ok with her, thereby forcing an unwanted and potentially harmful label upon her. Further, resentment is apparent in that not only was she forced to assume this victim label/identity, but nothing was done to make it better. There were no attempts to address or correct the wrongdoing, thereby leaving her stuck or 'locked in' this state of victimhood (Van Dijk, 2009). In a strongly emotive turn of phrase, the woman describes "the carnage inside of me", which is likely linked to the emotional and psychological impact that the crime has had on her. Carnage elicits images of destruction, a war zone, where a battle rages between the forces attempting to preserve old world views and the new information brought about by the victimisation (that the world is not safe, etc).

Thus, we see that a strong emotional reaction to the word 'victim' is common among respondents, which seems linked to the motivation to avoid the label:

"Yes, I mean, I wouldn't generally describe myself as a victim just for the reasons I said it can be seen as a sort of you're feeling sorry for yourself, but maybe that's just the sort of connotation society puts on that word, it's to do with emotions but it's not the word I would generally use." (P011, female)

Like the participants before her, this woman would also not describe herself as a victim. Also, like the young man mentioned previously, she has an awareness of the societal stigma attached to the word. Feeling sorry for oneself is not acceptable and highly undesirable. Also noteworthy here is the statement that "it's to do with emotions". Is she referring to her own emotions or the emotions that the word 'victim' elicits from society? I would suggest that it could apply to either, but that she is referring to her own emotions. That she, like the others, is avoiding the victim label to protect herself from the negative, shameful and unwanted emotions that are associated with victimhood.

Psychological explanations

A subconscious process of self-preservation against the negative and typically unwanted emotions associated with victimisation goes some way in explaining the rejection of the victim identity. Victims who engage in this process, who not only do not fit the ideal victim criteria, but actively engage in the dismissal of the victim identity, are the embodiment of the non-ideal.

As mentioned previously, Frieze et al (1987) suggested victimhood to be undesirable for a number of reasons, both social and personal, irrevocably altering the person's identity and social status (Goffman, 1963; Pilgrim, 2017: 191). Thus far, we have seen how personal factors might potentially help to explain this, though the explanations examined focus on personal characteristics, such as physical strength, repeat victimisation or initiation of the incident. Only Fohring (2015) has focused on the potentially harmful psychological consequences of assuming the victim identity.

What is it about experiences of criminal victimisation that leave people feeling a state of internal carnage? As suggested earlier, there may be a struggle to integrate the experience of victimisation with our existing beliefs about ourselves and the world around us. Criminal victimisation acts as a significant challenge to these beliefs, thereby creating the opportunity for considerable psychological distress. Avoiding victimisation, or at least avoiding the victim identity, is thereby potentially an effective means of protecting one's foundational belief systems and maintaining personal well-being.

These beliefs, commonly called cognitive structures or schemas, encompass the working beliefs and assumptions that we hold about ourselves and the world in which we live (Fohring, 2015). Although the number of these assumptions is likely to vary from individual to individual, Janoff-Bulman (1992) and Frieze et al (1987) suggest that people typically possess three core beliefs: the belief in personal invulnerability; the perception of the world as meaningful and benevolent; and a positive self-view. Self-confidence and feelings of security rely on the basic principle of the world as a safe place: that it is meaningful, just and ordered. This, in turn, relies on the belief that the people we encircle ourselves with are trustworthy and good, and do not pose a threat. Taken together, these beliefs emulate a conceptual system that has been developed over the life course in order to guide us through our immediate environment.

Rudimentary though these beliefs may seem, they allow us to live day to day without constant worry and fear, and it is by virtue of these schemas that we are able to adjust and adapt to new and challenging situations (Pilgrim, 2003). Some (see Taylor, 1990) go so far as to purport that these beliefs are both necessary and beneficial to the maintenance of healthy emotions, as well as both physical and psychological well-being. Janoff-Bulman (1992) argues that when a person is faced with a traumatic experience, such as criminal victimisation, it is the challenging (or shattering) of this belief system that leads to the psychological impact typically associated with victimisation, such as the feelings of weakness, fear and loss of control discussed by the participants.

Therefore, a major coping task confronting victims is a cognitive one: that of assimilating incongruous trauma-related impressions into their experience and/or changing their basic schemas about themselves and their world (Janoff-Bulmann, 1992: 113; Pilgrim, 2003). The man quoted earlier clearly demonstrated a struggle with admitting his own vulnerability, which is understandable as this may make a sense of security as well as trust in other people difficult to achieve. Admitting vulnerability may be associated with feelings of fear, focusing on the risk of future victimisation and potentially exacerbating existing feelings of stress (Pilgrim, 2003).

This demonstrates the tendency to distort information in order to protect established cognitive structures. If the information is indisputable, in order to recover, individuals must adapt cognitive structures to facilitate its assimilation. This may be further achieved via the use of various defence mechanisms, as outlined by Taylor et al (1983) and elaborated on by Fohring (2015). These cognitive mechanisms, referred to as 'selective evaluation', offer routes to integrate traumatic experiences by lessening the amount or seriousness of trauma-related information. Examples include: the tendency to belittle or downgrade the seriousness of the incident (Fohring, 2015); making social comparisons with less fortunate others (downward comparisons); selectively focusing on attributes that make one appear advantaged; creating hypothetical worse worlds; construing benefit from the victimising event; and manufacturing normative standards of adjustment that make one's own adjustment appear exceptional (Taylor et al, 1983).

This demonstrates a possible route by which victims can reassess their situation, thereby avoiding the victim identity and label. This is thus another explanation for non-reporting, in addition to those discussed by Brennan (2016) and Weiss (2011). Alternatively, those who are either unable to integrate their victimisation experience or successfully employ any of the outlined defence mechanisms will be more inclined to adopt the victim label, resulting in fewer barriers to engagement with the criminal justice system.

In summary, the non-ideal victim may take many forms, but, arguably, the victim who refuses both acknowledgement and the label represents the quintessence of the non-ideal. Previous work has offered explanations as to why victims choose to avoid acknowledgement, but much of it has failed to consider the impact of motivations to maintain our foundational beliefs and the undesirable consequences of victimhood on these behaviours. The qualitative data presented here have added to the weight of evidence suggesting that many victims wish to avoid the label; however, the explanation posed here is novel. Instead of focusing on physical strength or crime characteristics, it is suggested that victims are inherently aware of the negative social stereotypes of victims. Additionally, as evidenced by reference to wanting to avoid weakness and vulnerability, the results suggest that participants may be seeking to uphold their pre-existing foundational belief systems. Further references to internal damage and carnage reinforce the image of a shattered belief system.

Conclusion

This chapter has endeavoured to expand upon Christie's now-classic work on the ideal victim, a concept that has shaped victimological literature and research since it was first published over 30 years ago.

The need for the expansion arises out of growing awareness of how the ideal actually describes very few victims, and how, until recently, discussion of the non-ideal has been dominated by those excluded (for one reason or another) from achieving victim status. A growing body of evidence has, however, demonstrated that many victims prefer not to be recognised or acknowledged as victims, but may actively shun the label to the best of their ability.

Victimologists have been slow to investigate this phenomenon. Here, I have reviewed three pieces of survey-based research into the impact of victim retaliation, crime labelling and emotional responses to the acquisition of the victim identity or label. Additionally, this chapter has used qualitative data from crime victims to further the argument that many victims are, in fact, non-ideal in that they seek to avoid the victim label. The implications of this are wide ranging for the criminal justice system, though of primary concern is arguably the influence on reporting behaviour. The dark figure of crime has been a criminological mainstay since the advent of the first crime surveys, yet novel explanations for the reasons surrounding non-reporting remain few and far between. The social-psychological explanation suggested here is in its infancy, yet deserves further investigation given the potential to explain (at least partially) aversion to the victim label and non-reporting.

Additionally, though unintentionally, the discussion here may also feed into ongoing debates around the use of the word 'victim' as compared to alternatives, such as 'survivor'. The first and somewhat obvious recommendation coming from this discussion is no doubt a need to re-examine the use of the word 'victim'. This, however, is not a new suggestion, and is one that has led to much controversy, of which I do not intend to add to here. A more practical suggestion may be to instead target resources at those victims who do not label themselves as such (whatever the reason may be) and are therefore less likely to access the criminal justice system and support services. Like those victims who do, in fact, aspire to acknowledgement as 'real' victims but are barred from doing so, victims who reject the label face the same problems, that is, lack of justice, protection, care, support and compensation. The question, then, is whether or not these problems are offset by the psychological benefits of maintaining one's core foundational beliefs and values?

The motivation to protect these beliefs is robust and enduring. It places victims at odds with societal expectations, and therefore at risk of blame, derogation or worse. Society's image of the ideal, weak, helpless and vulnerable victim is, however, in direct contrast to the image that we like to hold of ourselves: strong, independent and in control. Therefore, these inconsistent characteristics must be either adopted into our foundational belief systems or rejected. Those who choose to reject these attributes of the ideal represent a new category of the non-ideal victim. As Christie himself said, 'ideal victims do not necessarily have much to do with the prevalence of *real victims*' (Christie, 1986: 27, emphasis in original).

References

Brennan, I.R. (2016) 'When is violence not a crime? Factors associated with victims' labelling of violence as a crime', *International Review of Victimology*, 22(1): 3–23.

Bryant, S.A. and Spencer, G.A. (2003) 'University students' attitudes about attributing blame in domestic violence', *Journal of Family Violence*, 18(6): 369–76.

Christie, N. (1986) 'The ideal victim', in E.A. Fattah (ed) *From Crime Policy to Victim Policy: Reorienting the Justice System*, Basingstoke: Macmillan, pp 17–30.

Coxell, A. and King, M. (1996) 'Male victims of rape and sexual abuse', *Sexual and Marital Therapy*, 11(3): 380–91.

Fohring, S. (2015) 'An integrated model of victimization as an explanation of non-involvement with the criminal justice system', *International Review of Victimology*, 21(1): 45–70.

Frieze, I., Greenberg, M. and Hymer, S. (1987) 'Describing the crime victim: psychological reactions to victimization', *Professional Psychology: Research and Practice*, 18(4): 299–315.

Goffman, E. (1963) *Stigma: Notes on a Spoiled Identity*, New York, NY: Jenkins, JH and Carpenter.

Grubb, A. and Turner, E. (2012) 'Attribution of blame in rape cases: a review of the impact of rape myth acceptance, gender role conformity and substance use on victim blaming', *Aggression and Violent Behavior*, 17(5): 443–52.

Herman, J. (2003) 'The mental health of crime victims: impact of legal intervention', *Journal of Traumatic Stress*, 16(2): 159–66.

Janoff-Bulman, R. (1992) *Shattered Assumptions: Towards a New Psychology of Trauma*, New York, NY: The Free Press.

Jordan, J. (2004) *The Word of a Woman? Police, Rape and Belief*, Basingstoke: Palgrave Macmillan.

Lea, S., Hunt, L. and Shaw, S. (2011) 'Sexual assault of older women by strangers', *Journal of Interpersonal Violence*, 26(11): 2303–20.

Lynch, O. and Argomaniz, J. (2015) *Victims of Terrorism: A Comparative and Interdisciplinary Study*, London: Routledge.

Maguire, M. and Bennett, T. (1982) *Burglary in a Dwelling: The Offence, the Offender, and the Victim*, London: Heinemann.

McEvoy, K. and McConnachie, K. (2012) 'Victimology in transitional justice: victimhood, innocence and hierarchy', *European Journal of Criminology*, 9(5): 527–38.

Miller, J. and Schwartz, M.D. (1995) 'Rape myths and violence against street prostitutes', *Deviant Behavior*, 16(1): 1–23.

Pilgrim, D. (2017) *Key Concepts in Mental Health* (4th edn), London: Sage.

Pilgrim, H. (2003) 'Cognitive perspectives on early reactions to traumatic events', in R. Orner and U. Schnyder (eds) *Reconstructing Early Intervention After Trauma*, Oxford: Oxford University Press.

Richardson, D. and May, H. (1999) 'Deserving victims? Sexual status and the social construction of violence', *The Sociological Review*, 47(2): 308–31.

Rock, P. (2004) 'Victims, prosecutors and the state in nineteenth century England and Wales', *Criminal Justice*, 4(4): 331–54.

Smith, R., Pine, C., Hawley, M. and Smith, R. (1988) 'Social cognitions about adult male victims of female sexual assault', *Journal of Sex Research*, 24: 101–12.

Spalek, B. (2006) *Crime Victims: Theory, Policy and Practice*, Basingstoke: Palgrave Macmillan.

Taylor, S.E. (1990) *Positive Illusions: Creative Self-Deception and the Healthy Mind*, New York, NY: Basic Books.

Taylor, S.E., Wood, J.V. and Lichtman, R. (1983) 'It could be worse: selective evaluation as a response to victimization', *Journal of Social Issues*, 39(2): 19–40.

Tesseling, I. van (2001) *In het Oog van de Storm: Slachtoffers in Actie [In the Eye of the Storm. Victims in Action]* (In Dutch) Veen: Amsterdam.

Van Dijk, J. (2009) 'Free the victim: a critique of the Western conception of victimhood', *International Review of Victimology*, 16(1): 1–33.

Weiss, K.G. (2011) 'Neutralizing sexual victimization: a typology of victims' non-reporting accounts', *Theoretical Criminology*, 15(4): 445–67.

Whatley, M.A. (2005) 'The effect of participant sex, victim dress, and traditional attitudes on causal judgments for marital rape victims', *Journal of Family Violence*, 20(3): 191–200.

ELEVEN

Conceptualising victims of anti-social behaviour is far from 'ideal'

Vicky Heap

Introduction

Since Christie produced his seminal paper on 'ideal victims' in 1986, one of the most significant developments in UK criminal justice policy has been the creation of anti-social behaviour (ASB) legislation to govern nuisance and sub-criminal conduct. From 1998, a vast number of ASB tools and powers have been introduced to tackle behaviour that 'caused or was likely to cause harassment, alarm or distress to one or more persons not of the same household as [the perpetrator]' (Crime and Disorder Act 1998 (s.1(1a))). This broad legal definition allows a wide range of behaviours to be interpreted as anti-social, extending from noisy neighbours and verbal abuse, to graffiti and fly-tipping. This chapter will critically deconstruct notions of ASB victimisation by focusing on conceptualising individual and community experiences of ASB in order to determine the extent to which Christie's ideal victim framework applies to these contemporarily controlled phenomena.

In order the set the scene, an overview of the extent of ASB victimisation is provided. This highlights the subjective nature of ASB and outlines some of the issues associated with trying to measure the amount of ASB victimisation. A summary of the prevalence of ASB in England and Wales follows, alongside details about the characteristics of those people that are most likely to be victims. Once the context of ASB victimisation has been established, attention turns to individual victims of personal ASB. The definition of personal ASB is explored before the degree to which these types of victims are conceptualised as ideal and non-ideal victims is considered, with specific reference to real-life cases and the impact of wider political and social policy discourses. The final section explores an area that Christie (1986) did not consider: communities as victims. His ideal victim framework is applied to communities that suffer from nuisance and environmental

ASB in public spaces to determine the utility of his thesis in these circumstances.

Contextualising and understanding ASB victimisation

Christie's work focuses on victims of *crime*. When he wrote his piece, ASB was not defined in its current form and so could not be discussed alongside the crime-related examples used to demonstrate the ideal victim framework. However, Christie (1986: 18, emphasis in original) made an important point about victimisation that resonates with ASB, he said: 'Firstly, being a victim is not a thing, an objective phenomenon. It will not be the same to all people.... *It has to do with the participant's definition of the situation*'. This appreciation of the interpretation and meaning of being a victim demonstrates that victimisation does not have to be restricted to the narrow black-letter-law definition of crime, or any other definition of crime. The idea of a personally defined victim status is particularly relevant to victims of ASB because the legal definition requires an individual to make a judgement about whether the behaviour they are experiencing causes them harassment, alarm or distress. As such, the creation of ASB legislation in 1998 marked a turning point in a conceptual sense. The powers introduced to tackle ASB provided significant recognition of the harms caused by sub-criminal behaviour, which can often occur over a long period of time, increase in severity and have an acute impact on the victim's quality of life. The definition of what constitutes ASB was kept deliberately broad because the flexibility allows victims' individual concerns to be raised and responded to.

Around the same time that ASB policies and procedures were established, the deployment of victimisation surveys facilitated a greater understanding of what constitutes criminal victimisation (Walklate, 2007). However, knowledge about ASB victimisation has failed to keep pace, chiefly fuelled by the difficulties associated with defining and counting ASB incidents, which have occurred as a result of the broad legal definition (Armitage, 2002; Whitehead et al, 2003; Harradine et al, 2004; Wood, 2004). Furthermore, over the years, most ASB research has tended to focus on how policy developments impact upon perpetrators rather than victims (see Cracknell, 2000; Brown, 2004; Matthews et al, 2007; Lewis et al, 2016). Therefore, what we know and understand about the characteristics of ASB victims is limited. This has been exacerbated by the use of *perceptions* of ASB as a proxy measure to determine the extent that certain behaviours are thought to be causing a problem. The Crime Survey for England

and Wales (known as the British Crime Survey until 2012) creates the proxy by capturing information about seven types of ASB, namely: noisy neighbours or loud parties; teenagers and young people hanging around; rubbish or litter; vandalism and graffiti; people using or dealing drugs; people being drunk or rowdy; and abandoned or burnt-out cars. These seven measures combine to create an overall index of perceptions of ASB, which details the proportion of respondents who perceive there to be high levels of ASB in their area (for a full discussion of the methodology, see Heap, 2010). Crime Survey for England and Wales data from 2017 shows that 9% of respondents perceived high levels of ASB in their local area (ONS, 2017a), a figure that has steadily decreased from a record high of 21% in 2002/03 (ONS, 2013). Due to the proxy measure being used, we do not have a clear picture of exactly how or why these changes are happening, nor do we know the type(s) of ASB that victims are truly experiencing or who is experiencing it, though we can see that perceived high levels of ASB are decreasing. The most in-depth, and recent, analysis of the perception data from the British Crime Survey by Flatley et al (2008) identifies the top five personal characteristics most likely to perceive high levels of ASB, which are:

- 10% most deprived areas;
- unemployed;
- living in 'hard-pressed' ACORN[1] areas;
- social renters; and
- victims of crime.

This investigation highlights some key ASB victim characteristics, such as high levels of deprivation, unemployment and being a tenant in social housing. National-level public perception data is complemented by a smaller-scale study, which replicated the British Crime Survey findings about deprivation, as well as uncovered that perceptions can vary wildly between different deprived areas of the same city (Heap, 2009). From 2012 onwards, police-recorded ASB incidents have also been reported by the Crime Survey for England and Wales, with data from 2017 showing that 1.8 million ASB incidents were recorded, a 1% decrease on the previous year, which compares to nearly 5 million recorded crimes (ONS, 2017b), a 10% yearly increase. The police National Standard for Incident Recording (NSIR) categorises ASB incidents as: personal – which are incidents deliberately targeted at an individual or group; nuisance – where behaviour causes trouble, annoyance or irritation to the local community; or environmental – which represents incidents by individuals or groups that have an impact on their surroundings (ONS, 2012). Where data have been provided, the nuisance category has always had the highest proportion of incidents (around 65%), followed by personal (around 30%) and environmental (around 5%) (ONS, 2012, 2013, 2014). Reporting on only three categories of ASB still prevents us from understanding the exact types of behaviours that victims are suffering from and the people that are most likely to experience different forms of ASB. Informal conversations with practitioners suggest the behaviours that are currently causing the most problems include: nuisance car parking, scrambler bikes, boy racers[2] and dangerous/status dogs. Nevertheless, the NSIR categories will be used as a starting point for the discussions about conceptualising individual and community victims of ASB that follow. Some could argue that adopting such an administrative approach to classifying ASB fails to capture and highlight the nuances of ASB victimisation. However, given the constraints associated with a stand-alone chapter, it provides a useful lens through which to apply Christie's ideas in a way that reflects how ASB is conceived in practice. Furthermore, the NSIR categories of ASB are broad enough to allow a wide range of ASB victimisation to be considered.

In sum, the sheer volume of ASB incidents demonstrates that ASB victimisation is experienced by many people. Our understanding about the types of ASB suffered by victims is unclear and does not have the same status or insight as criminal victimisation. By utilising a combination of British Crime Survey/Crime Survey of England and Wales data, high-profile ASB cases and media portrayals of ASB victims, we can start to apply Christie's ideal victim framework to determine the extent to which it is relevant to nuisance and sub-criminal behaviour today.

Conceptualising victims of 'personal' anti-social behaviour

Christie (1986: 19) characterised what he believed exemplified an 'ideal victim' of crime, based (initially) on five attributes, namely:

(1) The victim is weak. Sick, old or very young people are particularly well suited as ideal victims.
(2) The victim was carrying out a respectable project – caring for her sister [Christie's example].
(3) She was where she could not possibly be blamed for being – in the street during the daytime.

(4)   The offender was big and bad.
(5)   The offender was unknown and in no personal relationship to her.

The sixth, and lesser discussed, attribute is that: 'you are powerful enough to make your case known and successfully claim the status of an ideal victim. Or alternately, that you are not opposed by so strong counter-powers that you can not be heard' (Christie, 1986: 21). This section will initially consider the extent to which Christie's ideal victim framework can be applied to individual victims of 'personal' ASB. The police NSIR suggests that personal ASB 'includes incidents that cause concern, stress, disquiet and/or irritation through to incidents that have a serious impact on people's quality of life', with the impact of this behaviour ranging from 'minor annoyance', through to 'an inability to conduct normal day to day activities through fear and intimidation' (ONS, 2012: 39). Some examples of the types of ASB that this encompasses includes: verbal abuse, bullying, nasty or obscene communications, and/or groups/individuals making threats (Harradine et al, 2004). People suffering from these kinds of behaviours *could* be conceived as ideal victims, and some have been conceptualised as such in the national media.

ASB does not have many famous cases, unlike the vast array of notorious crimes that are well known to the general public, such as the murder of James Bulger or the Great Train Robbery. This may be because ASB as a type of harm has not become established in the public consciousness, and/or because society is not as concerned or interested in sub-criminal behaviour or the people it affects. Undoubtedly, the most high-profile ASB case to date is that of Fiona Pilkington from 2007, and those involved could be conceived as ideal victims. Pilkington took her own life and that of her severely learning-disabled daughter, Francecca Hardwick, as a result of her family suffering sustained harassment and bullying by a group of young people, which lasted nearly 10 years. Pilkington, her disabled daughter, disabled son and mother endured a catalogue of abuse, including: having snowballs and stones thrown at their windows, which were repeatedly broken; having their gates set on fire and their bins knocked over; having rubbish dumped in their garden and young people jumping over their hedges; having young people sit on their car and mooning[3]; and being subjected to threats to kill, verbal abuse, obscenities shouted at them and physical attacks (Independent Police Complaints Commission, 2011). These types of behaviours epitomise the sustained terror that victims of personal ASB often suffer, and even though ASB is sub-criminal, it can, and does, have a devastating impact on people's lives.

Fiona Pilkington and her family can be considered to be ideal victims according to Christie's framework in a number of ways. First, they could be considered weak, due to both of Pilkington's children being disabled and also, some might argue, because the majority of victims were women.[4] The family were carrying out a respectable project; they were harassed while in and around their home, and similarly could not be blamed for the treatment they received. The youths that perpetrated the behaviour were not involved with the family (initially), so they could be deemed as unknown offenders, with no personal relationship. However, not all of Christie's attributes are met because the perpetrators in the Pilkington case would not necessarily meet the 'ideal' criteria relating to the big, bad offender. As young people conducted the ASB, they might not be considered to be physically 'big' enough to pose a significant threat. Furthermore, and perhaps most tellingly, Pilkington did not meet Christie's sixth attribute as she was seemingly not powerful enough to secure her ideal victim status, make her case as a victim known and have it properly resolved by the police. However, she was not particularly opposed in her pursuit of justice, mainly ignored. The circumstances surrounding the case were referred to the Independent Police Complaints Commission as there were concerns that Leicestershire Police did not provide a sufficient response to their complaints. Overall, there is a strong argument for the Pilkington family to be conceptualised as ideal victims.

The Pilkington case is *atypical* when considering whether Christie's ideal victim framework can be applied to personal ASB because not many ASB victims meet the same number of ideal victim criteria. A further complicating factor is that the victimisation endured by the Pilkingtons should have been treated as a disability hate crime (as argued elsewhere; see Heap, 2016). Christie (1986: 27, emphasis in original) was right when he said that 'ideal victims do not necessarily have much to do with the prevalence of *real victims*'. Drawing on Flatley's analysis of perception data from the British Crime Survey, we know that *typical* victims of ASB display certain personal characteristics, namely, living in deprived areas, being a social renter and being a victim of crime (Flatley et al, 2008). Furthermore, it has been acknowledged in a Home Office report that ASB principally occurs in social housing (Brown, 2004), and Millie (2007) suggests that the 'ASB industry' is concentrated in these areas. From the (limited) data, we can fairly confidently argue that typical victims of personal ASB reside in social housing. As such, the following analyses will focus on personal ASB victimisation that occurs in these spaces. In stark contrast to Pilkington's case, archetypal victims of personal ASB are conceptualised as non-ideal as they are not perceived to display enough ideal victim attributes, and are also seen as undeserving due their social status (Christie, 1986).

Due to the pervasive connection between ASB, social housing and deprivation, both the media's portrayal and society's conceptualisation of typical ASB victims are often *defined* by their low socio-economic status, thus constructing them as non-ideal victims. In fact, often, the media do not portray these people as ASB victims at all. A clear example of personal ASB victims represented as non-ideal as a result of their perceived level of deprivation comes from a local newspaper. A family in the south of England wanted to move from their council[5] house, reportedly because they were being victimised by anti-social neighbours. Instead of the family being portrayed by the press as genuine or deserving ASB victims, the headline above the victims' story read 'Shameless scrounging parents with eight kids demand bigger council house for their growing family', despite a spokesperson from the area confirming that ASB was a problem (*Southend News Network*, 2016). This exemplifies how many victims of personal ASB are portrayed and consequently conceptualised as non-ideal victims, especially when they reside in social housing. It is important to clarify that there is not a *causal* link between living in social housing and socio-economic deprivation, although 43% of social renters live in poverty after housing costs (Tunstall et al, 2013). However, this notion has been socially constructed to become the dominant discourse, particularly in recent times (Hodkinson and Robbins, 2012). To put this into a broader context, social housing and ASB have always been inextricably linked, since long before ASB legislation was formulated in 1998. Flint (2006: 7) states that 'social housing provides the most long-standing example of how acceptable and unacceptable behaviour, rights and responsibilities and conditionality in welfare are defined and governed'. Social housing estates are often identified as problem areas that house problem people (Papps, 1998; Card, 2006; Johnston and Mooney, 2007), which is compounded by the growing residual tenure of marginalised groups (Brown, 2004; Hancock and Mooney, 2013). Subsequently, those who live in social housing are not given any sympathy when they are victimised because they are judged by society as all being as bad as each other, and therefore guilty by association. This, combined with our knowledge that ASB victimisation is concentrated in deprived areas, is likely to shape the perception of ASB victims as non-ideal because they are not viewed as respectable and they do not have the power to make their case heard and be conferred with an ideal victim status (Christie's sixth attribute).

The ASB–social housing–deprivation link is complex and it is beyond the scope of this chapter to fully explore the history and evolution of ASB-related social housing policy. However, a brief overview of two pivotal events – the shift in housing policy following the election of a Conservative-led Coalition government in 2010 and the rhetoric surrounding the 2011 English riots – will help us to better understand why many victims of personal ASB are consequently conceptualised as non-ideal. In addition to the standard ideal victim framework, ASB victims are also perceived as non-ideal because of their lack of power (attribute six), as well as Christie's suggestion that being non-ideal is a result of others' contrary interests, which both examples demonstrate. When the Conservative–Liberal Democrat Coalition government came to power in 2010, their chosen method to deal with the ramifications of the 2008 global financial crisis was to employ austerity politics. This resulted in severe cuts to unprotected public spending budgets and real-terms cuts of, on average, 20.5% between 2010 and 2016/17 (Institute for Fiscal Studies, 2016). In social housing terms, housing benefit 'was portrayed as "out of control" across the UK and unsustainable to the public purse' (Hodkinson and Robbins, 2012: 67). This was accompanied by a political discourse led by the (then) Prime Minister David Cameron, which stressed that the 'system' was unfairly favouring housing benefit claimants at the expense of hard-working families (Cameron, 2012). This perspective formed part of the 'broken society' narrative, pursued by the Conservative Party since 2006, which 'focused on social and moral decay which manifested in anti-social behaviour, crime and assorted "problematic" social practices in disadvantaged working class communities' (Hancock and Mooney, 2013: 47). One of the key drivers of the 'broken society' ideology was considered to be the reliance on welfare benefits, which created divisions within society. Tyler (2013a: 9) neatly explains that 'in such a climate public anxieties and hostilities are channelled towards those groups within the population, such as the unemployed, welfare recipients and irregular migrants, who are imagined to be a parasitical drain and threat to national resources', all of whom would likely be social housing tenants as a result of the residualisation of tenure. This division is evidenced by the British Social Attitudes Survey, which shows that public opinions towards welfare claimants have hardened, with people more likely to believe that poverty is caused by individual factors rather than societal ones (Taylor-Gooby and Taylor, 2014). These attitudes contrast public views in previous times of recession (Joseph Rowntree Foundation,

2013) and demonstrate how political rhetoric has impacted upon the public's general belief system. Consequently, when members of these marginalised groups become victims of ASB, which they are more likely to do because of their tenure, they are unlikely to receive public sympathy because of the stigma associated with their socio-economic and housing statuses.

Not long after the advent of austerity politics, the 2011 English riots took place. Unrest broke out in London following the fatal police shooting of Mark Duggan, and subsequently spread to many major towns and cities across the country over a period of five days. Without delving into the causes of the riots (see Lewis et al, 2011; Briggs, 2012), the government's immediate reaction was to blame a combination of actors, which included social housing tenants. This resulted in demands to stop the benefits of convicted rioters who lived in social housing, as well as the benefits of the family members they lived with. The public applied pressure on the Coalition to execute this move via a government e-petition (Tyler, 2013b). It received a total of 258,276 signatures, which meant that it easily passed the 100,000 signature threshold required to necessitate a response (Petitions UK Government and Parliament, 2017). After much protraction, the final outcome was to introduce the 'riot clause' into the Anti-Social Behaviour, Crime and Policing Act 2014, which provides powers to social landlords to evict tenants that have been convicted of rioting, including evicting the family if a child is the offender. Young (2016) outlines how this creates a two-tier punishment system as social housing tenants are doubly punished compared to those who reside in private tenure. The creation of this legislation adds further weight to the notion that those living in social housing are stigmatised, and builds on the idea that when they are victims of ASB, they are conceptualised as non-ideal victims.

The focus on personal ASB victims' socio-economic status and tenure can be further related to Christie's ideal victim framework, with society not perceiving these victims to meet certain attributes. For example, 'as the role of council housing has changed and anti-welfare discourses have gained ascendency ... all council tenants have become perceived as irresponsible, work-shy and "undeserving"' (Card, 2006: 54). Hence, when they are victimised, social renters would not be considered as 'carrying out a respectable project' (criteria two) or living where they could 'not possibly be blamed for being' (criteria three). However, Christie's ideal victim framework is unhelpful when victims have *multiple identities* as some of the attributes appear to be more important than others. Multiple identities make it difficult to predict who will be seen as 'ideal' when applying Christie's framework.

For example, some disabled people are disproportionately more at risk of ASB victimisation because we know that there are high numbers of disabled social housing tenants who also live in deprived areas (Wood and Edwards, 2005). Disabled people would be reasonably conceived as ideal victims if they experienced ASB (like in the Pilkington case) because they would be perceived as weak in relation to the offender. However, these conceptualisations may be based on *assumptions* about the victims' identity (or identities). For example, some disabled people have a hidden condition, such as a mental illness. If victimised, they may not be immediately judged as weak in relation to the offender, although their condition may render them as such. Furthermore, when considering multiple identities, disabled people claiming benefits are increasingly portrayed as 'scroungers' by the government and media (Hancock and Mooney, 2013). The changing views towards disabled benefit claimants demonstrates how conceptions of the ideal are *dynamic* over time, and can be overshadowed by a dominant non-ideal trait, which is at the mercy of wider societal discourse. At present, it appears that fulfilling the respectability criteria is the most important factor when considering whether someone is conceived as an ideal ASB victim or not. For example, social housing tenants who are in low-paid work may be conceptualised as ideal victims (based on the notion that they were carrying out a respectable project), compared to someone claiming unemployment benefits, who would be viewed as non-ideal, despite both sharing the same socio-economic status. This is problematic from a victim perspective because unemployed people could be some of the weakest and most vulnerable in society, but that does not seem to matter because they are not undertaking a respectable project. These judgements, whether based on a correct or incorrect assumption, determine whether the victim is seen as deserving or undeserving of public sympathy.

The underlying narratives of ASB-related social housing policy developments have created a climate where certain groups that (are likely to) live in social housing, and are more likely to experience ASB, are viewed as the undeserving poor. This social division has been reinforced by a discourse in popular culture that utilises the word *chav* as the 'pejorative and ubiquitous term of abuse of and abhorrence at Britain's poor' (Tyler, 2013a: 162). This has created an 'us' and 'them' situation (Jones, 2011), which may result in some victims of ASB rejecting or resisting their victim status in order to avoid being seen as part of the 'problem'. The flexible perception-based definition of ASB permits this to happen, allowing victims to suggest that behaviour which could be interpreted as ASB is considered 'normal' in that particular location (Heap, 2010). This tolerance of certain behaviours in a social housing context, which would not be acceptable elsewhere, may reinforce public stereotypes about the nature of the people that live in social housing, and the perceived lower standards to which they live. Regardless of how the foundations for the conceptions about ideal and non-ideal victims of ASB have been constructed, the fact that there is such a polarisation between perceptions of deserving and undeserving victims creates a hierarchy of victimisation. From a victimological perspective, this is damaging as it demarcates and prioritises certain victims depending on their identity (or identities), which is unfair (Duggan and Heap, 2014). Ultimately, given that the statistics show that we do not always know what types of ASB individual victims of personal ASB are suffering from, coupled with the way in which people who are most likely to be victims of ASB are portrayed, we can assume that society does not necessarily care.

Conceptualising communities as victims of anti-social behaviour

Unlike many crimes that have a discrete victim or victims, some types of ASB conducted in public spaces can be considered to have a negative impact on a *whole community*. Nuisance ASB, according to the police NSIR, occurs 'where an act, condition, thing or person causes trouble, annoyance, irritation, inconvenience, offence or suffering to the local community in general rather than to individual victims' (ONS, 2012: 40). Types of nuisance behaviour could include actions such as urinating in public, taking drugs, loitering, cycling/skateboarding in pedestrian areas and drunken behaviour (Harradine et al, 2004). Similarly, the NSIR environmental category 'deals with the interface between people and places ... where individuals and groups have an impact on their surroundings, including natural, built and social environments' (ONS, 2012: 40). Examples of environmental ASB include graffiti, damage to buildings/street furniture, dropping litter and fly-tipping (Harradine et al, 2004). Subsequently, ASB in public spaces can potentially affect *anyone* who uses that space, although the context, location, community tolerance levels and quality of life expectations will affect which behaviours are deemed to be anti-social or not (Nixon et al, 2003).

Christie's ideal victim framework is only applicable when the victim is *identifiable*, which is usually dependent on the type of space the nuisance and/or environmental ASB has been conducted in. When these types of ASB occur in a neighbourhood setting, the victim is more likely to be known. For example, if a street continually suffers from graffiti, the occupier/owner of the property that has been damaged can be conceived as the victim. Similarly, if the behaviour involves groups 'loitering' or creating noise nuisance, the individuals affected would be considered the victims. In these cases, Christie's ideal victim framework can be applied in a similar way to personal ASB. As a consequence of the socio-economic undertones that are apparent in ASB discourse, the perception of a neighbourhood as being 'rough' or 'respectable' (Watt, 2006) will be considered when its victim status is being assessed. If the area contains social housing, the victimisation will most likely be conceptualised as non-ideal due to the long-standing stigmatisation of these areas. Neighbourhoods that constitute primarily owner-occupiers are more likely to be perceived as ideal victims because of their conformity to Christie's second and third attributes: carrying out a respectable project and not being to blame for their victimisation.

When attempting to apply Christie's ideal victim framework to ASB, the scenario that proves most testing is when nuisance or environmental ASB occurs in urban public spaces, such as town centres. This is predominantly because in numerous situations, it is difficult to establish exactly who the victim is. It is also extremely challenging to determine if the one or more individuals in question identify as a victim themselves. These factors add further complexity to the aspiration to quantify ASB because nuisance and environmental ASB are likely to have multiple victims. To confound matters further, the types of behaviours that are sometimes considered to be problematic in public spaces are not necessarily perceived to be anti-social by all the users of that particular area. A relevant example here is swearing; this behaviour is currently attracting widespread attention in the UK because it is increasingly being legislated against in town-centre spaces. A contemporary (and controversial) ASB power, a Public Spaces Protection Order (PSPO), gives local councils the power to prohibit or require certain behaviours in a designated area where they negatively affect the 'quality of life'.[6] At the time of writing, several local councils in England have created PSPOs that prohibit swearing. Perpetrators can receive a fine of up to £100 from a fixed penalty notice, or be fined up to £1,000 on summary conviction. For example, a PSPO created by Salford City Council (2015) prohibits 'using foul and abusive language' in and around Salford Quays. This relates to swearing in general, not swearing at someone, although no list of 'banned' words or phrases has been produced. Despite Christie (1986: 18) stating that victimisation is 'an objective phenomenon', this is a bold step in the defence of the 'quality of life' because research conducted into swearing in public suggests that it 'is not an infrequent act, and most instances of swearing are conversational; they are not highly emotional, confrontational, rude, or aggressive' (Jay and Janschewitz, 2008: 268). Clearly, Salford City Council perceives there to be victims whose quality of life has been impaired or offended by the presence of swearing. However, this perception is unlikely to be based on reports of swearing to the local council or police as it is probably very unlikely that a victim will make a report based on the 'quality of life'. It has been argued that Salford City Council has created this prohibition in the regenerated 'posh' part of town frequented by visitors, with the perpetrators likely coming from the neighbouring deprived areas (*Guardian*, 2016), which resonates with previous discussions about class and stigmatisation. Whether deliberately or as a by-product, Salford City Council has decreased behavioural tolerance levels and (further) widened the net of the criminal justice system (for a more detailed discussion of PSPOs, tolerance and civility, see Heap and Dickinson, forthcoming). By prohibiting, and hence criminalising, something that is impossible to universally define (Jay and Janschewitz, 2008), it appears that an ideal victim of swearing has been constructed by Salford City Council: someone whom they wish to protect; someone weak[7] in relation to the offender; someone carrying out a respectable project; someone blameless; and someone with a big, bad, unknown swearing offender. Christie (1986: 29) himself expressed how 'to me it seems an important ideal to help create social systems where people are so close to each other that concepts such as crime and criminals are seen by everybody as being of very limited usefulness'. Prohibiting swearing through PSPOs appears to be the antithesis of this statement.

Overall, applying Christie's ideal victim framework to conceptualise communities as victims of ASB has been possible when the identity of the victim or victims has been known. In contrast, when the identity of the victim is unclear, it is difficult to apply the framework, although it appears to have been employed by proxy by those who wish to prevent victimisation (even when the extent of that victimisation might be minimal).

Concluding thoughts

On paper, it looks like many individual victims of personal ASB, and communities affected by nuisance and environmental ASB, could be conceptualised as ideal victims as they meet many of the attributes; weak (due to marginalisation or disability); carrying out a respectable project; blameless; and with a big and bad unknown offender. However, in practice, it seems that external factors, such as government and media discourses, have the power to influence which of the ideal criteria are deemed most important. At present, this has resulted in many ASB victims being portrayed as unrespectable, chiefly because of the stigmatisation surrounding social housing and claiming welfare benefits. Despite the notion of an ideal victim being inherently hierarchical, these added socially constructed layers of deservedness reinforce and extend this hierarchy of victimisation, and cast off a section of society considered to be undeserving of sympathy and, in some cases, our help. This is extremely problematic and likely to doubly victimise those people who are part of this conceptualised non-ideal residual group.

The operationalisation of Christie's ideal victim framework results in many victims of ASB being conceptualised as undeserving, which mirrors several other chapters in this volume. This highlights how ASB victims are perceived in a similar way as victims of crime, by both the criminal justice system and the public. Unfortunately, the current trend for criminalising acts of ASB, coupled with the government's commitment to austerity, means that any prospect of changing perceptions of ASB victims in the near future looks unlikely. Considering that Christie's (1986) victim framework and broader ideas about victimisation were outlined long before ASB became the central part of the criminal justice system it is today, the aspects that relate to ASB victimisation are impressive. It underlines how the foundational principles of Christie's theory have stood the tests of both time and context. However, the extent to which his framework can be accurately *applied* to victims of ASB is limited by the fact that not all the attributes are perceived as equally important.

Notes

[1] 'ACORN' (an acronym for A Classification of Residential Neighbourhoods) categorises households into five main groups according to their demographic, housing and employment characteristics. More information is available at: www. acorn.caci.co.uk

[2] 'Boy racer' is the term applied to young men driving high-powered cars in a fast and/or aggressive manner.

[3] In the UK, traditionally and in this context, the meaning of 'mooning' is to expose one's buttocks to someone in order to offend or insult them. Not to be confused with the action of putting one's mobile phone into 'do not disturb' mode, which is also known as mooning.

[4] Christie's (1986) chapter has an underlying gendered narrative, which is beyond the remit of this chapter to explore further.

[5] Throughout this chapter 'council housing' and 'social housing' are used interchangeably, with both terms referring to affordable housing that is provided at low rents to those who are in need and/or have a low income (Shelter, 2017).

⁶ What the 'quality of life' means, whose quality of life and how much it needs to be affected is not defined any further in the legislation or accompanying Home Office guidance.

⁷ Weak physically, although not necessarily weak in terms of social or economic capital given the suggestion that the PSPO has been created in the 'posh' part of town.

References

Armitage, R. (2002) *Tackling Anti-Social Behaviour: What Really Works*, London: Nacro.

Briggs, D. (2012) *The English Riots of 2011: A Summer of Discontent*, Hampshire: Waterside Press.

Brown, A.P. (2004) 'Anti-social behaviour, crime control and social control', *The Howard Journal*, 43(2): 203–11.

Cameron, D. (2012) 'Speech on welfare reform', Kent, 25 June. Available at: https://www.gov.uk/government/speeches/welfare-speech (accessed February 2017).

Card, P. (2006) 'Governing tenants: from dreadful enclosures to dangerous places', in J. Flint (ed) *Housing, Urban Governance and Anti-Social Behaviour*, Bristol: Policy Press.

Christie, N. (1986) 'The ideal victim', in E.A. Fattah (ed) *From Crime Policy to Victim Policy: Reorienting the Justice System*, Basingstoke: Macmillan, pp 17–30.

Cracknell, S. (2000) 'Anti-Social Behaviour Orders', in D. Morgan and I. McDonald (eds) *Journal of Social Welfare and Family Law*, 22(1): 108–15.

Duggan, M. and Heap, V. (2014) *Administrating Victimization: The Politics of Anti-Social Behaviour and Hate Crime Policy*, Basingstoke: Palgrave.

Flatley, J., Moley, S. and Hoare, J. (2008) *Perceptions of Anti-Social Behaviour: Findings from the 2007/08 British Crime Survey. Supplementary Volume 1 to Crime in England and Wales 2007/08*, Home Office Statistical Bulletin 15/08, London: Home Office.

Flint, J. (2006) 'Introduction', in J. Flint (ed) *Housing, Urban Governance and Anti-Social Behaviour*, Bristol: Policy Press.

Guardian (2016) 'You want to stop people swearing in the posh part of town? ★#?! off!', 10 March. Available at: http://www.theguardian.com/commentisfree/2016/mar/10/swearing-fine-salford-quays (accessed February 2017).

Hancock, L. and Mooney, G. (2013) '"Welfare ghettos" and the "broken society": territorial stigmatization in the contemporary UK', *Housing, Theory and Society*, 30(1): 46–64.

Harradine, S., Kodz, J., Lemetti, F. and Jones, B. (2004) *Defining and Measuring Anti-Social Behaviour*, Home Office Development and Practice Report 26, London: Home Office.

Heap, V. (2009) '"I don't say that bored kids hanging about are bad, but they are scary!" Exploring attitudinal factors that affect public perceptions of anti-social behaviour', *Papers from the British Criminology Conference*, 9: 71–91.

Heap, V. (2010) 'Understanding public perceptions of anti-social behaviour: problems and policy responses', doctoral thesis, University of Huddersfield. Available at: http://eprints.hud.ac.uk/9209/

Heap, V. (2016) 'Putting victims first? A critique of Coalition anti-social behaviour policy', *Critical Social Policy*, 36(2): 246–64.

Heap, V. and Dickinson, J. (forthcoming) *Public Spaces Protection Orders: a critical policy analysis*.

Hodkinson, S. and Robbins, G. (2012) 'The return of class war conservatism? Housing under the UK Coalition government', *Critical Social Policy*, 33(1): 57–71.

Independent Police Complaints Commission (2011) 'IPCC report into the contact between Fiona Pilkington and Leicestershire Constabulary 2004–2007'. Available at: http://www.hampshiresab.org.uk/wp-content/uploads/2009-Fiona-Pilkington-Leicestershire.pdf (accessed February 2017).

Institute for Fiscal Studies (2016) *Winter is Coming: The Outlook for the Public Finances in the 2016 Autumn Statement*, London: Institute for Fiscal Studies.

Jay, T. and Janschewitz, K. (2008) 'The pragmatics of swearing', *Journal of Politeness Studies*, 4: 267–88.

Johnston, C. and Mooney, G. (2007) '"Problem" people, "problem" places? New Labour and council estates', in R. Atkinson and G. Helms (eds) *Securing an Urban Renaissance: Crime, Community and British Urban Policy*, Bristol: Policy Press.

Jones, O. (2011) *Chavs: The Demonization of the Working Class*, London: Verso.

Joseph Rowntree Foundation (2013) 'Tough on people in poverty – new report shows public's hardening attitudes to welfare'. Available at: https://www.jrf.org.uk/press/tough-people-poverty-%E2%80%93-new-report-shows-public%E2%80%99s-hardening-attitudes-welfare (accessed February 2017).

Lewis, P., Newburn, T., Taylor, M., Mcgillivray, C., Greenhill, A., Frayman, H. and Proctor, R. (2011) *Reading the Riots: Investigating England's Summer of Disorder*, London: London School of Economics and Political Science and *The Guardian*. Available at: http://eprints. lse.ac.uk/46297/1/Reading%20the%20riots%28published%29.pdf (accessed February 2017).

Lewis, S., Crawford, A. and Traynor, P. (2016) 'Nipping crime in the bud? The use of antisocial behaviour interventions with young people in England and Wales', *British Journal of Criminology*, 57(5): 1230–48.

Matthews, R., Easton, H., Briggs, D. and Pease, K. (2007) *Assessing the Use and Impact of Anti-Social Behaviour Orders*, Bristol: Policy Press.

Millie, A. (2007) *Anti-Social Behaviour*, Maidenhead: McGraw Hill.

Nixon, J., Blandy, S., Hunter, C., Reeve, K. and Jones, A. (2003) *Tackling Anti-Social Behaviour in Mixed Tenure Areas*, London: ODPM.

ONS (Office for National Statistics) (2012) *User Guide to Crime Statistics for England and Wales*, London: ONS.

ONS (2013) *Crime in England and Wales, Year Ending March 2013*, London: ONS.

ONS (2014) *Crime in England and Wales, Year Ending March 2014*, London: ONS.

ONS (2017a) *Crime in England and Wales: Bulletin Tables*, London: ONS. Available at: https://www.ons.gov.uk/ peoplepopulationandcommunity/crimeandjustice/datasets/ crimeinenglandandwalesbulletintables (accessed August 2017).

ONS (2017b) *Crime in England and Wales, Year Ending March 2017*, London: ONS.

Papps, P. (1998) 'Anti-social behaviour strategies – individualistic or holistic?', *Housing Studies*, 13(5): 639–56.

Petitions UK Government and Parliament (2017) 'Convicted London rioters should loose [sic] all benefits'. Available at: https://petition. parliament.uk/archived/petitions/7337 (accessed February 2017).

Salford City Council (2015) 'Salford Quays Public Spaces Protection Order'. Available at: https://www.salford.gov.uk/crime-reduction-and-emergencies/anti-social-behaviour/public-spaces-protection-orders/salford-quays-pspo/ (accessed February 2017).

Shelter (2017) 'What is social housing?'. Available at: http://england. shelter.org.uk/campaigns_/why_we_campaign/Improving_social_ housing/what_is_social_housing (accessed February 2017).

Southend News Network (2016) 'Shameless scrounging parents with eight kids demand bigger council house for their growing family', 2 June. Available at: http://southendnewsnetwork.com/news/shameless-scrounging-parents-with-eight-kids-demand-bigger-council-house-for-their-growing-family/ (accessed February 2017).

Taylor-Gooby, P. and Taylor, E. (2014) 'Benefits and welfare: long-term trends or short-term reactions?', British Social Attitudes 32. Available at: http://www.bsa.natcen.ac.uk/media/38977/bsa32_welfare.pdf (accessed February 2017).

Tunstall, R., Bevan, M., Bradshaw, J., Croucher, K., Duffy, S., Hunter, C., Jones, A., Rugg, J., Wallace, A. and Wilcox, A. (2013) 'The links between housing and poverty: an evidence review', Joseph Rowntree Foundation. Available at: https://www.york.ac.uk/media/chp/documents/2013/poverty-housing-options-full.pdf (accessed February 2017).

Tyler, I. (2013a) *Revolting Subjects: Social Abjection and Resistance in Neoliberal Britain*, London: Zed Books.

Tyler, I. (2013b) 'The riots of the underclass? Stigmatisation, mediation and the government of poverty and disadvantage in neoliberal Britain', *Sociological Research Online*, 18(4): 6.

Walklate, S. (2007) *Imagining the Victim of Crime*, Maidenhead: Open University Press.

Watt, P. (2006) 'Respectability, roughness and "race": neighbourhood place images and the making of working-class social distinctions in London', *International Journal of Urban and Regional Research*, 30(4): 776–97.

Whitehead, C.M.E., Stockdale, J.E. and Razzu, G. (2003) *The Economic and Social Costs of Anti-Social Behaviour: A Review*, London: London School of Economics and Political Science.

Wood, J. and Edwards, K. (2005) 'Victimization of mentally ill patients living in the community: is it a life-style choice?', *Legal and Criminal Psychology*, 10: 279–90.

Wood, M. (2004) *Perceptions and Experience of Anti-Social Behaviour: Findings from the 2003/2004 British Crime Survey*, Home Office Online Report 49/04, London: Home Office.

Young, G.J. (2016) 'Pushing the boundaries: urban unrest as anti-social behaviour', *Safer Communities*, 15(4): 202–12.

TWELVE

The 'ideal' rape victim and the elderly woman: a contradiction in terms?

Hannah Bows

Introduction

The 'ideal victim' was described by Christie (1986) as embodying a number of attributes, including weakness, age (old or very young), respectability and blamelessness; these attributes are nowhere more important than in rape cases. In particular, rape myths and stereotypes (Burt, 1980) have depicted the 'real-rape' victim to be young, female and attractive, and the perpetrator to be male, usually a stranger, who attacks the vulnerable woman late at night as she walks home. Decades of research has challenged these myths and stereotypes, and it is well known that the majority of rapes occur in the context of a relationship in the victim's home (ONS, 2015). Despite this, the 'real-rape' stereotype persists in society and is perpetuated by the popular media, who tend to report cases of rape that are in keeping with this stereotype (Korn and Efrat, 2004; Franiuk et al, 2008; Mahria, 2008).

Despite feminist efforts to challenge these dominant myths, there has been very little research or activism focusing on the myths concerning victim age. As Jones and Powell (2006) point out, feminists have largely distanced themselves from issues relating to older women. It remains the case that older rape victims do not fit the real-rape stereotype of a young attractive woman who is attacked, late at night, because of her sexual desirability. However, when cases of rape involving older women hit the headlines, the ideal victim that Christie describes is crucial in framing and conceptualising their victimisation. Older people in general are portrayed in the media as inherently vulnerable, old and frail, making them ideal victims. The contrasting dynamics of age and gender in assigning legitimate victim identity when it comes to sexual violence will be addressed in this chapter. Drawing on data from the first national study to examine the extent of recorded rape offences involving a female victim aged 60 or over, this chapter challenges the depiction of the ideal older rape victim that dominates the media coverage of such cases. This chapter will demonstrate that reported cases of rape involving an older woman are broadly similar to those involving younger women; the offences usually take place in the victim's home and the perpetrator is usually known to the victim. However, unlike younger victims, older women are afforded legitimate victim status due to their inherent vulnerability, which is crucial in framing these cases and developing a 'real-rape' stereotype of *older* people.

Background

Sexual violence is a global pandemic. The World Health Organization (2013) estimates that more than 35% of women experience at least one incident of sexual violence during their lifetime. Over the last four decades, there has been extensive research conducted to examine the extent, nature, impacts and causes of sexual violence. The most significant theoretical contributions about the causes of sexual violence have been from feminists, who have located sexual violence on a continuum (Kelly, 1988), constituting different forms and behaviours experienced at different times across the life course. This continuum operates within a broader patriarchal structure that subordinates women while simultaneously empowering and privileging men. The oppression and subordination that women experience facilitates and normalises the extent and range of sexual violence that women experience. Thus, rape is not about sex, but power, control and domination (Brownmiller, 1975), and we consequently need to tackle the societal and cultural gendered structures instead of individual men (Schwartz and DeKeseredy, 2008).

Importantly, the gender roles, norms and values that women and men are socialised into both contribute to and perpetuate the structures that create what has been termed 'rape culture', that is, 'the social, cultural and structural discourses and practices in which sexual violence is tolerated, accepted, minimized, normalized, and trivialized' (Henry and Powell, 2014: 2). As Hayes, Abbott and Cook (2016: 1541) describe, 'rape culture is derived from rhetorical patterns that are entrenched in conscious or unconscious hetero-normative, White male, privileged traditions'. Thus, in a rape culture, rape and other forms of sexual violence are common but the prosecution and conviction of these acts are not (Messina-Dysert, 2015). Furthermore, sexual violence is eroticised in the popular media, literature and film. Perpetrators are rarely held accountable in fiction or real life, and victim blaming is rife: women are told they deserved it, they asked for it and they should take responsibility for it (Henry and Powell, 2014).

These attitudes and victim-blaming perspectives are strongly associated with rape myths and stereotypes. Burt (1980: 217) defined rape myths as 'prejudicial, stereotyped, or false beliefs about rape, rape victims, and rapists'. Some prevalent myths include: people provoke rape by the way they dress or act; rape is a crime of passion and based on sexual desire; rape occurs between strangers, at night in dark alleys; women cry rape when they regret having sex; women fight and scream if they are raped; and if the victim did not complain immediately, then it is not rape (Burrowes, 2013). Rape myths are not just inaccurate assumptions about rape, victims and perpetrators; they also have socio-legal consequences for victims. A significant body of literature has emerged over the last two decades that has explored rape myths and the links between belief in such myths and increased likelihood of raping (Bohner et al, 2005; Chapleau and Oswald, 2014). Similarly, Ellison and Munro's (2009) work on jurors' belief in myths and the impact on decisions in (mock) trials have illustrated the depth of denial in accepting that a victim is telling the truth about what happened to them. Such research has demonstrated the negative consequences of rape myth acceptance: people who have not been raped tend to consider stranger assault to be more of a 'real' crime and distressing than rape where the victim knows the perpetrator (Whatley, 1996) and are more likely to blame the victim in acquaintance rape compared to stranger rape (Abrams et al, 2003; Monson et al, 2000; Westmarland and Graham, 2010). In other words, these myths form together to create an ideal victim and a real-rape model that must be conformed to in order for victims to be believed and given victim status.

The 'real-rape' stereotype and the 'ideal victim'

The concept that there exists a 'real-rape' victim was first introduced by Estrich (1987) to describe the dominant stereotype around what constitutes rape. This stereotype involves a particular victim (female, young, white) raped by a particular perpetrator (male, young, stranger) in particular circumstances (at night/in the dark, dragged away from a public place, such as a park or alleyway). This model involves what Williams (1984) described as the 'classic' rape situation, involving a stranger, severe force and physical injury. Moreover, the race of both the victim and perpetrator is central to this stereotype and influences rape blame attribution (Donovan, 2007). As Donovan (2007) points out, research has consistently shown that rape is seen as more serious when the victim is white rather than black. Moreover, racial factors are more detrimental for black men accused of raping white women, reflecting the stereotype that black men are sexual predators of white women (Donovan, 2007).

The classic rape stereotype largely echoes the characteristics identified by Christie (1986). It is important that the victim is ideal in order for the rape to be real: the victim should be physically weaker than the offender, there should be no previous relationship, the victim must be acting or doing something considered respectable, and the victim cannot be blameworthy in any way – to some extent, this includes being white. As Stevenson (2000) argues, it is vital that rape complainants are 'unequivocal victims'.

In addition to the rape myths described earlier, which support the classic rape stereotype, the media and popular fiction continue to perpetuate this model (Adelman, 1989; Brinson, 1992; Bufkin and Eschholz, 2000; Korn and Efrat, 2004; Larcombe, 2005; Franiuk et al, 2008; Mahria, 2008). Television, film, literature and mass media contribute to a dichotomy where women are either innocent or whores; if the rape conforms to the classic rape and the victim embodies the ideal attributes, then they are viewed as legitimate victims. However, if the woman wears revealing clothing, acts in a way that is viewed as provocative (consuming alcohol, flirting, inviting the perpetrator back for coffee, etc), then they are depicted as whores and the rape is instead portrayed as a (regretted) sexual encounter. Moreover, Kahlor and Morrison (2007) demonstrated an association between the consumption of general, everyday television programmes and the acceptance of rape myths, including that only women portrayed as promiscuous are raped. Additionally, they report a positive relationship between television use and perceptions that rape accusations are false.

However, despite widespread perpetration of, and belief in, the classic rape scenario and ideal rape victim, research has overwhelmingly shown that very few rapes conform to this narrow model and, consequently, very few victims conform to this idealised typology (Rennison and Rand, 2003). In the UK, national data suggest that only 15% of rapes involve a stranger (ONS, 2015) and research has observed that women are most likely to be assaulted by a partner or acquaintance, often in social situations that involve the consumption of alcohol by the victim and/or perpetrator(s) (Kelly et al, 2005). Despite this evidence, the classic rape stereotype persists in society.

One of the important components of this stereotype, the victim's youth, has remained relatively unchallenged in the literature. Perhaps influenced by the age–crime curve, which sees offending and victimisation peak in late adolescence and decline thereafter (see Bows, 2016), the majority of efforts to challenge rape myths and stereotypes have not given consideration to the older victim. Some scholars have gone as far as to describe this as a form of rape denial (Jones and Powell, 2006); this has been coupled with calls for a critical, feminist analysis of sexual violence that incorporates older victims (Whittaker, 1995; Penhale, 2003; Lea et al, 2011; Mann et al, 2014).

The 'ideal' older rape victim

Older rape victims do not fit the classic rape stereotype of a young, attractive woman who is attacked by a stranger because of her sexual desirability (Bows and Westmarland, 2017). Older people may be less likely to be out in public spaces at night, where rape occurs according to the classic stereotype. Moreover, society tends to view older people as not sexually desirable, largely based on ageist attitudes that view old age as a process of decay, decline and deterioration (Jones and Powell, 2006). As I have highlighted elsewhere (Bows and Westmarland, 2017), sexuality in old age continues to be a taboo subject in society, and the existing academic literature has predominantly focused on sexual health and physiological issues in older age (Kleinplatz, 2008), giving the impression that sex in later life is either non-existent or associated with negativity.

However, despite not fitting the classic rape stereotype, older people do meet several of the criteria for being an 'ideal victim' that Christie (1986) identified. Similar to the example that Christie gives of an older women being mugged by a male stranger in public, older rape victims can be seen as frail and weak, and are more likely to be viewed as blameless and respectable as they are less likely to be engaging in activities or behaviour that are known to lead to higher levels of victim blaming (such as being drunk, flirting with the rapist or wearing clothes that are constructed as provocative).

These personal and situational characteristics underpin the construction of what we have argued elsewhere is a specific 'classic' or 'real-rape' stereotype *specifically for older people* (Bows and Westmarland, 2017). This is particularly evident in media reports; the vast majority of cases that make the news headlines involve a younger male stranger who rapes an elderly woman either at home (usually in the pursuit of another crime, such as burglary) or in public. The emergence of this *specific* stereotype of offences involving older victims is almost identical in criteria to Christie's description of the 'ideal victim', relying heavily on the inherent vulnerability assumed of older people to make sense of their victimisation. A quick news search of recent reported cases involving elderly victims of rape conforms to this model. For example, *Press Telegram* reported on an incident involving a man who raped five elderly women after breaking into their homes and stealing personal belongings from each victim (Dobruck, 2017). In Albertville, Waay TV reported that a man was arrested for the rape and burglary of an 82-year-old woman (Aiello and Christmas, 2017). In October 2017, *The Express* reported on a case in Germany of a 90-year-old women who was raped by a 19-year-old man (Rogers, 2016). In March 2017, a 41-year-old man admitted raping an 81-year-old woman in public after he sat next to her on a bus before following her and dragging her into a secluded area in Tooting, London. In a report of the case and subsequent community support for the victim, the *Wandsworth Guardian* included quotes from local residents, who described their horror at the attack on a 'vulnerable' victim (Cuffe, 2017).

Importantly, in all of these cases, the victim was white. There are few reported cases of rape involving an older woman from a minority ethnic group in the media, contributing to the ideal 'white' victim. In a number of these cases, the perpetrator is not white, and this is at the forefront of the media construction of the case. In the German example provided, the perpetrator was a male migrant, originally from North Africa. The chief of police is quoted in the article as stating that criminal migrants from North Africa despised the country and were 'laughing' at the German justice system. This racialisation of sexual violence is bound up with wider socio-political stigmatisation of migrants and societal racism. The headline for this article in another newspaper (*The Daily Star*) read 'Migrant rapes 60-year-old woman'. In another example, *The Express* reported on a separate rape of a 69-year-old woman by a 'Romanian migrant' (Sheldrick, 2016) in Worthing, England. The status of the perpetrator (migrant) and his length of time in the country (less than three months) are described before the details of the rape or that of the victim. It is interesting that in this report, the perpetrator is quoted as telling the court that if he was going to commit a rape, it would be against someone his own age.

The implied vulnerability of older people (especially women) is particularly important in the media coverage of cases of elderly victims of rape. Emotive terminology alluding to frailty and vulnerability is often used, alongside moralistic terms such as 'shocking', 'horrifying' and so on to describe the event, despite there often being no evidence that the victim is 'vulnerable'. For example, in a report by *The Age*, an Australian newspaper website, the rape of an 80-year-old woman by a 56-year-old man is described as 'incomprehensible'. The judge described the rape as 'an abhorrent violation of a vulnerable woman' (Cooper, 2016). As there is no explanation or further detail given as to what made the victim vulnerable, one assumes that this qualification was based on her advanced years. In a *Guardian* report of the rape of an elderly woman in her own home by an 18-year-old man, the senior prosecutor is quoted as describing the victim as 'extremely vulnerable' and the attack as 'abhorrent'. However, what makes these elderly victims any more, or less, vulnerable than younger victims? What makes the attacks more horrifying, abhorrent or shocking than *any* sexual attack?

Fundamentally, it appears that the framing of these offences reflects the dominant depiction of rape being fundamentally about sex, and, importantly, sexual desirability. It is therefore unbelievable, shocking or horrifying that an older woman could be raped; after all, older people are not sexy, or desirable – especially to younger men. Thus, the only way that the rape of older people can be understood is through the lens of vulnerability. In an analysis of the concepts of vulnerability and victimisation, Walklate (2011) identifies age as a structural dimension that has been key to a number of influential theories or models for understanding who is victimised. Drawing on the work of Sparks (1982), Walklate also points out that vulnerability has been used to describe a state in which victims find themselves vulnerable because of attributes they possess rather than anything that they actually did to put themselves at risk. Therefore, being old *and* 'frail' are examples of such attributes; however, as Walklate (citing Pain, 2003) points out, this approach fuels ageist stereotypes even though – and because – not all older people are frail. This inherent vulnerability is narrowly constructed and one dimensional. In the case of older rape victims, despite not conforming to the 'classic, real-rape' stereotype afforded to younger women, they can legitimately claim victim status through their positioning as 'ideal victims' due to age, inherent vulnerability (blamelessness) and respectability. As Walklate (2011) indicates, a hierarchy of victimisation exists and the assumed vulnerability of older people places them at the top of it.

Challenging the stereotype

Despite international news stories of rape involving older victims, sexual violence perpetrated against women aged 60 and over has only recently begun to attract scholarly attention. Over the last two decades, a small but growing number of studies or papers have considered this issue, although it is often examined alongside other forms of abuse within the definitional parameters of domestic violence or 'elder abuse' (for an overview, see Bows, 2017). Few studies have specifically examined sexual violence against this cohort, with only three studies published in the last decade in the UK (for a review of the literature, see Bows, 2017).

In order to address the gaps in existing research, I conducted a national study to examine the extent, nature and impacts of sexual violence against people of all genders aged 60 and over. The first phase of this mixed-methods study involved analysing police-recorded data on rape and sexual assault by penetration offences (the two most serious offences under the Sexual Offences Act 2003) involving a victim aged 60 or older, recorded between 1 January 2009 and 31 December 2013. The data were collected from all police forces in England, Wales and Northern Ireland using Freedom of Information requests (for reflections on the use of this method, see Bows, 2017).

Overall, there were 655 cases recorded by police during this period, equating to around 150 offences per year. Most victims were female and most perpetrators were male. Reflecting the existing knowledge on younger populations, sexual violence against older people is similarly gendered. The vast majority of victims were female (92%), which reflects the national statistics. Men were victims in 7% of cases, a slightly lower figure than reported in national police-recorded figures on rape and sexual assault (11.5%). Data on the gender of the perpetrator were available from 41 forces, relating to 570 offences. In 73 cases, the gender of the perpetrator was unknown. The main reason for this was that the crime was still undetected and no suspect had yet been found. For the remaining 497 cases, the vast majority of perpetrators were male. Overall, just 12 cases (2%) involved a female perpetrator. At least four of those cases also involved a male co-perpetrator.

Two thirds (66%) of offenders were aged under 60 years of age, with 42% of these aged between 40 and 59 years. Victims, by contrast, were aged between 60 and 98 years of age, with the majority in their 60s and 70s. Most perpetrators were known to the victim. The most common relationship was acquaintance (26%), followed by partner or husband (20%) and stranger (20%). The fact that the majority of victims knew the offender is consistent with national data, which estimate that 80% of victims know their perpetrator. However, whereas national statistics (ONS, 2015) report that the majority of perpetrators are partners or ex-partners (47%), followed by other family members (33%), the present study found that the broader category of acquaintance was the most common relationship, followed by partner and stranger.

The type of relationship had obvious links to the location of the assault. Most of the assaults took place in the victim's home, with some occurring in the perpetrator's home. Where the offence took place in one of these two settings, the perpetrator was most likely an acquaintance or the victim's partner; when the offence occurred in a care home, the perpetrator was usually an unrelated carer. However, it is interesting to note that despite care homes being the second most common location, in the overall sample, unrelated carers were the fourth most common relationship group, suggesting that a significant proportion of the rapes in care homes are perpetrated by people other than carers – possibly by other residents or by visitors to the care home.

Police forces were asked to indicate where the rape or sexual assault by penetration offence was linked to another, recorded offence. Importantly, very few of the sexual offences were also linked to another crime. This indicates that the sole purpose or intention of the perpetrator – however planned or opportunistic the situation – was to commit a sexual offence. Only 51 of the cases had a positive link to one or more other offences. Details of the type of secondary offence were not requested; however, two of the police forces who provided details of a secondary crime noted that they were assault (by the suspect towards the victim) and theft of money.

These findings show that, as with younger victims, rape cases involving older victims usually involve a perpetrator who is known to them, take place in the victim's home and are not linked to another crime (such as a burglary). Thus, the rape of older women does not conform to either the 'classic, real-rape' stereotype afforded to younger women, *or* the dominant media depictions of what constitutes the 'classic, real-rape' stereotype constructed around older victims. While older women generally do not conform to either model, they do embody some characteristics of the ideal victim that Christie identified: they are older, respectable and blameless, theoretically placing them at the top of the victim hierarchy. However, notwithstanding the age dynamic, some older victims of rape cannot avail of this ideal victim status as their familiarity with the perpetrator and the location of the offence contradict the requirements of the typology. Instead, victimhood is conferred via the vulnerability associated with old age, the respectability afforded to older generations and the *blamelessness* of older victims, who are less likely to engage in behaviours or display the characteristics that feed into the dominant rape myths.

Arguably, older victims are at an advantage by being afforded the legitimate status of victim because of these attributes, yet are systematically disadvantaged by the widespread belief and acceptance of the 'classic, real-rape' stereotype, which has led to the invisibility of older victims. This is compounded further by the reporting of cases involving older people that narrowly construct these offences to involve the ideal victim (elderly, vulnerable, white, respectable) and the 'classic' rape (male, stranger, younger, often commits another offence, such as burglary). This serves to further marginalise and obscure the majority of older rape victims, who do not conform to this model.

Conclusion

Despite decades of research and activism by feminists, the 'classic, real-rape' stereotype involving the ideal victim persists, for older and younger victims, with damaging implications for women outside of this rubric. The overall lack of protest about the age of victims in the predominant 'classic, real-rape' stereotype means that the focus has disproportionately been on young women, with older victims of sexual violence receiving very little academic or policy attention. Age, and its association with vulnerability, is particularly important in the framing and understanding of rape against older women, especially in media reporting of cases. However, while some of the victims may be vulnerable, the assumption that all people over the age of 60 are inherently vulnerable reflects ageist attitudes and stereotypes that must be challenged.

The majority of offences involving older victims reported in the news involve aged female victims who are raped or sexually assaulted in their homes by younger male strangers during the course of a burglary, or in a public space. In this sense, these cases share many of the same characteristics of the 'classic, real-rape' stereotype afforded to younger women, although it is the construction of vulnerability that is at the forefront of these reports. In reality, the majority of police-recorded rape offences involving older victims do not reflect media reporting as the female victim is usually in her 60s, the male perpetrator is usually known to her and no other crime (such as burglary) occurs. Therefore, the rape of older women appears to share many of the same characteristics as cases involving younger women, rendering the lack of feminist or other scholarly research into this cohort both problematic and puzzling.

References

Abrams, D., Viki, G.T., Masser, B. and Bohner, G. (2003) 'Perceptions of stranger and acquaintance rape: the role of benevolent and hostile sexism in victim blame and rape proclivity', *Journal of Personality and Social Psychology*, 84(1): 111–25.

Adelman, S. (1989) 'Representations of violence against women in mainstream film', *Resources for Feminist Research*, 18: 21–6.

Aiello, C. and Christmas, L. (2017) 'Albertville Police charge man with rape; Victim 82 years old', *WHNT News 19*. Available at: http://whnt.com/2017/03/02/albertville-police-charge-man-with-rape-victim-82-years-old/

Bohner, G., Jarvis, C.I., Eyssel, F. and Siebler, F. (2005) 'The causal impact of rape myth acceptance on men's rape proclivity: comparing sexually coercive and noncoercive men', *European Journal of Social Psychology*, 35(6): 819–28.

Bows, H. (2016) 'Characteristics of offenders', in P. Davies, J. Harding and G. Mair (eds) *Criminal Justice in England and Wales: An Introduction*, London: Sage.

Bows, H. (2017) 'Sexual violence against older people: a review of the empirical literature', *Trauma, Violence and Abuse*, DOI: 10.1177/1524838016683455.

Bows, H. and Westmarland, N. (2017) 'Rape of older people in the United Kingdom: challenging the "real rape" stereotype', *British Journal of Criminology*, 57(1): 1–17.

Brinson, S. (1992) 'The use and opposition of rape myths in prime-time television dramas', *Sex Roles*, 27: 359–75.

Brownmiller, S. (1975) *Against our Will*, New York, NY: Simon & Schuster.

Bufkin, J. and Eschholz, S. (2000) 'Images of sex and rape: a content analysis of popular film', *Violence Against Women*, 6(12): 1317–44.

Burrowes, N. (2013) *Responding to the Challenge of Rape Myths in Court. A Guide for Prosecutors*, London: NB Research.

Burt, M.R. (1980) 'Cultural myths and supports for rape', *Journal of Personality and Social Psychology*, 38(2): 217–30.

Chapleau, K.M. and Oswald, D.L. (2014) 'A system justification view of sexual violence: legitimizing gender inequality and reduced moral outrage are connected to greater rape myth acceptance', *Journal of Trauma & Dissociation*, 15(2): 204–18.

Christie, N. (1986) 'The ideal victim', in E.A. Fattah (ed) *From Crime Policy to Victim Policy: Reorienting the Justice System*, Basingstoke: Palgrave Macmillan, pp 17–30.

Cooper, A. (2016) 'Masseur jailed for raping 80-year-old woman' *The Age* (Australia). Available from: https://www.theage.com.au/national/victoria/masseur-jailed-for-raping-80yearold-woman-20161216-gtczqr.html

Cuffe, G. (2017) 'Crowdfunding page set up for 81-year-old woman who was raped and kidnapped in Balham', The Wandsworth. Available at: http://www.wandsworthguardian.co.uk/news/15154338.Crowd_funding_page_set_up_for_81_year_old_rape_and_kidnap_victim/

Dobruck, J. (2017) 'Man charged with robbing, raping elderly Long Beach women held without bail', *Press Telegram*. Available at: http://www.presstelegram.com/general-news/20170215/man-charged-with-robbing-raping-elderly-long-beach-women-held-without-bail

Donovan, R.A. (2007) 'To blame or not to blame: influences of target race and observer sex on rape blame attribution', *Journal of Interpersonal Violence*, 22(6): 722–36.

Ellison, L. and Munro, V. (2009) 'Of "normal sex" and "real rape": exploring the use of socio-sexual scripts in (mock) jury deliberation', *Social & Legal Studies*, 18(3): 291–312.

Estrich, S. (1987) *Real Rape*, Cambridge, MA: Harvard University Press.

Franiuk, R., Seefelt, J.L., Cepress, S.L. and Vandello, J.A. (2008) 'Prevalence and effects of rape myths in print journalism: the Kobe Bryant case', *Violence Against Women*, 14(3): 287–309.

Hayes, R.M., Abbott, R.L. and Cook, S. (2016) 'It's her fault: student acceptance of rape myths on two college campuses', *Violence Against Women*, 22(13): 1540–55.

Henry, N. and Powell, A. (eds) (2014) *Preventing Sexual Violence: Interdisciplinary Approaches to Overcoming a Rape Culture*, Basingstoke: Springer.

Jones, H. and Powell, J.L. (2006) 'Old age, vulnerability and sexual violence: implications for knowledge and practice', *International Nursing Review*, 53(3): 211–16.

Kahlor, L. and Morrison, D. (2007) 'Television viewing and rape myth acceptance among college women', *Sex Roles*, 56(11/12): 729–39.

Kelly, L. (1988) *Surviving Sexual Violence*, Oxford: Polity Press.

Kelly, L., Lovett, J. and Regan, L. (2005) *A Gap or a Chasm? Attrition in Reported Rape Cases*, London: Home Office.

Kleinplatz, P.J. (2008) 'Sexuality and older people', *British Medical Journal*, 337: 121.

Korn, A. and Efrat, S. (2004) 'The coverage of rape in the Israeli popular press', *Violence Against Women*, 10(9): 1056–74.

Larcombe, W. (2005) *Compelling Engagements: Feminism, Rape Law and Romance Fiction*, Sydney: Federation Press.

Lea, S.J., Hunt, L. and Shaw, S. (2011) 'Sexual assault of older women by strangers', *Journal of Interpersonal Violence*, 26(11): 2303–20.

Mahria, N. (2008) *Just Representation: Press Reporting and the Reality of Rape*, London: Eaves/The Lilith Project.

Mann, R., Horsley, P., Barrett, C. and Tinney, J. (2014) 'Norma's project: a research study into the sexual assault of older women in Australia', Australian Research Centre in Sex, Health and Society, La Trobe University.

Messina-Dysert, G. (2015) *Rape Culture and Spiritual Violence: Religion, Testimony, and Visions of Healing*, Abingdon: Routledge.

Monson, C.M., Langhinrichsen-Rohling, J. and Binderup, T. (2000) 'Does "no" really mean "no" after you say "yes"? Attributions about date and marital rape', *Journal of Interpersonal Violence*, 15(11): 1156–74.

ONS (Office of National Statistics) (2015) *Focus on Violent Crime and Sexual Offences, 2013/14*, London: ONS.

Pain, R. (2003) 'Old age and victimisation', in P. Davies, P. Francis and V. Jupp (eds) *Victimisation: Theory, Research and Policy*, London: Palgrave, pp 61–78.

Penhale, B. (2003) 'Older women, domestic violence and elder abuse: a review of commonalities, differences and shared approaches', *Journal of Elder Abuse and Neglect*, 15(3/4): 163–83.

Rennison, C. and Rand, M.R. (2003) 'Nonlethal intimate partner violence against women: a comparison of three age cohorts', *Violence Against Women*, 9(12): 1417–28.

Rogers, J. (2016) 'Migrant arrested in Germany after 90-year-old grandmother rape whilst returning from church', *The Express*. Available at: http://www.express.co.uk/news/world/722188/Migrant-arrested-Germany-90-year-old-grandmother-raped-church

Schwartz, M.D. and DeKeseredy, W.S. (2008) 'Interpersonal violence against women: the role of men', *Journal of Contemporary Criminal Justice*, 24(2): 178–85.

Sheldrick, G. (2016) 'Romanian migrant jailed after raping and robbing a 69-year-old woman', *The Express*. Available at: http://www.express.co.uk/news/uk/702051/romanian-migrant-jailed-rapped-woman-robbed-elderly-mcdonalds-crown-court-gabriel-lupu

Sparks, R.F. (1982) *Research onvictims of crime*, Washington, DC: US Government Printing Office.

Stevenson, K. (2000) 'Unequivocal victims: the historical roots of the mystification of the female complainant in rape cases', *Feminist Legal Studies*, 8: 343–66.

Walklate, S. (2011) 'Reframing criminal victimization: finding a place for vulnerability and resilience', *Theoretical Criminology*, 15(2): 179–94.

Westmarland, N. and Graham, L. (2010) 'The promotion and resistance of rape myths in an Internet discussion forum', *Journal of Social Criminology*, 1(2): 80–104.

Whatley, M.A. (1996) 'Victim characteristics influencing attributions of responsibility to rape victims: a meta-analysis', *Aggression and Violent Behavior*, 1: 81–95.

Whittaker, T. (1995) 'Violence, gender and elder abuse: towards a feminist analysis and practice', *Journal of Gender Studies*, 4: 35–45.

Williams, L.S. (1984) 'The classic rape: when do victims report?', *Social Problems*, 31(4): 459–67.

World Health Organization (2013) 'Global and regional estimates of violence against women: Prevalence and health effects of intimate partner violence and non-partner sexual violence', World Health Organization. Available from: http://www.who.int/reproductivehealth/publications/violence/9789241564625/en/.

THIRTEEN

Denying victim status to online fraud victims: the challenges of being a 'non-ideal victim'

Cassandra Cross

Introduction

Victimhood is a contested space. Far from being a fixed category, 'the "victim" label is contingent and complex, shifting frequently according to social practices, race, gender, and class relations' (Spalek, 2006: 31). Not all persons who experience harm and trauma associated with criminal acts will see themselves as victims or be afforded victim status. Similar to crime, victims can 'be seen as *social* categories' (Sanders, 2002: 206, emphasis in original), which are contingent upon economic and political processes (Green, 2007: 91). Nor should being a 'victim' be understood as a neutral process (Walklate, 2007: 52) and there is both desirability and resistance to the embracing of the term and the connotations that derive from it (Spalek, 2006: 10–11).

Nils Christie (1986) recognised the complexity surrounding the social processes involved in ascribing individual victim status when he wrote his seminal piece entitled 'The ideal victim'. This provided a detailed examination of the processes surrounding victims and their ability to claim legitimate victim status. It identified the factors that influence the acceptance or otherwise of the victimhood of a person who has experienced crime. Christie put forward his concept of an 'ideal victim', involving five characteristics whose presence, he argued, was more likely to readily identify a person as a genuine victim, worthy and deserving of 'victim' status, and with the ability to use the status to trigger a variety of services and outcomes. The five characteristics can be briefly summarised as follows: a focus on the weakness and vulnerability of the victim; the respectability of the victim's actions at the time; the location of the victim at the time of the incident; the 'big and bad' nature of the offender; and the non–existence of a prior relationship between the victim and offender (Christie, 1986: 19). In contrast to this, Christie argues that an absence of these characteristics will usually mark a person as ineligible for victim status, or viewed as 'non-ideal victims'.

The concept of the ideal victim is an enduring framework that is arguably still of relevance and importance in contemporary society. This chapter takes the concept of the ideal victim and applies it to a specific category: online fraud victims or those who are defrauded in a virtual environment. There is little existing research that explicitly focuses its attention on online fraud victims (Button et al, 2009a, 2009b; Cross, 2015; Cross et al, 2016). Of the current work, there is an overwhelming consensus on the negativity associated with online fraud victimisation and the inadequate responses by the current criminal justice system and the fraud justice network more broadly (Button et al, 2009a, 2009b; Cross et al, 2016). This has significant consequences for the individuals who are subjected to online fraud.

In applying the attributes of Christie's ideal victim to those who have experienced online fraud, this chapter will provide a better understanding of the reasons underpinning the current negative experiences and challenges faced by online fraud victims seeking to attain legitimate victim status. Each of the five attributes will be examined in the context of online fraud to determine how (or if) they apply to this particular group of victims. In doing this, the chapter will demonstrate how online fraud victims are overwhelmingly understood as 'non-ideal victims', and how, as a consequence, they struggle to achieve external recognition of what has occurred and the related impact from the fraud. This occurs across both private and public spheres, with family members, friends, law enforcement and other organisations collectively unresponsive to the individual's attempt to claim victim status. In understanding why online fraud victims are not afforded victim status, this chapter details some of the resulting consequences. Overall, this chapter will argue that online fraud victims are primarily understood as non-ideal victims, a status that restricts their ability to gain recognition and support for their experiences and one that further justifies a systemic response that causes additional harm and trauma to this particular category of victims.

Defining a 'victim'

As previously stated, the term 'victim' is neither a straightforward nor taken-for-granted concept. Rather, it is shaped by various social, economic, cultural and political forces. In seeking to understand how victims are defined, it is common to recognise victims in terms of the 'harm they endure' (Hall, 2010: 30). This is perhaps best exemplified in the 1985 definition put forward by the United Nations in their 'Declaration of basic principles of justice for victims of crime and abuse of power'. Article 1 of the declaration asserts the following:

> 'Victims' means persons who, individually or collectively, have suffered harm, including physical or mental injury, emotional suffering, economic loss or substantial impairment of their fundamental rights, through acts or omissions that are in violation of criminal laws operative within Member States, including those laws proscribing criminal abuse of power. (United Nations, 1985)

The focus on the experience of harm is further illustrated by the European Union, as noted by Hall (2010: 30–1), which states that '"victim" shall mean a natural person who has suffered harm, including physical or mental injury, emotional suffering, economic loss, directly caused by acts or omissions that are a violation of the criminal law of a Member State'. Hall (2010: 31) argues that there are two implications that result in understanding victims in terms of the harm and suffering that they have experienced. The first is the broad nature of those who can be included within the term, specifically arising from the inclusion of emotional suffering and not simply restricted to physical injuries. Second, the inclusion of harm enables victims to self-define their status given that there is no requirement for legal processes to be present or enacted in order to claim this status. In this way, 'the focus is therefore on the *outcome* and *impact* of the crime, rather than the legal process' (Hall, 2010: 33, emphases in original). Having explored some of the issues underpinning current definitions of 'victim' across a variety of contexts, the following section examines a brief history of victims within the criminal justice system and the role of victimology in seeking to better understand the victimisation process.

A brief history of victimology and the 'ideal' victim

For many decades, victims were seen to be the forgotten actors within the criminal justice system (Sanders, 2002: 200). Interest in victims emerged in the 1940s, with early scholars using a positivist approach to victimology, one that focused on individualistic explanations. This early work focused on developing typologies that sought to differentiate victims from non-victims, usually based on the individual characteristics of the victim, rather than any structural or societal factors (Burgess et al, 2013). Consequently, popular concepts, such as victim precipitation and lifestyle theory, 'both implicitly and explicitly focus our attention on the behaviour of the individual victims and the extent to which their behaviour puts them at greater or lesser risk of victimisation' (Walklate, 2007: 51). This has arguably contributed to high levels of victim blaming that are often directed at particular categories of victims, notably, those of rape, sexual assault and domestic and family violence (see Suarez and Gadalla, 2010; Thapar-Björket and Morgan, 2010; Bieneck and Krahé, 2011). It will be demonstrated later in this chapter that online fraud victims also suffer from a high degree of victim blaming in societal attitudes towards their victimisation.

Christie's chapter on the ideal victim can be understood within the context of individual attributes and how they apply to victimisation. In it, Christie analysed the concept of victimhood more broadly, and sought to reconcile why the victim label was not always given to people under a variety of circumstances. His example of the ideal victim is a little old lady on her way home from caring for her sick sister who is robbed by a stranger during the day. The power behind Christie's five ideal victim characteristics lies in the projection of a stereotypical image presented of a person who is deemed a worthy victim, deserving of such status and therefore eligible for support and acknowledgement. It operates on the premise that there is a clear distinction between victims and offenders, whereas the reality of the situation sees a much larger nexus concerning both groups. It is important to note that while Christie presents the characteristics of what he perceives to be the ideal victim, he is not subscribing to such a narrow conceptualisation himself. Rather, his analysis uses this as a means to challenge understandings of who a victim is and how the process of being labelled a victim unfolds.

Many scholars have argued that the image presented by the ideal victim is not an accurate depiction of victims and offenders within the criminal justice system. For example, Green (2007: 91) observes that 'Christie (1986) argues that this idealisation provides an image of the victim, and correspondingly the offender, which is out of kilter with messy social realities…. The ideal victim represents an abstraction of what it is to be a victim'. Despite the inaccuracy of the ideal victim, it arguably still has relevance and has had an enduring influence on society's understanding and response to different types of victims.

The remainder of this chapter elaborates on how the ideal victim framework can be applied to the current example of online fraud victims. Importantly, it argues how these characteristics operate to deny online fraud victims recognition, and therefore to refuse to bestow the victim label to this category of individuals. However, before undertaking this, the next section provides an overview of online fraud and some of the challenges associated with victimisation that are relevant to the subsequent analysis from within the ideal victim framework.

Online fraud in context

Online fraud causes substantial harm to millions globally. In Australia, a report from the Australian Competition and Consumer Commission (ACCC) indicated that in 2016, Australians recorded losses of almost AU$300 million to fraud (ACCC, 2017). Similarly, there are large levels of losses recorded in the US (estimated at US$1,070,711,522 by the Internet Crime Complaint Centre in 2015) (IC3, 2016: 12) and Canada (estimated at over CA$74 million by the Canadian Anti-Fraud Centre in 2014) (CAFC, 2015). The Office of National Statistics for England and Wales included statistics for fraud and computer crime for the first time in 2016. This saw an additional 5.8 million new offences added to the existing 6.3 million, effectively almost doubling the overall crime figures (ONS, 2016). In combination, these figures demonstrate the global reach of victimisation and the large degree of financial losses.

Research indicates that fraud has one of the lowest reporting rates of all crime types, with many estimating that less than one third of fraud is ever actually reported (Reibovich and Layne, 2000; Copes et al, 2001; Button et al, 2014), with figures for online fraud being even less (Smith, 2007, 2008). It is realistic, then, to assume that the previously cited figures are likely to represent only a small amount of the actual losses incurred through fraud. Additionally, these figures do not incorporate the non-financial harms associated with fraud victimisation, which include a decline in physical health and well-being, emotional and psychological problems (namely, depression), relationship breakdown, unemployment, homelessness, and, in extreme cases, suicide (Button et al, 2009a; Cross et al, 2014, 2016; Button and Cross, 2017a).

Online fraud is not new; fraud in an offline context has been documented for centuries. However, the evolution of technology, namely, computers and the Internet, has seen fraud significantly evolve (Yar, 2013; Button and Cross, 2017b). Technology has opened up the ability of fraud to be committed in an online environment, with a greater level of anonymity and making the most of its transnational nature to largely avoid police detection. A potential offender can easily target victims globally with any number of fraudulent pitches, and for very little cost and initial outlay. In this way, the patterns of fraud offending and victimisation have changed substantially.

There are an endless number of fraudulent approaches or 'pitches' that offenders can use, and these are often tailored specifically to target an identified weakness or vulnerability in a potential victim (Cross and Kelly, 2016). Some of the most common approaches are known as 'advanced fee fraud'. This is when a victim is asked to send a small amount of money in return for the promise of a larger amount of money in the future (Ross and Smith, 2011). A derivative of advanced fee fraud is romance fraud (also known as dating and relationship fraud). In this context, offenders will use the guise of a legitimate relationship with the victim to coerce them into sending large amounts of money over a period of time (Rege, 2009; Whitty and Buchanan, 2012). Romance fraud is particularly insidious, with victims suffering what is termed a 'double hit', where they must grieve the loss of the perceived relationship as well as any financial loss incurred (Whitty and Buchanan, 2012).

There are challenges posed by online fraud to police and other agencies in their ability to investigate, arrest and prosecute offenders as they would for terrestrial offences. This stems from: the transnational nature of the offence (whereby offenders in one country can target a victim from another country and request money to be sent to a third country); the prevalence of identity crime (whereby offenders will steal legitimate identities or create fictitious ones to commit their crimes); the lack of adequate legislation across jurisdictions; and a lack of resources and skills dedicated to the investigation of these crimes (Cross and Blackshaw, 2015).

Fraud is unique in that there are several authorities other than the police that victims can report to, including banks, other financial institutions, consumer protection agencies and other government and non-government agencies. This is termed the 'fraud justice network' (Button et al, 2012). There is a small but consistent body of research that examines the experiences of online fraud victims with the fraud justice network and asserts the negativity associated with their interactions and attempts at reporting (Button et al, 2009a, 2009b; Cross et al, 2016). In fact, it has been asserted that attempting to report online fraud to those agencies across the fraud justice network can actually incur additional trauma or exacerbate the existing trauma associated with the victimisation itself (Cross et al, 2016). One of the reasons underpinning this negativity can be argued to arise from the understanding of who a victim is and the discourses surrounding the victimisation of this particular group. This point forms the basis of the current discussion.

Victims of online fraud individually experience a large degree of shame and embarrassment, as well as encounter strong victim-blaming attitudes from those around them. In addition, there are common negative stereotypes that assert fraud victims to be greedy, gullible and somewhat responsible for their own victimisation (Cross, 2015). These are some of the many challenges that colour the experiences of victims in their interactions with family, friends and those in the fraud justice network in the aftermath of their victimisation. The application of the ideal victim framework helps to understand better the reasons behind these challenges and current responses, and understandings of online fraud victimisation. It is to this analysis that the chapter now turns.

Applying the 'ideal victim' framework

As noted, Christie (1986: 19) advocated five factors argued to contribute to the successful attainment of ideal victim status. Each of these will be detailed, with an analysis of how they are relevant (or not) to the context of online fraud victims, and, more importantly, how they contribute to this particular group of victims, more often than not, being seen as non-ideal victims.

Characteristic 1: 'The victim was weak (sick, old or very young people are particularly suited as ideal victims)'

Fraud victimisation cuts across all demographics; however, there is a general assumption that older victims are more likely to be victims of fraud (in both online and offline contexts) (Cross, 2016). While there is conflicting evidence on the validity of this statement, there is agreement that older persons are certainly *attractive* targets for fraud offenders. This stems from their high level of financial attractiveness, with many older persons having access to life savings and superannuation, owning their own homes, and having a good credit rating. The popularity of self-managed superannuation has also contributed to offenders specifically targeting schemes to retirees, who are deliberately looking for an opportunity to invest their money and are therefore open and vulnerable to fraudulent pitches.

Noting the low reporting rates of fraud, of that which is reported, the most common group for victims is those aged 45–54 years, with 40% of reports made by those aged over 55 years (ACCC, 2016). This can be explained through the particular stage of life of these people, many of whom may have ended a long-term relationship (with their children having grown up), with a newly single person being vulnerable to fraudulent pitches. Despite these statistics, the impact of online fraud on the elderly can be devastating. The financial impact of losing substantial amounts of money for an older person is exacerbated by their inability to recoup their losses. Many are forced to return to work or live off the pension (Cross et al, 2016).

The first characteristic – that the ideal victim is weak and vulnerable – is evident in the example of online fraud victims. As an offence, fraud is premised upon deceit, lies and manipulation. Offenders portray themselves and situations falsely to unsuspecting victims in order to gain their trust, and subsequently gain ongoing compliance to their requests for money. A case study exemplifies how offenders will target specific vulnerabilities in a potential victim in order to exploit them for financial gain (see Box 13.1).

Box 13.1: Case study 1 – targeting older fraud victims

'Frank' had recently lost his wife to a brain haemorrhage. He had started using various social networking websites to chat to women across the globe and in particular, started communicating with a woman in Ghana. During their conversations, Frank had shared details about himself and more importantly, details about his wife's death. After a few months, Frank received a request for money from the brother of the woman he had been communicating with, after being advised she had been in a car crash and was suffering from the same illness that had taken his wife.

> ... Then her brother calls me, sends me an email under her name and said she got hit by a car, her brain's bleeding anyway, I just lost my wife with a brain hemorrhage, and they wanted $1000 for the doctor to operate, they won't do anything unless you pay, so I sent them $1000 [or] $1200, then it started ... (Frank, 73 years).

Frank was suspicious ... but was willing to send the money on the off chance that the situation was legitimate and that this woman was sick. He had also been in phone contact with the alleged doctor who was treating her, which added to the plausibility of the situation.

Frank's situation illustrates the insidious way that offenders will manipulate a person's emotions and circumstances to obtain financial benefits.... The use of the same illness that had claimed his wife also reinforces the ways that offenders will specifically target victims to gain compliance to financial requests. (Taken from Cross, 2013: 33)

Characteristic 2: 'The victim was carrying out a respectable project'

There are many misconceptions about who becomes a victim of online fraud and how it is perpetrated. In particular, there is a strong negative stereotype which generally posits that the victim is greedy, uneducated, gullible and somewhat deserving of their victimisation (Cross, 2013, 2015). Consequently, online fraud victims are often held responsible for their actions and are seen to have actively contributed to their own victimisation. Fraud is a unique offence in that it requires the active participation of the victim to enable an offence to occur. In all circumstances, victims of online fraud (regardless of the approach used) have, at some point, sent money to offenders, and this has resulted in their financial losses. However, it is vital to remember that victims have done this under false pretences. Victims have been deceived into undertaking actions that they would not normally have done and blaming the victim for their actions completely ignores and negates the role of the offender and their ability to manipulate victims into complying with their requests.

As stated, there are an endless number of 'plotlines' that offenders can use to defraud an individual (Cross and Kelly, 2016). Some of the most common approaches include investment fraud, romance fraud and lottery and inheritance notifications. In each of these examples, victims who respond to these approaches are seen to be greedy and gullible. The aspect of greed is particularly relevant to investment fraud, where it is argued that those who invest in these opportunities are chasing ridiculously high returns compared to genuine investment options. However, in reality, many fraudulent investment schemes mirror legitimate companies through their operations, as detailed in the case study in Box 13.2.

Box 13.2: Case study 2 – the complexity and sophistication of investment schemes

The following outlines the circumstances that led one man to put in over $200K to a fraudulent investment scheme.

> **Participant:** It was basically phone and email contact and they [offenders] had a website and a trial set up so I didn't just go straight into it and I put 1000 bucks into it to start with as I am a bit cautious about these things. I ran that for a couple of months and then said that it was doing alright and let's get my money out. So I got my money out and then ...

Interviewer: So you were actually able to retrieve your money at that point?

Participant: Yeah and I think that's what actually did me in. Because I was quite happy to risk a thousand bucks and thought if it is bogus I am not going to get my money back and that's the end of it but when I said ... give me my money back, they did.... Then I ramped it up and put in 10,000 bucks. You can basically watch on the website to see how your money is going on a daily basis so after about another month I put it up to 100,000 and then let it go for 3 months, something like that. Then I put another 100,000 into it and let it run for another 3 months. Then I sat back thinking I am doing alright here, that was a good investment. Then the updates stopped on the website and I rang the guys up and the phone calls didn't work then the next thing the website disappeared. All this happened in a week, so the updates stopped, the phone calls stopped coming, then a week later the website disappeared. I think it was the day before the website disappeared that I recognised that this was a scam. (unpublished quote, Interview 26, Cross et al, 2016).

Lottery and inheritance victims are also seen to be greedy in that they are chasing money which is not theirs to begin with. This is exemplified in the following quotation: 'They [victims] are greedy. They are out for money that they don't earn, they didn't earn. The money that they shouldn't claim and really if they respond to them [fraudulent emails], they are being dishonest' (Cynthia, 65 years, taken from Cross, 2013: 30). In reality, offenders can target schemes to individual victims with known relatives in order to increase the likelihood of a response, as was the case of 'Martha' (as cited in Cross, 2013). 'Martha' received a beneficiary notification of a relative on her ex-husband's side of the family, a name that she recognised and believed to be legitimate. Not all schemes represent the stereotypical 'Nigerian prince' scenario commonly associated with such victimisation (ACCC, 2017).

In contrast to these types of online fraud, discourses surrounding romance fraud victims are not focused on greed. In this case, the focus is on the use of the Internet for online dating and the establishment of a relationship in this context. While online dating platforms are popular and are increasing in their usage, a certain degree of shame and stigma associated with online dating still exists, particularly from an older person's perspective. For example, Cross et al (2016: 61) provide details of a small number of victims who had not disclosed their online dating activity to their families, based on the fear and stigma associated with dating in a virtual environment. To illustrate, one woman stated:

'I've got adolescent kids…. They knew about it, they knew I was on a [dating] site…. But they're not real comfortable talking about it' (interview 5, quoted in Cross et al, 2016: 61).

In this way, those who are defrauded through online dating platforms are seen to have been foolish in their actions and gullible to have sent money to a person that they have likely not met. However, this contradicts established research that documents the existence of 'hyperpersonal relationships' or those relationships that grow more quickly and more intensely online compared to offline (Jiang et al, 2011). The dynamics of communication and dating in a virtual environment, and the increased willingness of victims to disclose personal details, contributes to the strong levels of trust and rapport developed by the victim to the offender and therefore enables compliance with the resulting requests for money.

In summary, online fraud victims are generally not seen to have been carrying out a respectable project, due to the nature of the contexts that they find themselves in. Therefore, this second characteristic of Christie as it relates to the ideal victim is not seen to be present for victims of online fraud.

Characteristic 3: 'The victim was where they could not possibly be blamed for being'

Similar to the previous characteristic, despite the saturation of the Internet and the prevalence of Internet usage, interactions using online platforms are still not always accepted by society as a whole. As noted, this is particularly the case for older persons and the use of the Internet for online dating (Cross et al, 2016: 61).

Victims who are defrauded through an online relationship are often isolated and ostracised from their family and friends, and carry a large degree of shame over what has happened. This encompasses their financial losses as well as their presence on an online dating site. This is further illustrated through the following excerpt of an interview with a male romance fraud victim:

> The stigma is twofold. One is to admit to your family that you have gone onto an international dating site, which is socially something which most Anglo-Saxon children would struggle with…. It's the whole stigma of being on a site that's a problem with the mail order bride thing…. The other thing is I got stung. That is two things there

that you will emotionally not share. (Interview 4, quoted in Cross et al, 2016: 61)

Further to this, Christie (1986: 19) argues that to be considered an ideal victim, an individual must have put reasonable energy into protecting themselves. For victims of online fraud, the fact that the victim has facilitated the loss of their finances through their own actions voids any potential of sympathy or belief that they have been wronged. Online fraud victims are held accountable for their actions in being on the Internet and communicating with offenders in the first place, as well as enabling their financial loss through money transfers. In this way, the third characteristic is not seen to apply to online fraud victims.

Characteristic 4: 'The offender is big and bad'

As stated, fraud offences are defined through the use of lies and deception. Offenders employ many social-engineering techniques in order to gain the trust and compliance of victims (see Drew and Cross, 2013). Offenders can also be seen to implement grooming techniques over a period of time in order to increase the likelihood that a victim will send ongoing and often escalating amounts of money (Whitty, 2013a, 2013b). There is also evidence from victims to suggest that offenders will use techniques of abuse, aggression and threats to their safety in an attempt to maintain control over their victims and guarantee financial rewards for their efforts (Cross et al, 2016; Whitty, 2013a, 2013b).

In the case of online fraud, offenders intentionally set out to identify a weakness or vulnerability in a person, and once they achieve this, they will do whatever necessary to exploit this for their own financial benefit. There are several cases where the offenders have targeted the specific attributes of a person in order to initiate and develop a relationship with their victim. This was previously seen in the example of Frank and the use of his dead wife's illness as a means of securing his initial cooperation in sending money.

There is also anecdotal evidence to suggest that offenders work collaboratively with each other to assist the ongoing success of their engagements with online fraud victims. This was observed by the following female victim:

Participant: Clearly from the emails there was [sic] at least three people talking to me.

Interviewer: What makes you think that?

Participant: Because of the toning's of the wordings and stuff. I said to him [offender] on one day that I feel like I am talking to at least two people here, and all of [a] sudden it changed again. (unpublished quote, Interview 42, Cross et al, 2016)

Overall, this indicates the morally corrupt nature of many online fraud offenders and their willingness to do whatever it takes to destroy and devastate the lives of their victims without hesitation. This also demonstrates adequate evidence to suggest the 'big and bad' nature of the offender in the context of online fraud.

Characteristic 5: 'The offender was unknown and in no personal relationship to the victim'

One of the challenges associated with online fraud is the way in which it can provide a greater level of anonymity compared to interactions in a terrestrial environment. There are significant hurdles in being able to verify or authenticate an online identity. Many offenders will use stolen identities of legitimate persons or businesses, while others will create fictitious identities. The nature of the Internet and the difficulties associated with gauging whether or not the information being presented is true or not strongly favours offenders rather than victims.

While the unknown aspect of this characteristic can be established, there is a distinct tension in the second part to this: the presence of a personal relationship. The success of most online fraudulent approaches relies upon the ability of the offender to establish a relationship with their victim. While in romance fraud, this is through the development of an intense, romantic relationship, other fraudulent approaches will still require a strong level of trust and rapport in order for the offender to gain compliance. In this way, victims genuinely believe that there is a strong relationship between themselves and their offender(s), and it is only when the presence of this relationship exists that victims will send money. Once victims start to question the truth of what they are being presented and the authenticity of the relationship between them and their offender(s), this is the point where most victims will cease contact and refuse to send any further financial transactions.

The tension of this characteristic lies in the fact that the majority of fraudulent transactions, despite the victim believing that they know the person, are conducted with unknown identities. Therefore, no authentic relationship is established. In most cases, victims will not have met with their offenders face to face; instead, their communication will be restricted to a variety of written and verbal platforms. In this way, while there is a strong relationship between the victim and the offender that facilitates the fraud to occur, this relationship is based upon lies and deceit and is a tool used by offenders to gain financial reward for themselves. In the context of Christie's ideal victim characteristic, the applicability of this to the context of online fraud can be argued from both sides.

Summary of the five characteristics in the context of online fraud

The analysis has sought to apply the five ideal victim characteristics advocated by Christie in presenting the stereotyped image of a pure victim, who is most readily able to claim victim status. The arguments presented indicate mixed support for these characteristics and their applicability to victims in an online fraud context. Some were clearly evident, others were to the contrary, and the last one, in particular, is difficult to determine either way. Despite online fraud victims fitting some of the ideal victim characteristics, the contested nature of the remaining characteristics appears to override any ability for online fraud victims to achieve the ideal victim status.

For victims of online fraud, the greatest areas of disparity relate to their own actions and the location of the offence (being online). The culpability and perceived motivations for victims to engage with offenders in an online environment are clearly construed within the current framework as violating the ideal victim image. Rather, online fraud victims are cast as non-ideal victims, refused victim status and denied any societal acceptability for the harm and suffering that they have endured (across financial and non-financial realms).

In coming to this conclusion, it is therefore important to consider why this is a relevant issue for online fraud victims. What are the consequences for this group in being classified as non-ideal victims? Why would online fraud victims want to be understood as an ideal victim? It is the answers to these questions that the final section of this chapter explores.

The implications of 'non-ideal' victim status

So far, this chapter has illustrated how those who experience online fraud are understood to be non-ideal victims. In refusing to ascribe victim status, there are concrete consequences experienced by this group of victims that extend beyond the simple adoption of the victim label. Rather, an inability to claim legitimate victim status has significant negative impacts. Each of these will be detailed in turn.

The first consequence stems around recognition of what online fraud victims have experienced. In denying their victimhood, there is also a denial of how they have been wronged, which can also manifest itself in a trivialisation of the incident as non-fraud-related behaviour (Cross et al, 2016). An example of this can be seen in the following quotation of an investment fraud victim and his interaction with a police officer:

> I said it was an investment fraud and she [police officer] said she had much more important things than that to deal with. [She said] 'We have people robbed at knife point'. I said [I had been defrauded of] $20 000. She said, 'but you gave it away sir', and I said, 'I didn't give it away, it was an investment'. She said it was voluntary and I gave it away. I ended up phoning up a few times but got nowhere. (Interview 27, quoted in Cross et al, 2016: 48–9)

This interaction indicates how the police officer refused to frame the victim's loss of money as fraud, and instead saw it as a voluntary transaction.

The second consequence of being refused victim status concerns the ability of online fraud victims to access both formal and informal mechanisms of support, in that 'being able to claim a victim status is connected to benefits, in terms of both financial compensation and emotional support' (Jägervi, 2014: 73). The attainment of an accepted victim status can afford an individual access to a range of services to assist with their recovery and can trigger a criminal justice response (Hall, 2010: 28). As noted by Spalek (2006: 31), 'victimhood is … a complex concept, being contingent upon intricate psychological and social processes, its construction helping to determine what forms of victimisation and what kinds of people are helped'. In the previous analysis, it is clear that given victims of online fraud are not seen as genuine victims, they are subsequently not identified as a group of worthy victims, deserving of support services and assistance. This is further reiterated by Walklate (2007: 44):

> Acquiring the label and/or status of victim, especially that of a 'deserving' victim, is crucial in some circumstances if the victim is to receive appropriate agency response and support. So how and under what circumstances people

acquire the label and the possible access to resources is of great importance.

It is acknowledged that the label of 'victim' can have negative connotations to it, primarily around the assumption of passivity (Spalek, 2006: 10). Many advocate the term 'survivor', in that this 'acknowledges active resistance on behalf of the victim, thereby challenging idealised notions of victim passivity' (Spalek, 2006: 11). Regardless of one's position on the term itself, it is evident that the victim label is a prerequisite to enable positive outcomes from the criminal incident:

> Becoming a victim can have its rewards: sympathy; attention towards being treated as blameless; the ability to bestow meaning and control on an untoward and disturbing experience; the receiving of exoneration, absolution, validation and credit; exemption from prosecution; mitigation of punishment and financial compensation. (Rock, 2002: 14)

The absence of these identified incentives to acquiring victimhood leads to the final negative consequence associated with the non-ideal victim status: secondary victimisation. There is an established body of research that has documented the additional trauma sustained by many different types of victims as they attempt to navigate 'an unsympathetic criminal justice system – which ignores the views, perspectives and needs of victims' (Hall, 2010: 40). The existence of secondary victimisation has been demonstrated to exist for online fraud victims (Button et al, 2009a, 2009b; Cross et al, 2016) and this can be seen as a direct result of the inability of online fraud victims to assert genuine victim status.

Conclusion

This chapter has examined the example of online fraud victims against Christie's (1986) notion of the ideal victim. In doing this, the chapter has clearly illustrated the non-ideal victim status currently ascribed to online fraud victims. In examining the characteristics associated with the ideal victim, this chapter has outlined the 'social conditions under which some people are not only assigned victim status, but are seen to deserve it' (Walklate, 2011: 183). Sadly, online fraud victims are not currently afforded ideal victim status, and in denying their victimhood, they are subjected to a number of negative consequences.

Despite the prevalence of online fraud, the substantial financial losses associated with it, the significant impact it has on the physical and emotional well-being of victims, and the skill in which this crime is perpetrated against victims, those who experience online fraud are not seen to be worthy or deserving victims. Their own actions and behaviours are seen to violate the ideal victim characteristics and this renders them unable to access any of the benefits and rewards associated with the attainment of legitimate victim status.

Not all victims accept the victim label and all that is associated with it. Not all victims are even striving to be recognised as ideal victims as this is impracticable. However, casting all those who experience online fraud as non-ideal victims deliberately seeks to silence and limit the ability of victims to access support activated through shared community understandings of victimhood.

The attainment of an accepted victim label ensures that this group can access much-needed support to move forward with their recovery. The example of online fraud victims demonstrates the current cultural and social factors that are in operation. It is clear that online fraud is not well understood, and that there are elements of it being a cyber-offence that are not well accepted. Rather, the behaviour and interactions of these victims in an online environment are seen to exist on the fringe of normal, acceptable behaviour. The focus is also centred on their individual actions as voiding their claim to victim status. There is a pressing need for this to change, and for online fraud victims to be afforded recognition of their experiences and the harms that they have suffered, in order to allow them access to support services (formal and informal) to assist in their recovery.

References

ACCC (2016) *Targeting Scams: Report of the ACCC on Scams Activity 2015*, Canberra: Australian Competition and Consumer Commission. Available at: http://www.accc.gov.au/publications/targeting-scams-report-on-scam-activity/targeting-scams-report-of-the-accc-on-scam-activity-2015

ACCC (2017) *Targeting Scams: Report of the ACCC on Scams Activity 2016*, Canberra: Australian Competition and Consumer Commission. Available at: http://www.accc.gov.au/publications/targeting-scams-report-on-scam-activity/targeting-scams-report-of-the-accc-on-scam-activity-2016

Bieneck, S. and Krahé, B. (2011) 'Blaming the victim and exonerating the perpetrator in cases of rape and robbery: is there a double standard?', *Journal of Interpersonal Violence*, 26(9): 1785–97.

Burgess, A., Regehr, C. and Roberts, A. (2013) *Victimology Theories and Applications* (2nd edn), Burlington: Jones and Bartlett Learning.

Button, M. and Cross, C. (2017a) *Cyber Frauds, Scams and their Victims*, London: Routledge.

Button, M. and Cross, C. (2017b) 'Technology and fraud: the "fraudogenic" consequences of the Internet revolution', in M. Maguire and T. Holt (eds) *The Routledge Handbook of Technology, Crime and Justice*, London: Routledge.

Button, M., Lewis, C. and Tapley, J. (2009a) *A Better Deal for Victims*, London: National Fraud Authority.

Button, M., Lewis, C. and Tapley, J. (2009b) *Fraud Typologies and the Victims of Fraud Literature Review*, London: National Fraud Authority.

Button, M., Tapley, J. and Lewis, C. (2012) 'The "fraud justice network" and the infrastructure of support for individual fraud victims in England and Wales', *Criminology and Criminal Justice*, 13(1): 37–61.

Button, M., Lewis, C. and Tapley, J. (2014) 'Not a victimless crime: the impact of fraud on individual victims and their families', *Security Journal*, 27(1): 36–54.

CAFC (Canadian Anti-Fraud Centre) (2015) 'Annual statistics report 2014'. Available at: http://www.antifraudcentre-centreantifraude.ca/reports-rapports/2014/ann-ann-eng.htm

Christie, N. (1986) 'The ideal victim', in E.A. Fattah (ed) *From Crime Policy to Victim Policy*, Basingstoke: Macmillan, pp 17–30.

Copes, H., Kerley, K., Mason, K. and Van Wyk, J. (2001) 'Reporting behaviour of fraud victims and Black's theory of law: an empirical assessment', *Justice Quarterly*, 18(2): 343–63.

Cross, C. (2013) '"Nobody's holding a gun to your head...": examining current discourses surrounding victims of online fraud', in K. Richards and J. Tauri (eds) *Crime, Justice and Social Democracy: Proceedings of the 2nd International Conference*, Brisbane: Crime and Justice Research Centre, QUT, pp 25–32. Available at: https://eprints.qut.edu.au/61011/

Cross, C. (2015) 'No laughing matter: blaming the victim of online fraud', *International Review of Victimology*, 21(2): 187–204.

Cross, C. (2016) '"They're very lonely": understanding the fraud victimisation of seniors', *International Journal for Crime, Justice and Social Democracy*, 5(4): 60–75.

Cross, C. and Blackshaw, D. (2015) 'Improving the police response to online fraud', *Policing: A Journal of Policy and Practice*, 9(2): 119–28.

Cross, C. and Kelly, M. (2016) 'The problem of "white noise": examining current prevention approaches to online fraud', *Journal of Financial Crime*, 23(4): 806–28.

Cross, C., Smith, R.G. and Richards, K. (2014) 'Challenges of responding to online fraud victimisation in Australia', *Trends and Issues in Crime and Criminal Justice*, 474: 1–7.

Cross, C., Richards, K. and Smith, R. (2016) *Improving the Response to Online Fraud Victims: An Examination of Reporting and Support*, Canberra: Criminology Research Grant Final Report. Available at: https://eprints.qut.edu.au/98346/

Drew, J. and Cross, C. (2013) 'Fraud and its PREY: conceptualising social engineering tactics and its impact on financial literacy outcomes', *Journal of Financial Services Marketing*, 18(3): 188–98.

Green, S. (2007) 'Crime, victimisation and vulnerability', in S. Walklate (ed) *Handbook of Victims and Victimology*, Cullompton: Willan Publishing, pp 91–117.

Hall, M. (2010) *Victims and Policy Making: A Comparative Perspective*, Oxon: Willan Publishing.

IC3 (Internet Crime Complaint Centre) (2016) '2015 Internet crime report'. Available at: https://pdf.ic3.gov/2015_IC3Report.pdf

Jägervi, L. (2014) 'Who wants to be an ideal victim? A narrative analysis of crime victims' self-presentation', *Journal of Scandinavian Studies in Criminology and Crime Prevention*, 15(1): 73–88.

Jiang, L., Bazarova, N. and Hancock, J. (2011) 'The disclosure–intimacy link in computer-mediated communication: an attributional extension of the hyperpersonal model', *Human Communication Research*, 37(1): 58–77.

ONS (Office for National Statistics) (2016) 'Crime in England and Wales: year ending March 2016'. Available at: https://www.ons.gov.uk/peoplepopulationandcommunity/crimeandjustice/bulletins/crimeinenglandandwales/yearendingmar2016

Rebovich, D. and Layne, J. (2000) *The National Public Survey on White Collar Crime*, Morgantown: National White Collar Crime Centre.

Rege, A. (2009) 'What's love got to do with it? Exploring online dating scams and identity', *International Journal of Cyber Criminology*, 3(2): 494–512.

Rock, P. (2002) 'On becoming a victim', in C. Hoyle and R. Young (eds) *New Visions of Crime Victims*, Oxford: Hart Publishing, pp 1–22.

Ross, S. and Smith, R.G. (2011) 'Risk factors for advance fee fraud victimization', *Trends and Issues in Crime and Criminal Justice*, 420: 1–6.

Sanders, A. (2002) 'Victim participation in an exclusionary criminal justice system', in Hoyle, C. and Young, R. (eds) *New Visions of Crime Victims*, Oxford: Hart Publishing, pp 197–222.

Smith, R.G. (2007) 'Consumer scams in Australia: an overview', *Trends and Issues in Crime and Criminal Justice*, 331: 1–6.

Smith, R.G. (2008) 'Coordinating individual and organisational responses to fraud', *Crime Law and Social Change*, 49(5): 379–96.

Spalek, B. (2006) *Crime Victims: Theory, Policy and Practice*, Basingstoke: Palgrave.

Suarez, E. and Gadalla, T. (2010) 'Stop blaming the victim: a meta-analysis on rape myths', *Journal of Interpersonal Violence*, 25(11): 2010–35.

Thapar-Björkert, S. and Morgan, K. (2010) '"But sometimes I think ... they put themselves in the situation": exploring blame and responsibility in interpersonal violence', *Violence against Women*, 16(1): 32–59.

United Nations (1985) 'Declaration of the basic principles of justice for victims of crime and abuse of power'. Available at: http://www.un.org/documents/ga/res/40/a40r034.htm

Walklate, S. (2007) *Imagining the Victim of Crime*, Berkshire: McGraw Hill and Open University Press.

Walklate, S. (2011) 'Reframing criminal victimisation: Finding a place for vulnerability and resilience', *Theoretical Criminology*, 15(2): 179–94.

Whitty, M. (2013a) 'Anatomy of the online dating romance scam', *Security Journal*, 28(4): 443–55.

Whitty, M. (2013b) 'The scammers' persuasive techniques model: development of a stage model to explain the online dating romance scam', *British Journal of Criminology*, 53(4): 665–884.

Whitty, M. and Buchanan, T. (2012) *The Psychology of the Online Dating Romance Scam*, Leicester: University of Leicester. Available at: https://www2.le.ac.uk/departments/media/people/monica-whitty/Whitty_romance_scam_report.pdf

Yar, M. (2013) *Cybercrime and Society* (2nd edn), London: Sage.

FOURTEEN

Male prisoners' vulnerabilities and the ideal victim concept

Jennifer Anne Sloan Rainbow

Introduction

Christie's (1986) conception of the ideal victim has been highly influential within victimological circles since its publication. Since then, numerous changes have occurred to address the victimisation of many marginalised groups, which arguably extends the notion of the ideal victim beyond what it was initially held to be. The development of hate crime legislation and high-profile cases of harms with intersecting characteristics go beyond Christie's initial thoughts, resulting in more people recognised as 'deserving victims'. Yet, routinely omitted from this ideal victim discourse is the male prisoner. Men in prison have often experienced high levels of physical, sexual, emotional and structural victimisation before, during and after their incarceration. Indeed, male prisons are presumed to be highly violent and harmful places; they are represented as such within popular cultural fictitious (see Wilson and O'Sullivan, 2004) and factual (BBC, 2017) depictions. Yet, rarely is the victim status of the non-vulnerable male prisoner recognised in popular or academic discourse. While those who have been institutionally recognised to be vulnerable are given a certain amount of attention – which, in itself, has potentially harmful implications through the impact of the acknowledgement of vulnerability upon notions of masculinity (see Sloan, 2016[1]) – there is a distinct lack of attention given to the victim status of the general male prison population.

In this chapter, I address this conflict between prisoner and victim labels, and draw upon ethnographic data from time spent within an adult male category C prison in England for a doctoral study into masculinities in prison (Sloan, 2011; see also Sloan, 2016) to develop the argument of why men in prison should perhaps be seen more as victims and could, dare I say it, even fit into the 'ideal' victim construct when considered with a broader mindset. I focus on men in prison for two key reasons: (1) they comprise 95% of the prison population of England and Wales while simultaneously receiving very little direct (gendered) attention relative to women, young people or other distinct minority groups in prisons (see Sloan, 2018); and (2) my research focuses on men in prison and I thus have qualitative interview data to support my discussions from men rather than from women.

Male prisoners, vulnerability and victim status

The male prisoner has traditionally struggled to be seen within the victim sphere. I was recently asked to speak at an event under the title 'Citizenship: what are the challenges of engaging marginalised populations within inclusive communities?', in which I argued that men in prison struggle to be seen as 'marginalised' populations, often by virtue of the fact that they are the cause of others' marginalisation – they are the marginalisers (see also SIPS, 2017). One of the main problems that men in prison suffer from is that they are generally seen to be the 'other' to problematised dichotomies: they are the victimisers rather than the victims, the marginalisers rather than the marginalised, the other rather than 'one of us'. This becomes even starker when placing the male prisoner against the attributes detailed by Christie for the 'ideal victim'. As such, men in prison are seen to be the creators of victims and positioned as completely opposed to the ideal victim construct. Yet, many men in prison are actually victims themselves – physically, mentally and emotionally in their past, present and future lives (see Sloan, 2016). This is a problem given that Christie has problematised the position of those victims who are also offenders, stating: 'Offenders that merge with victims make for bad offenders, just as victims that merge with offenders make for bad victims' (Christie, 1986: 25). Yet, it is necessary that we confront male prisoners' victimisation and vulnerabilities in order to attempt to address the future offending and harm that results from this vulnerable positionality.

In essence, the crux of the ideal victim construct seems to be an acknowledgement of the vulnerability of the victim – those who are clearly vulnerable seem to be accepted as being victims. On the face of it, in the main, men in prison have all the characteristics that directly oppose the notion of vulnerability: 95% of the prison population is male, a place where constructions of maleness and masculinity tend to shy away from any connection to vulnerability. Vulnerability is 'feminine'; vulnerability is 'weakness'. Prison, on the other hand, demands being masculine and strong:

"You put a wall up to everything, d'you know what I mean, you make people think that you're not ... or otherwise you're just going to get walked all over, if you're seen as a weak person in prison, then you're going to get, you're going to get trampled on, no matter what, I don't care what anybody says, in this, in normal mainstream prison, you cannot be seen as being weak because people will just walk all over.... You know, so ... even though it might not seem that way, it is isn't it, I know, I know it's a no, it's pretty obvious in my mind that ... the reason that I have to put a front on every day is so, is letting other prisoners know that I'm not a certain way myself.... You know, so they, in actual fact, are forcing me to do that, coz if I were to be myself, then people would think 'Oh you're weak' or 'You're vulnerable to this' or ... 'Can we, can we get round him that way?', d'you know what I mean?" (Kai[2])

Indeed, victimisation and vulnerability can actually lead to further victimisation and vulnerability within the prison, hence the need (and general revulsion within the prison population) for Vulnerable Prisoner Units (VPUs). VPUs are areas of certain prisons (not all prisons have a VPU) where groups of individuals in need of segregation are kept in one segregated location:

> because of the nature of their offences, or for some other reason, are a target for hostility and possible attack by other prisoners. These prisoners (the men on 'Rule 43 own protection') need to be segregated in their own interests, and in the majority of the long-term prisons this means that they will be held in the ordinary segregation unit. This has two disadvantages. First, they take up space in the segregation units, and cannot be unlocked at the same time as the other prisoners there. This is a major limitation on the segregation units' operational use. Second, the quality of life available to these men in the segregation units (sometimes for virtually the whole of their sentence) is of necessity very poor, with little or no access to association, work or education. This is very difficult to justify, particularly since without a degree of association they will have no opportunity to gain the confidence and social skills which might enable them to end their self-imposed isolation. (Home Office, 1984: 23)

These individuals are often subjected to victimisation within the prison by virtue of their offence type, for example, sex offenders are particularly reviled within the prison population and are often the subject of serious violence from other prisoners (see Priestley, 1980; Mann, 2016):

> "Coz I don't want to be banged up with a rapist. Coz other people wanted to beat him up, yeah, and I was his cell mate, so it don't look good on me coz, obviously, if you're cell mates, you're going to look after each other, yeah. But I can't look out for a rapist coz a rapist … and plus you can get hurt. You can get hurt coz I've seen people get hurt, get stabbed in prison, pool balls in their heads, all sorts of things, they get jumped as well, loads of people rush them and that, all sorts and cues, people get hit with cue sticks and that. People get bullied, robbed." (Jack)

The label of being a vulnerable prisoner in this instance is highly negative, as one research participant described:

> "it's not good for your self-, your self-respect…. I mean because, obviously, when I get out, I wanna get, I wanna have a relationship with a woman and all that and it's … it's gonna be bad enough saying I've been in prison, if somebody says 'Ah yeah, he was on the Vulnerable Prisoners Unit', it's not good for the old, uh, ego." (Benjamin)

As another noted:

> "I'll be honest with you, it's embarrassing…. It is, and there would, it's like, um, there's a stigma attached to that kind of thing, and in my whole set, in my whole life so far, in and out of custody, I've never been in that situation." (Zachary)

Other personal characteristics may generally imply personal weakness, such as a lack of cleanliness (see Sloan, 2012a, 2012b). In addition, many would presume men in prison to be getting their 'just desserts' if victimised while incarcerated. This is particularly evident in reactions along the lines of the offender's victimisation by other prisoners as 'punishment' for their crimes: popular cultural depictions of criminal justice, using phrases like 'In prison, he'll be the pie' (*Jay and Silent Bob Strike Back* [Smith, 2001]) (also available on a T-shirt), and the acceptance of prison sexual violence in popular culture as part of the punishment process (see Sloan, 2013) emphasise the general acceptance of such experiences for certain groups, rather than outright revulsion.

Within the prison in particular, victimisation experiences are often seen against the fact that these individuals (may have) victimised another to be in prison in the first place. It is interesting that such notions of victim precipitation are still seen to be culturally acceptable forms of humour when directed against men in prison. Elsewhere, this may invite critique and even outright uproar (McCleer, 1998). Berg and Johnson (1979: 61–2) discuss victim precipitation as follows:

> the offender selects his or her victim on the basis of certain clues provided by the potential victim. Presumably these clues include the various 'dispositional factors' involved in precipitating the offense, along with certain physical or social characteristics of the potential victim (e.g., race, age, sex, manner of appearance, or patterns of behavior). In some cases these clues may also involve the assumption that the victim is already a victim; he or she is perceived by the offender to be performing the role of victim and is, therefore, an appropriate target.

With this in mind, it could be argued that men in prison are subject to 'dispositional factors' of showing forms of weakness and committing certain offences that 'predispose' them to being victimised by other prisoners. Indeed, considering some of the structural inequalities (and violences) that determine which men end up in prison, we can see that Berg and Johnson may have a point.

The offender-as-victim is already a victim of structural inequalities and violence, and becomes an appropriate (and often publicly acceptable) target in ways that other victims would never be seen within modern discourses of victimisation. When discussing the sexual abuse and exploitation of women prisoners in Hawaii in the 1990s, Baro (1997: 79) noted that 'the social status of women in general and women inmates in particular is probably not high enough to generate the political will to comply with equal protection or sexual assault laws'. Whereas, arguably, women in prison today do receive more appropriate protection and attention (certainly in England and Wales, they tend to receive a greater proportion of the attention given to prisoners in general) (see Sloan, 2018), men in prison do not receive the same degree of equality of discursive attention with regard to their victimisation and vulnerability. Put bluntly, fewer people care about male prisoners suffering at the hands of each other when incarcerated (see French, 1979; Sennot, 1994; Dumond, 1995).

Male prisoners as vulnerable

Given that men in prison are often there by virtue of their having created victims themselves, it can be difficult to see how they can fit into the definition of being vulnerable enough even to begin to be seen as 'good' (let alone 'ideal') victims. Heber (2014: 418–19) notes that, at least in Sweden, offenders who are also victims are dominated by their offenderhood:

> they differ from authentic, innocent crime victims who are in need of redress.... Offenders who are also crime victims are thus included among the group of pitiable poor things. They are described as offenders who have been exposed to crime, not as crime victims who have committed offences. In chronological terms, their victimhood precedes their offenderhood.

As such, they cannot easily be seen as victims alone; where they achieve a degree of victim sympathy, this is aligned with notions of weakness through the notion of them being 'pitiable poor things' (Heber, 2014: 417), which, in itself, is a label that many wish to avoid when in prison – this being an identity marker that can lead to further victimisation by others.

Yet, men in prison who avoid the 'weak' and 'vulnerable' labels imposed through institutional processes of segregation do suffer from a substantial number of vulnerabilities before, during and after their incarceration (see Sloan, 2016). The structural inequalities and sad life stories of many men in prison are well known. Indeed, the Prison Reform Trust (2017: 22) reports that 24% of men in prison were taken into care as a child, 27% of men experienced abuse, 40% observed violence and 43% were expelled or permanently excluded, experiences that became apparent in the course of my discussions with men in prison:

> "Just to say there's a boy like on the last wing, the lives he, the life he's had, like he tells me about his life and its bad, I mean, his mum had died, his dad had died, he had no one, he started to turn to drugs, he ... all sorts of things, now you know he's got no one, he's on his own, you know....

But, um … yeah, but some people have just got nothing. I'm not saying I've got, coz I'm no better than anyone, but at least I've got something to get out to, got a job and I've got parents who, you know, care about me, and I've got a girlfriend to get out to. I've got summink, I think, I'm quite lucky to be honest, compared to some people, coz they really haven't got, they haven't got anything." (Oliver)

Elsewhere, I talk about the 'audience that matters' affecting the life course and masculine performances of men in prison (Sloan, 2016) – men perform their masculine identities (Kimmel, 1994) for particular audiences that matter to them at that particular point in their lives. This argument aligns with the notion of social capital within desistance discourses (Coleman, 1988). Positive social capital/audiences that matter often stem from early relationships – parents, grandparents, loved ones, close friends – even the dynamics of gender and relationships that one develops with a partner stem from behaviours learned at a young age (Tolson, 1977; McHale et al, 2003).

As such, having a lack of positive audiences to whom men are able to perform their masculinities in a positive and aspirational manner has implications for the development and behaviours of those men later in their lives. This can lead to potential criminality as a means through which to perform masculinity when other, more legitimate, means (and audiences) are unavailable (Messerschmidt, 1993), which, in turn, can lead to future vulnerabilities. This is not to say that men's criminality can be blamed on the presence or absence of others – it cannot. Men are autonomous beings who make conscious decisions. What the discussion seeks to do is to highlight the ways in which early relationships – or the lack of them – and the associated vulnerabilities that can be seen from having few people that matter in a man's life *even before imprisonment*, can result in criminality and vulnerability working in tandem and have serious implications for an individual during (and after) their prison experience(s).

During incarceration, there are many behaviours that can be seen to demonstrate inherent vulnerabilities within the prison population. In the 12 months ending September 2016, there were 30,465 self-harm incidents in male prisons in England and Wales, resulting in 2,449 hospital attendances, and there were 107 self-inflicted deaths (Ministry of Justice, 2017). Similarly, the Prison Reform Trust (2017: 22) notes that 23% of men in prison are suffering from anxiety and depression, and 21% have attempted suicide:

> "You have to be, you have to have a joke and a laugh about things and keep your sense of humour, d'you know what I mean, because if you don't and you lose that and just depressed all the time, then you can wind up killing yourself.... If you laugh a lot outside and you're used to being with your mates and you sit down and have a laugh and that and always having a joke, then in jail, you try and … maintain don't you, you want to try and have a laugh."
> (Henry)

In addition, the use of illicit substances within the prison estate has been seen as a means through which some men cope with their sentences (Cope, 2003) – prison, in itself, has implications in terms of reducing prisoners' abilities to cope with the additional stresses imposed upon men in prison (Liebling, 1999). Upon release, these stresses continue:

> Of the 66 non-natural deaths recorded following release from prison over the period of 2010–15, 44 died from drug overdoses and 14 were unclassified. The majority of those who died of a drug overdose did so within 10 days of release. This suggested a lack of continuity of care where, for example, records or referrals for treatment were not passed on or acted upon. (Phillips et al, 2016: 2–3)

Yet, whereas most individuals suffering from mental health problems are seen as vulnerable and potential ideal victims, men in prison are not, despite the intense emotional, mental and structural stresses and pressures placed upon them in prison and upon release.

Not only have many men in prison been victims of mental illness, structural inequalities and crime prior to their incarceration, but they are also at risk of physical victimisation in the course of their prison careers. In the 12 months ending September 2016, there were 17,886 incidents of prisoner-on-prisoner assault, and three cases of homicide in men's prisons in England and Wales (Ministry of Justice, 2017). In addition, in 2013, there were 170 cases of reported sexual assault incidents within prisons in England and Wales (including female prisons – the statistics are not broken down according to sex) (Ministry of Justice, 2015). Such stories of violence were common in my discussions with men in prison:

> "my pal got stabbed up, um, and he's in a, he's in a wheelchair now and he got like … stitches in his neck, face,

back, all over, but they'd doubled the razor, so they doubled the razor up so they couldn't stitch it so he had months of … um, where he just had gauzes on him so they had to change them every day, plus where they'd been kicking him, he couldn't walk again, so he was in a wheelchair as well, so that was over, phh, a stupid bit of debt, do you know what I mean … after that, I just calmed down a bit." (Bailey)

As such, men in prison suffer intense physical and mental harms (and the fear of succumbing to them), which results in them having to amend their behaviours and put on 'fronts' (Crewe, 2009) to appear 'big and bad' (as Christie's ideal victim construct dictates the offender to be) as a self-preservation mechanism, that is, 'Putting reasonable energies into protecting self' (Christie, 1986: 19). Indeed, placing oneself as the 'big and bad' offender is arguably often as a result of suffering from (or attempting to avoid) personal victimisation, be that physical, emotional or structural.

Victims of structural violence

Men in prison have often been subject to substantial inequalities throughout their lives (as noted already), which has subsequently led to their eventual movement into criminal activity and consequent incarceration. Indeed, Messerschmidt (1993) posits that men use crime as a means of demonstrating their masculinities when other, more socially legitimate, forms of masculine demonstration are unavailable to them. This is not even beginning to cover the structural violence that certain groups of male prisoners experience, for instance, there has been found to be a direct association between being a member of an ethnic group and the probability of receiving a custodial sentence (Hopkins et al, 2016), and black, minority ethnic and Muslim prisoners are more likely to report negative experiences of prison and staff relationships (HMCIP, 2016). Another excellent example is the over-representation of the Traveller population within prisons (HMIP, 2014).[3] This ethnic group has been found to be highly excluded, with issues concerning low literacy rates and high levels of alcohol and substance misuse, yet they make up 5% of the prison population (HMIP, 2014: 4). More generally, the Prison Reform Trust's 'Bromley Briefings' regularly compare the structural inequalities visible when comparing those in prison with those who are not. In the categories of being taken into care as a child, observing violence in the home as a child, regularly truanting from school, being expelled or permanently excluded from school, having no qualifications, being unemployed and jobless, and being homeless, for instance, the rates for people in prison are much higher than for their non-prisoner counterparts (Prison Reform Trust, 2017: 22). These individuals are clearly highly excluded and suffer from substantial inequalities as a result of such disparities.

Christie (1986: 21, emphasis in original) notes that the ideal victim 'must be strong enough to be listened to, or dare to talk. But she (he) must at the very same time be *weak enough not to become a threat to other important interests*'. The weakness of the ideal victim is not just physical in nature; it is also structural. Yet, Christie (1986: 24) claims that this structural victimisation does not align well with the ideal victim construction process due to the offenders not being visible individuals. Perhaps this is the key to why men in prison cannot successfully be placed within the ideal victim construct: the imposition of a prison sentence is, in itself, structural violence. This violence may be justified by legislation and sentencing guidelines, but it is violence nonetheless.

Christie (1986: 24) argued that structural violence does not work for constructing the ideal victim due to the lack of a visible 'offender'; using his example of the shorter life expectancy of certain classes, he states that 'no particular individual is – more than others in his class – responsible for the shorter life-expectancy among workers'. Yet, this argument is problematic in itself because there is the assumption that merely because a class or group of people is responsible, then the ideal victim label cannot be applied: there is a lack of an individual offender. Yet, in reality, there are many instances where groups have been blamed for the sins of an individual and the ideal victim label has been readily applied. Owen Jones recognises this process of differential application of blame according to class and power:

> Ever since Britain was plunged into economic disaster in September 2008, there has been a concerted attempt to redirect people's anger – both over their own plight, and that of the nation as a whole – away from the powerful. Instead, the British public are routinely encouraged to direct their frustrations at other, often more visible, targets, who have long been vilified by elite politicians and the media alike: immigrants, unemployed people, benefit claimants, public-sector workers, and so on. (Jones, 2014: xi)

Previously, Christie (1986: 20) argued that 'beaten wives are not such ideal victims because we – males – understand the phenomena so extraordinarily well, and because we can get our definition of the situation to be the valid one'. So, groups (of men), as opposed to individuals, actually dictate the notion of the ideal victim. These are generally the same groups of men responsible for the structural violence applied to individuals that 'cannot' be seen to create ideal victims. In essence, Christie's argument is that individual men can create ideal victims, and groups of men (such as men in prison) can be ideal offenders, yet groups of men who have structural power to delineate definitions are able to escape any offender label because they themselves define the victim state. While Christie eloquently made this point, it seems to have gone missing from most discussions of the ideal victim.

In actuality, this argument fundamentally undermines the ideal victim construct, and highlights its state as yet another mechanism of patriarchal control designed to enforce 'valued' qualities of masculinities through processes of subordination and marginalisation (Connell, 2005). Indeed, Bibbings (2014) notes that men in power have historically controlled the behaviours of other, less powerful, men through criminalisation, while Kimmel (1994) argues that men act out their masculinities for audiences of other, more powerful, men who grant them their masculine identities relative to others.

Conclusion

One of the key issues with seeing men in prison as victims is that this could potentially undermine the victim status of their own victim(s). In essence, the ideal victim construct applies the simplistic binary of one victim = one offender: to have an offender who is also a victim is problematic. Yet, this overlap is common (Reingle, 2014). That said, looking at the qualities of the ideal victim through the lens of the male prisoner, we can see considerable overlap with the categories discussed by Christie, particularly those categories of: weakness; offender as big and bad; putting reasonable energies into protecting self; weak enough not to be a threat to other important interests; and fear of being victimised.

- *Weakness* and *fear of being victimised*: One of the main worries seen by men in prison is the concern with being seen to be 'weak' and thus the potential target of harm. Many tools are used by men in prison to distance themselves from such labels, and yet men in prison have inherent vulnerabilities (and, by association, weaknesses) by virtue of being men in prison:

vulnerability in prison is intrinsically linked to masculine identity – rather than simply seeing vulnerability in terms of physical or mental harms, potential harms to gendered identity are seen to result from imprisonment due, in part, to a lack of control or certainty over the self. (Sloan, 2016: 153)

Ricciardelli et al (2015: 509) also note that 'where physical vulnerability is salient, prisoners may be more likely to use overstated aggressive masculine presentations to minimize harm, which in turn perpetuates or exacerbates existing physical risks'.

- *Offender as big and bad*: In many instances, men in prison are victimised by those who they find themselves incarcerated alongside: 'big and bad' men (who are often using crime as a means to show that they are 'big and bad' men) (Messerchmidt, 1993). Indeed, public discourse around prisons, and the inherent aversion to placing men in prison within the ideal victim status, is centred around the simplistic notion that men in prison are just that 'big and bad'.
- *Putting reasonable energies into protecting self*: As noted already, many tools are used by men in prison to attempt self-preservation, whether that be the use of violence and reputation to protect the self from others (McCorkle, 1992) or whether that be self-harm and the use of illicit substances as a means to protect the self. Ultimately, men in prison spend hours using various means to protect themselves and their identities (Schmid and Jones, 1991) so that they can get through the prison experience.
- *Weak enough not to be a threat to other important interests*: Although men in prison attempt to distance themselves from the label of weakness, in essence, prison imposes states of weakness upon them. Sykes's (2007 [1958]) pains of imprisonment (deprivation of goods and services, autonomy, heterosexual relationships, security, and liberty) demonstrate the ways in which men in prison are 'othered' and imposed upon by the state, which can also be seen through processes of disenfranchisement (Behan, 2017) and stigma imposition upon release. As such, the process of incarceration aims to remove the potential threat that these men impose upon society primarily through incapacitation, and subsequently through the continued imposition of stigmatising labels of 'prisoner' and 'offender' (regardless of their 'ex' status). Their social power is undermined and inhibited to such a degree that they fail to be able to be a significant 'threat to other important issues'.

Men in prison have not been, and probably never will be, seen as 'ideal victims' in any true sense – to do so would be to recognise the structural inequalities that belie the prison and justice system and processes, to undermine our entrenched understandings of what it is to be a 'victim', and to make society face up to some very uncomfortable truths. Yet, there are some clear alignments between the experiences of men in prison and Christie's notion of the ideal victim that allow us to place a critical lens on our understandings of men's experiences of prisons and punishment, and some of the common assumptions made about gender, offending and punishment. Their victimhood may not be 'ideal', but it should certainly not be ignored.

Notes

[1]   To avoid confusion, it should be noted that authors J. Sloan and J.A.S. Rainbow are one and the same.

[2]   All names of participants are pseudonyms to protect anonymity.

[3]   The terms 'Travellers', 'Gypsies' and 'Romany' refer to individuals who belong to certain (often highly stigmatised) communities; 'the group history, lifestyle or occupation of some, but not all, of these groups may involve or may have involved a nomadic lifestyle' (HMIP, 2014: 3). The terms are sometimes used interchangeably, yet generally refer to distinct ethnic groups (for more detailed definitions, see HMIP, 2014).

References

Baro, A.L. (1997) 'Spheres of consent: an analysis of the sexual abuse and sexual exploitation of women incarcerated in the state of Hawaii', *Women and Criminal Justice*, 8: 61–84.

BBC (2017) 'Panorama: behind bars: prison undercover'. Available at: https://www.bbc.co.uk/iplayer/episode/b08fn2sv/panorama-behind-bars-prison-undercover (accessed 10 March 2017).

Behan, C. (2017) *Citizen Convicts: Prisoners, Politics and the Vote*, Oxford: Oxford University Press.

Berg, W.E. and Johnson, R. (1979) 'Assessing the impact of victimization: acquisition of the victim role among elderly and female victims', in W. Parsonage (ed) *Perspectives on Victimology*, London: Sage, pp 58–71.

Bibbings, L.S. (2014) *Binding Men: Stories about Violence and Law in Late Victorian England*, Abingdon: Routledge.

Christie, N. (1986) 'The ideal victim', in E.A. Fattah (ed) *From Crime Policy to Victim Policy*, New York, NY: St. Martin's.

Coleman, J.S. (1988) 'Social capital in the creation of human capital', *American Journal of Sociology*, 94: S95–S120.

Connell, R.W. (2005) *Masculinities* (2nd edn), Cambridge: Polity Press.

Cope, N. (2003) '"It's no time or high time": young offenders' experiences of time and drug use in prison', *The Howard Journal of Criminal Justice*, 42(2): 158–75.

Crewe, B. (2009) *The Prisoner Society: Power, Adaptation, and Social Life in an English Prison*, Oxford and New York, NY: Oxford University Press.

Dumond, R.W. (1995) 'Ignominious victims: effective treatment of male sexual assault in prison', paper presented at the 103rd annual conference of the American Psychological Association, August, New York.

French, L. (1979) 'Prison sexualization: inmate adaptations to psycho sexual stress', *Corrective and Social Psychiatry and Journal of Behavior Technology Methods and Therapy*, 25(2): 64–9.

Heber, A. (2014) 'Good versus bad? Victims, offenders and victim-offenders in Swedish crime policy', *European Journal of Criminology*, 11(4): 410–28.

HMCIP (Her Majesty's Chief Inspector of Prisons) (2016) *Annual Report 2015–16*, London: The Stationery Office.

HMIP (Her Majesty's Inspectorate of Prisons) (2014) *Annual Report 2013–14*, London: The Stationery Office.

Home Office (1984) *Managing the Long-Term Prison System: The Report of the Control Review Committee*, London: HMSO.

Hopkins, K., Uhrig, N. and Colahan, M. (2016) *Associations between Ethnic Background and Being Sentenced to Prison in the Crown Court in England and Wales in 2015*, London: Ministry of Justice.

Jones, O. (2014) *The Establishment: And how they get away with it*, London: Penguin.

Kimmel, M.S. (1994) 'Masculinity as homophobia: fear, shame, and silence in the construction of gender identity', in H. Brod and M. Kaufman (eds) *Theorizing Masculinities*, Thousand Oaks, CA, and London: Sage.

Liebling, A. (1999) 'Prison suicide and prisoner coping', *Crime and Justice*, 26: 283–359.

Mann, R.E. (2016) 'Sex offenders in prison', in Y. Jewkes, B. Crewe and J. Bennett (eds) *Handbook on Prisons* (2nd edn), London and New York, NY: Routledge.

McCorkle, R.C. (1992) 'Personal precautions to violence in prison', *Criminal Justice and Behaviour*, 19(2): 160–73.

McHale, S.M., Crouter, A.C. and Whiteman, S.D. (2003) 'The family contexts of gender development in childhood and adolescence', *Social Development*, 12(1): 125–48.

McLeer, A. (1998) 'Saving the victim: recuperating the language of the victim and reassessing global feminism', *Hypatia*, 13(1): 41–55.

Messerschmidt, J.W. (1993) *Masculinities and Crime*, Maryland, MA: Rowman and Littlefield Publishers, Inc.

Ministry of Justice (2015) *Management Information Bulletin on Sexual Assaults in Prison Custody*, London: Ministry of Justice.

Ministry of Justice (2017) 'Safety in custody quarterly: update to September 2016', safety in custody summary tables to September 2016. Available at: https://www.gov.uk/government/statistics/safety-in-custody-quarterly-update-to-december-2016 (accessed 10 April 2017).

Phillips, J., Gelsthorpe, L., Padfield, N. and Buckingham, S. (2016) *Non-Natural Deaths Following Prison and Police Custody: Executive Summary, Data and Practice Issues*, Equality and Human Rights Commission Research Report 106, Manchester: Equality and Human Rights Commission.

Priestley, P. (1980) *Community of Scapegoats: The Segregation of Sex Offenders and Informers in Prison*, Oxford: Pergamon Press.

Prison Reform Trust (2017) 'Bromley Briefings Prison Factfile', Autumn 2017, London: Prison Reform Trust.

Reingle, J.M. (2014) 'Victim–offender overlap', in J.M. Miller (ed) *The Encyclopedia of Theoretical Criminology*, Malden, MA: Wiley-Blackwell, pp 1–3.

Ricciardelli, R., Maier, K. and Hannah-Moffat, K. (2015) 'Strategic masculinities: vulnerabilities, risk and the production of prison masculinities', *Theoretical Criminology*, 19(4): 491–513.

Schmid, T.J. and Jones, R.S. (1991) 'Suspended identity: identity transformation in a maximum security prison', *Symbolic Interaction*, 14(4): 415–32.

Sennot, C.M. (1994) 'Poll finds wide concern about prison rape', *Boston Globe*, 17 May, p 22.

SIPS (Sheffield Institute of Policy Studies) (2017) 'Marginalisation, inclusion and research: academic challenges?' Available at: https://sheffieldinstituteforpolicystudies.com/2017/03/29/marginalisation-inclusion-and-research-academic-challenges (accessed 10 April 2017).

Sloan, J. (2011) 'Men inside: masculinities and the adult male prison experience', unpublished PhD thesis, University of Sheffield, UK.

Sloan, J. (2012a) '"You can see your face in my floor": examining the function of cleanliness in an adult male prison', *The Howard Journal of Criminal Justice*, 51(4): 400–10.

Sloan, J. (2012b) 'Cleanliness, spaces and masculine identity in an adult male prison', *Prison Service Journal*, 201: 3–6.

Sloan, J. (2013) 'Inter-prisoner sexual harm: representation vs. reality' in G. Meško, A. Sotlar and J. Greene (eds) *Criminal Justice and Security in Central and Eastern Europe – Practice and Research*, Ljubljana: University of Maribor, pp 261–77.

Sloan, J. (2016) *Masculinities and the Adult Male Prison Experience*, Basingstoke: Palgrave Macmillan.

Sloan, J. (2018) 'Saying the unsayable: foregrounding men in the prison system', in M. Maycock and K. Hunt (eds) *New Perspectives on Prison Masculinities*, Basingstoke: Palgrave Macmillan.

Smith, K. (Director) (2001) *Jay and Silent Bob Strike Back* [Motion picture], Dimension Films, View Askew Productions and Miramax.

Sykes, G. (2007 [1958]) *The Society of Captives: A Study of a Maximum Security Prison*, Princeton, NJ: Princeton University Press.

Tolson, A. (1977) *The Limits of Masculinity*, London: Tavistock Publications Limited.

Wilson, D. and O'Sullivan, S. (2004) *Images of Incarceration: Representations of Prison in Film and Television Drama*, Winchester: Waterside Press.

FIFTEEN

A decade after Lynndie: non-ideal victims of non-ideal offenders – doubly anomalised, doubly invisibilised

Claire Cohen

Introduction

My present orientation is towards victimology, but I am not a victimologist. I am a critical criminologist and Foucauldian – my interest in victimology is part of a broader interest in problematising knowledges constructed within criminology and the allied disciplines. As a Foucauldian I am sensitised to recognising knowledges as socially constructed, and serving particular forms of power, in the creation of subjects for the purpose of governance – or, more accurately, governmentality. Which is to say that, for the purpose of this chapter, victimology is the target of my research, and victimological practices are the object of my study. In so doing, I am guided by Foucault's admonition that 'people know what they do, they know why they do what they do, but what they don't know is what what they do does' (Foucault, personal communication, cited in Dreyfus and Rabinow, 1982: 187), and his imperative for us to 'think differently' (Foucault, 1984: 8).[1] In essence then, it is useful to understand that Foucault requires that we are cognisant of the ironies incurred through the practices of 'experts', be they ever so well meaning, and that we free ourselves from the shackles of established 'truth' or truisms, recognising that these might be best understood as reflecting and perpetuating existing power relations.

Ostensibly, the focus of this chapter is Lynndie England, but the key issue for me in examining Lynndie England is not Lynndie England – not at all. My ongoing research is into male rape and male victims of sexual violence, in all forms. What I am really concerned about is their neglect, a concern inspired, in no small part, by the lack of progress in this area – particularly over the last two decades, despite key sociocultural and legislative changes in various Western contexts that really should have remedied this.

I note, with dismay, that there are recurrent patterns in research that contribute to discursive regularity around this issue. In particular, interest is frequently inspired in regards to male victims of rape and sexual violence, usually boys, in response to certain cases, which results in a momentary popularisation that then quickly wanes. This cycle, regarded as 'treading water' (Scarce, 1997: 104), ensures a 'forgotten history' for the male rape victim (Cohen, 2014: 29). Over and over again, this pattern can be seen, contributing to a perpetual state of (re)discovery for the male victim of sexual violence (Cohen, 2014). I am particularly interested in this phenomenon, and question why it is that this interest in male victims is not sustained. After all, what we would expect to happen in such instances is that they would leave a legacy of some sort – resulting in a permanent change both in how we 'see' and what we 'do'. There should be a cumulative impact arising from that initial flurry of attention and activity. Those of us interested in discourse, in various guises, expect certain things to happen – be they conceived of as revelation, momentum, critical mass, rupture, intervention, insurrection or shift. Female rape is an excellent case in point here, for example, consider the progress made in regards to victims of rape within marriage; however, for male rape, there has been little or no change. Many of the concerns and criticisms that colleagues had some 10 and even 20 years ago – around neglect, marginalisation and de-prioritisation – still persist. So, my concern is: what is it that makes us focus on some victims and not others, and why is it that substantive and enduring change is not happening? Perhaps more importantly, how is this so? I have started to think of discourse as the placid surface of a lake, where it reaches a lovely equilibrium. We would expect that there would be this 'swim, swim, swim' to breach the surface of the lake, and once it has been breached, there is a wave, a rupture that is very obvious, and some type of permanent change to the landscape – but there is not. Instead, its 'swim, swim, swim' and – seemingly – 'Drag!', as the issue is pulled back down, disappearing from view once again. There is no breach, no rupture, no permanent change. We thought it was coming, but then it was gone. It is the mechanisms that serve to protect the equilibrium that I am now interested in.

Although the draw of my attention is male victims vis-a-vis criminology and victimology, what I am really examining is the dark figure – not just in terms of criminal justice practice, but also in terms of our academic practice – in order to query why it is that the great bulk of our endeavour focuses on some offenders and some victims, and not other offenders and other victims. In this chapter, I am using a particular case to enable me to highlight, track and problematise this phenomenon. For sure, the ideal victim construct is of considerable importance here – after all, conformity to its ideal assures hyper-visibility for some victims (see Hua, 2011). However, my concern is not with the 'ideal victim' per se; it is with the binaristic position of the 'non-ideal victim' (which Christie depicts in relation to two historical examples: 'witches' and 'workers') and the invisibilisation that ensues from the failure to conform (an issue that Christie touches on only briefly in relation to the lack of attention that his own work received some decades previously). Moreover, it is the non-ideal binaristic subject positions of non-ideal offender (female) and non-ideal victim (male), or, rather, the relational non-ideal subject position occupied by male victims of female offenders, that guarantees double-invisibilisation for these 'pariah'[2] subjectivities. In so doing, I score the gendered ideal victim binary as a governmentalised gender-normative taxonomy that regulates and deploys gender.

Thus, this chapter will examine both the concept and the construct of the ideal victim, positing, ultimately, that the latter serves to regulate discourse in its operation as a regime of knowledge, and that the former, while an incisive contribution that has left a considerable impact within the conceptual academic toolkit, has nevertheless left a negligible impact on the academy itself. I will illustrate this with regards to the case of Lynndie England, arguing that academic priorities illustrate the continued influence of the ideal victim on the very people who should be best placed to resist it, and even in work that purports to do so.

The ideal victim - new concept, old construct, enduring problem: the ideal victim binary/ies as a normative taxonomy

Christie's conceptualisation of the 'ideal victim' articulates a discursive construct that serves to accord or deny the ascription of 'victimhood', and thus justice, based not on the material qualities of a criminal act, but on the innate characteristics of the actors in any given crime scenario. In so doing, Christie's concept lays bare the precarity and contestation inherent in the application of that label, and in securing that identity. Christie revealed that, whether conceived of as the 'credible' victim (Graham, 2006), 'legitimate' victim (Fattah, 1979), 'innocent' victim or 'deserving' victim (Christie, 1986), the mantle of victimhood is awarded dependent on the satisfaction of the internal logics of this construct, or, more accurately, conformity to its 'ideal' – rather than any objective assessment of harm. This serves to establish binaries of ideal versus non-ideal victim, be that understood as legitimate versus non-legitimate victim or credible versus non-credible victim – it amounts to those deserving versus not deserving of recognition as a victim.

Key to one's position in the ideal victim binary is the extent to which one can be construed as embodying culturally loaded perceptions of vulnerability and innocence, versus strength and culpability (see Rainbow, this volume). As others have noted, these components – passivity (Quinney, 1972), innocence (McShane and Williams, 1992) and vulnerability (Walklate, 2007) – are also components of femininity. Indeed, it can be said that the ideal victim is comprised of facets of ideal femininity. For Christie, the ideal victim – in the behavioural and characterological signs and signifiers he outlines as necessary preconditions for securing this status – is feminised. Indeed, there has been a normalisation of femininity as a trait of victimity, and likewise – as epitomised in the 'women-and-children' narrative (Enloe, 2000) – there has emerged a normalisation of victimhood as a feminine trait. It is unsurprising, then, that in the original exemplification of the ideal victim, that victim was a woman; furthermore, the ideal offender was a man – a clear demarcation by gender, then, for Christie's proto-'ideals' (what might be regarded as the paradigmatic 'little old lady' in his original piece).

As discussed and illustrated at length in my previous work (Cohen, 2014), this gendering of claims to legitimate victimhood, or, more accurately, this feminisation of victimhood and gendering of subject positions within the ideal victim binary, reaches its zenith in regards to crimes of sexual violence and particularly rape – operating as a barrier to justice for those women who fail to conform to normative values of ideal femininity, and as something of a brick wall for men. After all, to paraphrase Clover (1987, 1992), the hegemonic male is the hero or the villain, but never the victim.[3] Thus, by dint of their sex, male victims of rape and sexual violence fail full stop. So, while it cannot be claimed that all women are readily cast as legitimate victims, it can certainly be asserted that all men are not – which is to say that women are more inclined to gain such recognition because of their gender, while for men, any recognition at all is in spite of it. Most assuredly, male victims are far from 'ideal' in Christie's context.

As a system of thought, the ideal victim construct draws on various related normative gendered knowledges – including the Just World Thesis, myths, scripts, schemas, stereotypes, tropes and narratives (see Bosma, Mulder and Pemberton, this volume). These contiguous knowledges intermesh, mutually reinforce and sustain one another, operating as circular logics, to afford victim blame or exoneration. Of these, the most significant is arguably the Just World Thesis (Lerner and Matthews, 1967) and its associated cognitive biases – confirmation bias, hindsight, cognitive dissonance and so on. Redolent of the maxim that 'you get what you deserve and deserve what you get' (Anderson and Doherty, 2008), this functions to accord causality and responsibility to the individual, simultaneously 'Othering' them and responsibilising them for their fate – thus underscoring the ideal victim binary by legitimising notions of victim precipitation and victim blame. Hence, while it is commonly assumed that we have come a long way since early criminologists sketched typologies apportioning direct blame to victims (eg Garofalo, 1885; Sutherland, 1924; Schafer, 1968; Ferri, 1971 [1892]; Beccarria, 1997 [1764]; Lombroso, 2006 [1876]), and since victim precipitation was explicitly advocated as a explanatory model by those now regarded as the – somewhat regrettable – forefathers of victimology (Von Hentig, 1940, 1948; Mendelsohn, 1956, 1974; Wolfgang, 1958; Amir, 1967, 1971), the continued relevance of Christie's framework suggests otherwise.

As a concept, the ideal victim is startling in its simplicity and insight. Feminist criminologists, focusing on female victims of rape, have long recognised that the ideal victim's diametrically opposed categories serve to police women's behaviour in line with patriarchal gender norms. Research into male rape has extended existing analyses by focusing on men's precarious positioning as the 'non-ideal victim' vis-a-vis hegemonic masculinity (Graham, 2006; Cohen, 2014). As this is a situated construct that reflects the normative values of its socio-historical context, it is discriminatory in its application, and is thus regulatory in its effects – key 'governing through crime' (Crawford, 1997 and Coleman, 2004, cited in Walklate, 2007).

The notion of the ideal victim, in its construction and power effects, lends itself readily to examination with Foucauldian tools. By delineating individuals in line with normative behaviours and attributes, this construct ensures that we 'know' the victim, and they 'know' themselves – thus delimiting what Foucault termed the 'conduct of potential conduct' by incurring self-regulation. As a Foucauldian, I recognise that 'discourse is a violence which we do to things, or, at all events, as a practice we impose upon them' (Foucault, 1972 [1969]: 229). Simply put, knowledges are reified in the construction of subjects – who are the vehicle for power, not its point of application – for the purpose of governance. The power effects of such truth claims go beyond the merely linguistic or rhetorical in the service of governmentality.

My ongoing research in this area is concerned with problematising established truth claims, and disrupting discursive regularities. In particular, I take issue with knowledges that are taken for granted and/or held sacred. As such, it is interesting for me to note that the great weight of academic work that utilises Christie's concept contrasts that construct against its antithesis, the ideal offender, but neglects its necessary counterpart: the *non*-ideal victim. Indeed, at the time of writing this chapter (7 May 2017), the search term 'non-ideal victim' in Google Scholar returned just 30 hits – including Christie's original piece – whereas 'ideal victim' returned 2,130 relevant publications. However, one cannot 'know' the ideal without 'knowing' the non-ideal – in constructing one, we inevitably construct the other. To fail to give due attention to the non-ideal victim is to miss, or, more accurately, to elide, a significant part of the discursive puzzle. These are symbiotic and dialectical, and together they comprise part of the machinations that operate contra to the achievement, or not, of justice.

In my previous work (Cohen, 2014), among other things, I built on Christie's work to elucidate the gendered ideal/non-ideal victim binary as a governmentalised construct. I argued that the male rape victim faces a struggle for justice that in no small part is attributable to his struggle against a gendered regime of truth epitomised in the ideal victim. In its particularised, binaristic and relational knowledges around rape, predicated on gender norms, the ideal victim functions to sustain discursive regularities that are key to the deployment of gender, and thus serves to preserve and perpetuate existing asymmetric gender-based power relations that shore up patriarchy. I also detailed the irony of contemporary criminology's push to deconstruct the ideal victim for female rape complainants while simultaneously (re)constructing the male rape victim as the repository for these erstwhile disqualified knowledges, which – revalidated – 'write back' to the female (Cohen, 2014).

In this chapter, I turn my attention to another neglected aspect of the ideal victim. I note that, as an operating schema, this construct is actually comprised of four subject positions – ideal victim, ideal offender, non-ideal victim and non-ideal offender – which therefore operate not as a single binary, but as six superordinate co-constitutive binaries: ideal victim versus ideal offender; ideal victim versus non-ideal victim; ideal victim versus non-ideal offender; non-ideal victim versus ideal offender; non-ideal offender versus ideal offender; and non-ideal offender versus non-ideal victim. Building on my previous work, I propose that, together, these gendered binaries within the ideal victim constitute a gender-normative taxonomy. The power effects of this ideal victim taxonomy can be deduced by traces left in the social sphere – its influence can be seen in our criminal justice system, in the media, in our data and in the academy. Certain subject positions are hyper-visible and others are invisibilised. Those that languish on what might be regarded as the dark side of the binary, as non-ideal victims and/or non-ideal offenders – specifically, female offenders and male victims – are subject to mechanisms of elision and processes of redaction, becoming (in Foucauldian terms) subjugated knowledges in order to satisfy the imperative of, and to restore, what I term discursive equilibrium – an ineluctable reversion to the norm. While a fulsome examination of this is beyond the scope of the present chapter, what will be presented here is a problematisation of knowledge production in the academy, through which the influence of the taxonomy might be discerned.

The ideal victim taxonomy and discursive equilibrium: the stubborn persistence of the gendered binary in sexual violence

The ideal victim is not a man because the 'ideal', in this instance, is comprised of ideal femininity; the ideal offender is not a woman because the 'ideal', in this instance, is comprised of ideal masculinity – these two subject positions languish on the dark side of the ideal victim binary. While the ideals are hyper-visible, the non-ideals are readily invisibilised – co-constitutive discursive practices that serve to regulate and reify normative gender. What better case to illustrate this process of redaction in action than that of Lynndie England?

In 2005, Lynndie England was dishonourably discharged from the US military, and subsequently served a prison term, for her part in the abuse and torture of Iraqi prisoners of war detained in Abu Ghraib. In the years prior to this, photographs documenting these acts, which included crimes of sexual violence – all of which were targeted at male detainees in her charge – were widely disseminated in the media. As the female face of appalling human rights abuse, Lynndie became notorious, and her photographs of the atrocities – showing sexual degradation and molestation, including coerced masturbation – became iconic and, indeed, were pivotal in the public backlash against the Iraq war (see Mason, 2005; Harp and Struckman, 2010).

The case of Lynndie England dominated global, but particularly Western, media – being prime-time, front-page news in both the UK and US for over a year. More than a decade on, in the public sphere, Lynndie has been of sustained interest – the subject of numerous magazine articles and television interviews, documentaries, books and blogs, and she has even been the subject of a song (*Dangerous Beauty*) by rock band The Rolling Stones (2005). By any standard, this is a high-profile case, with a lasting impact on the public 'imaginary' (McLaughlin and Muncie, 2013). On the face of it, while this case sits within the dark side of the ideal victim taxonomy, it does not illustrate the process of redaction in action, or a return to discursive equilibrium. However, such an interpretation requires that we overlook the fact that Lynndie's male victims were readily effaced – being largely absent from media representations and public discourse, except for Lynndie's enthusiastic victim blaming and the recurrent use of their images – rendering them dehumanised, objectified, nameless, faceless targets known only in relation to Lynndie herself. These trends surely satisfy any measure of secondary victimisation and, at the very least, illustrate a cost to victims in languishing on the dark side of the taxonomy, where one is anomalised and anomalous. Facets of such phenomena in relation to this case have been examined by others (see, among others, Cohler, 2006; Howard and Prividera, 2008; Holland, 2009; Harp and Struckman, 2010). However, they are certainly worthy of further inquiry in relation to the ideal victim taxonomy, and, for the purposes of this chapter, I would suggest that we need to look a little closer to home.

Given the high-profile nature of coverage regarding the case of Lynndie England, and the enduring interest in it, it would be reasonable to assume that this case marked a watershed moment in knowledge construction relating to sexual violence, which leaves a lasting legacy in the academic discourse – it did not, and it does not. This event did not disrupt orthodox discourse; it did not breach the gendered binary that casts men as offenders and women as victims. It does, therefore, illustrate the mechanisms underlying the move towards 'discursive equilibrium' in the preservation of those gendered, normative, binaristic, subject positions that serve to cast men outside of legitimate victimhood, particularly men assaulted by women. The ideal victim taxonomy, as a regime of truth, is epitomised in this case and its impact on knowledge construction, or – rather – lack of it.

In order to ascertain the impact of the case of Lynndie England on the academic community, I interrogated online repositories of academic publications, principally by conducting data mining in Google Scholar on 4 December 2016. I undertook key word searches relating both to this specific case and to broader categories of offending behaviour, which could then be compared with other variants in order to identify trends in published research and thus ascertain priorities in scholarly activity, which could be tracked by year.[4] When I initially approached this task, I had expected to find – in line with my previous research – that male victims were quickly redacted. That much was readily satisfied. However, I had also expected to find, in line with feminist research on 'monstrous' women and, indeed, the vast amount of research on female criminality and criminalisation, that the academic community would have formed a critical mass around the female offending behaviour highlighted within this case. In this aspect, I was to be bitterly disappointed. Instead of the 'doubly-deviant' principle, whereby 'monstrous women' experience enhanced visibility in the media (see Lloyd, 1995; Heidensohn, 2000), it seems that – for the academy – where both actors are on the dark side of the ideal victim taxonomy, doubly anomalised is to be doubly invisibilised.

Unsurprisingly, I found a steady rise in interest for 'Lynndie England' in the year following the breaking of this case in the news media, but this interest was not sustained. The peak year for the academic community to reflect an interest in this was 2010, with a total of 153 articles published. In order to maximise returns, and isolate the generalised impact of this case, I broadened my search criteria. The first alternate search comprised three separate inquiries for 'female perpetrators' + 'male victims' + rape, rape, and, finally, 'female sexual offenders'. For 'female perpetrators' + 'male victims' + rape, I found a substantially lower level of interest than in Lynndie herself. This was, most assuredly, not what I had been expecting. The peak year for this broader search was 2014, with a total of 122 articles. Some of the lack of visibility here might be explained by the fact that legislative constructs for rape have historically excluded males from being recognised as victims, and some jurisdictions still fail to recognise women as offenders in regards to this crime. For example, the crime of rape on statute in England and Wales currently requires penile penetration to be committed by the offender, and, as such, is far from gender-neutral (see Rumney and Morgan-Taylor, 1997a, 1997b; Rumney, 2007).

With that in mind, I broadened the search criteria, contrasting the previous search with the gender-neutral category 'rape', and then with 'female sexual offenders'. I found that interest in 'rape', across the full time period, was consistently strong, with a peak year in 2008, totalling 37,200 articles. In line with my previous research, this indicates that although seemingly gender-neutral, in actuality, 'rape' is gendered female. This reflects a discursive normalisation around the gendering – or, rather, feminising – of 'rape' that persists despite the case of Lynndie England. For female sexual offenders, a category that easily accommodates Lynndie and has none of the legislative limitations around female rapists, there was – inexplicably – a similar rate to that search, with a peak total of 146 articles published in 2014. At the very least, this is interesting; even more so when one considers that this period encompasses several high-profile cases in the UK where female sexual offenders hit the headlines, such as Rose West in 1995 and Vanessa George in 2009. Not only did Lynndie have a minimal impact in garnering and sustaining the attention of the academy, but so did others.

Alternate search number two comprised three separate searches for: 'female perpetrators' + 'male victims' + military + rape; then military + rape; and, finally, 'male victims' + military + rape. This search deliberately shifted the focus of inquiry to the military as the context for knowledge production, in order to better reflect what was assumed to be the main field in which the impact of this case would be felt. The search category "female perpetrators" + "male victims" + military + rape gave a peak year of 2013, with a total of 49 published works. Given that in 1990, there were zero publications in this area, and indeed interest didn't reach double-figures until 2002, at least it can be stated that interest grew during this period, and that there was a steady rise. The contrast with the search for military + rape however, is stark – those 49 articles pale into insignificance versus the 17,300 published in this area during 2014, and indeed there is a consistently high level of sustained interest in this, rising from 1,870 in 1990, to 6,770 in 2002. In order to ascertain if the supposedly gender neutral search was actually gender neutral, I then searched for "male victims" + military + rape. I found a greater level of interest here than the first explicitly gendered criteria, but it still falls far short, at a peak year of just 333 in 2014. So, despite the military being the pertinent context for Lynndie England, there remains a stark neglect of the issues her case raises, the supposedly gender-neutral category of 'rape' is fundamentally gendered female, and even where female offenders are removed from the equation, interest in male victims remains low. Academia then is far more comfortable with male rape than with female perpetrators, but only by increments, and both are dwarfed by interest in rape proper (understood as normatively gendered - male offender, female victim).

Alternate search number three comprised the following four searches: 'female perpetrators' + 'male victims' + military + 'sexual assault'; military + 'sexual assault'; military + 'female victims' + 'sexual assault'; and, finally, military + 'male victims' + 'sexual assault'. This search was intended to shift the focus to sexual assault in the hopes that it might prove more inclusive than the implicitly gendered category of rape, and could thus raise the hit rate. At this point, I conscientiously took steps to unearth any and all research inspired by this case and its variants. The first search – 'female perpetrators' + 'male victims' + military + 'sexual assault' – produced as disappointing a set of results as the gendered search terms in alternate search number two – a peak of just 50 papers published in 2013. So, there are gross limitations in 'seeing' female sexual offenders, male victims of sexual violence and, indeed, both. Military + 'sexual assault' returned a peak of 4,740 articles published in 2014, so – once again – the seemingly gender-neutral is the most popular orientation in the academy. The female-specific search military + 'female victims' + 'sexual assault' returned a peak of just 444 articles published in 2015, but rather than indicating that females are likewise neglected, and the great mass of research is dedicated to male victims, or even that the research is genuinely gender-neutral, this instead reveals that, once again, there is a gendered norm at work underlying the construct of sexual violence to feminise this – what this search reveals is that gendering female where the term is already assumed to denote female is a nonsense. The final search in this data set – military + 'male victims' + 'sexual assault' – gives a peak year of 2015 at a rate of just 346 articles returned. This is on par with female-specified and reveals this gendering of the search criteria as equally anomalous, but instead of interpreting this as revealing that sexual assault is gendered male, to my mind, this simply points to a lack of orientation to the male in current research.

Alternate search number four comprised the following three searches: 'male on male rape' + military; military + rape; and 'male rape' + military. This search was intended to shift the focus to male victims of rape, male-on-male rape and male rape in order to bypass the linguistic and rhetorical limitations incurred by including female sexual offenders in the search. I had assumed that it might be the case that the academy is more comfortable with men as victims of other men, rather than men as victims of women – a prioritisation that could simply be said to reflect a lag in academic fashions and relevance. However, the results for this data set are startlingly low given that this form of sexual violence against men, especially within institutional contexts, is the assumed normative variant insomuch as our legislative and historical constructs dictate. Indeed, there has been a lengthy history of acknowledgement of this within the military and militarised contexts such as war and conflict (Scarce, 1997; Cohen, 2014). However, in this instance, a total of 36 returns were achieved in 2013; compare this with the results for military + rape, at 17,300 in 2014. Interestingly, the terms 'male rape'

+ military return slightly more, at 183 in 2015. There are more pieces oriented to male rape than male-on-male rape. Logically, it should be the former that is more popular, until one realises that the male offender indicated in the terms 'male-on-male' is actually the assumed norm and thus does not necessitate denotation.

Alternate search number five comprised the following search terms: 'male on male sexual assault' + military; 'sexual assault' + military; and, finally, 'male on male sexual assault'. This search was intended to focus on the 'lesser' and more inclusive category of sexual assault in the hopes that more men might be included here. In essence, perhaps this is where all the academic attention in regards to this issue is hiding – no, not at all. In fact, this is the most blatant illustration of gender-normative values at work in the academy – the peak year for 'male on male sexual assault' + military was 2013, at a measly six publications. This reveals a level of interest so slight that it is less than that for male victims of female perpetrators in the military – at least that made it into double figures. This is not at all what I had expected. Compare this to the supposedly gender-neutral/implicitly gendered 'sexual assault' + military, at 4,740 in 2014, and the implications are galling. In the meantime, 'male on male sexual assault' itself achieves only a high of 14 in 2013. This is bewildering; after all, the case of Lynndie England is most readily understood as one of sexual assault rather than rape, so that case should have had rather more impact within these categories, and this area.

What these data reveal is that, certainly, the minimising of sexual violence for men is profoundly apparent, as it is likewise for female sexual offenders. This is plausibly the product of two interrelated phenomena: a gendered hierarchy of harm in relation to sexual violence; and a gendered rape model that posits men as offenders and women as victims. Each phenomenon is underscored by the binaries within the ideal victim taxonomy. This pattern of neglect within academic knowledge production constitutes a redaction of cases such as Lynndie England from our disciplinary scapes, and reflects a redaction of such from our respective imaginaries. It is damning: at the very least, it indicates the alignment of research interests and funding along gender-normative lines; at worst, it indicates the academy as a site for the preservation and perpetuation of the ideal victim construct, and illustrates redaction in action. At which point, we had best be mindful of Foucault's conceptualisation of discourse as 'a violence which we do to things' (Foucault, 1972 [1969]: 67); I would argue that this is especially the case in our silences, where subjugated knowledges bear the brunt of this epistemic violence.

So, what can be said in summation? That Lynndie England did not really have much of an impact, that there is still gendering at work in knowledge production and that there is evidence of redaction on a grand scale. For me, of great concern is that the construction of issues raised by this case is largely taking place outside of the academy – we are not addressing this, but this is certainly being addressed. Female sexual offenders, female rapists, male rape victims, male victims of sexual assault and so on – there is abundance of 'information' online, so there is engagement with this issue. It is being constructed, but we are most assuredly not leading this construction. It is happening largely without academic involvement. This raises a significant issue as well: as public or activist intellectuals, do we not have a responsibility to provide some type of counterbalance to this? After all, 'the work of an intellectual is ... to question over and over again what is postulated as self-evident, to disturb people's mental habits, the way they do and think things, to dissipate what is familiar and accepted, to re-examine rules and institutions' (Foucault, 1988: 265). From this examination of the literature, it is fair to say that we are failing in our responsibility. At best, it can be said that modern victimology has not travelled as far from its historical roots as one might have hoped. Far worse though, it could be said that our gaze – refracted through institutionalisation of the ideal victim taxonomy – makes us complicit in such injustice, and renders the academy a key site for the recuperation of gender norms.

Concluding thoughts

My initial interest in the case of Lynndie England was in regards to how this might impact on knowledge production around male victims of rape and sexual violence. When I began assembling and interrogating data sets for this chapter, I had expected to unearth enough to enable me to build on my previous research in respect of the construction of the male rape victim, and the existing work in this area that considers the (mis)representation of Lynndie England in popular discourse, in order that I might examine the construction of male victims of female offenders. This was intended to enable me to develop my concept of the ideal victim taxonomy. Instead, it quickly became apparent that the rather more significant trend was not how this case and its related issues were being represented in the academic discourse, but that they were not – relative to those subject positions that occupy the 'ideals'. It is that gendered prioritisations and proscriptions continue to constitute our disciplinary scape, despite cases such as Lynndie England, which has captured my interest – not least because, in itself, the fact that we are inured to the cacophony of silence in the academy for the 'non-ideals' roundly illustrates the influence of the ideal victim taxonomy, and the pull of discursive equilibrium, in its ineluctable return to the norm. In closing, let it be noted that Nils Christie gave us the tools we needed to tear the ideal victim framework down, but that we can only succeed in doing so if we first turn those tools on ourselves.

Notes

[1] These deceptively simple statements form the basis of a complex and extensive Foucauldian methodology, which is integral to my ongoing research in this area. Unfortunately, it is beyond the scope of this chapter to adequately reflect this (see Cohen, 2014: esp ch 2, 'Problematisation', and ch 3, 'Investigation – a Foucauldian triangulation?').

[2] À la 'pariah femininities' (see Schippers, 2007).

[3] For a fulsome analysis in respect of Christie's (1986) and Clover's (1987) precepts as extended through a Foucauldian analysis of male rape, see Cohen (2014: esp ch 4, 'Representations – knowing victimhood').

[4] This method of key word searching exploits Boolean searches in Google. It must be noted that Google changes search commands on a frequent basis. Neither + nor AND are now supported, instead, Google automatically inserts this specific command utility into a search where no other modifier is specified. For the sake of clarity for the reader, I retain + in the account of my method, although its explicit use in Google is redundant. In addition, where inverted commas are denoted around search terms in this chapter, this indicates that this precise phrase was searched. In a Google Boolean search, these should be replaced by double quote marks (at least at the time of writing). See Google support for up to date guidance.

References

Amir, M. (1967) 'Victim precipitated forcible rape', *Journal of Criminal Law, Criminology and Police Science*, 58(4): 493–502.

Amir, M. (1971) *Patterns in Forcible Rape*, Chicago, IL: University of Chicago Press.

Anderson, I. and Doherty, K. (2008) *Accounting for Rape: Psychology, Feminism and Discourse Analysis in the Study of Sexual Violence*, London: Routledge.

Beccaria, C. (1997 [1764]) *On Crimes and Punishments*, Indianapolis, IN: Hackett.

Christie, N. (1986) 'The ideal victim', in E.A. Fattah (ed) *From Crime Policy to Victim Policy*, Basingstoke: Palgrave Macmillan.

Clover, C. (1987) 'Her body, himself: gender in the slasher film', *Representations*, 20: 187–228.

Clover, C. (1992) *Men, Women and Chainsaws: Gender in the Modern Horror Film*, London: BFI Publishing.

Cohen, C. (2014) *Male Rape is a Feminist Issue: Feminism, Governmentality and Male Rape*, Basingstoke: Palgrave Macmillan.

Cohler, D. (2006) 'Keeping the home front burning: renegotiating gender and sexuality in US mass media after September 11', *Feminist Media Studies*, 6(3): 245–61.

Dreyfus, H.L. and Rabinow, P. (1982) *Michel Foucault: Beyond Structuralism and Hermeneutics*, Chicago, IL: University of Chicago Press.

Enloe, C. (2000) *Maneuvers: The International Politics of Militarizing Women's Lives*, Berkeley, CA: University of California Press.

Fattah, E.A. (1979) 'Some recent theoretical developments in victimology', *Victimology*, 4(2): 198–213.

Ferri, E. (1971 [1892]) 'The positive school of criminology: three lectures', in S.E. Grupp (ed) *Theories of Punishment*, Indiana, IN: Indiana University.

Foucault, M. (1972 [1969]) *The Archaeology of Knowledge* (trans A.M. Sheridan Smith), New York, NY: Pantheon Books.

Foucault, M. (1984) *The Use of Pleasure: The History of Sexuality Volume 2* (trans R. Hurley), London: Penguin.

Foucault, M. (1988) *Politics, Philosophy, Culture: Interviews and Other Writings, 1977-1984*, (trans L.D. Kritzman), New York, NY: Routledge.

Garofalo, R. (1885) *Criminologica*, Turim: Bocca.

Graham, R. (2006) 'Male rape and the careful construction of the male victim', *Social Legal Studies*, 15(2): 187–208.

Harp, D. and Struckman, S. (2010) 'The articulation of Lynndie England to Abu Ghraib: gender ideologies, war, and the construction of reality', *Journal of Magazine & New Media Research*, 11(2): 1–23.

Heidensohn, F. (2000) 'Women and violence: myths and reality in the 21st century', *Criminal Justice Matters*, 42(1): 20–1.

Holland, S.L. (2009) 'The enigmatic Lynndie England: gendered explanations for the crisis at Abu Ghraib', *Communication and Critical/Cultural Studies*, 6(3): 246–64.

Howard, J.W., III and Prividera, L.C. (2008) 'The fallen woman archetype: media representations of Lynndie England, gender, and the (ab)uses of US female soldiers', *Women's Studies in Communication*, 31(3): 287–311.

Hua, J. (2011) *Trafficking Women's Human Rights*, Minneapolis, MN, and London: University of Minnesota Press.

Lerner, M.J. and Matthews, J. (1967) 'Reactions to suffering of others under conditions of indirect responsibility', *Journal of Personality and Social Psychology*, 5: 319–25.

Lloyd, A. (1995) *Doubly Deviant, Doubly Damned: Society's Treatment of Violent Women*, London: Penguin Books.

Lombroso, C. (2006 [1876]) *Criminal Man* (trans M. Gibson and N. Rafter), North Carolina, NC: Duke University Press.

Mason, C. (2005) 'The hillbilly defence: culturally mediating U.S. terror at home and abroad', *NWSA Journal*, 17(3): 39–63.

McLaughlin, J. and Muncie, E. (2013) *Criminological Perspectives* (3rd edn), London: Sage.

McShane, M.D. and Williams, F.P., III (1992) 'Radical victimology: a critique of the concept of the victim in traditional victimology', *NPPA Journal*, 38(2): 258–71.

Mendelsohn, B. (1956) 'A new branch of bio-psychosocial science: la victimology', *Review International de Criminologie et de Police Technique*, 10: 782–9.

Mendelsohn, B. (1974) 'The origins of the doctrine of victimology', in I. Drapkin and E. Viano (eds) *Victimology*, Lexington, MA: Lexington Books.

Quinney, R. (1972) 'Who is the victim?', *Criminology*, 10(3): 14–323.

Rolling Stones (2005) *Dangerous Beauty*, produced by Don Was and the Glimmer Twins (audio CD), Virgin Records, US.

Rumney, P. (2007) 'In defence of gender neutrality within rape', *Seattle Journal of Social Justice*, 6: 481–526.

Rumney, P. and Morgan-Taylor, M. (1997a) 'Recognizing the male victim: gender neutrality and the law of rape part one', *Anglo American Law Review*, 26: 198–234.

Rumney, P. and Morgan-Taylor, M. (1997b) 'Recognizing the male victim: gender neutrality and the law of rape part two', *Anglo American Law Review*, 26: 330–6.

Scarce, M. (1997) *Male on Male Rape: The Hidden Toll of Stigma and Shame*, Cambridge, MA: Perseus.

Schafer, S. (1968) *The Victim and His Criminal*, New York, NY: Random House.

Schippers, M. (2007) 'Recovering the feminine other: masculinity, femininity, and gender hegemony', *Theory and Society*, 36(1): 85–102.

Sutherland, E.H. (1924) *Criminology*, Philadelphia, PA: J.B. Lippincott Compan.

Von Hentig, H. (1940) 'Remarks on the interaction of perpetrator and victim', *Journal of Criminal Law and Criminology*, 31(3): 303–9.

Von Hentig, H. (1948) *The Criminal and his Victim*, New Haven, CT: Yale University Press.

Walklate, S. (ed) (2007) *Handbook on Victims and Victimology*, Devon: Willan.

Wolfgang, M.E. (1958) *Patterns in Criminal Homicide*, Philadelphia, PA: University of Pennsylvania Press.

SIXTEEN

Towards an inclusive victimology and a new understanding of public compassion to victims: from and beyond Christie's ideal victim

Jorge Gracia

Introduction

Victimology is about human suffering. Its interests are fundamentally focused on the consequences generated by crime and how it affects all kinds of victims and their lives. It analyses, using different social and scientific methodologies, how we can manage pain as a society. In that sense, concern about victims' statuses and needs ought to be an important issue in open and democratic societies. However, victimology has an undeservedly bad reputation (Karmen, 2010) in some academic circles, often being accused of exercising a kind of 'commiseration' towards certain victims while forgetting others. Similarly, it has been criticised by some as providing an excuse for punitive turns in criminal policy (see Cressey, 1992; Elias, 1996; Garland, 2001; Fatah, 2012).

In the context of the increasing importance of emotions in victim-oriented policies, challenging some of the inadequate understandings of 'compassion' and its limits may help provide scholars with a useful policy of compassion as a public virtue. In turn, this may generate stronger and more accurate institutions for victim support. Such an approach requires being especially aware of the processes of differentiation and hierarchies of victims (Tamarit, 2013) that ultimately distinguish between 'good' and 'bad' victims: those victims worthy of support and compassion, and those that inspire only oblivion or contempt. To achieve this goal, further reflections about the impacts and negative effects of the stereotype of the 'ideal victim' present in Nils Christie's (1986) work could be a good starting point in order to achieve a truly inclusive victimology.

Human suffering, compassion and crime victims

According to Van Dijk (2009: 9), the use of the word 'victim' in most Western languages to name the people affected by the consequences of crime implies the idea – in the shadow of Jesus Christ and the Christian tradition – that 'they are socially constructed both as suffering objects worthy of society's compassion and as the active subjects of a sacrifice'. Once they have been labelled as crime victims, the community can acknowledge their deep and innocent suffering and, at the same time, express its firm expectation that victims will sacrifice their right of revenge. General compassion and respect for people who comply with the label's expectations are expected, while the victim, as an ideal, remains 'innocent, suffers deeply but is ready to forgive their offender nevertheless' (Van Dijk, 2009: 8).

However, the compassion that some victims receive is not easy to define. Most authors dealing with the issue have as a starting point the definition that Aristotle gave of pity[1] or compassion (ἔλεος) in *On Rhetoric*:

> Let pity be [defined as] a certain pain at an apparently destructive or painful event happening to one who does not deserve it and which a person might expect himself or one of his own to suffer, and this when it seems close at hand; for it is clear that a person who is going to feel pity necessarily thinks that some evil is actually present of the sort that he or one of his own might suffer and that this evil is of the sort mentioned in the definition or like it or about equal to it. (Aristotle, 1991: 139)

From Greek philosophers to contemporary neuroscientists, there is a considerable amount of literature dealing with the complexities of compassion. Obviously, this body of work cannot fully be explored here. Instead, we will focus on the writings of Martha C. Nussbaum (1996, 2001, 2015) regarding the role of emotions in democratic and open societies. She has repeatedly explored, in a very compelling way, compassion as a basic social emotion (Nussbaum, 1996) and key political emotion (Nussbaum, 2001, 2013). Similarly to Aristotle's conception, Nussbaum (2001: 301) defines it as 'a painful emotion occasioned by the awareness of another person's undeserved misfortune'.

For Nussbaum (2001, 2013), compassion includes three cognitive requirements: the belief that the suffering is serious rather than trivial; the belief that the person does not deserve the suffering; and the belief that the possibilities of the person who experiences the emotion are similar to those of the sufferer. These three beliefs are present in the development of compassion from Aristotle, but Nussbaum adds what she calls the 'eudaimonistic judgment' which implies that 'this person, or creature, is a significant element in my scheme of goals and projects, an end whose good is to be promoted' (Nussbaum, 2001: 321). She basically argues that when people fail to fully acknowledge the relevant compassion-composing beliefs, they fail also to experience compassion. The belief that consequences of crime are serious, at least some kind of crime affecting some kind of victims, is, at some point, easy to achieve because crime is nowadays generally regarded as a source of serious suffering for victims. It would be more problematic to complete the belief that the person 'is not at fault for his/her own misfortune or suffering'. This difficulty resonates, when related to criminal victimisation, with Christie's exploration of the ideal victim. The ideal victim, as we will explore further, is an innocent one that no one can honestly blame. Nevertheless, the social representation of victimhood is frequently underpinned by a tendency towards 'victim blaming' (see Cross, this volume).

Some authors disagree with Nussbaum (2001) at this point. For Weber (2004: 490), it is not enough for the denial of compassion that the person is at fault for their suffering; 'it requires that his mistake is a particularly egregious or stupid one, one that most people would not make'. Weber (2004: 490) gives the example of a driver who oversleeps and suffers a car accident, whose suffering probably would be, nevertheless, an object of compassion. However, speaking about crime victims, the doubt arises about whether this judgement of fault is not frequently 'harsher', at least in some cases. Think, for example, of cases of female victims of sexual violence. From the beginning, since the work of Amir (1971) about rape victims, the way in which traditional victimology has addressed female victims of sexual violence has been a controversial issue (Walklate, 2014). Cates (2003) criticises that regarding these assessments of innocence and fault as an integral and necessary condition, as Nussbaum does, would make compassion very rare. However, as Cates (2003: 338) also notes, Nussbaum sees this difficulty and seems then to encourage compassion by encouraging people not to be so quick in assuming that people are substantially and inexcusably 'at fault' for their own suffering and are thus undeserving of compassion (Nussbaum, 2001: 311–15). This is closely related to the need to create an extended public compassion, which Nussbaum (2001, 2013) encourages. It is also connected to the need to resist victim differentiation and hierarchies, as we will try to explore further in this chapter.

The third requirement associated with compassion is that of the 'similarity of possibilities'. The person who feels compassion usually thinks that the one who suffers resembles them or at least has possibilities in life similar to their own. According to Nussbaum (2013: 144), this thought 'may do important work removing barriers to compassion that had been created by artificial social divisions'. However, she thinks that this is not absolutely necessary as a conceptual condition. So, we can perfectly 'feel compassion for others without seeing his predicament as one that we could experience' (Nussbaum, 2013: 144). In fact, creating an extended compassion that also includes those whose lives are very different from ours will allow us to avoid traditional 'ideal victims' as the only legitimate object of our sympathy. This leads us to the 'eudaimonistic judgment' that Nussbaum (2001, 2013) adds to the structure of compassion, which implies an extension of the field of our interests by including concern for the fate of distant others that we consider important and valuable. The people who stir up deep emotions in us, including compassion, are those to whom we are connected, so to speak, through our imagination of what a valuable life means. They are part of what could be called our circle of interest or concern. As Alicia Villar (2008: 70) concludes, compassion 'allows us to discover that, if concern about common well-being is a question for all, radical misfortune is also a matter for us all'.

Compassion critics have always regarded it as an unreliable emotion because our sympathy to others in pain is easily exhausted. Compassion involves attention at an external focus to oneself or our immediate circle. Furthermore, although it can seem strong at an initial time, it is difficult to hold it for a long time. Compassion exhausts us and fades itself over time. Finally, contact with suffering, even in our imagination, generates more suffering. We must think here of the personal difficulties that professionals in direct contact with victims could face, like 'compassion fatigue syndrome' (see Figley 2002; Machado, 2004) or 'staff burnout' scenario (Freudenberger, 1974). As Sennet (2003: 64) notes, there is a kind of 'compassion which wounds'. For him, 'the compassion which lies behind the desire to give back can be deformed by social conditions into pity by the weak, pity which the receiver experiences as contempt' (Sennet, 2003: 64). The view of victims of crime as weak people, passive objects of pity if they fulfil some idealised characteristic that inspires our public compassion, can be disempowering and fuel inequality while being completely disconnected with social justice. This is why it is paramount to critically analyse the mechanisms of differentiation and hierarchy that are involved in order to select which victims deserve public compassion.

Which victims? The 'ideal victim' as an object of compassion

As Garland (2001: 11) notes, the new political imperative 'is that victims must be protected, their voices must be heard, their memory honoured, their anger expressed, their fears addressed'. This 'return of the victim' (Garland, 2001) has created a context of increasing political concern for and the social prestige of victimhood; becoming a victim generates, to some extent, some benefits. However, in any case, not every victim can benefit from the growing social visibility and importance of victims; only those close to ideal actually do. Consequently, finding a way to present oneself as an innocent crime victim and a legitimate object of social and public compassion could, hence, be necessary for those who need help and support after a crime (Tamarit, 2013; Herrera, 2014; Jägervi, 2014). The problem is that, in the 'real world', not every person that had been victimised fulfils the stereotype of the ideal victim portrayed by Christie (1986). Christie's ideal victim is primarily innocent and faultless. In his seminal work, Christie (1986: 18–19) provides an example of the ideal victim in his own culture: a little old lady on her way home in the middle of the day after having cared for her sick sister who is attacked by a big man that takes her money away in order to use it for liquor or drugs. These attributes are closely connected with the judgement focusing on whether the person is 'at fault' or not for their misfortune included in Nussbaum's (2001, 2013) analysis of compassion. If the community finds that the victim's misfortune has something to do with his/her fault, it would be harder for compassion to exist, according to Nussbaum (2001). To put it in other words: 'Where the forgiveness of the victim is supposed to be unconditional, the offer of compassion is not' (Van Dijk, 2009: 8).

However, the ideal victim stereotype, as every social construction, is not 'set in stone' and changes over time, moving some victims towards that status. For example, Christie suggested that, at the time he wrote about the ideal victim, this could be happening to women victims of intimate partner violence. Thirty years later, it seems that he was right and concern about gender and family violence has effectively moved this kind of victim to the status of ideal victim, which brings considerable amounts of general and public sympathy. Therefore, according to Walklate (2011: 183), the 'ideal victim' captures the social conditions under which some people are not only assigned victim status, but are also seen to deserve it. In this regard, Carrabine et al (2004: 157) enlighten us as to how some victims enjoy a higher status in the crime discourse and, consequently, their victimisation is taken more seriously.

This creates a kind of 'hierarchy of victimisation': at the top, we have the victims considered weak, innocent and deserving of help, care and compassion (like children or elderly ladies, the least prone to being a victim of crime, but assumed to be vulnerable); at the bottom, we have the less ideal victims, or not ideal at all, which are seen as less deserving of sympathy because of their physical characteristics (physical strength), action (risk-taking behaviours) or inactions (not protecting themselves). In this group, we have, for instance, young men, homeless people, drunken victims of an assault, the drug addict or the street prostitute, in short, all those 'for whom their lifestyle renders them prone to victimization and that are vulnerable but their victim status is denied' (Walklate, 2011: 183). The ideal victim stereotype is so powerful in creating this hierarchy of victims that it operates even when the law implicitly claims that prejudice is wrong, as in the case of hate crime:

> The ideal victim of hate crime, for symbolic purposes, is one who can lend their good name, so to speak, to this call for social justice by engendering compassionate thinking for their plight and thereby challenging the sentiments that drive prejudiced and discriminatory perceptions of them in individual, social and institutional domains. (Mason, 2014: 13)

Therefore, only the minority groups that have the greatest capacity to do this can convince others that they are the undeserved targets of a kind of harm that deserves collective concern (see Corteen, this volume). In particular, Christie remarks how ideal victims, assumed also as more vulnerable, do not necessarily have to do with the prevalence of real victims grounded in empirical victimological research or public statistics. In short, Christie's theory of the ideal victim could be viewed as 'an attempt to capture the master narrative defining a good crime victim in more general terms' (Jägervi, 2014: 74).

However, being labelled as a crime victim close to the ideal stereotype, despite the benefits it could incur in terms of being a suitable object for public compassion, may not be desirable for every real victim. For instance, in a study about victim narratives, Jägervi (2014) found that a considerable amount of the real victims participating in the research did not want to become 'ideal victims', mainly because of the perceived weakness inherent in this role. He also warns that 'crime victims' reluctance to present themselves as weak should not be understood as an admission of guilt, but rather as an expression of a wish to maintain integrity and a positive self-image, in both women and men' (Jägervi, 2014: 86; see also Forhing, this volume).

Finally, we have to notice that there is an undeniable role of social media in shaping and building an extended and public compassion about crime victims. For example, we can think here of Susan Sontag's (2003) work about photojournalism and the way in which disaster and war photography can help in cultivating emotional identification with others, avoiding the hazards of photographic objectification. Similarly, for Yeong (2014: 16) 'the challenge for us as viewers seems to involve interpreting photographs in a way that allows us to cultivate our empathy, by consciously recognizing the obstacles to emotional identification that the medium of photography inherently imposes'. However, we can also bear in mind the importance of 'talk shows' to the way in which the general public regards victims.[2] Therefore, as Woods (2012: 41) claims, 'journalists have as much or more to tell us than do (rationalist) philosophers about the scope of a moral community'. Here, we have to agree with Karmen (2010: 37) when he observes that skilful reporting and insightful observations allow the public to better understand the actions and reactions of those who suffer harm. However, social media coverage also has its dangers if we reflect on the ways in which journalists might present those whose suffering should elicit our sympathy (Woods, 2012: 41) and could reinforce victim hierarchies. Furthermore, we have the challenge of being overexposed to victim suffering, whereby 'misfortune is one more ingredient of our informational consumption against which we have developed a great capacity of indifference' (Innerarity, 1994: 64).

Politics of compassion

As Susan Sontag (2003: 101) warns us, compassion is an unstable emotion: 'It needs to be translated into action, or it withers. The question is what to do with the feelings that have been aroused, the knowledge that has been communicated'. It seems necessary, then, to address compassion as the basis of policy and, specifically, victim-oriented and victim support policies. By and large, there can be certain resistance to the idea of compassion as the basis of policy, mainly because it is associated with charity and due to its demeaning rather than empowering effects. The point here is to determine if we can build compassion as a democratic political virtue.

According to Collins et al (2012: 252), 'philosophical and theological definitions of virtue focus on qualities of moral excellence and characteristics that are valued as promoting individual and collective well-being'.[3] As Innerarity (1994: 68) concludes, 'the legitimacy of compassion lies in the fact that one would be willing to eliminate evil from the one they sympathize with if he could'. In other words, 'when people suffer due to unjust conditions, the compassionate agent, concerned about both alleviating and eliminating suffering, would recognize this injustice as a cause for suffering as well' (Frakes, 2010: 96). In that sense, the active-oriented meaning of virtue might be suited here to policy discussions by connecting compassion necessarily to political action. For Whitebrook (2014a: 25–6), this kind of compassion-oriented political action:

> is exercised specifically in respect of the causes of suffering and vulnerability, thus distinguishing between the political agent active within the political system and the victim of systemic injustice effectively excluded from the exercises of political agency by their socio-political conditions.

She also suggests that for the building of compassion as a (potentially) political virtue, vulnerability rather than suffering might be the proper location or occasion for exercising the virtue (Whitebrook, 2014b: 537). Furthermore, as we have discussed earlier, vulnerability is a very complex matter related not only to biological or psychological characteristics, but also to social conditions.

To sum up, in order to fully understand the increasing role of the victim in criminal policy, we cannot avoid the sentimental or emotional turn experienced in the social sciences and politics shaping the content and meaning of contemporary democracy.[4] Although it has deniable strengths and obvious fragilities[5]:

> the sentimental turn invokes sentiment not at a trivial level in which we are easily manipulated one way and then another, but rather at a level that reflects on the sort of people we are, or perhaps that we should be. (Woods, 2012: 45)

Among these emotions, compassion seems especially important in order to achieve a true understanding of the victim's needs, as well as to enforce victims' rights and build efficient victim support systems. However, this 'sentimental turn', which highlights the political use of compassion as a public virtue, may be not simply instrumental, but also critical.

As Nussbaum (2001: 405) beautifully concludes: 'compassionate individuals construct institutions that embody what they imagine, and, in turn, institutions influence the development of compassion in individuals'. Compassion, as an important political emotion, could help to reinforce community. This could be important in fighting against victim hierarchies because, as Christie points out, fragmented societies with isolated individuals are ideal for creating ideal victims and ideal offenders.

Taking compassion seriously: new paths for victimology

When talking about victim-oriented policies, it is important to address the role of victimology, not only in the past, but also its implications for the future. Although its institutionalisation as a discipline is relatively recent, there have been strong criticisms around victimology. For instance, several years ago, Donald Cressey (1992) claimed that victimology is characterised by a clash between two equally desirable orientations to human suffering: the humanistic and the scientific. Cressey (1992) argues, according to Elias (1996), that humanistic victimology has inappropriately politicised the field, undermining scientific victimology, becoming too dominated by victim advocates whose zeal for promoting victim policy has biased our ability to conduct objective scientific research. Richard Harding (1994) also argues that a politicised victimology has distorted criminal justice, with harmful consequences for both. The victims' rights movement has promoted rights selectively for certain victims, and also the unwarranted assumption that victim rights are more important than competing rights or values in society. It perpetuates a false, zero–sum contest between victim and offender interests that promotes ineffective, conservative crime policies. As Herrera (2014: 368) concludes, on the one hand, 'from the discourse of victim rights, victimhood is identified as a socially valuable and empowering position; on the other hand, from a critical view, it strives to highlight the negative elements and a constructed victimhood'.

With regard to victim support policies, Collins et al (2012) focus on the mature empathy that implies compassion-oriented work for professionals and advocates (not simply devolvement to community volunteers) and the appropriate understanding of 'shared suffering' from a policy perspective. For them, it has three different elements: first, there needs to be administrative infrastructure to support the interpersonal element of shared suffering[6]; second, there needs to be formal policy recognition that suffering does occur and that those suffering have a right to the alleviation of suffering as a component of justice; and, third, there needs to be sustained funding to allow continuity of assistance throughout the period of suffering. It is also important to continue focusing on the concept of vulnerability in a more subtle and complex way than mainstream victimology usually does (see, for instance, critical analysis by Green, 2007; Walklate, 2011). We must also focus on the structured and socially constructed vulnerability of people belonging to certain groups that, when objects of criminal victimisation, experience difficulties to be seen as victims and, therefore, legitimate objects of public compassion.

Regarding the future of victimology, Dussich (2015) recently offered some interesting proposals that could help to build a better scientifically strong victimology, being critical and also oriented to social action that enforces victims' rights. Among others, he suggests passing victim advocacy professionalisation *certification laws* so that victims (from crimes or other stark misfortunes) would only be treated by licensed professionals based on required levels of education, viably managed internships and national or state licensure, as well as passing laws that require all police prosecutors and judges to have *a basic victimology course* as it applies to their profession in their training prior to becoming licensed. He also remarks the importance of strengthening victims' rights laws so that victims are *ensured of legal standing* in the courts and then creating an enforcement mechanism to hold those in the criminal justice system accountable. This would reinforce the use of compassion as a political virtue by linking it clearly to justice and transformative political practices.

When speaking of intervention with victims, it is crucial to deal with secondary victimisation. At that point, the kind of 'compassion that wounds' (Sennet, 2003) is closely related to 'secondary victimisation', which may exacerbate harm to victims through the inaccurate intervention of the institutions dealing with them. If, as it has been outlined here, concern about victims is a characteristic of a 'decent society', which Margalit (1996: 10–11) regards as a kind of society that fights conditions that constitute a justification for its dependants to consider themselves humiliated, then we must consider how an inaccurate use of compassion can humiliate people, and how secondary victimisation, although not always connected with this, could be seen as a failure to create truly compassionate institutions. A 'decent society', therefore, must create 'compassionate institutions' greatly concerned with avoiding secondary victimisation. Victimological research therefore plays an important role in resisting the limiting stereotype of the ideal victim. An expansion of the research agenda should also be encouraged to cover the study of other forms of victimisation that are not well analysed and these less visible 'other victims'. To do so, as Tamarit (2013: 26) points out, in addition to promoting interdisciplinary dialogue, 'specific studies are useful using standardized instruments that can be adapted to the reality to be studied'. We must include here qualitative research, through in-depth interviews with victims, which can complement the limitations of quantitative studies in order to gain a deeper understanding of the specific problem of victims in groups highly exposed to victimisation and difficult to access through conventional victim surveys.

As the media are crucial in creating public compassion for crime victims, it seems important to acknowledge the important roles of journalism and, at the same time, curb the excesses in the coverage of victims' plight. Nevertheless, this is a controversial issue because of people's right to know about crime. Karmen (2010: 48) enumerates three different remedies that have been used: first, to enact new laws to shield those suffering from unnecessary public disclosure; second, to rely on the self-restraint of reporters and their editors; and, third, to adopt a code of professional ethics for the media. Finally, an accurate use of compassion regarding victim support must also be concerned with facing the problems that appear when compassion fades. A compassionate institution dealing with victims must know that we cannot only rely on advocates' and professionals' individual sense of compassion. There have to be instruments in order to deal with issues like 'compassion fatigue' and 'burnout' by creating more accurate victim support structures capable of dealing with these problems. As Frakes (2010: 95) claims, this results in people 'becoming physically and psychologically incapacitated, unable to respond well in the face of so much suffering does not represent the achievement of compassion but rather its deficiency'.

Some concluding thoughts: towards a more inclusive victimology

In sum, while being aware of the well-deserved criticism of the contemporary cult of victimhood, it is important to review the circle of victims so as to be, maybe in a different way, more inclusive and the object of a balanced compassion centred on the consequences of crime for real victims, all kinds of victims. Concern about victims, in spite of its paradoxes and contradictions, appears as an important characteristic to build a 'decent society', as Margalit (1996) wanted.

Hence, we ought not to 'throw the baby out with the bathwater' and, consequently, not to belittle the advances in terms of rights and justice for victims that victimology and victim support movements, even in their most activist aspects, have brought. We do not have to dismiss the criticisms of the constructed victim identity and its distortions that have led to an inaccurate and manipulative use of public compassion by recognising vulnerability and suffering only for those victims that we presume close to the ideal victim stereotype. At this point, the criticism implicit in the stereotype of ideal victims, as Christie advanced in his important work, ought to be fully embraced and their changes over time analysed by scientific victimology. Furthermore, it is crucial to think in what ways an accurate and compassionate understanding of victims could be useful in order to transform victimology and victim support movements and structures.

Finally, the use of compassion as a public political virtue is closely related to the need for a victimological approach that, as Herrera (2014) claims, does not give up on the purpose of open non-essentialist paths that transcend the exigency of perfect victimhood, as reflected in Christie's ideal victim. Instead, 'the path to an imperfect victimhood could reach the needs of those less sublime but more real victims as a legitimate object of extended and accurate compassion' (Herrera, 2014: 403). Another victimology, a much more inclusive one, would then be possible.

Notes

[1]   Nussbaum (1996: 29), as Weber (2004: 488) observes, thinks that 'pity' and 'compassion' are basically the same emotion, only with subtle differences. She prefers to use 'pity', which took connotations of condescension and superiority in the Victorian era, when talking about the historical debate and 'compassion' when discussing contemporary issues. However, Hannah Arendt, for instance, claimed that 'compassion, to be stricken with the suffering of someone else as though it were contagious, and pity, to be sorry without being touched in the flesh are not only not the same, they may not even be related' (Arendt, 1963: 85, in Von Tevenar, 2014: 38). Whereas Whitebrook (2014a) thinks that 'pity' denotes feelings towards suffering and compassion refers to feelings together with action. Consequently, compassion 'is a matter of acting on the basis of feelings of pity rather than feeling an emotion' (Whitebrook, 2014a: 22).

[2]   For instance, Marshall and Pienaar (2008) studied the way in which *The Oprah Winfrey Show*, recognised as the most successful television talk show of all time, presented victim suffering to its audience. For them, one of the most revealing features of the show is its reliance on a belief in the universality of suffering, and its success hinges on the practice of putting a suffering individual on display in

order to emphasise our shared humanity and potential victimisation. The aim is to alleviate pain, initiate change and validate the agency of the victim in overcoming their suffering. Hence, Oprah's influence may lie in her role not only as an entertainer and media mogul, but as a therapist to the masses. She also presents selected victims to the audience as legitimate objects of social compassion. The essential message of the show seems to be 'you are not alone', and so 'democracy is defined by the number of people who are "empowered" by knowing that their sadness and frustration is shared by other people' (Siegel, 2006: 21).

3   They go on to add: 'Virtue requires the inculcation of habit, not merely the occasional exercise of goodness. Virtues are acquired, stable dispositions. They are applied morals; they require behaviours' (Collins et al, 2012: 252).

4   For an excellent Spanish reflection on this issue, see Arias (2016).

5   For a critical view of this sentimental turn in criminal policies, see, for instance, Walklate (2009) and Karstedt (2002).

6   It is important to highlight that the goal of compassionate victim support ought to imply public policies and efforts and should not remain only upon private initiative: 'Without the sustained infrastructure of national policy to provide funding and coordination, the grassroots efforts of community and faith-based groups do not elevate compassion to the societal level. This is in opposition to compassionate conservatism, which advocates a high reliance on volunteers and removal of a government role' (Collins et al, 2012: 262).

References

Amir, M. (1971) *Patterns of Forcible Rape*, Chicago, IL: Chicago University Press.

Arendt, H. (1963) *On Revolution*, London: Penguin Books.

Arias, M. (2016) *La Democracia Sentimental* [*Sentimental Democracy*], Barcelona: Página Indómita.

Aristotle (1991) *On Rhetoric: A Theory of Civic Discourse* (trans G.A. Kennedy), New York, NY: Oxford University Press.

Carrabine, E., Cox, P., Lee, M., Plummer, K. and South, N. (2004) *Criminology: A Sociological Introduction* (1st edn), London: Routledge.

Cates, D.F. (2003) 'Conceiving emotions: Martha Nussbaum's *Upheavals of Thought*', *The Journal of Religious Ethics*, 31(2): 325–41.

Christie, N. (1986) 'The ideal victim', in E.A. Fatah (ed) *From Crime Policy to Victim Policy: Reorienting the Justice System*, Basingstoke: Macmillan.

Collins, E.M., Cooney, K. and Garlington, S. (2012) 'Compassion in contemporary social policy: applications of virtue theory', *Journal of Social Policy*, 41(2): 251–69.

Cressey, D. (1992) 'Research implications of conflicting conceptions of victimology', in E.A. Fattah (ed) *Towards a Critical Victimology* (1st edn), New York, NY: St. Martin's Press, pp 57–73.

Dussich, J. (2015) 'The evolution of international victimology and its current status in the world today', *Revista de victimología/Journal of Victimology*, 1(8): 37–81.

Elias, R. (1996) 'Paradigms and paradoxes of victimology', in C. Sumner, M. Israel, M. O'Connell and M. Sarre (eds) *International Victimology: Selected Papers from the 8th International Symposium* (1st edn), Canberra: Australian Institute of Criminology, pp 9–34.

Fatah, E.A. (2012) 'From victimology of the act to victimology of action. And the resulting impoverishment of the scholarly discipline of victimology', in S. Hazenbroek, R. Letschert and M. Groenhuijsen (eds) *K.L.M. Van Dijk: Liber Amicorum Prof. Dr. Mr. J.J.M. Van Dijk*, Nijmegen: Wolf Publishing, pp 85–98.

Figley, C.R. (2002) 'Compassion fatigue: psychotherapists' chronic lack of self care', *Psychotherapy in Practice*, 58(11): 1433–41.

Frakes, C. (2010) 'When strangers call: a consideration of care, justice and compassion', *Hypatia*, 21(1): 79–99.

Freudenberger, H.J. (1974) 'Staff burnout', *Journal of Social Issues*, 30(1): 159–65.

Garland, D. (2001) *The Culture of Control: Crime and Social Order in Contemporary Society*, Chicago, IL: University of Chicago Press.

Green, S. (2007) 'Crime, victimisation and vulnerability', in S. Walklate (ed) *Handbook of Victims and Victimology*, Cullompton: Willan, pp 91–118.

Harding, R. (1994) 'Victimisation, moral panics, and the distortion of criminal justice policy', *Current Issues in Criminal Justice*, 6: 27–42.

Herrera, M. (2014) '¿Quién teme a la victimidad? El debate identitario en victimología' ['Who is afraid of victimhood? Identity debate in victimology'], *Revista de Derecho Penal y Victimología*, 12: 343–404.

Innerarity, D. (1994) 'Poética de la compasión' ['Poetic of compassion'], *Comunicación y sociedad*, 7(2): 63–72.

Jägervi, L. (2014) 'Who wants to be an ideal victim? A narrative analysis of crime victims' self-presentation', *Journal of Scandinavian Studies in Criminology and Crime Prevention*, 15(1): 73–88.

Karmen, A. (2010) *Crime Victims. An Introduction to Victimology* (1st edn), Belmont: Wadsworth.

Karstedt, S. (2002) 'Emotions and criminal justice', *Theoretical Criminology*, 6(3): 299–317.

Machado, C. (2004) 'Intervenção psicológica com vítimas de crimes: Dilemas teóricos, técnicos e emocionais' ['Psychologic intervention with victims: theoretical, technical and emotional dilemmas'], *International Journal of Clinical and Health Psychology*, 4(2): 399–411.

Margalit, A. (1996) *The Decent Society* (trans N. Goldblum), Cambridge and London: Harvard University Press.

Marshall, C. and Pienaar, K. (2008) '"You are not alone": the discursive construction of the "suffering victim" identity on The Oprah Winfrey Show', *Southern African Linguistics and Applied Language Studies*, 26(4): 525–46.

Mason, G. (2014) 'The symbolic purpose of hate crime law: ideal victims and emotion', *Theoretical Criminology* , 18(1): 75–92.

Nussbaum, M.C. (1996) 'Compassion: the basic social emotion', *Social Philosophy & Policy*, 13(Winter): 27–58.

Nussbaum, M.C. (2001) *Upheavals of Thought: The Intelligence of Emotions* (1st edn), Cambridge: Cambridge University Press.

Nussbaum, M.C. (2013) *Political Emotions: Why Love Matters for Justice*, Cambridge and London: Harvard University Press.

Sennet, R. (2003) *Respect in a World of Inequality* (1st edn), New York, NY, and London: W.W. Norton & Company.

Siegel, L. (2006) 'Thank you for sharing: the strange genius of Oprah', *The New Republic*, 234 (21/22): 19–23.

Sontag, S. (2003) *Regarding the Pain of Others* (1st edn), New York, NY: Farrar, Straus and Giroux.

Tamarit, J.M. (2013) 'Paradojas y patologías en la construcción social, política y jurídica de la victimidad' ['Paradoxes and pathologies in the social, political and legal construction of victimhood'], *InDret. Revista para el análisis del Derecho*, 1: 1–31. Available at: http://www.indret.com/pdf/940.pdf

Van Dijk, J. (2009) 'Free the victim: a critic of the western conception of victimhood', *International Review of Victimology*, 16: 1–33.

Villar, A. (2008) 'La ambivalencia de la compasión' ['The ambivalence of compassion'], in M. García-Baro and A. Vilar (eds) *Pensar la compasión* [*Thinking Compassion*] (1st edn), Madrid: Universidad Pontificia de Comillas, pp 23–72.

Von Tevenar, G. (2014) 'Invisibility in Arendt's public space', in M. Ure and M. Frost (eds) *The Politics of Compassion*, London and New York, NY: Routledge, pp 37–50.

Walklate, S. (2009) 'Are we all victims now? Crime, justice and suffering', *British Journal of Community Justice*, 7(2): 5–16.

Walklate, S. (2011) 'Reframing criminal victimization: finding a place for vulnerability and resilience', *Theoretical Criminology*, 15(2): 179–94.

Walklate, S. (2014) 'Sexual violence against women: still a controversial issue for victimology?', *International Review of Victimology*, 20: 71–84.

Weber, M. (2004) 'Compassion and pity: an evaluation of Nussbaum's analysis and defense', *Ethical Theory and Moral Practice*, 7: 487–511.

Whitebrook, M. (2014a) 'Love and anger as political virtues', in M. Ure and M. Frost (eds) *The Politics of Compassion*, London and New York, NY: Routledge, pp 21–36.

Whitebrook, M. (2014b) 'Compassion as a political virtue', *Political Studies*, 2: 529–44.

Woods, K. (2012) 'Whiter sentiment? Compassion, solidarity and disgust in cosmopolitan thought', *Journal of Social Philosophy*, 43(1): 33–49.

Yeong, O.K.W. (2014) '"Our failure of empathy": Kevin Carter, Susan Sontag, and the problems of photography', *Think Pieces: A Journal of the Arts, Humanities, and Social Sciences*, 1(1): 9–17.

Conclusion

Marian Duggan

Back in 2013, my co-editors and I showcased the relevance of Howard Becker's (1967) seminal article, entitled 'Whose side are we on?', to a range of scholars working in and around the field of criminal justice. The resultant volume, entitled *Values in Criminology and Community Justice*, proved to be a rich tapestry of academic and practitioner insight into the strengths and weaknesses, and opportunities and impediments, of addressing how personal and institutional 'values' may or may not inform and impact upon processes of criminal justice. Fittingly, similar issues related to morality, ethics and justice have been demonstrated by the contributors in the present volume. Although they have merely scratched the surface of understanding how idealised constructions of victimhood manifest in contemporary society, the contributions in *Revisiting the 'Ideal Victim': Developments in Critical Victimology* excellently demonstrate how Christie's ideas continue to thrive in the contemporary victimological imagination.

This is important as, prior to writing about the ideal victim, Christie (1977: 1) had taken the criminal justice system to task in another influential piece, 'Conflicts as property', in which he suggested that 'Maybe we should not have any criminology. Maybe we should rather abolish institutes, not open them. Maybe the social consequences of criminology are more dubious than we like to think'. As a scholar who was (quite rightly) opposed to the term 'crime' and the punitive (as opposed to welfarist) treatment of people who had broken the law, Christie strove to present a different vision of 'criminology' that focused on processes of control rather than criminals themselves. He sought to reduce the infliction of pain – not just by individuals, but by institutions too. This shift onto the subject (rather than object) of harm is vital for ensuring that trauma, distress and hurt are eased rather than exacerbated.

While the victim-oriented model of criminal justice espoused by Christie may still prove evasive in many respects – not least due to the incompatibility of such a model in many current offender-focused systems – the ideologies behind it have informed a wealth of alternative and supplementary approaches to justice based on representation, reparation and restitution. The development of restorative and transitional justice movements in formerly deeply divided societies (such as Northern Ireland and South Africa) demonstrates the potential power that victims can have when given the space to have their voices heard. Indeed, as is evident in several of the chapters in this volume, such power may only manifest after great trauma, which, from a harm reduction perspective, implies something of a pyrrhic victory.

While illustrating the diversity of contexts in which the 'ideal victim' status is (or is not) ascribed, the authors have addressed issues of power, status, deservedness and legitimacy. This is important as we are currently living in an increasingly interconnected yet divided, globalised yet fragmented, and inclusive yet often judgemental world. In some ways, much has changed in the three short decades since Christie wrote his chapter, for example, developments in mobile and social technologies have revolutionised the way in which people share, receive and obtain information (not all of it accurate, of course). In other ways, less has changed; broadening the scope of the criminal justice system to recognise 'new' forms of victimisation – such as anti-social behaviour and hate crimes – does little to *reduce* harm, but instead offers additional ways to *punish* it (Garland, 2001).

As with any volume, this one has its limitations. Many of the contributions (and contributors) reflect the Global North/northern hemisphere. While this is not to suggest that the issues they discuss do not affect or impact on the Global South, it does indicate that we must be mindful of how and where knowledge is produced, disseminated and applied. As victimology and victim studies continue to develop in new and diverse directions, I hope the ideas presented in this collection offer a platform from which to infinitely develop our collective critical victimological imagination.

References

Becker, H. (1967) 'Whose side are we on?', *Social Problems*, 14: 237–47.
Christie, N. (1977) 'Conflicts as property', *British Journal of Criminology*, 17(1): 1–15.
Garland, D. (2001) *The Culture of Control: Crime and Social Order in Contemporary Society*, Chicago, IL: Chicago University Press.

Index

Printed and bound by CPI Group (UK) Ltd, Croydon, CR0 4YY

29/01/2025

14634972-0001